CONTENTS

✤

On the cover: (Top Row L. to R.) Magee Hickey, Roy Scheider, Ben Gazarra, Jerry Della Femina (Second Row) Rusty Leaver, Erica Abeel, Tom Paxton, John Weitz (Third Row) Martha Stewart, Tony Drexel Duke, Carl Spielvogel, Barbara Corcoran (Bottom Row) Bob Pittman, Mort Zuckerman, Aya Azrielant, Wilbur Ross

DEDICATION

✦

For Susyn Reeve, Jerry Finkelstein, Mike Schenkler
Charles Platkin and my parents

WHO'S HERE:
The Heart of the Hamptons

by DAN RATTINER

✤

Introduction by George Plimpton

Books by Dan Rattiner:

Dan's Book
Loose Change in the New World
Albert Einstein's Summer Vacation
Attack of the Space Creatures (Ill. by Richard Shephard)
What to Do if Gravity Fails
The Eat All You Want and Still Lose Weight Cookbook
It's All His Fault (with co-author Susan Atkinson)
It's All Her Fault (with co-author Susan Atkinson)
Computer Raider's News

This book was produced for the publisher by Ray Freiman & Company.

INTRODUCTION

by George Plimpton

✣

I have no doubt that Dan Rattiner and his newspaper, *Dan's Papers*, could very well be identified as being among the great institutions of the South Fork — right up there with the windmills, the Walking Dunes, the American Hotel, the Montauk Lighthouse (which still stands largely due to Rattiner's efforts), the Candy Kitchen, the Artists and Writers baseball game, the Sagaponack General Store, the Hampton Classic, the Parrish Art Museum, whatever.

There is little to suggest of an institution on meeting Dan Rattiner — a mild, unassuming, rather avuncular figure, hardly a Colossus astride the South Fork. In my mind's eye I see him umpiring the annual Artists and Writers game, white-bearded, whose motions to signify a strike or a close play at first are as thoughtful and measured as those of a cricket umpire.

There is very little of this placidity in Mr. Rattiner's newspapers — which as well as being informative are lively, irreverent, iconoclastic, often heightened with outrageous spoofs. In person it is difficult to connect these latter qualities with the publisher of *Dan's Papers* until by a sly smile, a glint in the eye, one suddenly becomes aware of a puckish turn of mind.

This interview was conducted in the cavernous Harvard Hall of New York's Harvard Club (Rattiner studied architecture at that institution) — its imposing row of large presidential portraits, solemn, heavy-lidded, seeming to preclude any high-jinks on the part of the person being interviewed.

Q: *What was your first journalistic enterprise?*

A: I was a college kid, a sophomore at the University of Rochester, when in the Summer of 1960 I started a paper in Montauk. For a couple of summers I had been working for my dad in his drugstore. It's awkward to work for your father because you can never tell whether you're being talked to as an employee or a son. I was a clerk. I handled the register. I managed the fountain at one point — malts and so forth — which was great. It wasn't working out. I thought, next summer I'll make my own business. I'll start a town newspaper.

Q: *The concept was a very novel one — to give the paper away free. Was that the idea from the very beginning?*

A: Oh yes. There hadn't been anything of the sort prior to that time. It was really questioned whether a publication given away free could actually work. People would not know it was a newspaper. It was said they would pick it up and just throw it away. So there was no sense of the value of advertising. The first awareness that I had a readership was when one night I got a call from the Montauk stationmaster. He said he was holed up upstairs, an angry crowd below because I had printed the wrong train departure times in my paper. And I thought, "Wait 'til my ad customers hear this!"

Q: *What was the first issue like?*

A: It was eight pages long, a run of 5000. I distributed it myself in a 1953 Oldsmobile. It was printed in Freeport — the printing expenses about $350. I made about $2000 that first summer. In 1960 Montauk was really a bunch of ticky tacky boxes on a main street with no curbs or sidewalks. I called the paper The Montauk Pioneer because what it represented looked like a western town. To have that town blossom, which it has, into a full-grown community with street boxes and lots of landscaping in the center of the town, a library, a museum, a police annex, a chamber of commerce building...it's like watching a flower bloom. Now the paper is no longer just a newspaper for the tourists; it's a newspaper representing the interest of the whole community.

Q: *What were some of the stories in the first issue?*

A: There was a story about a 3000 pound shark that had been landed at Montauk, a real fish. Also the first of a series of history pieces I did on the French-Canadian families who had been in the rum-running business. There was a column called "Trail-Blazing" in which I wrote about all the good things that would come to a town that had a newspaper. I wrote the features, news, history — everything in the paper — basically putting on one hat and taking it off and putting on another.

Q: *Other than your undergraduate days, had you had any newspaper experience?*

A: Those early winters I went into the city and worked briefly in the city room at the *New York Times*. I also worked as a cartoonist, selling little line drawings. Then I helped found the *East Village Other*, which was an underground newspaper on the Lower East Side.

Q: *When did you change the name to Dan's Papers?*

A: In 1966 I began publishing a paper called *The East Hampton Summer Sun*, and the next year I added the *South Hampton Summer Day*, and then *The Hampton Beach* in Westhampton and finally, the *North Fork Enterprise*. Though generally they had the same articles, they all had different names. I needed a name for the chain. That's when my friend Ron Zeil suggested we call it "Dan's Papers" as in "Joe's Hots."

Q: *What is the circulation now?*

A: It's 87,000. With 10,000 in New York City. It's distributed in about 20 street-boxes. There's one in front of the Pierre Hotel. The *Montauk Pioneer* which has remained separate has a circulation of 13,000.

Q: *What does a page of advertising cost these days?*

A: About eighteen hundred dollars. In the first issue it was $200.

Q: *And the number of employees now?*

A: About forty.

Q: *The hoax is very much a part of your literary makeup, isn't it? I would suppose April Fool's Day is heavily marked in your Daily Reminder.*

A: Yes, sometimes I run hoaxes on April first. We did a hoax some years ago where we had a fictitious town meeting where it was decided that the solution to the parking problem in the Hamptons would be to only allow parking for BMWs, Mercedes, Audis and Saabs. That got quite a stir. The most famous hoax story I wrote was when the movie *Jaws* came out. I published a letter on the first page of the paper that purported to be a notice from the Chief of Police. It advised readers that it was safe to swim in the ocean on Monday, Wednesdays, and Fridays, and in Gardiner's Bay on Tuesdays, Thursdays, and Saturdays. The Great White Shark was being fed by helicopter — the Hampton butchers supplying the meat — so the authorities knew where he was at all time. That hoax, as did many of them, got coverage by the national media.

Q: *What was the first hoax you pulled off?*

A: It was while I was at the University of Rochester. I was the editor of the humor magazine there. I decided to publish a parody of the student newspaper. We produced our parody overnight and substituted it for their papers in the morning. The front page headline was "U. of R. to Go on Tri-semester System. Summer vacation eliminated." It created a riot at the University. In the women's cafeteria people were dropping trays on the floor with a crash. In the men's dining hall there was fighting. The secretaries in the Administration Building walked off the job. You couldn't make a phone call because everybody was trying to call home at the same time. I remember the sheer joy of creating this utterly chaotic situation.

Q: *Did you get in trouble with the authorities?*

A: Oh, absolutely. I was accused of misuse of student funds publishing a newspaper with money earmarked for a humor magazine. They had just put together a student justice system. It was their first trial. The judge was a student. I had a defense attorney who was about 19. It was hilariously funny. The trial began at 8 p.m. because everybody had classes during the day and it went into the night. At two o'clock in the morning they arrived at the decision that I was guilty but because it was my senior year and I was graduating in two months they recommended only that I should be suspended from any student activities until graduation.

Q: *It would be interesting to hear from someone who single-handedly wrote an entire paper all those years what your writing habits are.*

A: These days I have a writing pattern that is probably is pretty unique. I have a van. And a laptop computer. Around noon I go down to the beach at the end of Sagg Main and I park by a dune. I write there for an hour and a half. Usually there's a half hour fiddling before I start and twenty minutes wrapping it up, so I'm down there between two and three hours. It's there that I'll put on one of my hats.

Q: *Your hats?*

A: Figuratively speaking. I put on a different hat depending what day it is. Usually in any one issue there'll be several different kinds of articles. So each day I get myself into a different mood, a different hat. I write an article a day. I'll write a light piece, a hoax, or an investigative piece, or a profile of someone I've interviewed either well-known or not — a group of which are what's collected in this book. I never did you, so you'll have to wait until volume two.

Q: *I'd be honored, at least I think so.*

A: Let me talk about these interviews. When I interview somebody I try to find a moment in their lives, generally occurring in their teenage years, when they got pointed in the direction they finally end up going. I talk to them about their families, where they're from and how they were raised. Then I relate that to their accomplishments today...what has put them in a position to be honored in my newspaper.

Q: *Have you done other types of writing?*

A: I've written nine books. The one I'm most proud of is *The Eat All You Want and Still Lose Weight Cookbook*. It is basically a series of travel stories about eating food that makes you so sick you lose weight. One entry is about eating raw clams on a beach in Mexico. Another is about eating octopus in the Canary Islands and not wanting to eat for days.

Q: *One of your "hats" is investigative reporting. What are some of the campaigns on the South Fork you can take credit for?*

A: I fought bitterly to stop East Hampton from "improving" the airport by creating a terminal in an architectural Mediterranean style. I won that fight and was credited so by angry architects. But probably the best-known thing I did involved the Montauk Lighthouse. I was doing a story about the erosion there and how it was threatening the Lighthouse. When George Washington ordered it built it was three hundred feet from the edge of the cliff. Now just sixty feet remained. I called the Coast Guard and asked if they had any plans to do anything about it. They said, "Oh, we go out and measure the distance from the lighthouse to the cliff edge every month. We keep track of it." I thought, the man is avoiding the question. Then he said, "The engineers from the Coast Guard are planning to put a steel tower about three hundred feet back from the edge. The lighthouse will be demolished. Then we won't have the problem. We expect it to happen within two years." I was horrified. It was like blowing up the Empire State Building. I called Governor's Island and got a confirmation from a mid-level official. "Yes, these plans are in the works."

Well, I talked to a number of people. Someone remembered there was a framed photograph hanging in a barber shop in Hampton Bays of a lighthouse in the process of being blown up...tilted at a 45° angle in a puff of smoke. It was the Shinnecock Lighthouse, which was dynamited in 1948. I said to myself: "There's my front cover: *Lighthouse Dynamited.* It looked like a hoax, but it was a serious article. The idea was, "This can happen here." We published it and called for a protest.

Q: *What was the result?*

A: The newspaper held a protest and a candlelight vigil for three years. Finally, the Coast Guard rescinded the order and then two months later made a commitment to fund the lighthouse's restoration and preservation. They invited me to the Coast Guard headquarters on Governor's Island to give me an award. By the way, this is a story I tell my children...proving it with back issues. And with the plaque I received.

Q: *What is the genesis of your splendid Flight to Portugal extravaganza in which contestants fly rubber-propelled aircraft from the Montauk cliffs out over the ocean?*

A: We had started a Manhattan circulation of *Dan's Papers*. It was in the fall. The idea was to target a city-wide audience. So I wrote, "Come out every winter weekend. We have wonderful festivals for you to enjoy in the Hamptons." I listed nine fictitious events in January and February. One of them was the "Flight to Portugal" in which I described how young men take old cars to Montauk where they gun the engines and peel out up a wooded ramp over the ninety foot cliff to splash out into the sea. The drivers are rescued by helicopter. No one had ever been injured. We'd been doing it for years. I wrote that the winners got six-packs of beer, laurel wreaths, and got carried around on the spectators' shoulders. To my astonishment, when my wife and I returned from a European vacation, all kinds of people had been phoning the office wanting to know more about the Flight to Portugal. They wanted to see it! Then a lot of things happened. The Portuguese National Tourist Board offered a vacation for two to the winners. ABC news called and wanted to send a crew. So we modified it to rubberband airplanes rather than old cars — flying them off the cliffs towards Portugal. It has turned out to be quite an annual event!

Q: *Your spiritual home then is really Montauk?*

A: I go out there and feel real good about being there.

Q: *Are you worried about the fate of the Hamptons?*

A: No. We've become a classy resort with an overlay of New York sophistication, unique in the world. *Forbes* just published their 400 richest men in America. 17 billionaires. Somebody checked the list and noted that four of the billionaires have houses in the Hamptons. So I don't think we have to worry about litter or trash. I think our heritage is in safe hands. Consider what could have happened: the Hamptons could have been swallowed up into some suburban situation like Lido Beach or Coney Island. Or we could have become a tacky, cheap Jersey shore resort. We didn't become either. And I don't think we will. I have a family that I am raising, four kids, and I think it's a great place to raise them. It's certainly a good place to run a paper!

Chapter 1

CHARLIE VANDERVEER

I took my daughter to a restaurant that evening. It was Thanksgiving break, she was home from college and I figured I'd treat her to a square meal. We chose Bobby Van's, the traditional watering hole in Bridgehampton, and were midway through the main course when one of my best friends walked in with his son, also home from college. They sat at a nearby table and we waved to one another. Then, after a bit, my friend Charlie Vanderveer got up and came over to our table.

"Want to hear something amazing?" he said.

I always wanted to hear something amazing from Charlie. He is a story teller. You can sit and listen to him tell his tales for hours.

"I have less than three months to live," he continued.

"This is a joke," I said.

"No joke. I have terminal leukemia. Doctors say there is nothing they can do."

I looked at Charlie. He is a big bear of a man, six foot four and 280 pounds. He looked like he always looked.

"I don't believe this," I said. "You look perfectly fine. Stop fooling around."

"I feel fine. That's the amazing part. But that's what they tell me."

"You don't seem very upset about it."

"Upset? Ha!" Charlie grinned and snorted. "Not much I can do about it." And he returned to his table.

We finished our dinner. Because Charlie didn't seem very upset we didn't feel very upset. Maybe it wasn't true. Maybe it was but he'd beat it. We ate. After paying our bill, we went over to the

Vanderveers' table and asked his son Stuyvie about school and how things were going.

"Well, we have to wind up dad's affairs," he said.

I walked up to Charlie from behind and stood over him. Then I reached down, hugged him, kissed him on the head and told him I loved him and I'd pray for him.

* * *

I interviewed Charlie in his home after Thanksgiving, on a Wednesday. The kids were gone back to school. He was in the main house — there are three houses — on his sixty acre farm on Scuttlehole Road. All the junk and antiques and curios he'd collected during the past twenty years as this community's auctioneer was gathering dust all around him. We sat in his bedroom. At one point he got up to boil some water for tea.

Many people think that Charlie Vanderveer, who has been a fixture in this community for more than a generation, is also a native. He isn't.

"I grew up in a big mansion in Jamaica, Queens," he said. "It's a bed and breakfast today, but back then it had lawns all around, maple trees you could swing off of to the garage roof, a porch off the living room. We had a separate garage where the gardener lived. And on the third floor my sister Shirley and I had a play room and there was a maid's room.

"My mother's father was Charles E. Culbert, President of the U. S. Title Company and he and his wife lived in Garden City. Sometimes my mother would take Shirley and me shopping in Garden City. We'd sit in the back of the Packard with a lap robe over us and the chauffeur would be up front driving. Mother didn't go in to the stores right away. The butcher would come out from the butcher shop and he'd take her order, then we'd do the same thing at the vegetable store and at the fruit market. We'd come to the end of town, then we'd turn around and the packages would be ready. She'd go in and inspect everything and sign for it, then the merchants would bring it out to the car. Sometimes I'd get a chocolate eclair from the baker for free.

"My father's father was a farmer. He also lived in Garden City, with his wife and his bachelor son, who was my Uncle John. My father, in 1927 when I was a year old, sold off about 61 acres of the farm he owned in Queens as house lots. Buy a lot 30x60 and grandfather would put a house on it. They were so close together. If you wanted to bring a lawnmower into the back yard you'd have to take it through the house. If you wanted to paint a window frame on the side of the house you'd have to go to the neighbor's and lean out his window.

"Grandfather Vanderveer, after selling off the farm, still liked working the garden. We had a garden at our house. And sometimes

2

grandfather would walk the six miles from Garden City early in the morning, mess in the garden, go home for lunch, then walk back and mess in the garden the rest of the afternoon.

"There were always lots of kids around. I remember throwing cherry bombs into the furnace. There was always a baseball game you could get into on a Saturday. And I figured out, early on, that if I went over to a friend's house on a tricycle at noon, they'd feed me.

"I grew up with lots of fathers and lots of mothers, all with different ideas. And it was just me and my sister. I considered it my home until I was thirty seven years old, which is when I got married."

Until he was eleven, Charlie went to the local public school. Then, he became ill with encephalitis and fell into a coma for three weeks. When he awoke and was well enough to return to school, it was decided it would be "good for him to be around kids but not challenged." He had to learn everything all over again: to walk, pick up a book, read. The family decided he would go to the nearby St. Paul's School and he went there until he was sixteen. Then he went to Choate. But before he could graduate, World War II broke out. Charlie, at six foot four and almost three hundred pounds, spent it as an MP at various bases in the Northeast. Toward the end of the war he was stationed at Fort Belevedere on the Hudson.

"I was trained for combat. At Fort Belvore near Boston I was sometimes assigned to Scollay Square, one of the roughest parts of that town. We'd go in four abreast. There were bars, fights everywhere. Our orders were they don't do what you tell them the first time hit 'em. Kick 'em in the crotch, push the head down. We were there with the Shore Patrol and the marines and so forth. Nobody wanted them all over the countryside.

"At Fort Dedens in Ayer, Mass., I worked teaching illiterates close order drills. Blacks, Puerto Ricans, hillbillies. We always had them separate and it was fine. Then we were told we had to integrate and all hell broke loose. We'd find people in the weeds two days later all beat up. We'd go out in the night, into the big field and we'd sit in a chair and wait for trouble. It'd come.

"Finally, I was assigned to Fort Slocum. This was being used as a warehouse at the time. And there were just three of us. A shipment of metal desks would come in and we'd carry them into a warehouse on top of other desks and walk them across the desks to line them up by other desks. We lived in the jail, swept it out, fired the cannon in the morning and raised the flag, fired the cannon at night and lowered the flag and that was it. I was there for three months. Nobody ever came except to do deliveries and pickups.

"One way we had of amusing ourselves was to put big rocks into the breech of the cannon, pull the lanyard and fire it off into the river.

3

Whizzzz, SPLASH. We'd shoot across the bows of fishing boats. Once, on a real foggy day we heard a boat and fired across the bow and it came out of the fog and it was Ripley's hundred foot long Chinese junk with the bamboo masts and booms. This was Ripley from 'Ripley's Believe it or Not.' Eventually a whole company came and just took over. They had come to convert Fort Slocum into a hospital. Who are you guys? They asked. What are you doing here? Get your gear together. You're leaving. The war is over."

Charlie was discharged from the service at Fort Dix, and now eligible for the G.I. Bill, decided to become a veterinarian. But first he had to get his high school diploma. He went at night, to Jamaica High School. During the day, he worked.

"I had a friend who had a motorcycle who worked carrying things for Levitt. They were building Levittown. I went down to see him one day and I walk up and this guy falls off a roof. An ambulance comes. They are putting him on the stretcher and they ask me 'can I do roofing' and I say yes and they stop the stretcher for a minute and take off his thick leather belt with all the tools on it and hand it to me. Then they put him in the ambulance and drove him away. I roofed."

He applied to Penn State and Cornell, but eventually settled on the New York State Institute at Farmingdale. They had an Ag school there and he could commute from home. He took courses in poultry, feed, machinery, horticulture and animal husbandry and he did graduate but not with a degree as a veterinarian.

"I met George Simmons. He taught farm shop at the school and they had set up a whole course around him. I learned how to make candles, harnesses, brooms, we studied where lanterns come from and why they were named that, he took me to the State Fair in Syracuse and because of my interest in his course asked if I would serve on the Board of the Early American Industry Association which I did. What really happened is I got interested in the same thing Mr. Simmons was interested in. One day, Mr. Simmons had me work as an assistant at an auction. I liked that."

After graduation, Charlie took a job at the Henry Ford Museum in Greenfield Village near Dearborn, Michigan. His job was director of crafts and he operated steam engines, printing presses and shops and he taught these skills to students. He lived in a rooming house at first and later an apartment. He stayed four years.

"It was during this period I got engaged," he said. "I became engaged to Anne Hooper of Garden City. We'd send tape recordings back and forth. I sent her a ring. But then she sent it back and said she would marry somebody else. I remember attending the wedding in Garden City. I was heartbroken. She was marrying this guy who owned a company

4

that made saw horses with the blinking lights on them. I stood there at the end of the day and watched as my love flew off in a helicopter for her honeymoon."

In 1955, at the age of twenty nine, Charlie left his job in Michigan to return to the family home. His father was ill. Discussions proceeded. And though father recovered, he was asked, what would make you happy? What would you like to do? I'd like to farm, he said.

And that is how Charlie Vanderveer came to the Hamptons. He came with his father, and for $1,100 an acre, his father bought the eighty acre Jablonski potato farm on Scuttlehole Road. There was no electricity, no plumbing. There was a barn and an unheated house. You could farm there but you couldn't really live there.

Charlie's father came out weekends, but Charlie lived here year around tending the farm. He lived, at first, at Baron's Cove in Sag Harbor, then he rented the Vail House on the Montauk Highway in Bridgehampton, finally he rented a house on Lumber Lane in Bridgehampton.

"We tore out the potatoes. What we planted was endive, wiltloff chicory. It was said you could get $90,000 an acre growing it but it never really worked out though we tried for years. There was something in the water. Maybe too much iron. The endive would turn pink. We sent it to Rutgers, Holland, Belgium, France, nobody could figure it out. But we grew it and we sold it. It took a lot of hard hand labor."

In 1962, Charlie married Natalie, a woman twelve years his junior who he grew up with in Garden City.

"I figured I already had one broken heart. Natalie was the kid next door. I had carried her in the house as a baby. I knew Natalie real well. Or so I thought. It was November 10th, my parents' anniversary. We were married in the same church, the Episcopal cathedral and the place was packed. It was, in fact, more like a coronation than a wedding. We kissed everybody and raced out. We had a suite at the St. Regis for the night."

Back on the farm, Charlie Vanderveer fixed up the farmhouse so he and his new wife could live in it. He started on a second house where his mother and father could move to. Meanwhile, his father continued to drive out half time to help him with the farming. Then Charlie had a run-in with the local clergy.

"The word around town was that we were working farmhands on Sunday. Well, we weren't working farmhands on Sunday. We had all these Cubans and Puerto Ricans and Blacks and on Sunday it was like a playground with picnics, blankets, food and music.

"The ministers from three churches, together with the Catholic priest, came driving up our driveway in a car and half way up who they saw was me. I was stark naked in the field, taking a shower. What

5

we had rigged up there was a 55 gallon drum overhead with a pull chain and nozzles and you'd stand under it and pull the chain and the water was nice and warmed by the sun. They honked the horn. I let go the chain and toweled myself off and then wrapped it around me and walked over. We had a discussion. They went up and saw for themselves. Then they left. They never came back. For THAT reason, anyway."

In 1968, Charlie's father died and Charlie decided not to continue farming without him. Instead, he began to spend more and more time developing his career as the town auctioneer. He leased out the farmland to other farmers. And most of the land was converted back to potatoes.

His marriage also did not prosper. There were no children and he and Natalie had different interests. They began to drift apart. It all came to a head in 1970.

"I had met a woman named Gypsy. She was married to her second husband, Sheridan Lord, and she lived in New York at 96th Street and Park Avenue and worked as the Assistant Public Relations Director at the *New Yorker* magazine. You know, you meet people and you just have to do something. I went to Mexico City with Natalie and we went to the Municipal Building and we got divorced. Then I walked across the hall and there was Gypsy and I married her. I was single for about ten minutes."

There were also young children to raise. Gypsy had three children from a first marriage. The father was in Argentina. And so they all moved in. Charlie took on the job of full time dad. He had an instant family.

"We got lots of animals. There was Petunia the pig who weighed 400 pounds. And there was Jenny the pony. Jenny had come our way as a result of a horse auction we ran for John Halsey at the Stony Hill Farm in Amagansett. At the end of the auction there was this pony unsold. The kind that pulls wagons at the coal mines in Pennsylvania. $50 and its yours, Halsey said. We got it home. You couldn't touch it because it would bite you. You couldn't get close because it would kick you. Nice horse."

It was the following year, 1971, that I met Charlie Vanderveer. I still remember it. We had talked on the telephone because my new wife and I had just bought the house on Lumber Lane that Charlie had once rented. We invited him down for dinner. Gypsy and the three kids came in a stationwagon. Behind them came a green Nash Metropolitan automobile. This was a car, made for about three years in the 1950's, that looked like something Donald Duck would drive. It was a perfectly proportioned sedan, but it was half size. The first compact car. I watched as the door opened and one of the biggest men I had ever seen unfolded himself out of it. I liked him instantly.

"There were two Metropolitans the year you met me," Charlie said.

"I had bought the contents of a house for $250 and it included these two little cars. Also included in the deal was that I had to clean the house out, including the coal in the coal bin. By 1971 it was hard to find people who liked coal. I don't think a scoop had come out since 1910."

Charlie would buy the contents of a house, tag and box everything up and put it into box lots and hold an auction. Once he bought the contents of a house in Springs for $75. He took in $40. Other times, the contents would be so vast he would not buy them but would contract to sell them. One such arrangement was the Rose de Rose house on Hill Street in Southampton. Mrs. de Rose had passed away. He was contacted by her estate.

"Here was a woman who was a real shopper. She had a servant, old Charlie, and they would go out to the Five and Ten and she'd need a cat litter tray and they'd buy ten. She'd buy twenty boxes of laundry soap. And old Charlie would put them on shelves in the basement. We got there and there was ivy growing over the windows but the place was just as she left it. The pillows and sheets were on the bed. There was an artificial leg, gold rim glasses, china and then all this stuff everywhere. We found, in the basement, for example, 144 boxes of Ivory Snowflakes with Marilyn Chambers on the box. She had been a model who had become a pornography film star and there was a whole scandal. Now Ivory was using another model on the box, but these old Marilyn Chambers boxes were worth a lot of money. They were marked 39 cents. We sold them for $5 each. I kept two. Recently, I read where they are fetching $75 a box.

"It took us three months to set up the Rose de Rose house for an auction. And then we had ten separate auctions. Seven for household items, two for the good stuff and one for farm equipment. It was the biggest auction I ever did. When it was over, we were able to give Southampton Hospital a check for $160,000."

There were lots of other auctions, both for charity and for profit. And there were other projects. Once, Charlie and I went for a walk through his farmland to a hollow. It was here, Charlie said, that he was thinking about having a rock concert. He had a promoter. It could be like Woodstock. What did I think? I didn't think much of it. Charlie purchased the Bull's Head Inn building right in the center of downtown Bridgehampton. But when he squabbled with the Town about how he might develop it, he sold it. Today this grand old building is an antique store. Charlie and Gypsy had two more children, Sarah and Styvie. And for several years, after a falling out with the Hampton Day School, Charlie and Gypsy ran their own school in a barn on the property for their kids and about twenty others.

And then there was the night of Charlie and the television. Gypsy was preparing dinner downstairs and asked Charlie to go upstairs and tell the kids dinner was ready. He did, but they didn't come down. They were watching television. He asked them again but they still didn't come down. When he asked them a third time and got no response, he walked upstairs, pulled the television set out of the wall and threw it out the window. Then they all came down for dinner.

"I got pretty good at auctioneering," Charlie said. "At first I could only do about thirty lots an hour. Later I could go through a hundred lots an hour. It really is fun. Especially when you can get two people who really want something — it is usually men and they usually give themselves away — and the bidding goes up and up and up because neither will let the other have it.

"And then there are the catastrophes. Once, I went to a big Post Office auction in New York City. The lot seemed to be a bunch of books in a canvas bag in a push around cart. I got it for $5. But when I showed them my number they said you take these in the bag and you go down the hall and you'll see three big rooms with the same number on it. Those rooms are also filled with your books. And they have to be out by nightfall or we charge you storage.

"I made lots of phone calls, got trailers and thirty guys and we worked all night loading up tractor trailers. I sold a bunch of the books to an outfit in New York that was in the business of coffee table books. I sold the rest to an outfit in Jersey City that bought paper for recycling. What a mess."

Unfortunately, by 1982, his marriage to Gypsy was also on the rocks. A bitter divorce followed. And though Charlie has had a relationship with another woman for the past ten years, he never remarried.

"I do like women," Charlie said. "How they smell, how they look, how they think. So devious. A few days later, they say something and it all makes sense. It's such a great world. So interesting. It never stops."

The interview was over. I commented again that Charlie seemed to look well. I asked how he felt.

"You remember about seven years ago the doctors told you you might die? We talked about it at the time."

I remembered.

"Well, that's how I feel. Only now it is really going to happen. Anyway, physically I feel good. They say I'm supposed to lose weight but I haven't. The only thing is that when I bump into anything I get a black and blue mark. Or I just start bleeding from my gums for no reason. Apparently, I'm losing my ability to clot." He paused for a moment. "Sometimes I think I'll just run into a tree and that will be it. Hee hee."

"And you are taking no medications."

"None. I take vitamin C. Massive amounts. But I don't think there's a cure for this disease."

"You don't think they could prolong it?"

"I don't want to prolong it. Life is all about lifestyle. You have your lifestyle. You live it as long as you can."

I took some pictures of Charlie Vanderveer and they accompany this article. They were probably the last pictures taken of him. Two days later, he was gone. He was sixty six.

January 22, 1993

Chapter 2

ROY SCHEIDER

Actor Roy Scheider (*Jaws, The French Connection, All That Jazz*) took a house in the Hamptons on the recommendation of his wife Brenda.

"It was 1988," Scheider says. "We had just gotten married and she said I know this beautiful place you should lease a house for the summer. And she went and leased a house in Sagaponack. Then she brought me out to it. And I fell in love with this area."

"I'd been coming out to the Hamptons since the early 1970's," Brenda says. "I had shares in summer houses in Amagansett back then"

"Where are you from originally," I ask.

"Buffalo."

We are sitting, Brenda and Roy Scheider and I, at a table in the Bridgehampton Candy Kitchen. It is nine o'clock on a Saturday morning. And, among other things, we discuss kids. The Scheiders have enrolled their son, now three, in the Hampton Day School pre-school program. And Scheider is in the process of starting a theatre club at the school to perform serious drama.

"The birth of our son changed things a great deal for me. Our plan was to settle in Manhattan and we were in the process of decorating an apartment. But the more we came out here the more we though, why do we have to be in Manhattan? We sold our very expensive apartment at a loss about a month ago. We will be year round residents."

Roy Scheider, 60, is perhaps best known in these parts as the star of the movie *Jaws*, a film fashioned after a book set in the Hamptons. But he also has had two Oscar nominations, one for *The French Connection* and the other for *All That Jazz*. He is an accomplished actor.

"What about the house in Los Angeles?" I ask.

"Three months ago, I got a call from Steven Spielberg. He said he'd like to fly me out to Los Angeles for a meeting. I said why? You have a compound in East Hampton. He said come on out, you'll see."

Spielberg, it turned out, had planned a TV show called *SeaQuest*. In fact, NBC had already bought 22 weeks. It's pilot will premiere in March. Spielberg wanted Scheider to have the starring role.

"The year is 2018," Scheider explains. "This is not intended to be fiction. It is intended to be a projection of what it will be like in 2018. Space travel has proven impractical. But undersea development is something else. Many cities have expanded underwater. For example, in Boston and New York, you can get in an elevator and go down under the sea just offshore where people are farming and mining.

"There are land grabbers and robbers down there, however, just like anywhere else. And so the government has built a big ship, the *SeaQuest*, to ply the seas and keep law and order. I have been asked to be the captain of this ship. I am a former marine geologist and submarine captain, now living as a recluse. I take on the job. It is somewhere between *Star Trek* and *Twenty Thousand Leagues Under the Sea*. So now, though we remain based in Sagaponack, I have to take a house for several months in Los Angeles."

Roy Scheider was born and raised in Maplewood, New Jersey, the son of a German immigrant who owned a gas station. He had a difficult childhood. A fat kid, he was the last chosen for anything and, in order to avoid being picked on, either had to run fast or be funny. "I couldn't run fast," he says. "But I could do impressions of practically every actor in Hollywood by the time I was ten."

His home life as a boy was not a happy one. In particular, he felt that his father was extremely critical of him. And so it was that when he went to Franklin and Marshall College in Lancaster, Pennsylvania, he was in absolute heaven. A professor, Daryl Larson who ran the theatre department there, encouraged him to act, told him he was talented and that if he worked at it he could be very good.

"Franklin and Marshall was a college for men back then. So we did plays that were easily done without a lot of women actors. *Coriolanus*, *Mr. Roberts*, *Darkness at Noon*, *Billy Budd*. What few women we needed came from town. Townies. With this encouragement I absolutely fell in love with theatre and for three years running won the actors award, the MVP, that was given out at Franklin and Marshall. When I graduated college I knew exactly what I would be. I told my father 'I'm an actor.' He said, 'you're a damn fool.' And that was that."

When Scheider graduated, however, the Korean War was on. He put three years in the Air Force and it was when he was stationed in Oregon that he married briefly. He married a second time, in 1962, and with his second wife Cynthia, had a daughter, now 29 and married and living in Alaska.

"I just became a grandfather," Scheider says.

For ten years, from 1960 to 1970, he worked the stock companies, touring from Boston to Washington, playing in Joe Papp's Shakespeare Festival, in the Hecshter Theatre in Manhattan and in the Arena in Washington.

And then, after a brief part in *Klute* starring Jane Fonda, he landed the co-starring role, along with Gene Hackman, in *The French Connection*.

"It came about in a very strange way," he says. "Several months before they began casting for *The French Connection*, I had gone to an audition for a British play. The notice said they wanted an actor six feet tall. It was a drizzly day and there was a long line of actors and we had to stand outside the stage door. After about an hour, it was my turn and I went in and the theatre was dark, except for a single worklite on the stage. I could hear rustling sounds in the audience."

* * *

"Good afternoon, Mr. Scheider is it?" this British accent said. "Would you please read from page 18?"

Scheider reads.

"That's very good, Mr. Scheider," the accent said. "Now how tall are you?"

"I'm five eleven, but I could be six feet in boots."

"Would you read the scene on page 27?"

He reads the scene on page 27.

"That's very nice. How tall did you say you were?"

"I'm five eleven, but I could be six feet in boots."

"Now please read the scene on page 77."

He reads the scene on page 77.

"And you said you were how tall?"

"I said I was five feet eleven but I could be six feet in boots."

"Would you please stand back to back with the stage manager?"

And that was it. Scheider threw the script out into the darkness. The pages floated down. "You people wouldn't hire Lawrence Olivier, James Cagney, or Marlon Brando because they are too short," he yelled and he walked out.

* * *

The British accent, it turned out, belonged to the director of the play. But the casting director Bob Weiner, who was overhearing this conversation, abosorbed it all. And, unknown to Roy Scheider, three months later when casting began for *The French Connection*, Weiner was given that casting job too. They were looking for a tough guy.

"I think I know who should have this part," Weiner told the producers. "I saw this actor. I don't know if you can handle him, but he'd be perfect."

The French Connection, which was, in Scheider's words "the first two guys in a car city western," won nine Oscar nominations, including Scheider's for the best supporting actor.   Gene Hackman won Best Actor.

Without a doubt the most financially successful picture of Scheider's career was *Jaws*, which cost about $12 million to make in 1974 and which brought in $400 million in its first six months.

"Steven Spielberg was at a Hollywood party with Tracy Keenan Wynn and I walked in on this conversation where the two of them were talking about this giant shark that comes out of the water and cracks a boat in half.   I thought they were crazy.   But a few days later, Spielberg called and asked me to take this part where I'd be essentially the same character as I was in *The French Connection* but in this resort where nobody would believe me.   It was intriguing.

"We spent three seasons, spring, summer and fall, filming this movie on Martha's Vineyard.   I loved Martha's Vineyard.   I loved the ocean, the weather, the food, the island.   It was like the Jersey shore which I was very familiar with, but much better.   Not a whole lot to do.

"It took so long to film because the techies couldn't get the model shark to bear up under ocean conditions.   Salt would get at it.   It would malfunction.   Waiting around, Richard Dreyfus and I and Robert Shaw would improvise these scenes on the boat.   Many of these scenes made the movie.   It really does touch everybody's fear of water.   Even for people who live in the Bronx.   Or Buffalo."

Scheider starred in *Blue Thunder*, *The Sorcerer*, *Marathon Man* and *All That Jazz*.

All That Jazz, directed by Bob Fosse and written by Fosse and Robert Alan Arthur, was the most challenging film Scheider ever made.   He plays the lead, a Broadway show director who is admired and loved.   And as the film turns into a battle between life and death, it becomes a fantastic and disturbing blend of fantasy and reality.   *All That Jazz* won the Grand Prize at the Cannes Film Festival when it appeared in 1980. It also earned Scheider his second Oscar nomination, this time for Best Actor.

And then came Brenda King, from Buffalo.   His second marriage, after twenty years, was on the rocks.   He and his wife had agreed to go their separate ways.

"We met in the Zimmer Drug Store on the corner of Madison and 76th Street." Scheider says.   "She came up to me while I was looking at a magazine and told me that *All That Jazz* was one of her favorite movies and that I was terrific in it."

The rest, as they say, is history.

Februrary 12, 1993

13

Chapter 3

BOB PITTMAN

My appointment is with Bob Pittman, Chief Executive Officer and President of Time-Warner Enterprises, also Chairman and CEO of Six Flags Theme Parks. I know he is a young CEO, having risen on his talents to the top of the heap in a very short time. And so I figure he will be a young looking 45, maybe 50. Pittman is credited with having founded MTV and was the head of MTV, Nickelodeon and VH-1. Today, he is the head of Time-Warner Enterprises and, of course, Six Flags.

I go into the main lobby of the giant Time-Warner building in Rockefeller Center, am taken to the 27th floor and a small meeting room with a polished table and a few chairs, I'm offered coffee by a secretary and I wait.

In a little while, the door opens and a young man in his thirties comes in and extends his hand. A secretary follows. Somewhere in here, I figure, there is my cup of coffee. And Bob Pittman will be here soon.

"Hi," the young man says. "I'm Bob Pittman."

As I talk with this young man, I am impressed not only with the quickness of his mind, but with the people at Time-Warner who have promoted him to such a high position at such a young age. But the more we talk, the more I realize that whatever promotions have come along, they have not been because Mr. Pittman has jockeyed for them. He just does the job at hand with his great focus and enthusiasm. If they make him in charge, great. It's not that big a deal. It is, I think, the Zen approach to the corporate ladder.

I do try to coax a little of the trappings of success out of him.

14

"Where do you live in Manhattan?" I ask.

"The Upper West Side."

"Married?"

"Yes."

"A penthouse overlooking the water?"

"No," he shrugs. "Just an apartment. My wife is a mountain climber. Right now she is off climbing the tallest seven mountains in the world. She's on the fourth. No woman has ever done this."

I back out gracefully. "Children?"

"We have a nine year old son."

Bob Pittman was born and raised in the rural south, in a series of small towns in Mississippi. His father was a minister. His mother a homemaker.

"My dad would be the minister in a church for a few years, then move on. Where I was raised was Brookhaven, Mississippi, 'the homeseeker's paradise.' It was a time when people were moving south. Brookhaven wanted to encourage them. We settled in this small town when I was eleven and I stayed there through high school. I went to Brookhaven High School.

"My number one interest as a kid, I guess, was raising hell. I drove a motorcycle through the woods. A lot too fast. We'd steal eggs from a farm and let them rot in the woods upwind. But I also played clarinet and I had a rock band. And I had good grades so they couldn't throw me out. I rarely agreed with my teachers about anything. I enjoyed that. A few years ago, my math teacher Blanche Matheson wrote me a letter. It said, 'I guess sometimes we worry about the wrong people.'"

Pittman became obsessed with airplanes. At the age of 15, he informed his parents that the following year, he was going to get his pilot's license. Sixteen was the youngest you could be and still get a license. They told him he'd have to find the money to take the flying lessons necessary to get the license.

"I went to Jack's Clothing Store and asked for a job but they didn't have any. Then I went to the Piggly Wiggly and asked if I could bag groceries and there were no job openings there. Then I went into the local radio station, Station 16. Would they have a job? 'Can you play commercials?' they asked. That was that."

In his last few years at Brookhaven High, Pittman worked as a disk jockey at the station, went to school and, on weekends, motorcycled over to the airport where he took occasional lessons and basically just hung around. He'd trade pumping gas for flying lessons, accompany a doctor who sometimes flew down to the Gulf Coast and back — he'd let him fly — he'd even make bets about how easily he could do certain things in an airplane in exchange for flying lessons if he won. He got his pilot's license.

He also had all sorts of other hobbies. He seemed to like absolutely everything.

"My brother used to call them Hobbies du Jour. Every day it was something else. Photography, shooting, boating, fishing."

I asked about his brother. He was an older brother and he was the town's high school hero. Valedictorian of his class, "Mr. Basketball." Today he runs a daily paper in Tupelo, Mississippi.

Pittman went off to college, Millsaps College, thinking he would like to become a physician. It was 1972. He grew a full beard and had his hair long. But almost immediately, in the middle of his freshman year, he took a sharp turn into another field entirely.

"In a nutshell," Pittman said, "I was bitten by the radio bug."

Pittman was offered a radio job in Milwaukee, Wisconsin. He took the job, transferred to a school near Milwaukee, then got offered a job as night d.j. of a radio station in Detroit. He went to college during the day, spent his evenings at the radio station and went home early in the morning to sleep on a mattress in a one room apartment for a few hours. He loved it.

"What most interested me," he told me, "was not being a disk jockey, but being the program director of a station. I realized it was the program director behind the disk jockey who really mattered. And I'd look at ratings and I'd look at positioning and I'd try to think, what could we do to become number one in the market. To me, the challenge was the fight. The fight to succeed."

In a short time, he was promoted from night d.j. to research director. He was nineteen years old, and he still had his full beard and long hair.

His first assignment, to completely re-program a radio station, however, came with an offer from WPEZ in Pittsburgh. He could not refuse it.

"I would be going up against my idol," Pittman said. "This was Buzz Bennett, who was the greatest programmer in history. A legend. He was the first programmer to beat Bill Drake for the number one spot. Drake was also a legendary programmer.

"What Bennett had done at a station called 13Q in Pittsburgh was to simulcast top forty music on both AM and FM. This brought the station to number one. But then, he decided to break away the simulcasting and do beautiful music on FM. I thought, here I am going into a market with the greatest programmer ever. He's probably doing everything right. How do I beat him?"

The answer was to make WPEZ, an FM station, sound just like 13Q AM. By running the top forty on WPEZ, he made listeners who were searching for that sound on FM wind up on his station rather than on Buzz Bennett's. Within a year he had taken over the number one spot.

Pittman thoroughly enjoyed telling this story. He was animated, laughing, moving his hands for emphasis. It was the challenge of the

16

competition.

"Whatever Buzz would do on his AM station as a promotion," Pittman said, continuing, "we would copy on FM. He'd do The Great Rip Off. 'Be the fifth caller and rip us off for a record album.' We'd do the same thing and call it the Great Zip Off."

His next challenge was in Chicago for NBC radio. They wanted a country music format, and Pittman wondered if he could do it. "You know research," they told him. "You figure it out."

Pittman discovered, with his research, that country music was far more popular than anybody realized. But the people who were listening to it, mostly city people, were embarrassed to admit it. The disk jockeys were all "howdy pardner, hee haw," and the listeners wanted only to get past that to the music.

Pittman's solution was to run Top Forty radio station marketing techniques — answer your phone and win $10,000 — and have everything about the station be Top Forty except the music, which was country. Again his station went to number one.

"This station was a big 50,000 watt thing," Pittman told me. "I was in Chicago, but my parents could hear it in Jackson, Mississippi. I'd call and ask them what they thought."

Pittman took on the job of rescuing NBC's FM station in Chicago which had been an all-news station and a complete disaster. He made it an album rock station and, thinking hard about the fact that there were very few commercials, decided to make something positive about that. He had the disk jockeys advertise frequent "commercial free hours." He kept it up for sixty days until the commercials, pouring in, made continuing it impossible.

At this point, his extraordinary success had come to the attention of Herb Schlosser, who was President of NBC. Schlosser called Pittman into his Rockefeller Center office and told him he wanted him to move to New York and get experience programming television. Schlosser also told his executives to put Pittman under contract. They offered him a lucrative package. He was twenty three years old and he decided it was time to shave off his beard and begin to look respectable.

In NBC's Manhattan studios, Pittman was put in charge of programming a TV show to follow *Saturday Night Live*. At that late hour he did a fifteen minute program called *Album Tracks*. The first half was music videos. The second half was commentary on the music scene. It was Saturday night at one in the morning. He figured, correctly, it would be the teens and early twenties up at that hour after *Saturday Night Live*.

It was 1979, Pittman was 25 years old, and several events were to happen that year that were important in his life. He got married. And Fred Silverman replaced Herb Schlosser as President of NBC.

"I got an offer to be head of programming for the Warner AMEX

17

Satellite Entertainment Company; a joint venture of Warner Communications and American Express. It was right here in Rockefeller Center. I wouldn't even have to move. If Schlosser had still been at NBC I might not have taken it. But with him gone, there was no reason not to."

The company had already put together the first independent cable network, The Movie Channel. Now, they thought they would make more. Steve Ross asked Bob Pittman to think of what the next network might be. Pittman's idea was MTV.

"At the time," Pittman said, "there was talk that there would eventually be some sort of video music on television. Music videos were indeed being made at that time, although not particularly good ones. They were being made by groups that hadn't wanted to take the time to tour Europe. They'd make a tape of a song and send that, and on European television it was an accepted thing for an announcer to say 'Today's guest is Hall and Oates,' and then they'd run the tape. We looked into it, counted the number of tapes available since they would be our inventory. There were only 250. If we did an all music video channel we would have to gamble that more would be made. And quick."

Pittman approached the problem in a revolutionary way. Don't sell the shows. Sell the network. Pittman gave MTV a look and a feel. It wasn't the *I Love Lucy* show they wanted you to watch, it was the network itself. The cable companies, that would have to carry MTV, balked. And so Pittman pushed harder.

"We just, um, rammed it down their throats," he said.

An ad campaign was created called I WANT MY MTV. And among those singing it or just saying it on television and urging viewers to call their cable companies were David Bowie, Madonna, Sting, Cindi Lauper and dozens of others. The number of viewers able to receive MTV rose from just over a million when it first went on the air, to sixty million today. And MTV has become one of the biggest success stories in home entertainment.

Pittman rewarded his viewers with absolutely outrageous contests. "It was the 80's after all," he said, "sort of an exercise in excess."

There was the "One Night Stand." Wherever you were in the world, on that one night a Lear jet would come, pick up you and a friend, and fly you to a Fleetwood Mac concert where you would have dinner with the band, watch their show, go with them backstage afterwards and then, early that morning be flown by the Lear jet back to wherever you had come from. It would be the Best 24 Hours of Your Life.

Outrageous indeed.

In 1983, the company re-launched the floundering children's network called Nickelodeon. Programming had been endorsed by the PTA and the NEA but was just not connecting with children.

18

"The kids thought it was spinach," Pittman said. "My contribution on this was to find Gerry Laybourne far down the programming pole in the company. She fashioned Nickelodeon into what it is today. It too has been a big success."

Time-Warner recently purchased the chain of the Six Flags theme parks around the nation. And Pittman is promoting them as an alternative to Disneyworld, but right in your back yard close to home.

"We are opening the Batman ride at our New Jersey park in April," Pittman said. "It's going to be wonderful."

"I'll go," I said.

I asked Pittman about the future of home entertainment. He took out a pad and pencil and began drawing boxes and relationships as he talked.

"Twenty years from now," he said, "I think people will say it was very clever they thought to put that wire in the home. We are about to enter the age of two-way communication on cable. And video on demand. You want a particular movie at a particular time, pick what you want. There it is. And the boundaries separating television and the computer and the telephone are about to become very blurry. This is going to be a very exciting, and it will present many opportunities."

Pittman and his family have rented homes in the Hamptons from time to time, in East Hampton one year, in Bridgehampton another. They are frequent visitors here when they don't rent and one of Pittman's favorite places to shop is Loaves and Fishes in Sagaponack. But he hates the traffic between Southampton and East Hampton.

Pittman also rides with the Hampton HOGS. This is a group of motorcycle riders that includes singer Billy Joel, Glen Dubin a commodities trader, *Rolling Stone* owner Jann Wenner and Michael Cinque who owns the Amagansett Liquor Store. They ride together all over. Pittman recently completed a motorcycle ride criss-crossing the country with Jann Wenner.

"What about your pilot's license?" I asked.

"I like getting new ratings," he said. "I have a Cessna 340. And I'm rated for commercial multi-engine. I fly helicopters."

"What about a 747?" I asked.

"No," he said. "Well, not yet."

March 12, 1993

19

Chapter 4

FRANCES LEAR

If there was ever an example of what a woman can do in a man's world in America, it is the example of Frances Lear. Once the Beverly Hills wife of Norman Lear (*All in the Family*), she separated from him, moved back to Manhattan to an apartment they jointly owned on the Upper East Side, and told everybody she would be starting a magazine for women. This was in 1985. She was 62 years old. She never had anything to do with magazines before.

Now what were the odds she would get anywhere with that? Well, today she is sixty nine, and I am sitting with her in her splendid old oceanfront Victorian mansion in Southampton on a stormy afternoon and I have to tell you she absolutely knocks me out. She looks forty. No. Take that back. She looks thirty. She's about five feet one, there isn't an ounce of fat on her and she looks like a ballet dancer. In fact, she moves like a ballet dancer, tucking her legs under her, perching on the edge of a sofa as she makes a point, leaping up and walking over to a window to look out. Before we can even discuss *Lear's Magazine*, which has taken the publishing industry by storm and has soared to a circulation of almost half a million, I have to find out how she keeps herself in such fighting trim. This is remarkable.

"Exercise," she says. "Diet and exercise. I take care of myself."

People had told me, as I discussed with them that I would be meeting with Frances Lear, that she was a difficult woman, that she could be a bitch to work for, that she would undoubtedly be nice to me since I was interviewing her for the paper, that I should watch for the rough edges. But what I came away with was the image of a determined, smart, opinionated woman – a quite beautiful woman – who set a goal for herself, trained herself into fighting trim, and went out and got what she wanted. If she was to bruise a few egos along the way, so be it.

And what she got was something that was quite important to her. For it was, and is, a message for the future of women, and men, in this country.

"In 1985 I was in a bar in Beverly Hills with Jim Autrey, who publishes Meredith Magazines out there, and we were talking about magazines. I told him that all my adult life I had been unable to find a women's magazine that I liked. I was offended by them. I'd read them and all they'd talk about was home, sex and family. Nothing about the issues in the world. And they'd talk about these things in a condescending manner, as if their readers had not got a brain in their heads and would have to be talked down to. But I read the news magazines. *Time. Newsweek.*

"I asked Jim Autrey why there wasn't a magazine for me, and he said that nobody in the publishing houses had my mind set. I told him that I had this mind set and I knew a lot of women that had this mind set. And then I said that since there wasn't a magazine I'd make one."

She came to Manhattan, set up a magazine office in her New York apartment, almost got thrown out by the co-op board, then went out and rented offices on Madison Avenue.

"I want to make a magazine that will improve the image of women to women and industry," she told people. "I want a magazine that deals in solutions. We're not going to deal in rehashing the old problems in *Lear's Magazine.*"

The people she talked to, privately, gave her the chances of a snowball in hell. Wife of a Hollywood producer? Never had any experience in publishing before? The Manhattan publishing industry would eat her alive. They didn't know Frances Lear.

"I'm originally from New York," she told me. "I was born upstate of an unwed mother and I was placed in an orphanage for the first eighteen months of my life. Then I was adopted by an unloving mother and a loving father and I grew up in Larchmont until I was ten. Then everything went wrong. My father had been in the manufacturing business, nurses and maids uniforms, and when the crash came in 1929 and wiped him out, he became depressed. In 1933, he killed himself."

Her mother remarried.

"My step father incested me for a number of years. I became difficult. I was sent to a psychiatrist because I was being difficult and I told this woman psychiatrist what my step father was doing to me and the psychiatrist gave this information to my mother and stepfather.

"I was sixteen years old. We were living on East 88th Street. My stepfather confronted me and told me I would have to swear to my mother that what I told the psychiatrist was not true. He brought me to her and I refused. She turned her back on me."

That was the last day Frances Lear was to spend with her parents. That evening she packed her things and moved out to a rundown hotel on 23rd Street. She had enough money for one night. The next morning she got a job as a sales clerk at B. Altman's. She was on her own.

"I saw my mother twice more before she died. She had become ill. When she died I was eighteen."

Frances Lear took any job she could get. She worked as a receptionist, she took classified ads on the telephone. She worked at ad agencies, perfume companies, department stores, newspapers. Her goal was to find a job where the money was, doing "men's work." But try as she might, she could not get a job outside of what was considered the traditional female job market: receptionist, secretary, clerk.

Eventually, she worked her way into the fashion industry where she became an apparel buyer for a large department store. It was an important job, though it didn't pay well. It seemed to be as far as she could go given her background and gender in those times.

She also married. Twice. "I was very lonely. I wanted desperately to have a connection with someone. I'd get married and then it wouldn't work out. I was married each time less than eighteen months."

And then one day a male friend of hers suggested she meet this young television producer. This was in 1957, in the early days of television, when it was black and white and not yet considered the dominant industry it is today. The man that was recommended to her was producing the *Martha Raye Show* on television. He was the same age as she was, which was 32, and her friend knew him because the two of them had been buddies together in the air force during the Korean War.

Norman Lear came to her apartment. They would have a blind date.

"The first time I saw him, I knew I would marry him," she said. "I don't know why. But I sometimes have the ability to see through events."

Norman Lear was separated from his wife at the time, dated Frances and fell in love with her. He got a divorce. They married, set up housekeeping in Manhattan, and began to raise a family. They had two children.

"I was deliriously happy with him," Frances Lear said. "I was deliriously happy to have children with him."

The focus of their lives together, and this was perfectly all right with Frances Lear, was to work together on the promotion of Normal Lear's career. Frances Lear described it to me as a kind of "cottage industry." They were a team.

Soon, Norman Lear became a star. They moved to Beverly Hills. They bought a big house with a swimming pool and a tennis court. And suddenly, Norman Lear had all sorts of advisors in every conceivable field. He had accountants, public relations people, secretaries, creative help, drivers, backers. And Frances Lear saw that she was out of a job.

"It was incredible," she said. "I was perfectly happy until he became famous. Then he didn't need me any more and I was miserable. We talked about it and he said make the best of it. This is the way it is.

"It's all about fame. Fame rewrites life. It changes people and circumstances and perceptions that others have. Almost everybody I know who has become famous has been hurt by it. As for me, I did not share Norman's life anymore but I shared it. I became depressed and afraid."

And then the women's movement came along. It was 1975 and suddenly she found something she could get involved in. She went to meetings, events and marches. She joined organizations and she gave money and she wrote letters to newspapers and magazines. For ten years, until her children were fully grown and out of the nest, she continued to live unhappily in Beverly Hills, unable to leave and go out on her own because she had always wanted a family and here it was.

"I spent ten years trying to leave Beverly Hills," she said.

By 1985, both her daughters were in New York. Maggie was working on a Masters of Social Work. Kate had gotten married and was partners with her husband in a software company. There was that apartment in Manhattan which she and Norman seldom used. And then, one day, there was the drink she had in the bar in Beverly Hills.

Lear's Magazine published it's first issue in 1988. It had been three years in the making.

"I'd never done anything like this before," she said. "I had to learn how to do it. Furthermore, I had no credibility. I was a housewife from Beverly Hills. I'd have to print a prototype for the ad agency people. In fact, it would have to be a smashing prototype."

Frances Lear solicited help from her Manhattan friends and began to put together the design and editorial structure of the magazine. She credits much of this to a longtime friend, Richard Durrell, who was at that time publisher of *People* magazine, and who is now retired.

"He started out just helping me as a friend. But he is a very brilliant man. I asked him to be a consultant. He said he would and he did."

The prototype came out and it was a sensation. Less than a year after that the first issue appeared and *Lear's* took off like a rocket. It has increased in size, circulation and advertising every year since it was founded, right through the longest recession this nation has had since the Great Depression.

"The reason it has been a success," she said, "was that I had a point of view. I was making an old fashioned general interest contemporary magazine for a market that had no magazine. It was for women. Women like me.

"My opinion? I think there is something that women do better than men, or at least women over forty do better than men over forty and that is CHANGE. All through time, women have adapted. Now women are discarding the old role of victim and, surprise, it is the men who are taking it up. Men are victimized by the changes that are taking place in women. They are confused."

At this point in our interview, a thunderstorm began, coming in from the west. There was a clap of thunder and the lights went out. In other parts of the house, I could hear people running this way and that.

"Oh dear," Frances said. "I hope I haven't lost anything."

"Lost what?"

"On my computer. It is on upstairs. I'm not sure that I saved everything."

"Want to go look?"

"Yes. Come with me. I want you to see where I work anyway. I work in the bedroom. I have a desk set up there. I always work in my bedroom."

I followed her up a flight of stairs, through a huge sitting room with the sea pounding the sand below, and the lights came back on. Then we went into a bedroom that was the size of a living room. There was a double bed along one wall, there were two walls of Victorian windows looking out at the storm and the sea. It was breathtaking.

"Everything seems to be all right," Frances Lear said, looking at the glowing monitor. "It's all here."

"I would kill for a room like this," I said. "This is wonderful."

"I'm writing a new book. Can't tell you what it is about." Her current book, *Second Seduction*, is an autobiography and just out.

We walked back out of the living room and I met one of her daughters. Also a grandchild about a year old. Some people were playing dominoes on a glass table. It seemed to be a very private household.

"I think I have enough for a story," I said. "But I am curious how you came to buy such a wonderful house."

"It was when I moved to New York," Frances said. "I have a friend who is a real estate agent, Ed Cave, and I told him I didn't have time to look at houses, I'd like to just see one and he showed me this and I bought it."

"Do you do much socializing when you are out here?" I asked. "Do you have a favorite restaurant?"

"I eat at home," she said. "I eat at home here and I eat at home in Manhattan. I have gone 'out' too much in my life."

Frances Lear walked me to the door. We shook hands. And I ran out through the rain and got into my car.

July 24, 1992

24

Chapter 5

NICK CHAVIN

There is nothing particularly unusual about Nick Chavin that would leave you to suspect anything. His appearance is that of your typical New York advertising executive. Tie, jacket, mid-forties, rapid patter. He is neither particularly handsome or particularly ugly. And he is partners with Lannie Lambert in the largest advertising agency in the City of New York specializing in real estate: Chavin/Lambert.

But then, there is this crazy look in his eyes. Humor is there. An unremitting glee. There is something else. A wildness...

* * *

The big changes in Chavin's life began when he was twelve years old and I will get to that. But I warn you they involve X-rated material and if you find this offensive I suggest you stop reading now. First, however, Nick Chavin's early life.

"Until I was in junior high school, I was raised in Skokie, Illinois just outside Chicago. My father was an attorney who worked for the Department of Justice on immigration cases. My mother was a housewife and, sometimes, a medical aide. My grandparents had all emigrated from Russia, specifically from a small Jewish town outside of St. Petersburg called Gomel. It was a very small town. When you were in St. Petersburg they had a joke when you did something wrong which went 'excuse my ineptitude. I'm from Gomel.'"

Chavin's childhood was particularly normal except for one thing. He kept getting in trouble, mostly inadvertently. He threw a snowball at Barbara Schneiman in the third grade and it broke her nose. In the seventh grade, a kid lent him a switchblade knife for the afternoon just so he could feel how it felt carrying it around and then somebody squealed on him. His parents were called into the principal's office. What followed was a suspension and twice a week visits to the school psychologist for inkblot tests. The ineptitude of Gomel was following him around.

The changes began when his father was transferred to Phoenix and the family moved. Two years later he was transferred again, this time to El Paso, Texas on the Mexican border. If you were a judge dealing with immigration papers, this was the place to be. Chavin was fourteen.

"Most healthy American boys at fourteen fantasize about sex," Chavin said. "In El Paso in the late 1950's, there was no need to fantasize. Two hundred thousand residents of El Paso lived just across the river from four hundred thousand residents of Juarez, Mexico. All you had to do was put two cents in a slot and you could walk across the bridge. You could get anything you could want in Juarez and it cost pennies. The El Paso girls didn't stand a chance.

"All our parents, for example, had maids. They were paid three dollars a day. We teenagers had a network of sleeping with our mother's friend's maids in exchange for our allowance. I could order drinks. I could get anything I wanted at fourteen. And I did. Juarez and El Paso were the ultimate meeting of the greedy and the needy. The border divided them."

Chavin went to El Paso High School and became the school paper's sports editor. Here he was, a kid recently moved from buttoned down Chicago. In the *El Paso Tattler* he tried to get away with writing articles with sexual references. It would be great fun tweaking the authorities.

"I wrote that a particularly good halfback ejaculated through the line, or that he failed to get through and the prophylactic-like line of the defense held."

At home, his parents grounded him for a week.

His grades in his freshman and sophomore years at El Paso High were terrible. They ranged from D to F. But then something intellectual caught his interest. He joined the school debating team and the school entered him in competitions in the extemporaneous speaking category. He won the division title, then he entered and won the regional title, then he went off to the State Championships, where he won second prize in the entire state. It was his junior year and he began getting A's and B's. He pulled an almost exact repeat performance in his senior year.

"It was the same kid that beat me out as State Champion in both my junior and senior years. Still, going from juvenile delinquent to second best in the State wasn't bad."

Chavin applied for admission to the University of Texas. "At that time," he said, "they had a policy that 'No Male Texan Can Be Denied Admission to the University of Texas.' That was me."

On November 22, 1963, Chavin had been assigned by the *Daily Texan* news editor to write the story of the speech President Kennedy was going to give that night at the Austin Municipal Center. The speech never came because in the middle of the afternoon Kennedy was gunned down in Dallas. Nevertheless Chavin walked over to the Municipal Center.

"In the kitchen, I saw all these platters filled with partially cooked steaks. They would never be eaten because the event had been cancelled. Fifteen hundred partially cooked steaks. I'll never forget what it felt like seeing that. Time stood still. That was what I wrote about in my article."

A few other stories from his University of Texas period. One day, working in the newspaper office, a yellow jeep pulled up and author John Steinbeck got out. He came in to the journalism building, asked if he could use the wire service which he did to wire something, then tipped his cap and left. He was a world famous author and all the journalism students were awed by his appearance. He had, in fact, left his home in Sag Harbor to travel around the country in his jeep with his dog named Charlie. Two years later they published *Travels With Charlie*.

The anger and violence began to seethe in campuses across the country just as Chavin was graduating the University of Texas. He remembered President Johnson coming to graduation day—Linda Bird was in Chavin's class—and everybody looked at him sitting there with all the Secret Service men and Lady Bird and George Hamilton. (Hamilton fell asleep during the ceremony.)

"The coincidences were beginning to build. One month later to the day, a student named Charles Whitman climbed to the top of the University of Texas bell tower and with a high powered rifle killed 32 people below. He was shooting at almost exactly where President Johnson had been sitting one month before."

Chavin planned to go to Hastings Law School outside of Los Angeles where he had been accepted. His parents had sent him the $100 acceptance fee. He went to the mailbox. And he was unable to put the acceptance letter in.

What he did instead was go to San Francisco State to study creative writing as a graduate student. It was 1967. He rented an apartment one block from Haight Street. The very heart of the San Francisco hippie district.

For those who were not around in the late 1960's, the hippie movement is a very hard thing to describe. It was bellbottom jeans and beads, headbands and camper buses, psychedelic colors, sex and marijuana. Chavin, the graduate of, shall we say, El Paso, came to it like a duck to water.

He became editor of a poetry magazine, the *Magdelyn Syndrome Gazette*, on Waller Street in San Francisco. He published the poetry of Alan Ginsberg, Philip Whalen, Gary Snyder, Lou Welch, Richard Brautigan and, of course, Nick Chavin. He published the poetry of Ho Chi Minh, smuggled out of China by a dissident. He published, as poetry, a memo from Lim P. Lee of the U. S. Postal Service urging employees to "try to avoid crippling disabling accidents during Disability Week." And he received his Masters Degree. It was 1968. It was time to get a job, a real job. He'd TRY anyway. Anti-war demonstrations were everywhere. Protestors threw stones at Chavin when he walked into the administration building to pick up his Masters Degree.

This degree entitled him, in the State of California, to automatic junior college teaching credentials. He was, by all accounts, a left wing hippie poet hot head. What would they do with him? They gave him a job at the Contra Costa Junior College in Oakland teaching creative writing. He also worked as a General Education Development teacher for CETA, helping adults get their high school equivalency. He got married to his girl friend, had a daughter, and, for $20,000 bought a four bedroom house in Marin County overlooking the valley.

He was a retired hippie. He hated it.

"My friends used to say I'd roam around in the woods at night. They tell me today they used to wonder what would become of me. How long I would last doing this?"

Nick Chavin could not be chained down. It all lasted about three years. Then, in 1974, an old college friend returned from Borneo where he had been in the Peace Corps. He invited Chavin to come down and see him perform at the Troubador in Los Angeles where he and his rock group were known as Kinky Friedman and the Texas Jew Boys. Chavin went, then went out onto Santa Monica Boulevard and began to cry. I want to do this, he thought. I want to be a rock star.

Chavin leaned forward now in his chair at his Fifth Avenue advertising office. "You know, a month later I dressed myself up as a rock star, open shirt, cowboy boots, chains. And I went out onto the stage and into the limelight. If you've got the balls do to it, you say you will do it and then you go ahead and do it, nobody stops you."

And that is how rock star Chinga Chavin, formerly Nick Chavin, was born. A week after his second performance, he was reviewed in *Playboy* magazine.

The reason for this was that Chinga Chavin wrote very original songs. What songs they were. With a country western beat from his Texas days, he mixed in X-rated lyrics that he was able to put on paper from his poetry days in San Francisco. The songs were outrageous, pornographic and were either wildly funny or utterly offensive depending upon which side of the sofa you sat on. He wrote, and I warned you this would be the X-rated part, "Asshole from El Paso," "Tit Stop Rock," "Dry Humping in the Back of a Fifty Five Ford," "Jailbait," and dozens more.

"I took my songs to Commander Cody trying to get more exposure than just me. They were afraid to do it. I tried Asleep at the Wheel.

I tried Clover. Nobody was interested."

And then he got a telephone call from Bob Guccione of *Penthouse* magazine based in New York. Guccione would back Chinga Chavin who would play his own songs and record them on an album. Guccione would promote the album in *Penthouse*, sell the records mail order and send Chavin around the country on tour. Guccione promised to pay for the production of one Chavin album a year. It was a match made in heaven.

In fact, the match lasted three years. The album *Country Porn* created outrage in Nashville, media attention on both coasts and anathema in the middle. It sold over a hundred thousand copies.

Here's a review, written at the time.

"Not everyone has been amused," wrote Country Scene. "Chavin was arrested in suburban Hayward, California for indecent exposure during a concert. At his debut at the prestigious Troubador in Los Angeles, the manager went into shock on hearing *Country Porn's* lyrics and pulled the plug on the amplifiers...And (Chavin) made angry headlines when his show at a divinity school homecoming dance featured porn star Gina Fornelli in and out of nun's habit."

More enthusiastic reviews appeared in the columns of *Penthouse* magazine. But you might have expected that.

The Chavin marriage did not survive *Country Porn*. Mrs. Chavin remained with the house and daughter in Marin County. Chinga moved to Manhattan. The following year, however, their daughter Brandi moved to New York City to be with her father. From 1980 to 1985 she attended PS 158.

Kinky Friedman and the Texas Jew Boys thrived for many years. In fact, they continue to do so with appearances on *Saturday Night Live* and other TV shows. Chinga Chavin's career, however, ended. His second album, *Jet Lag*, did not, repeat, did not contain X-rated material. It got a lukewarm reception. And the arrangement with Guccione terminated.

It was 1981. What was a rock star named Chinga, in New York without a contract but with a small daughter that he loved very much, supposed to do?

"I always had a passion for real estate," Chavin said. "I had bought the house next door to mine in Marin County and had rented it out. By chance I was dating a girl who worked at an advertising agency. I applied for a job there. It was a small agency called Great Scott. And they hired me. After a year, I asked the owner, Lorraine Borden, if we couldn't specialize in Manhattan real estate advertising. It was the early 1980's and the boom had not yet begun. She said no. So I spun it off and, along with Lannie Lambert, a great advertising writer I befriended at Great Scott, went into the business for myself."

Today, Chavin/Lambert has the reputation for writing some of the most effective real estate advertising in the City. They are now the largest agency in this specialized field in the City of New York. Some of their current accounts include Barbara Corcoran, Newmark Realty, Galbraith Riverbank, Donald Zucker and the Durst Organization.

"We have been producing real estate advertising consistently for more than ten years now. We know this business. I speak at schools about it. I am interviewed by reporters. One recently asked me, 'Is real estate dead?' 'Yes,' I replied. 'Shelter is no longer considered one of the necessities of life.' Of course it will come back. It has already begun to come back, though I think it will never again return to the 7% compounded annual growth years of the 1980's. Back then, *Manhattan Inc.* magazine was featuring real estate company owners as *Playboy* pin-ups for heaven sakes."

In the roaring real estate boom of the 1980's, the creative work of Chavin/Lambert was on the back burner behind their uncanny ability to select successful advertising mediums. Now, with budgets smaller, the ads have to shout louder. People are turning to Chavin/Lambert more for their creativity.

"But now," he said, "the city is beginning to come back to life. There is no new residential housing, so the seeds have been sown for a future shortage. Vacant commercial office space is rapidly becoming absorbed. I think the best idea for Manhattan residential real estate in 1994 might be to buy up studio and one bedroom apartments that are right next to each other and combine them into three and four bedroom units, which are virtually nonexistent in the City today."

And Chavin has remarried. In the mid-1980's he began coming out to the Hamptons in the summertime. "We'd share houses. It was the breeding season and we were looking to mate."

In 1988 he came out to a house in Westhampton Beach and, because he had forgotten his key, climbed in through an open kitchen window to fall at the feet of a young woman employed there to do the cleaning.

"She was taking a summer break from going to school at the Sorbonne. Her name was Terri. Originally from Long Island. I married her."

Terri and Nick (formerly Chinga) live in Manhattan on Central Park South. They have two children, Maxfield and Drew. They also have a unit at the Montauk Manor in the summertime. Chavin also has a daughter from a previous marriage, Brandi, attending UCLA.

"I love to swim. I physically need the beach. I body surf and if there are high breaking waves I find them. In the wintertime I scuba in the Caribbean."

Chavin opens a drawer in his desk.

"Care for a record album?" he asks.

July 2, 1993

Chapter 6

ALAN LOMAX

Few people have traveled the world like Alan Lomax. Since the early 1930's, he has lugged recording equipment all over America and Europe, recording and transcribing hundreds of thousands of folk songs and sea shanties, legends and oral histories. Now we are sitting in his suite of offices in Manhattan — he and his staff occupy an entire floor of a school building at Hunter College — and he is telling me about the Hamptons.

"I've never found anything to match the Hamptons, not even in the Mediterranean. I remember the first time. I had gone out to visit some psychoanalyst friends who had formed a kind of colony up in Springs — it was 1978 — and I rented a rowboat. I rowed out into the Three Mile Harbor, then out into the bay. It was September and about six o'clock and the sun was setting and then all of a sudden, along came this school of dolphins. Hundreds of them. Each glinting like gold as they arched through the water. The sun sparkling off them. Nothing like it."

Alan Lomax is now 75 years old. He is a big, burly man, black hair, white beard, and there is nothing about him that is 75 years old. He is sharp and alert, he moves quickly, directing his staff this way and that, and there is a sort of childish delight about him that makes him appear twenty years younger than his chronological age.

Here at Hunter, he has embarked upon a massive computer project to classify and interpret the song styles of the world. It is a project that will take several years to complete and which, already, has resulted in some startling discoveries. He is also producing a five part television series that is currently appearing weekly coast to coast on PBS. It is called *American Patchwork*, a celebration of America's cultural heritage, and it can be seen on all three public television stations in the metropolitan area. Channel 13 airs it Sundays from 7-8 p.m. through August 5.

Alan Lomax and I talk for several hours amidst the videotape, books, records, editing equipment and Apple Mac computers. He fends off calls from IBM, from computer programmers, a TV reporter and someone from the NEA so we can complete our interview. Approximately eight assistants are at work editing, programming and cataloguing here on West 41st Street in a suite of rooms that contain, arguably, the largest private collection of folk music in the world. And Lomax is not satisfied.

"What we're doing here on PBS, showcasing American folk music and music of the common man, is something they should have been doing all along. They've got hundreds of stations with their back turned on the real America. The wonderland of mankind is there in their lap and they have been ignoring it. Twain, Sandburg, Melville. This is what America is about. But PBS seems to think their mission is to provide ballets and operas and symphony over and over to a country that has no artistic traditions. Improve the cultural level of the Podunkians. And meanwhile ignore everything that Podunk might produce. Meantime American regional culture is sweeping the world with the blues, rock, mariachi and country music."

Alan Lomax, more than any other man in this century, has been responsible for bringing the cultural products of Podunk, New Orleans, Appalachia and a wide variety of lumberjack towns and seafaring villages into the consciousness of the world. He found, recorded and introduced Pete Seeger, Leadbelly, Burl Ives, Woodie Guthrie, Josh White and many others. He's written over a dozen books. In 1986 he was awarded the National Medal of the Arts by President Reagan for his work in pioneering American folklore.

The collecting of folk songs was actually begun by Alan's father John, who achieved considerable fame in his own right. One of 21 children, John lived in a house that sat right by the Chisolm trail in pioneer Texas. As a young man, he'd hear cowboys sing as they rode by and he's write down the songs they sang. He was a natural-born literati and was the first to appreciate American ballads.

John Lomax taught English and American Literature at the University of Texas and one year he got a fellowship from Harvard to collect cowboy songs. John did collect them, and he published them in a book in 1910 with an introduction by President Teddy Roosevelt, who commented that the work was a good piece of rough and ready Americana.

The President of the University of Texas, however, was not pleased that someone from that institution would publish the vulgar songs of the wild cowboys. Even though his work was endorsed by the former President. John Lomax was fired.

Alan was born, one of four children, in 1915. His father worked as a bond salesman and as an investment banker in Dallas after he left the University. It was the Roaring Twenties and, for the moment, the business of finding folk songs was forgotten.

And then the Crash of 1929 hit. John Lomax lost everything, his wife, Alan's mother died. Everything seemed to be coming apart. But the cowboy song book was still selling and John Lomax landed a book contract to compile a book about his nationwide collections of the whole range of American folk songs. John headed out across the country in a car to fill the gaps in his collection. Alan at this time was in his late teens and was up for helping out his father. He went along and he and his father were to travel the dusty American roads for five years.

"We went out in a Model A Ford," Alan told me. "The Carnegie Foundation had provided us with this huge Presto Field Recorder. It was in many pieces and all together must have weighed three hundred pounds. We'd pack it in the trunk of the car, along with a tent and bedrolls and all these huge Edison alkali batteries which powered the recorder and we'd take the back roads."

Lomax described this very early recording device. There was a microphone and a huge vacuum tube amplifier. The batteries powered a small motor which, connected to a series of belts, turned a turntable. There was a speed adjustment, and to get it at exactly 78 rpms, they had this armature affair which sat on top of the turntable and, by centrifugal force, extended its arms to a certain span when it was the right speed.

Onto the turntable they placed an annealed aluminum disk. There was an armature with a diamond needle on the end, and a worm screw that moved it from the middle of the aluminum disk to the end, cutting a groove, and laying down the sound track in its walls.

Father and son recorded in East Texas, Mississippi, New Orleans. In Canton, Mississippi they recorded the black man who said he had wiped the blood off the locomotive in which Casey Jones met his fate. They recorded at Mardi Gras.

"Most people had never seen anything like this contraption. They'd hear themselves and they'd say 'stop that ghost.' I remember one man spoke into it and said 'Hello Mr. Roosevelt...' and then just trailed off. I told him continue. He said 'I'm waiting for him to hello me back.'"

In 1937, the Lomax team of father and son worked to create a national archive of folk songs at the Library of Congress. Working separately (and enlisting the help of others), they made a recorded survey of the whole country. He recorded down into Mexico, Cajun territory, Haiti, the Bahamas.

Then in 1939, CBS asked Alan Lomax to do a radio show coast to coast once a week for a year introducing these folk songs to schools of the nation. Lomax agreed, but on the condition that he could have genuine folk singers to do most of the performing.

"That's how Woodie Guthrie was introduced to the world," Lomax told me. "There had been a rally here in the city to raise money for the Spanish Loyalists fighting the Civil War that year, and I was at this rally and so was Guthrie. He'd been bumming around the country for years and had come to New York to seek his fortune. I invited him to come on the show.

"Everything was performed live then, of course. And the way it worked was we'd do a rehearsal on Thursday afternoon and then the following morning, at 9 a.m., we'd have the actual performance. Guthrie came to the rehearsal and we're doing the songs and we're running over maybe a half an hour. The CBS Orchestra was there, waiting to rehearse the *Chesterfield Hour* which was this very serious show right after ours, and the producer of the *Chesterfield Hour* was there and all the actors and they were pacing around. The producer came up to Guthrie and told him speed it up a little, maybe cut some songs short. And Woody Guthrie, without a word, slung his guitar over his shoulder and just left. Right in the middle of the rehearsal.

"Now I pick up and follow him, because I didn't want to lose sight of him. Now CBS has neither of the two principals of the show at the rehearsal. Woody walked slowly through Manhattan and I caught up with him and pretty soon we were at Leadbelly's house for supper. Leadbelly invited us to sleep over. Woody got in bed and he slept on the inside and I slept on the outside. At 3 a.m., he gets up and puts on his clothes so I get up and put on my clothes. We walk all the way down to the Battery, to a diner there. It's dawn. We have flapjacks, bacon, syrup. We sit around. Finally it is 8 a.m. and Woody says 'What you say we get up there and try that goddamn broadcast.' That program which came out on the nose, was named the best music education program of the year."

"Woody Guthrie was something. He slept his way through the whole secretarial staff at CBS. He was irresistible. And indefatigable."

As for Alan Lomax, he married Elizabeth Harold, a poet and novelist, and with her wrote a number of radio plays. They were divorced in 1948. They had a daughter Anna who is currently doing her Ph.D in anthropology at Columbia University, and she has a five year old son Odysseus, Alan's grandson.

For the next thirty years, Lomax divided his time between traveling the world and recording more folklore and teaching and doing research at Columbia. Now he is at Hunter.

"Would you care to see this current project?" Lomax asks. I follow him through a tape library that must contain over ten thousand recording tapes (all made by Lomax) through a magazine and book library of approximately the same dimensions, into a computer room where programmers are busily entering everything into a database.

"We have all these songs described with approximately forty different measures. Geographically, by topic, whether they are solo or group, the kind of rhythm, the coordination, etc. And we are coming up with some remarkable discoveries."

Lomax presses some computer keys and on the screen there is a pie-shaped graph showing the distribution of 4,000 songs by cultural background and by type. Some are storyteller type songs sung by individuals, others are group songs with repetitive and relatively simple backgrounds.

"What we have found here," Lomax continues, "is that there is a striking difference between the kinds of songs sung in the north and the kinds of songs sung in the tropics. In the colder climates — Siberia, Alaska, Norway — people tend to work by themselves. Highly individualistic. The folk songs are largely sung solo, to a group. And they are complex, story-type affairs. Nothing you'd sing along to. Meanwhile, in the tropics, people tend to work in groups doing repetitive tasks. Hoeing, for example. The songs tend to be group chants. Everybody joins in. Very repetitive."

"What else have you found?"

"The data is leading us to interesting discoveries every day. We have discovered several historical migrations no one ever knew about before.

A programmer pressed some keys and a description of a pygmy song from Africa appeared along with the map of Africa. Then she pressed another key and the song played, just as it had been recorded in Africa years earlier.

"Every library and every school in the country could use this," I said.

"They will. Teachers want this data base to make their kids feel welcome in the classroom — kids from many cultural backgrounds can find their roots in the Global Jukebox. The whole world sings and dances in this gadget. It teaches cultural tolerance. It advocates a new democratic principal — cultural equity, allowing culture to have it's fair share of time on the air and in the classroom. The human environment is under threat, just like our physical and biological surrounds. We must learn how to protect our most important human treasures, the varied cultural patterns of the planet. The Global Jukebox sings and dances that lesson for the 21st century.

* * *

Watch for Alan Lomax on PBS these next few Sundays. Or you might see him — he looks very much like any Bonacker — steering his 30 foot sloop out the harbor on his way for a daysail to Shelter Island or Sag Harbor.

"Three Mile Harbor is my relaxation," he says.

Then, Monday, it is back to Hunter and to the work he loves.

July 27, 1990

35

Chapter 7

FRANK MacNAMARA

The President and CEO of MacNamara, Klein and Solin advertising on Fifth Avenue speaks in an Irish brogue, wears a tie and suspenders at work, and has a summer house in Sag Harbor where he and his wife have weekended for the past dozen years. He also has a small boat, and in the last three years has gotten hooked on playing polo. Among other things, Frank MacNamara is one of the principals in a group that wants to open a horse breeding farm and polo club in Bridgehampton.

All of this is a very long way from the small town in Ireland where Frank MacNamara grew up.

"The town was called Longford. It is in the center of Ireland in Longford County. When I was seventeen, I signed an 'article' to apprentice for an accountant for five years. I paid him a sum. And then over the next five years he would slowly pay it back to me in exchange for my learning the trade at his knee, so to speak. This is an accepted thing in Ireland. Instead of paying a tuition and going to college, you pay this to a professional and you apprentice to him and learn a trade."

"How old were you when you came to America?" I asked.

"Twenty-three. I really felt there was little future for me in Ireland. When you sign the 'article,' there is this little clause that says you can't ever work within fifty miles of the office where you are apprenticing. Ireland is a small country. Longford County is in the very center and so I knew I'd only be able to find work after my fifth year along the coast. And even then it would be hard because the accounting firms all prefer to hire apprentices because it costs them nothing. I went to England. To London. I sold hats and shoes for a year on Oxford Street.

"But my mother had already emigrated. She was living in New York near Fordham and was working for an employment agency on Madison Avenue and she kept writing me and telling me what a great country America was and what wonderful opportunities there were here. This was in 1963."

"So you went?"

"It took a lot of letters. I was having so much fun in England. I was a young man. I was out partying five nights a week. But finally, I went."

Frank MacNamara, age 23, got his first job in America as an office boy in the accounting department at ABC television.

"I was just flabbergasted and amazed. I had this idea that all Americans wore big hats and wide ties and spoke with a drawl — *The Ugly American* was very popular in Ireland in the early sixties — and here everybody was very busy and very motivated. I arrived on a Friday, had an interview at an agency on Monday, and I had a job on Tuesday paying me $58 a week which I thought was all the money in the world. And the people were all running around. Everybody was going to night school Everybody wanted to better themselves. We had nothing like that in Ireland."

"I don't understand."

"In Ireland, everything is formal and everybody has their place. I would call the secretary 'Miss.' She'd call me 'Mr.' But getting a promotion was almost unheard of. Everything is just the way it is supposed to be. For example, we'd have a coffee break, and we'd all stand around near the fire and the owner would be there and you wouldn't speak to him unless spoken to. It would be a scandal if you spoke to him."

"Where would you be if you had stayed?" I asked.

"I'd probably be married and living in Mullingar with four or five kids going every day to work five minutes away at the accounting office. Every time I'd have a kid I'd get a raise."

Frank MacNamara determined to become the best office boy ABC ever had. They promoted him to clerk. Then an opening came up at NBC and he joined the accounting department there. He stayed at NBC for three years.

In 1967, he was told about an opening at Bates Advertising in the media department. He knew about advertising agencies but he didn't know what media was. But he went and became a media planner at Bates. Two years later, he got a job as the head of media planning for the American Home Products Company, which makes Anacin and Dristan. American Home had their own in-house agency and made their own media decisions. After a number of years, Frank MacNamara was deciding on advertising schedules for commercials and advertisements that were costing about $150 million a year. He was steady, personable, honest, and good at what he did. He had a knack for choosing the best media in given circumstances.

Certainly the most extraordinary time in Frank MacNamara's life came in 1980. Frank was now 40 years old, had been married and divorced (no children), and was working hard at American Home. The President of the in-house advertising division was a man named Dan Rogers who got the idea, in 1980, to leave American Home and to buy one of the most famous, and at this point, one of the most failing advertising agencies in America and turn it around. Norman Kraig and Cummel was billing over $200 million at that time, but its brilliant founder, Norman Norman, had become more involved in the overseas divisions and in his absence the main New York part of the business had started to crumble. Dan Rogers took over in New York and among the people he brought with him was Frank MacNamara to be Senior Vice President in charge of Marketing.

"We walked into the middle of chaos and confusion. Clients were walking out the door. I was out there, getting new business, and as fast as I'd get the new business, the old business was leaving. I couldn't get it fast enough. There were about 100 people working there when we started. By the end, and this was two years later, there were just fifteen people left. The overseas branches were pumping money into the New York central office. They called a halt to it. Something would have to give."

Frank MacNamara talked to Dan Rogers that if they could bring in new clients in all this mess, then they certainly could bring in new clients on their own. Why not just drop this thing and start fresh? Start a new advertising agency?

Dan Rogers hemmed and hawed. They'd do it. Someday. But then, one of the biggest clients said look — either open up somewhere or WE are moving elsewhere. And Frank MacNamara, along with Jeff Clapp, decided to go into business together. Dan Rogers did not go along.

"What we did," Frank told me, "was rent a room at the Hyde Park Hotel at 70th Street and Madison Avenue. At first they wouldn't move the beds out of the room and so for four days people came in and we had them sit on the beds. Every morning I'd come in to work and stop at the hotel desk and pay the rent. They were no fools."

But MacNamara Klapp thrived and in a few days they rented a whole suite in the hotel. Then, after six months, they rented a suite of offices in an office building. The firm was underway.

One year into his new enterprise, Frank MacNamara married Patricia Stuart, a Long Islander who was also working in marketing in the advertising field. Today she is an Executive Vice President at Campbell Mithun and Esty. They have no children.

"The way we came to buy a house in the Hamptons was like this.

We had been renting an apartment in the East 70's and started looking for an apartment to buy in New York City. One day we went to see a co-op for sale in the Federal building at 11th Avenue and 10th Street. This had once been a prison so it was built like a fortress but now they had converted it with thirty foot windows overlooking the river. Every twenty feet or so, inside the apartment, there were these huge flying buttresses and so you had to bend double to get under them to get from one part of the apartment to another. They wanted $350,000 for this. I thought this is the height of insanity. You'd kill yourself in the middle of the night."

Frank took Patricia out to lunch after looking at this apartment.

"Lets not buy a co-op in the city," he said. "Let's buy a house in the country."

"Where?"

"In the Hamptons. I've heard of a nice little village called Sag Harbor."

That weekend Frank and Patricia MacNamara came out to the Hamptons, looked at five houses, bought one and that was it. They've been coming out to the Hamptons weekends now for twelve years. They have a small boat that in the wintertime they keep at the Redwood Marina.

Six years ago, Patricia took up riding at the Swan Creek Stables in Bridgehampton. Three years later, Frank took it up as well. It was in that year, 1988, that the MacNamaras were vacationing in the Dominican Republic that they took up polo.

"We were staying at Casa de Campo and there was a retired British General there by the name of Arthur W. Nugent who offered to teach us how to play polo. He had me stand on two milk crates and he handed me a mallet and had me hit the ball. Then we went out and tried it on polo ponies. I was hooked. I've been an avid polo player since."

After finding there was no place to play polo on eastern Long Island, Frank MacNamara got together with several of his friends and put a proposal together for a horse farm and polo facility on the Tiska farm in Bridgehampton. The application is pending.

Today, MacNamara, Klein and Solin is thriving. One of their largest accounts is English Leather. The Klein part of the name is Don Klein, who is the creative director. Clapp left in 1987.

"At the age of 50," MacNamara told me, "Jeff Clapp decided he just wanted to be a windsurfer. From what he made and what he had inherited he had enough to just quit. This was in 1987. Today he and his wife and kids live in Florida and they summer in Amagansett."

May 24, 1991

Chapter 8

FRED MENGONI

Fred Mengoni is not what you expect. In advance you learn that he is a real estate millionaire with properties around the world, that he sponsors the annual Mengoni bicycle race in Central Park every autumn, drawing thousands of cyclists, that he discovered and coached cyclist Greg LeMond to win the Tour de France, that he is a bachelor who loves the ladies and lives alone in a twenty room, five story townhouse with a private elevator opposite Gracie Mansion, and that he spent three years rebuilding one of the most visible summer homes in East Hampton, the mansion festooned with lights every Christmas on the corner of Woods Lane and the Montauk Highway opposite Town Pond.

Then you meet the man. He is a small, gleeful grandfatherly looking fellow with white hair, flashing eyes and an engaging smile, and as he takes you through his East Hampton mansion, all chandeliers and mahogany and marble, his poodle scampering a step behind him, he talks about every piece of paneling, every rug and chair excitedly as if he were the curator at a museum, or, perhaps more accurately, the owner of an antique doll house. For Fred Mengoni, at 69, an Italian immigrant who still can't believe he made all this money, still lives every day with his passions. And every day he sees them again for the first time.

"This barn, it was falling down," he says of the restored building out the window on the six acre property. "Now it is beautiful." Mengoni built a swimming pool, put in Italian statuary around it, he built a grand horseshoe of a driveway to the front door and made it of Belgian block, complete with heating coils underneath so it never needs snow plowing in the winter time. And he restored the house right down to the flower boxes in the windows in the grand early American English colonial

40

manner.

"I looked for this house for fifteen years," he says. "This East Hampton is one of the best places in the world. Some day, I think, I would like to have a property here. Then this came along. A lot of trees sick. I cut them down. Make new landscaping. I wish I could live here all the time."

I comment to Mr. Mengoni that, as a real estate developer, spending three years to renovate a home was not exactly usual. I note that the World Trade Center was built in less time than that.

"This is not to pick up and sell," he says.

Fred Mengoni was born and raised in the ancient Italian town of Osimo, just below Bologna. One of seven children, his father bought old musical instruments, fixed them up and resold them. His mother was a housewife.

As a boy, like many another young boy in Italy, he became interested in bicycle racing. He thought he might win his fortune as a bicycle racer and he raced every day, sometimes eighty miles in the morning, home for an early dinner and then ninety miles in the afternoon. But he soon realized he was too small to compete on a world class level, and he put the dream aside.

He was sixteen years old when World War II broke out. He was drafted into the Italian army, given a uniform and as part of Mussolini's army, was sent to Greece to fight the British.

"I skipped," he says with a smile. "Went to Turkey, then to Palestine. I worked there for the English. I drove a car, was a messenger. Then, when the war ended, I came home."

He took up his father's trade, then discovered an entrepreneur's heart. He went into the car business, buying used cars here and there and selling them to his friends. He made money. He made more money buying and selling musical instruments. Then, in 1954, he saw the American movie *Gentlemen Prefer Blondes*, starring Marilyn Monroe. It transformed him.

"I saw this movie, I want to come to America," he says.

First, however, he had a sobering experience in a casino in Monte Carlo. There at the tables one night, he lost all the money he had accumulated in his life. He was virtually broke. And so it was that in 1957, a small man from central Italy, with the equivalent of fifty dollars in his pocket, boarded the *Andrea Doria* in Genoa for the three day crossing to America. He had a one way ticket. And his visa was for thirty days. He was arriving as a tourist.

"In Italy, I met somebody in the musical instrument business who knew somebody in New York City in the musical instrument business. I had his name and address. I got off the boat and I went to look him up."

Mengoni knew rudimentary English from his days in Palestine with

41

the British. It was enough. He was taken to an apartment house at 305 West 50th Street where he was given a rented room for three dollars a week. He remembers the address very well because several years later he was involved in his first attempt at a real estate transaction with this property, which he bungled. First, however, he had to get a green card and get some money. He got a 30 day extension, then a six month extension, then he went with a priest from the community who vouched for him, filled out the forms and got his green card.

"I took three jobs. Sometimes four. Worked as a dishwasher, as a musical instrument repair man. First year was very hard and I had to tell the landlord I could not pay him for awhile. He was an Italian, too. He understood. I paid him, finally, after a year, and after three years, I had saved up $70,000. That's when I learned that the building was for sale."

There were actually two buildings for sale, and the seller wanted $85,000 for the both of them. Mengoni offered his $70,000. He had not gotten any financing. The building was sold to a woman who later turned it over at a considerable profit.

The lesson was not lost on Mengoni, but in the meantime, disaster struck. He had invested his money in the stock market and in 1964 when the market crashed, he was wiped out. He would have to start all over again.

A year later, he had saved up $8,000. And now Fred Mengoni tells of his first successful real estate transaction with great glee.

"The building was at 225 East 84th Street, a rooming house. They wanted $80,000 for it with $8,000 down. I had the $8,000. Then I moved the tenants out, hired two guys and we renovated it into nine apartments. This cost $32,000 and I got the money by getting a $24,000 FHA mortgage and paying them the balance at the end at $1,000 a month from money I could make buying and selling musical instruments."

His second real estate transaction involved a $550,000 apartment house in Queens that housed over fifty families. They wanted $55,000 and he did not have $55,000, but he did have an incident occur that was in the back of his mind.

"I was washing my building on East 84th Street one day with a hose," he said. "This old guy comes along, maybe 75, he says you own this building? I say yes. He says I'll put a second mortgage on it. I say no. He give me his card."

Here is how Mengoni bought the $550,000 apartment house in Queens without any money. He agreed to buy it. Then he called the old guy and asked if he'd give him $60,000 for a second mortgage.

"He says you have an accountant? I say I am the accountant."

He got the $60,000 second mortgage at twenty per cent interest, then he found a buyer for his Manhattan apartment for $90,000, receiving

$10,000 as a deposit.

"I go to buy the apartment house with a $10,000 check and another check for $20,000 which is post dated thirty days for when the second mortgage comes through. The seller says no deal. My lawyer says we walk. I say I want the building. I say I don't make good in one month for the rest of the money, keep the $10,000. I buy the building."

Today, Fred Mengoni owns eight buildings in Manhattan, one of which is a 93 apartment building on East 63rd Street, he owns properties in Seattle, in California, in Reno and in northern Italy. He has become a rich man.

I comment that real estate right now must be pretty tough.

"I think we are in a cycle," he says. "But I travel a lot. We are still the best. We had recessions in '64, '75 and '82. This one's a little deeper. But I think we will come back better than before."

The town house in which Fred Mengoni lives, at which I meet him on a second occasion, he bought in March of 1973. It is on East 83rd Street and it is filled with antiques and furniture from the Louis XVI period.

"I always wanted to live in a house like this," he says. "It had been in the Richelieu family. A widow owned it, and when I saw it it had been vacant for 24 years. Pigeons flying around inside. Roof leaking. They wanted half a million for it. I got a mortgage. Remodeled it a little. Five years ago an embassy offered me $5 million for it."

In the late 1970's, Fred Mengoni decided he would give back to this country some of the good fortune it had given him. He began to focus his energies on one thing. Bicycle racing. He would help young Americans to organize the sport and he would teach them to compete internationally. It was a sport virtually unknown at that time in America. No one here really knew of the fame and fortune that awaited on the streets of Europe at the Tour de France and other races.

Mengoni formed his own bicycle team, offering uniforms and stipends to those who would compete for the team. At one time, the United States Professional Racing Organization was nearly broke and Mengoni stepped in and provided thousands of dollars in funds. It survived. Today he is President of that organization.

In the mid-1980's Mengoni disbanded his bicycle team because so many American corporations were sponsoring teams that his was no longer necessary. "Besides, they weren't doing very well," Mengoni told a reporter from a bike magazine at the time. Instead, he began to focus on just a few extremely talented bike riders who he was convinced were capable of winning the Tour de France. He also started his annual race around Central Park, still known today as the Mengoni, which offers prizes in three classes, men, women and veterans.

Without a doubt, however, Mengoni's greatest accomplishment was his development and sponsorship of a young man who has become the greatest American bicyclist of all time: Greg LeMond.

Mengoni first saw him in Central Park when LeMond was seventeen. Immediately Mengoni liked his racing style. He went up and, out of the blue, introduced himself and asked LeMond if he would like to be on the Mengoni racing team.

"At first, I think, he thought I was crazy," Mengoni says.

At the time, and this was in 1979, LeMond was just one of several American racers that Mengoni was developing. He'd accompany the team to meets. He'd praise them, he would rail at them. If there weren't enough beds where the team was staying, it was Mengoni who would wind up sleeping on the floor.

In an article about Mengoni in Cycle magazine, published in 1985, a racer who requested anonymity, claimed that for days after Ed Bauer had lost the Olympic road race to Grewel, Mengoni was, by turns, devastated, furious and baffled at his performance. Another racer, California ace Harvey Nitz, said, "If I raced as well as I could, then I'd be happy. But to Fred, second was no better than tenth."

Greg LeMond, of course, won the Tour de France in 1986, 1988 and 1989 and became a legend in the bicycle racing world. He was the only American, before or since, to win the Tour. And he did it with Fred Mengoni with him morning, noon and night, at every stage of the race, encouraging him, shouting at him, praising him. Mengoni was with him during the early 1980's, at the Tour. Each year he did better than the year before. Finally, he was the champion.

"I help Greg," Mengoni says. "I help any young cyclist with talent. Three years ago, Greg was going to sign up with a Japanese sponsor. I told him, hold out for a European sponsor. You'll make more money."

Greg LeMond signed with the famous Z team and became the first cyclist in history to be given a multimillion dollar contract.

In 1990, at the duPont Cycling championships in Minneapolis, Greg LeMond presented Mengoni with the Crystal Ball Award. A one-of-a-kind trophy, designed especially for the man who had become the sport's grand patron in America, the award represented the heartfelt thanks of the entire American cycling community for what Fred Mengoni had done for them.

Today, you will find Mengoni bicycling around East Hampton or, in the City, bicycling up to Westchester and back. He still cycles thirty and forty miles a day. His equipment?

"I used to ride a Masterpiu with Campagnolo components," Mengoni said. "But Greg gave me a steel LeMond and so now I ride that."

Look for it on the streets of the Hamptons. On the seat will be a small Italian man in his late sixties named Fred Mengoni.

July 9, 1993

Chapter 9

JULIE WARNER

As this is written, the movie *Doc Hollywood* has just completed the first week of it's nationwide run. According to the trades, it was the third most successful movie of the week, grossing an impressive $7.5 million. It continues to skip along now at the rate of a million dollars a day, and it may be one of the most successful films of the year.

Not bad for a simple story of an East Coast intern, on his way across country to a multi-million dollar practice as a plastic surgeon in Beverly Hills, who gets sidetracked into becoming a country doctor in a small southern town.

Well, maybe it had to do a lot with who is doing the sidetracking. The surgeon, played by Michael J. Fox, finds himself face to face with a sturdy, handsome young southern woman named Lou, who in the movie drives an ambulance, but in real life is a New York City girl who summers in the Hamptons.

This is the first motion picture role for Julie Warner, age 26. And wouldn't you know she's got herself a starring role. From Georgica Beach to a female lead. You can go see Julie tonight if you wish at the East Hampton Cinema where *Doc Hollywood* continues to pack them in. Not long ago — she's been summering out here for fourteen years — she was a kid scooping ice cream in Amagansett for after-movie goers.

I spoke to Julie recently and learned that if her star has taken off like a shot in Hollywood, it has been largely of her own doing. She is a confident, determined young lady and she's made it happen herself.

"I was raised on the Upper West Side," she told me. "My dad is Neil Warner who is a free lance advertising jingle composer. My mom is the licensing director at Harry Abrams. I went to Dalton, then Brown.

In the summers, we'd come out to the Hamptons. We rented. Mostly in Amagansett or Springs or East Hampton."

"Which beaches did you go to?" I asked.

"My parents would go to the family beaches with my brother who is ten years younger. I liked to hang out at Two Mile Hollow or Georgica or Main Beach, East Hampton with my friends."

"Those are Village beaches. But you weren't in the Village."

"No, but my dad always bought the Village Beach sticker."

"Did you have summer jobs?"

"I was a chambermaid one summer at the Maidstone Club."

"What's your favorite place out here?"

"I like Sam's Pizza."

"Did you go to the nightclubs?"

"I'm not a night person. I'd go over and be with my friends. Mostly we'd be in private homes."

Julie studied acting at Brown. And when she graduated, she made a bold decision.

"I decided to move to L.A. and try to find myself. If I had thought more about it, I might not have done it. But I went. I wanted to be an actress. I wanted to see what would happen."

Another girl from Brown had gone to Los Angeles and was doing theater there. Julie called her and arranged to move in with her. She would have a base from which to read the trade journals and go off on auditions. She would also have an agent, as it turned out. She had sent her clips to a casting director in New York who gave her an introduction to Susan Smith and Associates in Los Angeles. They took her on.

"That was in 1987," she told me. "I moved in with my friend and after a while I got my own place. I auditioned. And I got began getting guest spots on television. I had a role in *Star Trek*. Another in *The Outsiders*. I played opposite Carol Burnett in an episode of *Carol and Company*. She was an aging soap opera star. I was the young ingenue that the directors were promoting to force her out. It was a funny piece."

And then came *Doc Hollywood*.

"A friend told me about it and said this part was just perfect for me. So I tried to get a tryout but at first they wouldn't let me. They were looking for a 'name' to be opposite Michael J. Fox. But apparently they couldn't get a name. So they called me in and I auditioned for the assistant casting director.

"What happened is that the director Michael Cayton-Jones saw the tape of my audition and that was it. He had interviewed 80 people. He told me that all the time he was looking he knew he would know the person for this part when he saw her. It was instantaneous. He heard my voice. 'This is the voice I heard in my head,' he said."

Another advantage was that Julie is only five foot two. They wanted somebody smaller than Michael. That was Julie.

"What's Michael like?" I asked.

"He's great. Very complicated, very well read, funny, down to earth. And hard working."

"Did you fall in love with him?"

"Oh no. No. We developed affections. I always feel affection with the people I work with."

That was as far as I was going to go.

The movie was made in just three and a half months last fall and winter. They worked for seven weeks in Gainesville in northern Florida, then finished up on a set in L.A.

And though the reviews have been mixed, there has been nothing but praise for Julie's performance.

"And the future?"

"I'm negotiating on a project. But I'm not at liberty to say anything about it just now."

Sounds like a movie star to me.

August 16, 1991

Chapter 10

MORT ZUCKERMAN

If people in the Hamptons know Mort Zuckerman, they know him as a very good baseball player. He is visible every Saturday morning at a sandlot softball game in Mashashimuet Park in Sag Harbor. And once a year, he is visible as the pitcher for the writers in the annual Artists-Writers Game at the Herrick Park ballfield in East Hampton that is played every August. (This coming Saturday afternoon.)

Mort Zuckerman is thin, wiry and dark and from the look of him he might be thirty five years old. One might guess if one didn't know anything else about him that he is a reporter for *The Wall Street Journal* or maybe for *The Washington Post*. What else would this intense young man be doing playing for the Writers anyway?

In fact, Mort Zuckerman is one of the wealthiest and most successful men in America. If you recall, two years ago, there was a battle between the City and somebody who wanted to build an eighty story building at Columbus Circle. The man proposing this one billion dollar project was Mort Zuckerman. If you recall about ten years ago somebody buying the *Atlantic Monthly* magazine, that was him. And if you are a regular reader of the *U. S. News & World Report* (2,500,000 circulation) then you know he is both the owner of the publication and its editor in chief and has been for ten years. He is, to judge by the years of his college diplomas, about fifty. And if he looks so much younger than his years it is because he keeps great discipline in his life. He plays many sets of tennis, he runs, he plays softball, and he plays and works hard. Except he does not consider it work.

We are sitting in the living room of one of the grandest oceanfront estate homes in the Hamptons. It is a great shingled and turreted affair, about 10,000 square feet on four acres, and on one side of us there are tennis courts and swimming pools and on the other side there is the Atlantic Ocean, roaring against 350 feet of Mort Zuckerman's private beach. Servants are scurrying around.

"Work?" Mort says. "I have spent my entire life avoiding work. I consider myself the laziest man alive. I try to do nothing other than what I completely enjoy. And I have so far succeeded with this."

What Mort enjoys most is studying and writing about world affairs, and developing and building urban settings. He has his column in *U.S. News* every week. (This week about Iraq.) And he has built some very interesting and remarkable buildings and urban spaces, primarily in the Boston area, but also in California, Washington and New York and several other locations around the world.

He was not born wealthy, but he was not born poor either. He was born and raised in Montreal, where his father owned and ran a wholesale tobacco and candy business. And when his father took ill his mother ran it.

From an early age, however, it was apparent that Mort was quite special. He did remarkably in school, graduating Magna Cum Laude at the Wharton Business School. He thought he should be a lawyer. He went to McGill and got his law degree, then he went to Harvard and got a joint degree between the Harvard Law School and the Harvard Business School. He got a certificate in Law from the University of Paris.

But the more he worked with the law, the less he liked it.

"I found it to be the exact opposite of sex," he told me. "Even when it's good, it's lousy."

For years and years, he kept on trying to believe that he would enjoy being a lawyer. And then, in 1962, three years out of law school, he just gave up. He got a job teaching a course at the Graduate School of Design at Harvard. It was called the Economics of Design and Planning. He found the idea of building things exhilarating. He wanted to build. He began looking for work with real estate firms that were buying commercial property and building on it. He'd learn more about how to do this.

That year, at the age of 25, he landed a job with Cabot, Cabot and Forbes, a Boston real estate development firm. They considered him a whiz kid, and they put him to work in their accounting department. Four months later, the Chief Financial Officer of the company left the firm, and the President of the company came to Mort Zuckerman and asked him if he would be willing to take on this job, just temporarily, until they could find someone else.

"They came to me, I guess, because they assumed that with all my education I knew what they wanted me to do," he said. "In fact, I

49

knew nothing. But I didn't tell them that."

Mort took on this opportunity with a vengence. And then, just ten months after that, the President resigned from the company, and at the age of 27, Mort Zuckerman was asked to take the reins of one of the largest real estate development firms in the Boston area.

Five years after that, Mort decided to go off on his own. He formed Boston Properties, and after four or five years of struggling, became the hottest and most successful developer in Boston.

"What projects are you most proud of?" I asked.

"At the present time we are building a complex of buildings behind M. I. T. in Cambridge. There are offices, apartments, stores, a hotel. We are developing in the rundown Kendall Square area. We have bought twenty five acres. We are building over two and a half million square feet." Mort leans forward in his chair. "I want to stress that we are not speculators. We are BUILDING this. Boston Properties does not buy existing properties to sell them at a higher price."

Mort has a house in Washington, a house in Aspen where he skis, an apartment in Manhattan, and, his pride and joy, the home he bought from Pete Petersen in East Hampton. He completely remodeled it when he bought it in 1980. He loves it because it is only a hundred feet or so from the crashing of the waves. And he tries to come out here every weekend he possibly can.

"What do you do when you are here?"

"I try to do absolutely nothing."

"What brought you out here?"

"A woman."

"Gloria Steinem?" Mort Zuckerman was linked with Ms. Steinem for half a dozen years.

"It was before I met her."

I wasn't about to ask who he was going out with today, but by any measure, looks, money, success, he is probably the most eligible bachelor in America.

"Ever want to have a family?"

"I'd love to have a family." Deadpan.

If Mort spends half his working week at Boston Properties, which now has headquarters in New York, and which he runs with his partner Ed Linde, he spends the other half of his working week at U. S. News & World Report, which he edits. He loves this editing.

"I write about 1,500 words a week," he says. "I research and gather information. I feel I have assembled a talented group of editors who made U. S. News an editorial success."

Mort shows me a news clipping from Forbes magazine which reviewed his tenure as editor of U. S. News. It says that many people in the magazine world were concerned when a real estate developer purchased the magazine, but now he has earned their respect. His views are now sought out in world affairs.

Mort leaves the financial side of the publication to his partner Fred Drasner, a lawyer who handled the sale of the magazine but who said afterwards he'd like to leave the law to take over the business end of *U. S. News.* Mort took him up on it.

Mort is helped in the editing by Mike Ruby and Merle McLaughlin who he considers excellent. Many people have been with him ten years or more. He values this loyalty, whether its his loyalty to them or their loyalty to him.

He is on the Council on Foreign Relations and within the past year traveled to Kuwait, Egypt, Jordan, London, Paris and Saudi Arabia. He has been to the Soviet Union perhaps a dozen times. He was on the President's Council for the Philippine election in 1986. And for the last four years, he has been the pitcher in the annual East Hampton's Artists/Writers Game.

And every bit of it has been fun.

August 17, 1990

* * *

Since this was written, Mort Zuckerman came to the rescue and is currently the owner of the New York Daily News.

Chapter 11

BEN GAZZARA

Actor Ben Gazzara clearly remembers the first time he ever came to the Hamptons. He'd just had four straight smash hits on Broadway — *A Hat Full of Rain, End As a Man, Cat on a Hot Tin Roof* and *Strange Interlude* — and a beautiful blonde had become enamored of him.

"I'd moved to East 53rd Street, started going out with East Side girls and drinking martinis."

It was 1956.

"Her family was Old Money. She took me out to East Hampton, we went to that club there on the beach, what is it? The Maidstone? A WASP situation. I thought I handled it rather well, but I think they knew where I came from. I remember the women drank a lot."

Where Gazzara came from, of course, was the Irish/Italian immigrant tenement ghetto of the East 20's. He may have been a shooting star on Broadway, but his name still wasn't in the Blue Book of the Hamptons.

"I loved it in the Hamptons," Gazzara says. "Go out on the beach, flirt, swim in the ocean, show off all your muscles. Well, we were young." Gazzara looks off into space which happens to be the boats rocking at anchor at Long Wharf, Sag Harbor. "Hey, I still love the Hamptons."

Gazzara bought his home in the Hamptons, in Sag Harbor, in 1979 largely because Elke, the woman he was madly in love with, wanted it.

"I was going through a terrible divorce, you know, all about money and everything, and my lawyer said this is the worst time to buy a house and I said Elke loves it and I'm going to buy it and I did."

To this day, wherever they are in the world, and whatever they are doing, Elke and Ben Gazzara still spend the entire month of August in

Sag Harbor.

* * *

Ben Gazzara was born in 1930 to Italian parents who had emigrated from Sicily to New York. His mother kept the house — an apartment in a tenement on East 29th Street. His father worked.

"He worked with his hands. He paved many of the Manhattan streets we walk on. He did carpentry. He'd do anything except something that involved electricity. He was afraid of electricity."

His mother and father had met in Manhattan in 1905, the year after they had emigrated. They had lived four kilometers apart in Sicily and had not known one another. Now they were a block apart and they fell in love.

"Whole villages in Italy moved to the same block of tenements in Manhattan," Gazzara said. "So everybody still knew one another. I have an older brother. He became a lawyer and still lives in Manhattan. I was born very late in life to my parents. My father was 51, my mother 46. If I had been born at the usual time, I'd be dead by now."

When Gazzara was about 20, he asked his parents why he had been born so late. Had there been a problem? What was the trouble? None of your business, his mother told him.

Gazzara went to Stuyvesant High School. Right away he was hit by the acting bug.

"It was not in the high school, actually, but at a drama group in a Boys Club across from the school. When I was fourteen years old, I was playing Francoise Villon in *If I Were King*. My leading lady was 35. People came. The house was packed. I loved it."

Gazzara could do this because, at 14, his voice was as big and as deep as it is today.

"Once, because of my voice, I got thrown out of confession. I was in the confessional and I had confessed my sins and the priest said 'how old are you' and I said 'fourteen' and he said 'get out of here' and so I got out. I went into another confessional. Tried to speak in more of a whisper."

Gazzara went to City College but left after a year and a half to join the Dramatic Workshop connected to the New School. He studied with Erwin Piscator. Then he applied to the legendary Actor's Studio. He had been told it was too tough to get into this studio, that it was the likes of Marlon Brando and Montgomery Clift that were at the Actor's Studio.

He auditioned anyway. And they accepted him. He could hardly believe it.

"There I was, learning from Strassberg and Kazan. Paul Newman was there. I'd hang out with Jimmy Dean. We'd meet at the NBC Drugstore in Rockefeller Center and make the rounds together."

53

Back on 29th Street, what Gazzara was doing didn't cut much ice. His father thought he was pursuing an acting career because he didn't want to work.

"He may have been right," Gazzara said.

His mother had wanted him to get an education and perhaps become an attorney as his older brother had. But she was a bit easier on him.

And then something sensational happened.

Gazzara got the lead in Calder Willingham's *End As A Man*, which was being performed at the Actor's Studio as an exercise.

"James Dean was in it too," Gazzara says.

It was so remarkable, it was put on for the membership. Then money was raised and it was put on Off-Broadway where the critics loved it and it went uptown. Gazzara's career was launched.

Four Broadway hits followed and for a while Gazzara thought his Broadway successes would go on forever. In 1961, he married Janice Rule. They had a daughter Elizabeth. Janice had a daughter, Kate, from a previous marriage.

From his base in Manhattan, Gazzara pursued his Broadway career and at the same time starred in a series of films. He was in *Anatomy Of A Murder* and he was in *The Strange One*, which was an adaptation of *End As A Man*.

And then, he got the leading role in a network television show called *Run For Your Life*. For three years he was to make episode after episode — there were 86 all together — about a man who is told he has six months to live, then goes off to various locales where, week after week, he solves crimes. It was a grueling, repetitious business and, according to Gazzara, it tended to drive him crazy.

He had pulled up stakes in Manhattan for this and he had moved to the West Coast. This was going to occupy all of his time.

"I had a villa in Holby Hills, two Mercedes, a wife in psychoanalysis, two pools, a blond pool man and a house man."

It was not acting as Gazzara had known it.

When the series finally ended, Gazzara met and began to work with the legendary film maker John Cassavetes. For Gazzara, this along with his later work with Peter Bogdanovitch, was to be the peak of his film career.

"I consider *Husbands*, the Cassavetes film, to be a masterpiece," he said. "I will put it up next to anything."

Cassavetes had developed a whole new way of making films. The actors would read the script and understand the direction of the film, but then they would LIVE their parts. Every night they would talk about what they had filmed that day and where they felt their character was going. New dialogue would be written, new scenes created. The film would take on a life of its own, take off in new directions.

"We were exploring," Gazzara said. "We actors were part of the creation of the movie."

Gazzara made numerous films with Cassavetes, among them *The Killing Of A Chinese Bookie* and others. He also made *St. Jack* and *They All Laughed* with Peter Bogdanovitch.

A major change in Gazzara's life came in 1979 in Seoul, Korea. He was making a very unmemorable film entitled *Inchon* about the military invasion of that city during the Korean War.

"Lawrence Olivier played MacArthur. I played the leading man who gets the girl. An interesting thing about this movie was that, although we were paid in American money back home, all the staff and all the crew were paid in cash. Once a week this Japanese guy would go to Tokyo and come back with a suitcase full of money which he'd then dole out to the staff. About six weeks into the film we found out that Reverend Moon was behind it all. Only the Reverend Moon would do this kind of thing."

There was a TV crew, in Seoul, to make a show about the making of the film. The film cost about $40 million. Just the TV show cost $6 million. And the producer of this TV show was a German woman by the name of Elke.

"I fell in love with her. She was then and is now the most beautiful, most wonderful, the sexiest woman I ever met. And you can write that down."

Gazzara's whole life expanded. He and Elke, who is half German and half Czechoslovakian, took an apartment in Rome, made new friends there. Gazzara became active in Europe, and although they travel all over the world now, they came to consider their home half in Rome and half in Manhattan — with their Augusts in Sag Harbor.

Gazzara starred in *Tales Of Ordinary Madness*, financed in Europe, made in Savannah, Los Angeles, Atlanta, New York and Rome.

And then, last year, some of his old New York friends persuaded him to come back to the theatre. The show would be *Shimada*, it would star Gazzara, Estelle Parsons and Ellen Burstyn and it would rehearse for five weeks and then open on Broadway.

"It only shows that I know nothing," Gazzara said. "I thought it would be a big hit. It opened, Frank Rich, the critic of the *New York Times* killed it, and it lingered on for a total of three more nights."

Gazzara looks out, once again, over the boats of Sag Harbor.

"That _____," he says. "Ahh, find a nicer word."

The interview comes to an end. We have been sitting at a table in the Amazon on a quiet rainy afternoon and the place is just half full. It has not passed my notice that people occasionally glance furtively over to our table for a quick look. They are certainly not looking at me.

I have, from the beginning of this interview, been struck by Ben Gazzara, not because I am starry eyed about him, but because of something else. He looks no more than forty.

Briefly, I think, well, there are plastic surgeons all over Beverly Hills and every other place, but as I look at his hands and the rest of him I know they can't do THIS. I am looking at a young man. I actually ask him about it.

"I think it is in my genes," he says. "A lot of olive oil."

Or it could just be a man still passionate about life, his career, his family, his art. I remember one particular thing he told me.

"Two years ago, in Europe, I adopted Elke's daughter. She is six foot two, blond and twenty five. We went to this judge, a woman judge, who couldn't have been much older than her, and we had to ask her whether it would be okay. It was quite a day."

August 21, 1992

Chapter 12

DANI SHAPIRO

It is almost impossible to get a first novel published. This is the standard advice given to all would be novelists. To get a second novel selected for the Book-of-the-Month Club would be beyond one's wildest dreams. Yet this is exactly what has happened to Dani Shapiro at thirty years of age. This month, with the publication of her second novel, she embarks on a tour around the nation to promote her Book-of-the-Month Club selection *Fugitive Blue* published by Doubleday.

It has been an extraordinary achievement. And for this New York City and Southampton resident, her career is just getting off the ground.

I sat with Dani Shapiro in a New York City restaurant last week and talked with her about her work. She is blond, beautiful, and her interest in writing goes back to her childhood in Hillside, New Jersey.

"We lived in a large, English Tudor house in the suburbs," she said. "My dad was a Wall Street stockbroker. My mom gave up a career in advertising to be a full time mother. And yet, at home, my mom continued writing. I remember lying in bed, I was ten years old, and it would be eleven o'clock at night and through my bedroom wall I could hear the clack, clack, clack of my mother working on her Smith Corona. She would write articles and send them off to magazines. They would reject them and send them back. After eleven o'clock, when all the housework was done, that was her time to do her writing. It was her territory. And I admired it."

To this day, Ms. Shapiro spends several hours every day, no matter where she is, writing her stories. She uses a Toshiba laptop computer. She can use it anywhere.

"I have to do it virtually every day," she said. "It is essential to me. Like breathing."

Ms. Shapiro went to grammar school at a Jewish Yeshiva in Union, New Jersey. Half her lessons were in religion, half in academics. She studied classical piano. Her father had a daughter from a prior marriage, but she was fifteen years old when Dani came along. Dani was raised essentially as an only child.

"We traveled a lot. And I kept journals. My mother and father took me to Israel, to Portugal, Italy, Hawaii, Spain. In Turkey we found ourselves in the middle of a cholera epidemic. We had to leave. But before we could leave we had to get shots. I was so frightened about getting the shots and I remember standing in line at the French Hospital and a nurse came over and gave me a gift, because I seemed so miserable, of a bronze dagger with green stones. I still have it."

She went to Pingry Prep School and then, thinking she might pursue a career in music, went to Sarah Lawrence College in Bronxville, New York. They had a strong music department. Music did not take with her, however. Next, still ignoring the fact that she liked to write every day, she decided to become a commercial actress.

"It came about by accident," she said. "At the end of my third year of college, some friends of my parents said they thought I could do very well making TV commercials. They suggested an agency and I went. A portfolio and a group of pictures of me were made up. I got a job at one of the very first auditions I went to."

Shapiro dropped out of Sarah Lawrence, took an apartment on the Upper West Side, and began making the rounds. Soon she was in numerous television commercials shown coast to coast. She took acting classes. Got work on one of the afternoon soaps on television. Even got a small part in a movie.

"Would I recognize you in TV commercials?" I asked.

"I don't think so," she said. "People would see me on TV and then they would meet me and they'd say I looked familiar, maybe we went to camp together or something. They couldn't quite pin it down.

"Anyway, I did this for four years. But it never felt right. I never really liked it and didn't think I was good at it. It was just torture for me to get up in front of a camera."

Realizations about her future came shortly thereafter. She had played the part of Philip Bosco's son's girlfriend in the Geraldine Page movie *Flanagan*. And she'd had an extraordinary experience trying out for a Broadway play.

"The role for the play required I play the piano well. Well, I played the piano. I went to the audition. They asked if I could play Chopin's 'Revolutionary Etude.' I told them I would learn it. This is a very difficult piece. I went home and chained myself to the piano for a week, learning what otherwise might have taken three weeks. Then they gave the part to Molly Ringwald who does not play the piano at all. I thought, here I have just been with Philip Bosco and Geraldine Page, really great actors, and what it was about was sitting in chairs eight hours reading a book waiting for the five minutes they would need you. Now I've been misled and then lost this part to Molly Ringwald. And besides all that I don't like what I'm doing. I think I will go back and finish school."

She returned to Sarah Lawrence with a vengeance, and it was in her fourth year, her senior year, that she decided to do the one thing that she had liked to do all the time. She would be a writer. She studied with Grace Paley and E. M. Broner. She wrote a short story.

"Mrs. Broner, without my knowledge, submitted my story to the Henfield Competition. It won the prize of First Runner Up. They thought I was a very good writer. And they convinced me I should stay on at Sarah Lawrence for two more years and get a graduate degree."

During this time, Shapiro also met and studied with Jerome Badanes at Sarah Lawrence. She discovered a very interesting connection with him.

"About ten years earlier, Badanes made a film about a tiny Jewish ghetto village in Poland at the turn of the century. He had advertised in the paper for anyone who had old movies of this village. And it turned out that my grandfather had been from this town, Haradock, and had taken footage with one of the earliest movie cameras. And the film *Image Before My Eyes* was released in selected movie theaters in 1982 with my grandfather's footage in it. Now I was studying with this man who had uncovered my past."

Shapiro wrote her first novel in graduate school. It was called *Playing With Fire*, and it was about a young woman college student who has an affair with the father of her roommate. Doubleday bought it. And in 1990, they published it. At the same time that Shapiro got her graduate degree, her book was selected as a Literary Guild Selection, it was optioned for a movie, translated into three foreign languages and the paperback edition published. The *New York Times* wrote, "Shapiro's language sings of Fitzgerald."

She moved from her apartment into an Upper West Side loft. When she is in the City, which she is for the writing classes she teaches at Columbia University, she works there today.

"It is a former artist's studio. It is large and quiet. It is not far from Lincoln Center. I get to be alone with my thoughts. I write."

Shapiro does not plan her novels. She develops her characters, gets what she calls her "voice" and begins to put the words down. The characters do what the characters do. She has no idea where the novel is going.

"Joan Didion said she writes to figure out what she is thinking. If

59

she knew what she was thinking ahead of time she wouldn't write. I feel the same way."

In writing *Playing With Fire* and with *Fugitive Blue*, there came a time when the characters did things that were so extraordinary that Shapiro thought the manuscript had gotten out of control. "Uh oh, any chance of getting this published just went out the window," she wrongly concluded one day while writing *Playing With Fire*.

Shapiro first came to the Hamptons ten years ago for her older sister's wedding. It was held on the beach in Amagansett with a reception afterwards at the 1770 House in East Hampton. She went down Huntting Lane and fed the ducks at the Nature Preserve. She was seventeen years old. The Hamptons took hold of her and never let go.

She rented for a while in Sag Harbor. Now she lives in Southampton, and she has a special room in her house that overlooks a farmer's field and it is here that she has begun work on her third novel.

Her occasional weekends in the Hamptons have turned into an every weekend affair and now four days a week.

"Southampton is about to become my home full time," she said.

February 5, 1993

Chapter 13

JEFF SILVERMAN

Jeff Silverman has just concluded a meeting with some Japanese businessmen. "Cookies," he says. "We always have cookies on hand for the Japanese. They like them."

We are standing by a round conference table that graces one end of Mr. Silverman's office. There is a plate of cookies in the center and Mr. Silverman asks if I'd like some.

"This is quite a view here," I comment.

The office is absolutely grand, thirty stories above Third Avenue, with a wall of windows on two sides that affords a sweep of a view from the tip of Manhattan Island all the way up to the Triboro Bridge. It is an office befitting the President and Chairman of a large international corporation.

"On a clear day," Mr. Silverman says, "we can see the monument at the Robert Moses State Park on the South Shore of Long Island."

"That must be thirty miles away."

A secretary serves me some cookies and we settle ourselves in comfortable chairs by Mr. Silverman's desk. He is an intense man, highly focused, and when he looks at you he looks right at you.

"What were you meeting with the Japanese about?" I asked.

"We produce certain building materials that we sell domestically. They run a worldwide distribution company. I was trying to interest them in an arrangement where we would increase our production and they would market the product around the world."

"Will it happen?"

"We shall see."

For the past twelve years, Mr. Silverman, who is 46 years old, has been the President and chairman of Ply Gem, a company that manufactures building materials and supplies. When he arranged to purchase the company twelve years ago — his brother had married the daughter of the founder — it was doing $57 million a year in business. This past year it did ten times that and was noted as the 501st largest corporation in America by *Fortune* magazine.

"If the Fortune 500 were the Fortune 501, the name of Ply Gem Industries of New York City would already be in lights," wrote Fortune in their cover story last month. "This company sold $546 million in home improvement products such as wood paneling, windows, tileboards and vinyl siding. When Jeffrey Silverman took charge in 1982, Ply Gem had been a $57 million a year business."

I did a little arithmetic. Jeffrey Silverman was 34 years old when he bought a $57 million a year company. This was a whiz kid. But how did he do it?

"I grew up in Forest Hills," he said. "My dad, Harry, was a financier in the drug and accessories business. When I was nine years old I was working in my dad's factory in Jackson Heights where he made ladies compacts. I've always wanted to go into business."

He more than wanted to go into business. From the time he was a little kid, his dream was to build one of the great corporations in America. He has largely succeeded in that goal.

"In high school I was voted the kid most likely to succeed," he said. "I went to college at L.I.U. and got a degree in finance. I became the youngest member of the New York Stock Exchange."

At the age of thirty, Jeff Silverman bought a small rural TV cable company. Cable was in its infancy then, but there was money to be made in the rural communities. He built the company up and sold it, bought another and sold that. There were lots of very tiny cable companies all over the country at that time, and Silverman soon came to the conclusion that only half a dozen major players were going to succeed at it and he was not large enough to be one of them. A real estate firm approached him about selling out in 1980 and he did so. He then spent two years looking for the place to make his next investment. Ply Gem came along.

"Does your brother work with Ply Gem?" I asked.

"No. He works in the insurance business in Connecticut. All together I have four brothers. The third is in real estate in Nevada. The fourth, who is my twin, is still active in cable television out in California."

"So you built Ply Gem."

"I saw there was a huge potential in the home improvement market, in do-it-yourself. I began to buy small but related companies. Companies that make vinyl siding, patio doors, skylights. Ply Gem now is a grouping of eleven independent manufacturing companies from coast to coast.

Independent, and yet together."

"Describe a typical day."

"I live here in midtown. My driver picks me up at five thirty in the morning. I am at my office by six. Then I have meetings all day, both here and outside. There might be a breakfast meeting. We meet with suppliers, analysts, bankers, Wall Street people. Then I go home."

"At five?"

"Sometimes at nine or ten. You know I absolutely love my work. Building this business, to me, is all the fun in the world." He reaches into his jacket pocket and pulls out a small electronic device. "I have a portable phone. I have two phones in the car. Two different lines. I am always hard at work.

"You know, I am a great believer that with hard work you can become successful at almost anything you do in America. Even if you do not have talent. I tell my people — do not bring me any well rounded individuals. Bring me people who are focused, who have financial goals, who love what they are doing. That is what success is all about in America."

"Do you have any hobbies?"

"I play tennis. But it has a lower priority. On weekends, we go out east — we have a house in Southampton — and I usually have a briefcase of work with me. I play tennis, sit by the pool. Friends come over."

"Children?"

"Four kids, ages 13 to 21. My three oldest are at college, Ohio State, George Washington and C. W. Post. One of my kids is a rock star. Here."

Silverman give me a CD. The group is called GENTLEMEN PREFER BLONDS.

"Try it, I think you'll like it," Silverman says. "My son is the lead guitar."

Silverman has been as active philanthropist on the East End, particularly for the Southampton Campus of Long Island University. He is on the Board of that school. And he has contributed money for the repair of the school windmill and he has contributed money for the upgrading of the school radio station.

"Where do you think Ply Gem is going from here?" I asked.

"In the eighties we built the business by buying. In the nineties, we are focusing on the strengths of each of our companies and adding the strengths together so that two and two equal five. For example, we have a vinyl frame window that sells very well in the Midwest but doesn't sell well anywhere else. It has a patented urethane foam lining which gives it excellent insulating properties. Now we are removing the foam and we find it sells in the South where they don't need the insulation.

"We are also becoming involved in a joint venture with the Russians. We've just signed an agreement to form a new company half owned by the Russians, half owned by us, which will be the agent for all transactions involving paper, pulp and forest products that are sold between the two nations."

"Have you been in Russia?"

"Not just yet. But I've been meeting with their officials here. It's certainly a tough time for them. We had a meeting in the World Trade Center a few weeks ago and I gave each of them a cookbook to give to their wives. One of them told me it wouldn't do much good because they are unable to get all the ingredients, but they thanked me anyway. Their wives would like to see what other people eat."

With Silverman's drive and dedication, it seems hard to imagine him not succeeding at anything he tries. And others agree. He recently received the award as the 1991 Entrepreneur of the Year, presented by Merrill Lynch, INC Magazine and the accounting firm of Ernst and Young.

July 5, 1991

* * *

Ply Gem is now ranked #477 by sales on the Fortune 500 roster of America's largest corporations. More importantly, the Company ranks #62 in total return to investors out of the Fortune 500.

Chapter 14

BARRY SONNENFELD

Barry Sonnenfeld, the director of the movie *The Addams Family* wears round glasses, looks like a bookkeeper, and has a runny nose. We are sitting on sofas in the living room of his ultramodern East Hampton home within walking distance of the center of town and he is busy with tissues.

"I apologize for my nose," he says.

"Your nose is forgiven," I say.

"My nose accepts your apology."

Barry Sonnenfeld offers me a choice of drinks.

"Seltzer without ice?"

He's got cold seltzer which I can have without ice but it's flat. Or he's got warm seltzer which is fizzy and he can put over ice. I take the latter. Now he is messing around in the kitchen.

At 38, this is the first movie Barry has ever directed. It is not, however, the first movie that he has felt he has directed. He has been the cinematographer for half a dozen big hits, including *Big*, *When Harry Met Sally*, *Throw Mama From The Train*, *Compromising Positions* and several films he has worked with the Coen brothers, Joel and Ethan, *Blood Simple* and *Raising Arizona*.

"You see I always thought we were all filmmakers," he says. "And so I would make comments about the pacing, the lighting, the angles, the coverage. I used to call myself the Director's Friend. Of course I wasn't in the credits as that."

Barry Sonnenfeld lives full time in East Hampton with his wife Susan and their two children. He is a shooting star in the movie business with all this success but it is something of a problem because he loves being home so.

"I was away for six months shooting *The Addams Family* and I hated it. We shot it in Los Angeles and I didn't get to be home hardly at all."

He is determined that if his career continues as successfully as it has he will insist his next film be made in New York so he can be home with his wife. And he has said this loudly and often.

"I love her very much and it is difficult not to be with her," he says. "At this party in L. A. Brandon Tarkitoff, President of Paramount, said to me I know, I know, everyone says the sequel has to be shot in East Hampton. GOMEZ BY THE SEA."

In fact, there are several opportunities presenting themselves for films to be made in the East, and Barry is pursuing them. One is *Liar's Poker*, which he might make for Warner Brothers. Another is something called *Forest Gump* which Tom Hanks, who he befriended while making *Big*, wants him to do with him for Paramount.

"Also there is a script making the rounds that might be shot entirely here in East Hampton. It is called *Father's Day* about three divorced fathers who have their six kids for the summer. It would be shot right here at the beach."

Barry Sonnenfeld was born and raised in the Washington Heights section of Manhattan. He went to the High School of Music and Arts where he played the French horn. He and the French horn were a couple for 12 years he says, and after that he went to NYU, the Bronx Campus, for three years studying political science because his mother said if he went off to school she would commit suicide. So he commuted from home.

In between his junior year and senior year, NYU shut the Bronx campus and Barry figured that if he moved downtown and finished at NYU in the Village his mother would kill herself and so he might as well finish somewhere else. He did his senior year at Hampshire College in Amherst. His mother survived.

After college, he drifted around Manhattan for a year perusing, unsuccessfully, his one interest, which was taking still photographs — he had a darkroom at home while growing up — and then for a lack of anything else to do he enrolled at the NYU Graduate Film School and in three years emerged with an MFA in filmmaking.

"I immediately went out and bought a 16mm camera figuring if I bought a camera I could legitimately be a cameraman."

He was right. *The Wall Street Journal* hired him to do promotional documentaries. Another documentary he photographed, *In Our Water*, was nominated for an Academy Award.

He obviously was a talented cameraman, and his career was underway.

And then one day, at a party in the East 30's, given by Hillary

Ney, the daughter of the CEO of Young and Rubican, he met Joel Coen.

"Actually, Hillary wanted me to meet him because I was farther along in my career than he was and she thought I could give him a job. I did give him a job, as a production assistant, running errands, getting coffee and so forth. He was the worst production assistant I ever had. He got three tickets the first time I sent him out in a car."

Joel Coen and his brother Ethan had an idea to make a film called *Blood Simple*. They would need three quarter of a million dollars and to get it, rather than show prospective investors a script, they decided to make a trailer of the film as if it actually existed. They hired Barry to shoot it.

"Making a trailer was a very good idea," Barry says. "Most investors look at a script and have no idea what they are looking at. But show them a trailer, a preview like they would see at a theater and they say hey, I know I'd like to see that movie."

At this time, Ethan, with a degree in philosophy from Princeton, was working as a statistical typist at Macy's. He did this rather than be a regular typist because they paid an extra fifty cents an hour. Joel Coen seemed unable to hold any kind of steady job.

"Joel Coen is an idiot savant. If Joel wasn't doing films I have no idea what else he would do. They hired me for a four-day weekend at $100, that's $25 a day, to make the trailer, figuring if they paid me the $100 then they wouldn't be obligated to have me make the film. They explained what they had in mind about the trailer. I made it."

It took a year to raise the three quarters of a million dollars and the big break only came when Joel went back to Minneapolis — the Coens are from Minneapolis — and spoke to some lady there who was head of Hadassah fundraising who gave him the list of the 100 biggest contributors.

What Barry Sonnenfeld added to the Coen brothers' films seems to be this rather wacky kind of cinematography where a camera runs along the floor following something or otherwise makes a wrong turn. It became a kind of Sonnenfeld style for all the movies he has made.

"What is the concept behind this kind of film making?" I asked him.

"Well, I just do it. I don't have an intellectual answer for you about this. I remember Penny Marshall meeting with me for about 45 minutes when they were considering me for cinematographer and she went over all these concepts about what they wanted to do for *Big* and I said can I make a suggestion? And she said sure, and I said why don't we just make it look NICE. The concepts go out the window anyway when you actually get down to doing it. And so that is what we did.

"I suppose when they hired me to be the director for *The Addams Family* they thought I would bring a certain visual style to it, and I suppose I did. But I really discovered that this was a lot more complicated. This film seemed to be more about costumes. More about visual effects."

I was curious about the fact that so many things connected with *The Addams Family* were from eastern Long Island. The late Charles Addams, the *New Yorker* cartoonist who created "The Addams Family," lived in Sagaponack. He was from East Hampton. Christine Ricci, who plays Wednesday, grew up in Montauk, the show had it's advance sneak preview and grand opening party at the East Hampton Cinema and in Oddfellows Hall on Newtown Lane.

"I was very aware of it. I wanted to get Peter Larkin of Sag Harbor to do the sets but he was busy. As for Christine Ricci, I had no idea she was from Montauk until after she was selected for the part. Her father is a Manhattan lawyer and commuted two or three times a week from Montauk, but it's such a long commute they moved to New Jersey recently and so that is where I thought she was from."

Barry told me an interesting story about the set. They had at first thought they would build an old Victorian house but the cost was so great that they decided instead to go looking. They found what they thought was the perfect house in New Haven, Connecticut, an old abandoned creaky thing owned by Yale University. At first, Yale was receptive to their using it, but then the movie people offered to make a financial contribution to New Haven and fix the thing up. Now it developed Yale was planning to tear this building down in the not too distant future to make way for a school building and the movie people's activities were stirring up environmentalists who now suggested the old building be saved. Suddenly, the building burned to the ground.

"Go figure that one out," Barry said.

"Sounds like the plot for a new movie right there," I said.

"So we wound up building the facade of an old Victorian house on a hillside up in Burbank. More reason for me not to get home to East Hampton with any frequency."

I asked how he first came to East Hampton.

"I had worked as an assistant to Elliott Erwitt, the photographer and he had a house out here. I took a summer house. Soon I found something very unusual. I would take naps. In the city, I would take a nap and feel very guilty. In East Hampton I would take a nap and not feel guilty. I love to take naps. I thought, I have to move to East Hampton."

Here is how the Sonnenfelds spend their days.

"We wake up at seven and get Amy off to school. Then we come home, read the *New York Times*, debate where we are going to have lunch, have lunch, then nap. We nap from one to three. Then we get up, get dressed, Susan helps Amy with her homework, I go to the studio out back and get storyboards over the fax for TV commercials that I do. Then we go out to dinner. My favorite restaurant is the

Laundry. Also Nick and Toni's. Also Fresno. I don't like to cook or clean so to get out of it and not feel guilty I volunteer to take everybody out to eat every night. From this house we can walk to all three restaurants.

"I feel very privileged to live out here. This really is paradise. There is something about the quality of light. You can go weeks without seeing the water but just seeing the sky you know its there. You go down to the beach every day in your car, even for a minute. I'll tell you it's true what they say about L. A. There is no weather in L. A. Here it is drizzling or it is stormy or it is hot. I love it. I think anyone who can make their living and live out here is incredibly lucky."

Barry has bought property on Gardiner's Bay at the Bell Estate. Someday he wants to build a house there and it might have been something he did rather soon except for the fact he was asked to direct *The Addams Family*. Turns out he has a very good reputation as a cinematographer and commands a very good fee for that work, but as a first time director he was paid the minimum guild scale. He has put the new house on hold.

"If this is a success, I can do better with my second film. Maybe then I'll build. As for filmmaking, I have this dream in life. You remember when the Bridgehampton High School was talking about merging? I thought — they merge and I'll take the place and turn the school into a studio. Well, that didn't happen. I'd love to have a studio in East Hampton. In fact, I was on Newtown Lane last Saturday and ran into Steven Spielberg and Kate Capshaw and I told Spielberg who seems as enamored with East Hampton as I am that if he wanted to go half with me on a studio he was on."

December 6, 1991

* * *

Barry has directed two more films. He and Susan have a beautiful new daughter, Chloe, born last May, and they are finally building their oft-dreamed of house on Gardiner's Bay.

Chapter 15

ERICA ABEEL

Erica Abeel, who has a home in Sag Harbor, has been aggravating, shocking and fascinating everybody with her writing for more than fifteen years. She is perhaps best known for the HERS columns she frequently writes for the *New York Times*. They have been collected in a book. She is also a best selling author whose works include *The Last Romance, I'll Call You and Other Lies Between Men and Women* and her first novel, a bombshell, published seventeen years ago, which was entitled *Only When I Laugh* about what it was like for a woman to have her man run out on her and leave her with a three-year old and one on the way. From the titles of these books, you can see that she is not what you would call a lockstep member of the women's movement. She is sort of a thorn shouting from the side of the women's movement, a heckler, and she is not going away.

Her latest book, *Women Like Us*, is about four Sarah Lawrence graduates and what happens to them and their idealism over 35 years. It's a Ticknor & Fields book and its publication date is February 23, 1994.

Erica Abeel, Sarah Lawrence class of '55, is a stunning woman with bright red curly hair, freckles and a quizzical look she aims right at you. She has been coming out to Sag Harbor since 1971 and she likes everything out here that does not have to do with people.

"I hate social life. I am not social. I'm a beach person. I walk the beaches. And I stay at home and I write."

I asked her what, of all her controversial writings, she thinks has brought the most reaction.

"The latest HERS column I just did for the *Times* got tons of mail," she said. "It appeared in December. I said that the sex life of middle-aged single women is not with single younger men as many of us kind of wish but with married older men who have no intention of divorcing their wives. These men find these relationships non-threatening and comfortable. The times are tough. The men cannot afford divorce. And so they just play these middle-aged women along. There's not even a grand passion about any of it."

Abeel has remembered something. Her eyes twinkle. "There was a line in the piece I wrote that people really liked, or really reacted to anyway. I wrote 'a grand passion shrivels when competing with the idea of losing a house in Santa Fe.'"

Erica Abeel was born in Queens, attended school in East Rockaway, then in Mineola, then went off to Sarah Lawrence and if there ever was a good argument that people are molded by their environment more than they are by their genes, then Erica Abeel is it. In suburban Long Island in the 1950's, in the world of tailfins and crinolines and majorettes, Erica was a rebel, or, sort of a rebel. This ambivalent attitude came from her parents who gave her two completely contradictory and competing messages to grow up with.

On the one hand, her parents were serious radicals from the 1930's. Her father wrote plays — one was produced at the Henry Street Playhouse — and he fought for social change and he sent his children, Erica and her brother, to a leftist summer camp in Phonecia, New York called Camp Woodland where, for example, the resident folk singer was Pete Seeger. Erica read Stendhal at an early age, and, beginning at the age of four, was sent in a black leotard off to the New Dance Group where she studied with Donald McHale and his black dance troupe.

Erica really loved dancing. It was the age of the blossoming of modern dance and Erica studied it, even majored in it in college. She even pursued professional dance as a lifetime goal all the way from age four until she got married at the age of 26.

"I still love dance," she said. "It is hard to describe. It is an ecstatic experience. There is something very difficult about it. It is very, very physical and you are totally in your body. It is exciting. Sublime."

At the same time Erica's parents were promoting the anti-establishment bohemian life to Erica, they were also promoting the mainstream establishment. There was suburbia itself. There was the fact that her father was an attorney and, later, a corporate attorney on Wall Street. There was the fact that her mother was a mathematics teacher. And both of them spoke to her and told her they wanted her to find a nice Jewish boy and settle down.

"They even had one in mind," Erica told me. "He was a nice Jewish boy from the Bronx. He is today a lawyer for a major publishing firm. You probably know him. Anyway, he was a kind, decent young man who was totally besotted with me. He pursued me relentlessly. I thought I wanted to marry Amery Blaine, the WASP hero in *This Side Of Paradise* by F. Scott Fitzgerald."

In fact, Erica did not know what she wanted. At high school, she says, she was this square peg in a round hole.

"My girlfriends worshipped Tab Hunter and hoped to be cheerleaders. My idea of a romantic object was Najinski — a dancer, a bi-sexual, a schizophrenic. And then there was the matter of the high school my parents wanted me to attend. They wanted me to go to Roslyn High School, and so we moved to Roslyn. But after we moved in it turned out they had purchased a house one block short of the district. And so I went to Mineola High School. Gangs roamed the halls."

Erica described Sarah Lawrence in the 1950's as a place where the off-beat children of the very rich went. She had wanted to major in modern dance. Sarah Lawrence was the only school she could find that had such a major.

"I was the only kid there who was not rich," she said. "We had Rockefellers going there, we had Yoko Ono, we had the daughter of Marshall Field in my class. The Yalies would come down like foxes looking at a hen house — Sarah Lawrence was an all-girls school."

Erica would take the 20-minute train ride from Bronxville where Sarah Lawrence was located to Grand Central Station and from Grand Central she would make her way to the studio of the Martha Graham Dance Company. She took classes there. One day Martha Graham came over and said 'you have presence,' and the phrase stuck with her a long, long time.

"Ultimately, however, I decided I just didn't want the life of a dancer. It would mean living in a world mostly populated by women. It would mean living a life of sacrifice and poverty. And my career would end by the time I was 35."

Seven days after Erica graduated Sarah Lawrence she went down to the docks and boarded the *Liberte* — this was still the age of oceangoing liners — and she went to Paris. Her parents approved. They said one year in Paris would be good for her.

"I boarded the *Liberte* with a girlfriend. We were going to spend the whole time in Europe together. Halfway across the Atlantic she got a cable from a guy that said come home I want to marry you and so when we got to Cherbourg she turned around and went back. He was a nice, young Jewish lawyer. Her mother had met him at Grossinger's and introduced him to her. She is still with him."

Erica arrived in Paris alone, registered for classes at the Sorbonne and started hanging around with a bunch of expatriate Americans on the Left Bank.

"There was this hotel that had no name. Everybody called it the

Beat Hotel. Near Git-le-Couer and down the way from Cafe de Deux Maggots. Allen Ginsberg lived there and he would cook potato spaghetti soup on a gas burner in his room and we'd order cous cous for one and make it feed three people. I was a 'beat' groupie. I had met Gregory Corso in Greenwich Village and when he had come to Sarah Lawrence to speak he carried on about how madly in love with me he was and it was a great day for me at Sarah Lawrence, but now he was in Paris and I looked him up at the Beat Hotel. He was very weird. He and William Burroughs and a bunch of us would go out to this suburb of Paris, Meudon, where Celine lived — he wrote *Journey To The End Of Night* — and they worshipped him and we'd go in past all these German shepherd guard dogs — Celine was a recluse — and we'd sit at his feet. Celine, I think, was the creator of what is known as black humor. He was also accused of being a Nazi collaborator and an anti-Semite. It was all fascinating to me."

Erica says she did not actually live in the Beat Hotel.

"I didn't live anywhere. I was a bum. I just floated around. There would be no heat and I'd sleep in my coat or with my coat on the bed. The whole time I was in Paris I had fleas. It was the best time of my life."

She was, in fact, only there for a year and it did make me wonder why she came back after such a short time.

"I got scared. I was all bravado. The Beat Hotel reeked. There were sinks in the halls and the men would piss in them. I certainly couldn't see a way to make a living there. So I came back, and I picked up the drumbeat of getting married and I got married. I was 26. My husband, just this incredibly handsome young WASP graduate student, was three years younger than me. My parents were shocked."

Erica had moved into an apartment on the Upper West Side — she couldn't afford the Village — had gotten a job as a publicity assistant at Grove Press, and had registered for classes in French Literature at Columbia University in pursuit of a graduate degree. She had found her young man in one of the graduate school courses.

Grove Press, in 1960, was on the crest of the wave of liberalism breaking the American Puritan literary barriers of the time. Grove published Genet, *Lady Chatterley's Lover*, Arthur Miller. There were arrests, lawsuits, civil rights disturbances.

"I had nothing to do with any of this," Erica said. "I was in Siberia. At Grove Press, my boss spent her whole day on the phone talking to realtors trying to find a real estate situation where her boyfriend could move out of a furnished apartment into a real apartment."

The meaning of this escaped me. I asked for, and got, an explanation.

"Boyfriends don't get married when they live in furnished apartments. Boyfriends get married when they live in a real apartment where you need furnishings. For furnishings you need a wife."

As for Erica, she loved being married to her young man. While she worked in the public relations department at Grove, he worked a job as a Manhattan real estate broker. They bought a brownstone on West End Avenue at 104th Street. She'd come home and he'd come home. She got pregnant.

"I loved it. I had come in from the cold. I loved the boredom, I loved the quarreling, the shopping and the cooking. My son was three years old and I was pregnant with our second when one day he just moved out. Friends later told me had been planning it for quite some time. I don't know. It hurt. Everything hurt."

From Erica's perspective, suddenly, at the age of 32, she was in the fight of her life. She had a minor league job, one and now two kids, no husband and an apartment on West End Avenue to support.

"I became cunning and resourceful. I got little teaching jobs here and there. I was home with the kids. I was out working. Finally, I got a full time job teaching French at John Jay College at Tenth Avenue and 59th Street. At that time, what this meant was that now with a full time job I would have medical insurance. I would work in the day and then I'd go to my room and I would work all night. I decided to write a novel about all of this."

Abeel's novel *Only When I Laugh* was a sensation when it appeared in 1977. It described the horror show of a woman going through a divorce with a young child, pregnant and with the limited opportunities in the job market there were at the time for women. It became a seminal book in the women's movement. It went into paperback. It is still read today.

"How was I as a parent? Well, I had to work all the time so they had to understand that. I became a disciplinarian. They learned to look after each other, find games to play, etc. They became very resourceful. I think I was a good role model for my daughter."

Erica Abeel, fifteen years later, still teaches at John Jay College. It is an anchor for her.

"I'm tenured and I'm an Associate Professor. I'm crazy about my students. And after all these years I am still excited to be at this school. I teach French, writing and literature. My job supports my writing. It works out very well."

Erica first came out to the Hamptons in 1971. Her ex-husband had been a sailor and had a boat at Fire Island. But they had many friends in Westhampton Beach. After her divorce, she began to live in the Hamptons at what, for many years through the 1970's, was known as "the Commune." There were about a dozen people involved and every year they would rent either the same house they had rented before or a new house. For the most part they were high-powered and interesting intellectual people. The whole thing was very loosely organized. People went about their business, whatever it was, and then came home at night to share their experiences.

"Betty Friedan was one of the members. There was Cy Goode and Betty Rollins and Arthur Herzog. There was Cynthia Epstein and Ross Wetzsteon who was an editor at the *Village Voice*. I was the only one with young children in the Commune and they gave me a hard time. This was not for kids. Drinks would be at six and dinner at nine. Nobody could understand why at six thirty I was in the kitchen cooking a separate meal. Why was I doing that?"

The Commune rented on Drew Lane in East Hampton, on Sheldrake Cove in Wainscott and on Jobs Lane in Bridgehampton. For a number of years they rented in Sag Harbor which was "a great town for raising kids — they could go around on bikes," but eventually it kind of faded away. Members got married and drifted off. Members got divorced and drifted off. Erica says that when Betty Rollins and Arthur Herzog split up it sort of ended it.

Since that time, Erica has lived in Sag Harbor, coming out weekends in the wintertime, enjoying the summers, generally avoiding all the social action. She writes articles and books.

"I have an old IBM clone computer and WordPerfect. I use it but I don't particularly like it. I don't like technology. A refrigerator will always be an icebox to me."

Her kids are, finally, grown and gone. Both of them have settled in Portland, Oregon. "I don't know what it IS about Oregon," Erica says. "Everybody's kids seem to be settling in Oregon."

Neilson, who is 26, is heading for a career in photography. Maud, at 23, is active in educational reform.

And now, as her latest book, *Women Like Us*, springs to life, Erica is melancholy.

"It's over for me. I worked on this book for six years. And now I miss all the characters I created. They're like dolls. I want to play with my dolls."

And so she will. There is another book in the back of her mind.

February 18, 1994

Chapter 16

JERRY DELLA FEMINA

By any measure, Jerry Della Femina is the most successful copywriter active today. His firm, of which he is President and CEO, employs over 300 people and last year billed over three quarters of a BILLION dollars. If you visit his New York office (there are four offices around the country), you will find his name not on the directory in the lobby, but over the revolving door as you come in from the sidewalk. This is a big building on Madison Avenue.

Jerry Della Femina has won every major advertising award there is. Many of his ad campaigns are household slogans (for the Mets: The Magic Is Back). He writes much of it himself.

I met with Jerry Della Femina at his huge oceanfront mansion in East Hampton. We sat in the library, with the sea raging outside the window. And what I found out was that this interesting looking man with the shaved head and moustache is, at the age of 55, still a kid. He's had a childhood that has lasted over half a century, he loves every minute of it and, maybe because of it, the people around him seem to love every minute of it.

"I'm fifteen years old. A student at Lafayette High School in Brooklyn. No. The worst student at Lafayette High School in Brooklyn and always getting into trouble. So we're down there shooting craps, me and the other kids, and here comes Mr. Tholfson, the Dean of Boys. Everybody runs. Now I am the slowest runner and so I start in the back but all of a sudden I am passing two kids, then three kids then all the other kids and I am trying to figure out why I am in the front when there he is, Mr. Grady the Principal, right in front of me. I plow right into him, knock him into the fence. His glasses go flying. And then I hear something I will never forget. 'Stop That Boy, He's Killed Mr. Grady!' And I run through the school and out the door and into the park where I hear that an alarm is out for a boy with blue pegged pants, a white shirt and long blond hair with a ducktail.

"So I go home. Change into brown pants and a tan shirt. I ask my grandmother for fifty cents and I go to the barber and he shaves my head. I put on thick dark glasses and now I walk back to school and I go to Mr. Santuro's Art Class and I wait for them to come for me.

"Now I'm in the principal's office. Mr. Tholfson and Mr. Grady are there who I am secretly glad to see and both of them have their heads down.

"'You know why you're here?'" Mr. Grady asks.

"'Yes. I cut art last week. I'm sorry.'"

"'That's not why you're here.'"

"Now they both look up and see me. Shock crosses their faces. There is a long silence.

"'You're gonna get away with it,' Mr. Grady says. He shakes a finger at me. 'But we're watching you.'"

According to Della Femina, this incident changed him. Although his grades did not improve — he says he graduated high school with the lowest grades in the school's history — he never got into trouble again.

Della Femina was not college material. Low grades, a blue collar family, a learning disability which, he says, gives him difficulty with spatial relationships. Reflecting on this, Della Femina decided he would make his jobs his education. Whatever job he would get he would try to learn something from. He got a job as a clerk in Macy's and learned about selling things. He got a job as a messenger and learned about all different kinds of lifestyles. Once, he got a job as a messenger with National City Bank carrying two twenty-pound satchels each filled with 10,000 checks from 11 West 42nd Street to 10 Exchange Place. He actually had to lug them. One trip, every day, using the subway.

"And I'm thinking, what could I possibly learn from this job? And I thought I will learn now to build up my shoulders. And so I did. I used these satchels to build strong muscular shoulders for myself."

On one messenger job, this was the Mercury Message Service, he delivered a package to an ad agency. Here were guys with their feet up on the desk, hands behind their heads, staring off into space.

"What do they do?" he asked someone.

"They're copywriters," he was told.

"Wow," he said.

And from that moment on, that is what became his goal in life. To write advertising copy. He was twenty years old. He began scissoring pictures out of magazines and sending them to advertising agencies asking for a job, any job.

An ad for an agency: Photo — a clown. Caption — SHOULD YOU ALWAYS LEAVE 'EM LAUGHING?

Another ad for an agency: Photo — chefs in a hotel kitchen. Caption: IS IT TRUE WHAT THEY SAY ABOUT TOO MANY COOKS?

He would become twenty seven years old before his efforts to break into the advertising agency would bear fruit. In the meantime he got married, had two babies, and continued to work the menial jobs he had held up until then.

He is at the advertising agency of Daniel and Charles at Madison Avenue and 35th Street. It is October of 1961. Mr. Daniel is looking at some of the ads he has written.

"I'll work completely for free."

"No. We'll pay you a token salary."

"You don't have to. I have another job at night."

"I've got to give you a token salary. It will be just a hundred dollars a week. I'm afraid that's the best we can do."

Della Femina walks past the receptionist and down the hall to the elevator. He gets in, presses one, gets out into the lobby and there, amongst the guards, the people at the newsstand and hundreds of other people he lets out a scream of joy that has been building in him for as long as he can remember.

* * *

To say that Jerry Della Femina took the ad agency business by storm would be an understatement. By his own description, Daniel and Charles was the Parris Island of the agencies, with everybody quaking with fear. He played the game with reckless abandon.

"I was as tough as they were," he says. "I had nothing to lose. I'd been out of work before. And I did everything my way, the way I believed in. For example, for the first three months, I refused to read any magazines because I didn't want to spoil my originality."

Just how striking Della Femina was at this time can be illustrated by his first meeting with the other principal in the firm, Charles. It was 10 p.m., and Della Femina gets on the elevator, and there Charles joins him.

"Working late tonight, huh kid?"

Della Femina replied with the Jewish song, in Hebrew, that is sung by kids around the world on Passover. Keep in mind Della Femina is Italian.

"Ma Neesh Ta Naw Ha Lilaw Ha Zeh."

Which, translated, means WHY IS THIS NIGHT DIFFERENT FROM ALL OTHER NIGHTS?

Della Femina was to be at Daniel and Charles for two and a half years and for the last half year was the Copy Chief, in charge of all the creative work at the entire agency. He was twenty seven years old.

He left for an interesting reason. He had become Charles' "son" and could do no wrong. He knew that if he was going to grow he would have to move on.

At the age of thirty three, with his art director partner Ron Travisano, he opened the firm Jerry Della Femina and Partners. The first office was in a three room suite at the Gotham Hotel. They had no clients. No prospects. At three in the afternoon, when the phone still hadn't rung yet even for the first time, they took a break and had a pillow fight.

Over the years, Della Femina wrote advertising copy for Meow Mix, Blue Nun Wine and Izusu (he created the liar Joe Izusu.) For McGraw Hill, the publishing house, he wrote an advertisement that headlined BEFORE HITLER COULD KILL SIX MILLION JEWS HE HAD TO BURN SIX MILLION BOOKS.

He decided to ask Moishe Dayan, head of the Israeli Army, to write the body copy. He called Tel Aviv and he got on the phone with his wife.

"I don't know if he would do that," she said. "But let me ask him. (Pause.) He says he'll do it."

The campaign won an award. On the plaque, Della Femina insisted the inscription read HEADLINE: JERRY DELLA FEMINA, BODY COPY: MOISHE DAYAN.

"That reminds me of another story. You know, when we write these campaigns we test them out by inviting people off the street to watch the commercials at our offices and give their opinions. We serve cake and coffee. There is an interviewer, usually a woman. And there is a one way glass and we sit behind the glass in the next room and we watch people's reactions. One time, I recall, we were testing a new product, a douche for women, which, oddly, I had named after myself. It was Feminique. We had a dozen women watch this test commercial and afterwards our interviewer is asking them questions. 'Would you use this before intercourse?' she asks. All the women say yes, except one woman named Mrs. Sullivan. She says no. 'Why wouldn't you use it?' the interviewer asks. 'Well, it is Mr. Sullivan. I never know when he is going to strike.'"

Della Femina and his first wife were divorced in 1980. In 1983, he met TV newswoman Judy Licht, who is his second wife. He knew the moment he met her he wanted to marry her. She was the toughest, nastiest interviewer he ever had.

"Judy and I watch the tape of this interview occasionally. It is pretty rare that a couple records the day they met. Ours ran on ABC. We had just gotten a new account, the New York Mets. And she asks 'How much are the Mets planning to spend with you this year?' and I reply 'a quarter of a million dollars,' and she says 'don't you think it might be better if they spent that money on a second baseman?'"

For a long time, Jerry Della Femina lived on the Upper East Side, but when he married Judy Licht he moved to the West Side because "she is a West Side person." They live on Riverside Drive.

They have had two children, which adds to the three Della Femina has had by his first wife. They range in age from 34 down to 2.

"I'm crazy about kids. I have a kid every decade whether I need one or not. Talk to Judy about the 90's. She say's I'm crazy."

The Della Femina family has been coming out to the Hamptons for almost thirty years. At first it was renting and just in the summertime. Now it is weekends, long weekends, year around.

"It is a great place to bring up kids. I play tennis, I love the beach. I love that this (East Hampton) is a small town. I love it in February, I love that I know the merchants by their first names."

Della Femina built his magnificent beachfront home about five years ago. It has seven bedrooms, a pool, it is almost 8,400 square feet. It is his retreat and, very recently, what he has come to call home.

"I'm starting to think this is my home and New York is where I go Monday to Thursday. This is happening with me and it is happening with many people. There are faxes, there are phones. Also, nobody wants to spend a whole lot of time in New York anymore."

"Any special plans for the future?" I ask.

"This is what I do. It is either this or heavy lifting. I do want to do business here in East Hampton, go into a number of things. I own property with Ben (Krupinski, who built the house). But basically, I'm a copywriter. I'll do this until they cut the uniform off me."

The phone rings in another room and Jerry Della Femina is called in to take the call. I look around this magnificent library. Books entitled *1876* by Gore Vidal, another called *Alien Sex*. Outside, not fifty yards away, a raging surf thunders against the sand. The view is as far as the eye can see.

July 3, 1992

Chapter 17

JERRY DELLA FEMINA
Revisited

The picture that accompanies this article is of Jerry Della Femina and he is cutting lox at his Jerry and David's Red Horse Market in East Hampton. Why he is cutting lox, he says, is that they have only recently opened and cutting lox is a special art and they have nobody to cut it yet and so they called him in to do it. It was something he learned how to do as a kid growing up in Queens.

Jerry Della Femina is no longer the President of a giant advertising agency in Manhattan. In fact, other than his wife and children who remain the same, just about everything else is different.

Two years since my profile, practically everybody in the Hamptons now knows Jerry Della Femina. He opened a restaurant in East Hampton that bears his name, then he opened a waterfront restaurant, boatyard and marina called East Hampton Point on Three Mile Harbor, now he has bought a small shopping center which was built but then because of lawsuits never opened its doors, and he's opened one of the stores in it himself which he has called Jerry and David's Red Horse Market. (He's partners here with David Silver.)

"You've come in just in time," he told me when I came in to find him behind the counter. "We are just about to introduce a new sandwich. It is called the Maidstone." He called to a clerk. "Have you put it up on the chalkboard yet?"

"Not yet," the clerk replied.

"Well, get it up there."

"How much you want to charge?"

"Twelve dollars. It's a special sandwich. The Maidstone consists of two pieces of white bread, watercress and margarine."

Another man in an apron wandered over. He seemed more of a manager. "Don't you think this will get certain people mad at you?" he asked Jerry.

"They're already mad at me," Jerry said. "What difference will it make?"

"How about ninety nine cents?" the other clerk asked.

With all his projects going on the East End, *New York* magazine recently wrote a story of it's own about him entitled THE AD MAN WHO ATE EAST HAMPTON.

Indeed, people have complained about him, saying that all you read about in the town is Jerry Della Femina, Jerry Della Femina and Jerry Della Femina. And indeed you do, and indeed here it is again. He is a brilliant marketing man. And once again he has gotten me to write about him.

But how can you NOT write about him? I have come to Jerry and David's Red Horse Market because of still another marketing ploy. I drive from my home in East Hampton to my office in Bridgehampton every morning. Jerry, to get people to stop at his market and see what it is all about, has advertised in my newspaper that during the week if you can stop in before 10 a.m. you get a free cup of coffee. And here he is cutting lox.

This man is not only good copy, he is a delight. He lights up the world. Three weeks ago he had an opening day party for this new store and had a band out on the lawn. Crowds came and people parked across Cove Hollow Road not noticing the newly put up NO PARKING signs there. And the police were everywhere writing tickets.

This was pretty unusual behavior on the part of the police. We have big fairs in this town and people park illegally and nobody bothers them. There are events at Guild Hall and firemen's fireworks on the beach and the rules are suspended. This party only went on for two hours. Nobody at all lives across the street — it is an open field — you would have thought they might have left all the cars alone, but they didn't.

Jerry's response? He is paying all the parking tickets. I think he is about to put notices in the different newspapers that he is going to do this. Just send your ticket to him and if it is on Wireless Road and at the time of his party he'll pay it.

This is not to say that Jerry Della Femina cannot afford all this. He established himself years ago as an advertising legend on Madison Avenue. He sold his agency for a few zillion dollars to some French businessmen. He's a wit, funny guy, is unusual looking as you can see and is constantly being interviewed in both the newspapers and on television. Also, five years ago, with his well gotten gains he built a large oceanfront mansion near Main Beach in East Hampton.

Furthermore, although prices at the market are quite inexpensive at this time one wonders if they will forever stay that way. He doesn't come cheap, at least in his restaurant ventures. My wife and I and two of our four kids ate cheeseburgers at East Hampton Point the other night. Total bill for four cheeseburgers, one salad and four diet cokes was $61. Prices are comparable at Della Femina's.

Well, all I have described is the Jerry Della Femina that lives on eastern Long Island. That is just four days a week. There is still the Jerry Della Femina that lives in Manhattan which is the other three days a week. Jerry did indeed sell his agency, but there has been nothing to stop him from opening a brand new, if smaller agency. New agencies happen in Manhattan all the time. Jerry's new one cannot say Della Femina of course. And so he calls it Jerry, Inc. One of his biggest accounts is *Newsweek*.

I did indeed say that other than the wife and kids practically everything else has changed. Even where he lives in Manhattan has changed. He sold one apartment and moved into another. His new ad agency has offices on Third Avenue, not downtown on Hudson Street.

There was a Broadway show a few years ago called IF THIS IS TUESDAY IT MUST BE BELGIUM. And indeed, I wonder if Jerry wakes up in the morning and first thing tries to figure out where he is.

My guess is that if Jerry Della Femina opens a car agency it will be to sell used DeLoreans. More power to him. He is not boring.

October 8, 1993

Chapter 18

RICHARD ADLER

Richard Adler, the composer, is almost seventy years old. I think he must be as astonished by this fact as almost everyone who knows him because even today he acts like this thin and wiry kid. Richard is full of energy. He leaps across the room to get something. He answers the phone and talks and laughs. His conversation is filled with feelings and ideas and he gestures when he talks. It's the phone again, this time the woman in his life, and his voice softens and he ends the conversation: "I love you very much too."

Under the circumstances, I think it very unlikely that Mr. Adler, the man who wrote the music to *Pajama Game* and *Damn Yankees* would ever be thinking about writing a book about his remarkable life. Autobiographies generally come at the end of a long life. And for all intents and purposes, Richard Adler has at least another fifty years to go. And yet, two years ago he was seriously ill and his life was in danger and it brought him up short. Maybe there was something to this. He would write a book. And he has done so and he has called it *You've Got To Have Heart*. It's been available in bookstores for about a month.

I met with Richard Adler at his apartment just off Fifth Avenue in the East 80s. We talked for an hour or so. I learned that, among other things, he has had a house near the beach in Southampton for over twenty years. I also learned that he swims every day. Forty minutes, beginning about seven in the morning, laps in a pool. He's not much for ocean swimming, where, he thinks, the water is too damn cold, at least until August. But swimming sets him up for the day.

It is fair to say that Richard Adler is an American icon and has

84

been considered one since the middle 1950s when *Pajama Game* and *Damn Yankees* became hits. If you do a little arithmetic, you realize that he was quite a young man when all this was going on, and no matter what happened after that, he would be held in great esteem from then on. In fact, what happened after that involved a considerable number of zigs and zags. First, his working partner on these musicals, Jerry Ross, developed tuberculosis, and, quite unexpectedly, died. He was twenty-nine. Adler was devastated and found that he was barely able to work. In the years that followed he wrote several other Broadway shows.

And yet, there was something else. When President Jack Kennedy entered the White House in 1960, he immediately noticed that all there were around him were diplomats and advisors and bureaucrats, and he decided to change all that. He would invite members of the arts to participate at the seat of government. He would have them entertain. There would be musicians, comedians, singers, actors. Since that time, of course, the John F. Kennedy Center has been built in Washington which acts as a formal and permanent institution for what Jack Kennedy began. But back then all there was was the one man who President Kennedy asked to put all these performances together: Richard Adler.

"President Kennedy loved the theatre and the arts. I'm convinced that if he had not gone into politics he would have been a writer or a performer. I would put together these great evenings of entertainment for him, for one occasion or another, and if the President called, of course, you came."

Richard recalled one evening that was in honor of a visit from Prime Minister Harold MacMillan of Great Britain. It was entitled "An Evening With President Kennedy And Friend" and Adler had brought in clarinetist Benny Goodman, actor Peter Sellers, and a comedian named Eliot Reid who did such a remarkable imitation of the President that the President nearly fell off his chair."

"Immediately following Peter Sellers, the President got up and gave a hilarious performance himself. He was very witty. He gave as good as he got."

Needless to say, Adler was a familiar figure in Camelot. He occasionally went for walks with the President in the Rose Garden and the conversation the President seemed most interested in involved the arts. On one of these walks, in the Summer of 1963, the President confided in Adler that at the next election, his Vice President candidate would be governor Sandford of North Carolina. This change, of course, was never made.

Adler was also instrumental in bringing the President, and then Bobby Kennedy, together with Marilyn Monroe, for whatever that was about. Adler was putting together a show for the President's birthday and got the idea that Marilyn Monroe, America's most popular actress, should sing "Happy Birthday" to the President. He suggested this to the President and the President thought this was a great idea. But then it made a great uproar around the country. Was this something appropriate to have happen in the White House?

Adler called on Marilyn — she was quite eager to do it — and told her that at the performance she should wear a formal and very unprovocative gown. And that she should sing it naturally and normally, not "breathlessly." She understood.

At the event, however, although she did sing his birthday wish simply and straightforwardly, she wore a low cut dress designed to knock everyone's socks off. Bobby Kennedy, who was at the event with his wife, asked Adler to introduce him to her which he did. Bobby Kennedy then spent much of the evening in animated conversation with her.

"Once when I went to see Marilyn, I commented on the fact that she had lost a lot of weight. She said, let me show you just how much, and she grabbed her shirt and pulled it all the way up to her neck. I sat down."

"Was she making a pass at you?"

"No. I think she was just being playful. But she was every bit as lovely as advertised."

In the back of Richard Adler's book, there is a listing of the people he has known over the years and it reads like a who's who and it occupies ten pages, just this listing alone. Through it all, by his own admission, Richard had a hell of a good time.

"One thing I liked," he says, "was being with women. I found them funny, fascinating, interesting, and I loved loving them."

He describes himself as an unrepentant, or anyway an only recently unrepentant womanizer. He married four times. He had two sons, one of whom tragically passed away a few years ago in his thirtieth year. Adler went on after the Kennedy years to write more serious music. He was commissioned by the National Parks Service to write a symphonic work which was nominated for a Pulitzer. He wrote another for the centennial of the Statue of Liberty, and then he wrote a jazz ballet for the Sesquicentennial of the City of Chicago. He wrote a ballet for Suzanne Farrell. All together, he has received two Tony awards and four Pulitzer nominations. Currently, he is back working on a Broadway play. Almost completed, it is partially cast and should open for tryouts shortly in New Haven. It is called *Off Key*.

In 1988, however, an event occurred in Richard Adler's life that changed him completely.

"I think cancer was put in my path for me to get over. What I have done about it has changed my life. I am in the best position I have ever been in."

Adler was in Chapel Hill, North Carolina, teaching at the university there, which he does for a month every year, when he learned he had throat cancer and should immediately have radical and disfiguring throat surgery. He got a second opinion, however, and it was decided to do exploratory surgery. Then he went to seek spiritual help in the person of Gurumayi Chiduilasanande at her ashram in Oakland, California. Gurumayi Chiduilasanande gave Adler a peach colored sash she was wearing around her neck and she told him to wear it right up to the time of the surgery, and then wear it right afterwards and she would see him in New York.

"Gurumayi changed my life," Adler told me. "She is a twentieth century saint, a Great Being, a Master. I learned that psychic energies could be transferred to me from her — the essence of God — and I could actually experience it. In fact, the experience of this transfer is the single most extraordinary experience of my entire life. I have been transformed."

Today, Adler is a follower of Gurumayi. The cure he has experienced — with radiation but without radical disfiguring surgery — has so astounded everyone, particularly his doctors, that several of them have become followers too. With the cancer gone, he is considered something of a miracle and has written about his experience in his book.

I found spending time with Richard Adler an experience in excitement and enthusiasm. He is straightforward, seemingly unaffected by his successes, and he is apparently as astonished as anyone else might be regarding the experiences that have befallen him.

You've Got To Have Heart I suspect, is just Adler's autobiography Part One. There will be another volume coming later on, much later on.

October 5, 1990

* * *

A new version of Damn Yankees opened on Broadway in March of 1994 to rave reviews. Adler and Ross' score was reproduced word-for-word and note-for-note.

Chapter 19

LEE BAILEY

As usual, in a cookbook by Lee Bailey, there is a whole section on the Hamptons. The book is entitled *Lee Bailey's Cooking For Friends*, it is hard cover, it is full color, and you can cook all sorts of delicious things, all from ingredients available in the Hamptons. This is Lee Bailey's eleventh book. About one million of them have been sold. Almost all of them are, at least in part, about the Hamptons. And that figures. Lee Bailey was one of the very first "summerpeople." A pioneer.

I do not make this claim lightly. And as I sit with Mr. Bailey, a man of charm and grace, in his Manhattan loft in 1992, he explains it to me.

"Lots of people had been coming out in the summertime before me," he says. "It was the 1960's and the Hamptons were just so beautiful and quiet. But what I noticed was that although there were a lot of people like me, interested in fashionable things and so forth, there was no place to shop for anything. If you needed a doormat for your second home, you'd go to the hardware store and they'd sell you a standard issue doormat. That was it."

What Lee Bailey did, in the late 1960's, was get the idea that stores selling designer goods could make it in the Hamptons. He opened such a store, called Bailey-Heubner, which was perhaps the first such store in all the Hamptons, in 1971. It was located on Main Street in Southampton.

"We sold furniture and accessories and kitchen utensils and tablecloths. All wonderful things. Turned out there were lots of people like me. We were a hit from the very start."

For those who remember the Hamptons back in the 60's and early 70's, there were a few high fashion stores such as Abercrombie and Fitch or Saks Fifth Avenue, which is still here, but all the rest were mom and pop operations. Silver's Cigar Store in Southampton was truly a cigar store with newspapers, magazines and a soda fountain. What Bailey-Heubner did in the Hamptons was start the community down the road to where it is today. It is hard to go down Main Street today and see any store that does not bear a European name.

Lee Bailey was a natural choice to pioneer this change in the Hamptons. Born and bred on a plantation in Louisiana, he was, by the time he had gotten into his mid-twenties, an accomplished designer.

"I went away to school at sixteen, joined the Army at eighteen. After World War II I studied at LSU in New Orleans, then at Parsons in New York City. I loved New York City from the very start, but I went back home. I had a hankering for home. You know, they say, if you really want to find out if you're any good you have to do it back home."

His stint back in Louisiana lasted seven years and spanned the 1950's.

"I went to work at a design studio but after eight months I didn't like it. I spoke to my dad. He said 'my advice is don't ever work for anybody,' and so I went out on my own. I started a party design company. Sets for the Mardi Gras carnival in New Orleans, designs for parties."

It was in 1957 that he moved to Manhattan. It would be, from this point on, his home base, with travels all over the world with his companions. And with summers in the Hamptons.

His business, in Manhattan, was designing sets for advertisements. He had a wonderful sense of it, and he rented a studio on Second Avenue at 60th Street.

"It had belonged to Fernand Fonssagrives, the fashion photographer. He was in the middle of a divorce with his wife Lisa and wanted to leave the city."

Bailey noted that Lisa Fonssagrives subsequently married the photographer Irving Penn, and it is then that I realized the circles Lee Bailey began to travel in. Dick Heubner, with whom he opened the store in Southampton, owned an advertising agency. Geraldine Stutz, the President of Bendels, was another friend, who also had a house in the Hamptons. And among Bailey's house guests, once he began renting on the beach in Quogue, were literary agent Gloria Safire and the actress Elaine Strich.

Lee Bailey is also a close friend, and has been for the better part of thirty years, with Liz Smith, the society columnist for *Newsday*.

"I built my own house in the Hamptons in 1963," Bailey says. 'It was on Sagg Pond. I had earlier considered building on the ocean but I had seen too much damage with the oceanfront homes in Quogue. I thought it would be much less turbulent on the Pond, and of course, it was. I paid $13,000 for my lot on the Pond back then. I could

89

have had beachfront for the same thing. This was a lot of money for real estate at the time and in my circumstances, but I mortgaged myself to the hilt and I built."

Liz Smith, according to Bailey, was "part of the house, there every single weekend. I was with her just the other day and we were looking at old photographs. You know, when you build a summer house you figure it has to be filled every weekend and so we filled it, and Liz was always taking pictures. So we looked at these pictures the other day and besides noting how ridiculously young we looked, we looked at these gangs of people and asked who is that? Who is that? There were so many, some of them we saw once and never saw again."

Bailey actually did not have the money to completely finish the house and so he and his friends did the last touching up themselves. One such "touching up" was to paint the entire interior.

"I had painted my share of New York City lofts. I've scraped my share of Manhattan bathrooms and painted them. White of course back then. Well, we painted the inside of this house and when we finished I put down the paintbrush and I vowed I would never paint the interior of anything ever again and I never have. I don't know about Liz."

In 1973, after just two years with the store on Main Street, Southampton, Geraldine Stutz of Bendel asked Lee Bailey to open a branch of Bailey-Heubner in Manhattan. Like the main store in Southampton, it too was an instant success. Still another Bailey-Heubner opened in East Hampton and for a time Lee Bailey was going off on his shopping trips to Europe and to South America and feeding three different locations. By the late 1970's the store at Bendel had become so successful that the two Bailey-Heubners, with such low volume in the wintertime, seemed no longer worth the effort. They closed in the early 1980's.

And then, friends persuaded Lee Bailey to write what was to become his phenomenal best selling book, *Country Weekends*.

"I thought, at first, it would be just something that would help business at the stores," Lee Bailey says. It did a whole lot more than that. New York summerpeople were absolutely fascinated with this magnificent, coffee table book that covered every facet of country living. Writing informally, Bailey gave design and fashion advice on a wide variety of subjects, illustrated with some of the most beautiful color plates imaginable, helping to guide people on how to make a charming and lovely second home in the country. It sold 100,000 copies within twelve months of its publication date in May of 1982. And Bailey has written almost a book a year ever since. He will have his next one out this month. It is called *The Tomato Book*.

"I make books that I would want," he says. "My dad was a wonderful cook. He did it to entertain friends and I know this because we also had a cook. The simplicity of it is what I wanted to get back to. I figured if I was a host, which I sometimes am, I want to be out front when the guests arrive. So I write about cooking you prepare in advance."

Bailey has other ideas about what cookbooks ought to be. "I travel a lot. My friends have homes in Greece, in Provence, in St. Barts and, of course, the Hamptons. And when I am there, since they know I can cook and I like to cook I become the sort of designated chef for a particular evening. So I go into a kitchen, this would be from a cooking point of view a "strange" kitchen, and there may not be a blender, or there may be some skittish sort of oven that I decide I better not mess with, and so I improvise. And that's how I write my recipes. Improvised, and for kitchens with just basic ingredients and with only minimal appliances.

"Also, I've always thought the best cookbooks were the ones that showed you beautiful photographs of what you have cooked, all artfully arranged on the plate. This is what you are trying to arrive at, after all. And so my recipes have these photographs of the completed dishes. And they include what to serve with it and how to attractively serve it. I really don't think cooking is an art. I think it is a craft, and that's how I treat it. Anybody can do it. It's a very fine craft."

Our interview over, Lee Bailey escorted me to the door of his magnificently appointed Union Square loft. I went out to the hall. We promised we'd see one another again. I pressed the button for the elevator and I looked back. Bailey was gone back inside. At the foot of his front door was one of the most beautifully designed doormats I had ever seen.

June 19, 1992

Chapter 20

JOHN WEITZ

John Weitz is a gentleman. He sits across from me in an impeccably tailored suit of his own design, with silk lapel handkerchief and matching tie and I am offered coffee or tea. He is a handsome man, even more handsome than he appears in the advertisements he models in for the clothes he designs and which bear his label, and he is polite to a fault. I am handed a sheet of biographical data on John Hans-Werner Weitz. He was born, it says, in Berlin in 1923. He couldn't be 67 years old. Must be a misprint.

As constant readers of this newspaper know, I am interviewing successful people who live both in Manhattan and out in the Hamptons. For the most part, these people have been in the Hamptons for five or ten years or, at the most it seems, twenty. Personally, I came here as a teenager in the mid-nineteen fifties which means I have a considerable perspective on most of these people. They are johnny-come-latelies to me. Certainly, John Weitz, the world traveler, former OSS (precursor to the CIA) agent, former race car driver, millionaire fashion designer, best selling novelist and photographer will be no exception.

"What do you like most about the Hamptons?"

"Being in my boat. I like to find an isolated cove, anchor about twenty yards offshore, and read. I am a member of the Sag Harbor Yacht Club. I've had a boat there many years."

"How long?"

"Since 1941."

Silence. Surely this is a mistake. I ask him again and he says it again. There is no mistake.

"I rented a little house in Sag Harbor then. Plunked a boat in Sag

Harbor. I was a young man, just over from Germany. The war was starting. It was very peaceful. One of my friends who also came out then was the late Mike Burke (New York Yankees, Madison Square Garden). He was later in the CIA. I was to join the OSS."

In 1941, John Weitz would have been 18 years old. How had he come out to the eastern end of Long Island? How, in fact, had he come to America? I asked him.

"I came like most German Jews. Fleeing Hitler. My father had been well educated, had started the manufacturing of rayon and he had mills. He was an industrialist. We lived well, in a home in the center of Berlin. Why Sag Harbor? When I was growing up, when I was a little boy, my family would go for vacation to the North Friesan Islands, a little strip of beach and fishing village in the north of Germany where it connects with Denmark. I had wonderful years there. Flat dunes, potato fields, dairies, huge rye country. If you were lucky the fishermen would take you out for a day in their big chunky sloops. They'd talk with one another in their own special dialect, their own language actually, called Plattdeutsche which is closer to Danish than it is to German when you hear it. Listen. (Weitz speaks in Plattdeutsche. It almost sounds Swedish.) I loved those islands and those people. Huge, phlegmatic, warm, giving, loyal.

"This language is to German something similar to what Bonac is to English."

"I suppose. Although Bonac is not a full-fledged language."

"So you had come to New York. How in the world did you ever find the East End?"

"It was easy. Every major city in the world has a place where the city dwellers go. Rome had its Ostia, Paris its Deauville. There's not much to be said today for driving a couple of hours on a grey, drizzly day in a Ferrari to Deauville. City dwellers, if they can find it, if it is in reach of salt, develop an affection for little fishing villages which they then proceed to destroy. I got a map. Drew a circle one hundred miles around Manhattan. It was obvious."

"And it was?"

"Yes, indeed. Farmers. Fishermen. You could go to a house in Sag Harbor and, just as in the north of Germany, be shown a war club brought back from New Zealand by someone's grandfather. There were the little schoolhouses, the general store in Sagaponack, the fishing stations. One difference, perhaps, is that in Germany from these islands came the great nautical men of Germany. The men who became the captains of the ships built in nearby Hamburg and Keil. On the east end, there seemed none of that. Too much coastline in America compared to Germany, I think.

"However, in one regard, what has happened to the Hamptons in the past fifty years has also happened to the islands. Today, you can go to the Island of Sylt, even further north of the islands I used to go to, and you can now buy a little thatched cottage for one million dollars, and you can wear a yellow slicker, everyone wears yellow slickers on the island and it is de rigeur you never complain about the weather. All German society is there, if you wish to play that game."

"Now you live in Remsenburg. Are you isolated enough?"

"Nobody is isolated enough. But I have no visual interference anyway. My home is surrounded by trees. Still, the property is not big enough. Who can afford big enough? Through the trees, I can hear four old men who think they are John McEnroe thwacking at a tennis ball and yelling and whooping. I can hear women whining from a neighboring pool making our lives miserable. Except in winter anyway. The worst crime, in my opinion, is that real estate people rent out these homes around you to people who don't give a damn. You spend your time knocking on doors asking them to consider those around them."

"So you prefer being on your boat."

"Nothing beats gunkholing to an anchorage nobody knows."

(We discuss some of the quietest anchorages on the East End nearby to Sag Harbor, the coves and inlets of Shelter Island. Weitz is familiar with every one.)

"How often do you come out to the Hamptons?"

"We come out every blessed moment we can. We take long weekends. Leave Monday mid-morning."

John Weitz has had one of the most extraordinary careers of any contemporary man. After arriving in Manhattan in 1941 with an English boarding school education, he did what all young German male and Jewish refugees did at the time: he volunteered into the American army. He was a platoon sergeant in the infantry when, in 1943, he was recruited into the OSS, the network of American spies during the war. The OSS lent him to the British, and he worked with the German resistence movement and, during the failed attempt to assassinate Hitler in July of 1944, he worked as a messenger behind the lines. He was 21 years old.

"How did you become a designer?"

"When I was sixteen, I was at St. Paul's in London and we used to go in to London on weekends to meet girls. This was in 1939. One day, I went into town with an Oxford man who had gone to St. Paul's, and we went to a design house. From that moment, I knew this was for me."

When the war ended, Weitz got a job as a designer for Dorothy Shaver of Lord & Taylor, who encouraged him to launch his own look. His early collections of car coats, tight jeans, fatigues, peacoats and chinos for women involved in an active, driving life, were, as Bill Blass was to say "the first sportswear as we know it today."

Weitz founded his own company in 1954, and in 1962, '63 and '64 launched separate menswear collections in the same concept. Function preceded fashion. "I am interested in the construction of style, Weitz has said. "A man must always look fit and he should wear his clothes as if they were old and valued friends."

Weitz walked what he talked. In 1967, he was one of the first men to appear on the International Best Dressed List. He is still on this list today.

In the late fifties and early sixties, Weitz was a race car driver participating in four world championship sports car races. He also designed an automobile, the two seat X600 which today is in the permanent collection of the Crawford Auto-Aviation Museum of the Western Reserve Historical Society.

In 1963, while doing a personal appearance at Bonwitt's in Palm Beach, he ran into Bill Blass, a friend of his, who was doing an appearance at Saks. Blass said he thought there was a woman he ought to meet. Blass made the introduction, and he came to marry Susan Kohner, an actress and academy award nominee, with whom he has raised two sons, Paul and Christopher, who are today students at Wesleyan and Cambridge (England) respectively.

Weitz also has written several books. He had met and was friendly with the late John Steinbeck when he lived in Sag Harbor in his later years, and Steinbeck, according to Weitz, encouraged him. He wrote Value of Nothing, published by Stein and Day in 1970, and it made the best seller lists. He wrote Friends In High Places in 1962 and a piece of non-fiction, Man In Charge, a book for executives, in 1974.

We talked now about a variety of subjects. Weitz mounted a spirited defense of the OSS and the CIA.

"There are those who truly believe that the people in charge, the people that run things and need the best information possible ought to get the best information possible, then you don't have things such as the Bay of Pigs."

We talked about the movie Jaws, out fifteen years ago, and how it epitomized the relationship between city dwellers and resort towns.

"The key to that movie was how the police chief couldn't decide which camp he was in," Weitz said.

We talked about his current advertising campaign, which seems to be on the back of every bus in Manhattan these days.

And we talked about the coming debate over German unification. Weitz had recently returned from Berlin and Letter From Berlin had been published in Travel magazine.

"I am in favor of the unification of Germany," he said. "I don't think what happened fifty years ago should ever be forgotten. But I believe it is over with and we must move on. Occasionally, I fly the German flag over my house in Remsenberg. It is time."

July 13, 1990

* * *

In 1992 Ticknor & Fields published Mr. Weitz's biography of Joachim von Ribbentrop, entitled Hitler's Diplomat.

Chapter 21

RUSTY LEAVER

When you go to get your tickets to the Paul Simon Concert in Montauk, now going on sale all over the East End this week, you might give a few moments thought to a man named Rusty Leaver. With all the benefits and all the promotions held on eastern Long Island every summer, this is the man who has raised more money for charity than anybody else. During the past three years, running one concert a year, he has raised between one and one and a half million dollars. Nobody else comes close. The beneficiaries include the Montauk Historical Association, the Nature Conservancy, the East Hampton Community Council, the Family Service League, the East Hampton Baymen's Emergency Medical Fund, the East Hampton Town Shellfish Hatchery, the Group for the South Fork, the Retreat, the Concerned Citizens of Montauk and I am only including those charities that have received $25,000 or more. There are about a dozen others.

Rusty Leaver stopped by the offices of *Dan's Papers* the other day in his trademark cowboy hat and boots, and I talked with him for a while about the upcoming concert. His manner of dress is not an affectation. He runs a horse and cattle ranch in Montauk. It is the oldest continuously run ranch in the United States.

He told me that this year's concert, like the three that have come before, will be held in one of the pastures at Deep Hollow Ranch. It will be on Monday, August 9 at 3 p.m. and will include, besides Paul Simon, the Allman Brothers Band and Mary Chapin-Carpenter.

Never in Rusty Leaver's wildest dreams did he imagine he would be raising millions of dollars for charitable organizations during his working career. He was, in fact, a New York City boy, the son of two Upper

West Side painters. And it wasn't until he was seven years old that he realized what he wanted to do when he grew up. That is not a misprint.

"It was the late nineteen fifties," he said. "My parents had become friends with a wealthy Manhattan businessman by the name of Hy Sobiloff. Mr. Sobiloff had a home in Montauk. He was also a major eccentric. Besides publishing volumes of his own poetry, much of it about Montauk, he decided that out at this ranch in Montauk, known as Deep Hollow Ranch, they ought to have some buffalo. He bought two and had them trucked out. He paid for their upkeep for many years."

The senior Leavers came to visit Hy Sobiloff at his home in Montauk and then, in the early 1960's, came to rent a house for the summer themselves. Rusty Leaver, age seven, would bicycle over to Deep Hollow Ranch. It is a spread near the Lighthouse of over a thousand acres and has been in continuous operation since the first settlers came to Montauk in the 1700's. Rusty would go horseback riding. That, as they say, was all-she-wrote.

"I fell in love with the ranch. I would bike out there, go horseback riding, help with the chores, do whatever they wanted until they threw me out. Then I'd go the next day."

Rusty Leaver's fixation with the Deep Hollow Ranch has remained from that day until this. At the age of 19, when a part of the ranch came up for sale, he persuaded a man named Elbert Edwards to go into partnership with him to buy it. There still wasn't enough money. Leaver, at 19, went around Montauk and sold bonds to private individuals at 8% interest. He would see to it that the ranch would always remain a ranch and would never be developed. Many people bought these bonds and all of them have since been paid off. Both partners came to Montauk for awhile. Then Edwards moved on. Leaver remains.

At 21, Rusty married Diane Dickinson, the daughter of Frank Dickinson, who was one of the three brothers managing and running the ranch. Today, Rusty and Diane have two children. They are raising them at the ranch.

"For many years, after I bought the ranch, I had to work in the City part time," Leaver told me. "I did project management for the Helmsleys. But let me tell you. In Montauk, waking up in the morning and going out to feed the horses and cattle and doing this on a site where this has been done for hundreds of years, well, there is nothing like it. Sometimes, even today, I ride up on top of Signal Hill and I look down at it all. The solitude of it, the ranching tradition. I think, hey, this is great. I'm so glad I had this desire at such an early age to do what I had to do."

The Deep Hollow Ranch, today, is a working cattle ranch. There are cutting horses, stables, boarding, riding, skeet shooting and camp fires in the evening, two major horse shows and all that cattle. In the summer season, about 15 kids work for the Leavers. In the winter, there is a skeleton staff of three.

Not far up the road from the ranch is the oceanfront home of Paul Simon. Simon came by occasionally to go horseback riding. He and Leaver struck up a friendship.

"One year, a rodeo came to town and set up in the pasture south of the Highway. I called Paul ahead of time and told him we are doing this and I hope you have no trouble getting up to your house. He came over to see the rodeo and we were standing in the field just talking and he said 'gee this is a great spot for a music festival,' and I thought that's nice. It was just an offhand remark.

"A few days later Dick White from the Montauk Historical Society came over and said they were going to have to raise a lot of money to preserve the Montauk Lighthouse. We talked about bake sales and other things, and then I thought of what Paul had said. I called him and asked if I could come over because there was something I wanted to talk to him about. He said sure. I went there and we had coffee and I asked him if I could get him to come down and maybe play a song or two if I got some musicians set up for a fundraiser in that pasture there. He thought for a moment and then he said, maybe I can do better than that."

What Leaver did not know was that this dovetailed with preparations Simon was making for his major world tour. Leaver did know that Simon needed a rehearsal space in the area, and he had helped get him one, in Westhampton Beach at a former Police Academy. Now Simon thought that setting up an outdoor concert in the Deep Hollow pasture might serve the dual purpose — besides raising money — of coordinating and working out technical problems for the tour.

And so the Paul Simon Concert was born. In August of 1990, people lay on blankets and enjoyed an afternoon picnic at Deep Hollow listening to the wonderful music of Paul Simon. Everything went smoothly. What they didn't know was that Leaver had almost killed himself to make this concert a success.

"I had no idea what this would entail," he said. "I had never done it before. But I kept thinking that here we have Paul Simon, an icon. One of the great songwriters of our time. I didn't want to let him down. And so what I decided was, well, I just won't sleep."

There were tickets to be printed, sound systems to install, tents to be erected, permits to be gotten, food arrangements to be made, traffic flow to be considered, marketing and promotion to be done. Leaver hired nobody that first year. "I really neglected my business for an entire year," he said. He, along with Dick White, the Montauk Police Department and a host of other volunteers pulled off one of the most wonderful music festivals of all time. And the concert raised more than a quarter of a million dollars for the Montauk Lighthouse.

The next year, the concert was put on by Paul Simon's friend Billy Joel, who lives in East Hampton, and it raised half a million dollars. The third year, last year, Simon ran it again and it raised almost three hundred thousand dollars.

Now there is this year.

"So many people have come forward. Tom Shine of Logo 7 is donating all the shirts. Tropicana is donating product and making a major financial contribution. Last year, Ann Glew, the wife of David Glew who is President of Epic Records, called up and said what could she do? They have a house in Montauk. She came down on concert day and answered telephones, did whatever had to be done. This year, David Glew has gotten the involvement of Epic's parent company, Sony, who will be a major sponsor. And then there is Gary Madison of Long Island Sound, who for three years now has handled the ticket sales in his stores without asking for a cent. It takes more than a hundred people now, erecting the stage, selling tickets and so forth, to run this event. And what it all does is raise a lot of money for charity. But what I remember is something that Paul Simon said — "the most important thing is that we provide a great day."

And here is a list of some more charities receiving donations: The Family Service League, the East Hampton Community Council, the Montauk Senior Nutrition Center, the Montauk Village Association, the East Hampton Town Police, the Montauk Volunteer Fire Department, the East End Arts Council, Montauk Youth, Bridgehampton Child Care, the Montauk Harbor Association, the East End Wellness Project, the Montauk Library, the East Hampton Day Care Center, the Montauk Food Pantry and on and on and on...

June, 11, 1993

Chapter 22

FRED ALGER

You might call it luck. You might call it being in the right place at the right time. But you also have to consider that Fred Alger, who I am sitting with in his Georgica home in East Hampton, is a man of great focus and determination. What is luck to one man is shoulder to the wheel to another.

"When I decide to do something, I do it intently," he says. He is referring to his decision a dozen years ago to run and complete the New York City Marathon.

"The event is run on a Columbus Day weekend. I started training on Memorial Day, not for the coming Columbus Day but the Columbus Day after that. I trained for a year and a half."

And he completed the run. Although it almost killed him. Having never run this distance before in his life, he collapsed across the finish line, was taken off to a medical tent and remained there for more than an hour. But he had done what he had set out to do, averaging nine minutes a mile.

Fred Alger, at the time of this 1979 run, was already a legend on Wall Street. His managed accounts, which he had run beginning in the 1960's, had been so successful that he was the subject of articles in *Time* and *Newsweek*. At the time of the run, he had already been head of his own business, Fred Alger and Co., for fifteen years. Today, twelve years after that, Fred Alger and Co. employs 65 people on Wall Street and manages more than two billion dollars worth of other people's money. And Fred Alger remains firmly at the helm.

I am seated with a slender, athletic looking man in his mid-fifties. He is soft spoken and thoughtful. And he is telling me how he came to begin this business of managing other people's money.

"I was raised in Grosse Point, a suburb of Detroit. We lived well. My father was in politics in Michigan — he was Secretary of State for a while and once ran for Governor, although he lost — and I was sent off to private school. I went to Milton Academy in Massachusetts, then to Yale. I took a degree in American Studies.

"It was during the summer of my Junior year at Yale that I determined exactly what it was I was going to do with my life. I had a summer job in a brokerage house called First Michigan. I was living at home. I was a golfer, really, but I made friends with the head of research at this firm, Dr. Sidney Bordon. He showed me how you did research on up and coming companies. It was solving a puzzle. You get all the clues right and you make money. It was fascinating."

Alger worked for a number of brokerage and money management firms in the Midwest, getting to know the ropes. In 1962, he was employed by Winfield and Company and was assigned the job of being portfolio manager of one of three mutual funds.

"An older man owned the company and wasn't much interested in it. His son had no interest. The Vice President was interested in politics."

In very short order, several of the customers of the firm pulled up stakes and when a third one threatened to do so, so the head of the company sent Alger, who was their best portfolio manager, to New York City to see if he could save it. He failed.

"But then I suggested that if they didn't like Winfield but liked the way I managed the portfolio, I'd move to New York City and set up my own business. They could be my first customer."

Fred Alger, his wife and three small children moved into a two bedroom apartment in Riverside Drive and 86th Street. He opened his firm, one room off the hall in a building near Wall Street.

"I had three thousand dollars saved up. My one customer would bring me seven thousand for the year. It wasn't much and I'd have to run things on a shoestring. Our baby sitter came in part time to do typing. I bought a desk for five dollars from the building super. We had cardboard filing cabinets and the guest chair in the office was a rocking chair from the kids' room."

"I was down to my last three hundred dollars when I got a second customer who wanted me to run a theoretical fund — one where no funds are involved, just see how I'd do — for which he would pay me one hundred dollars a week. And that was what got us through. I should say that the entire firm at the time consisted of just me."

And then, it was a matter of Fred Alger being in the right place at the right time. The opening of his firm coincided with the birth of the active money market funds. Laws had been reinterpreted. And suddenly, in the early 1960's, people were taking their money out of banks and putting it into the hands of money market managers where they could make greater returns.

"My business became an overnight sensation. In 1965, my work with the Security Management Company led all of Wall Street in returns. A 78% increase. I received all sorts of publicity, national magazine interviews and so forth."

With his sudden success, Alger moved to 91st Street and Park Avenue. He also bought a house on Georgica Road in East Hampton. Talk about being in the right place at the right time. Listen as Alger talks about this house and what it was like to come into the Hamptons in the 1960's.

"We'd been coming out to the Hamptons since we first moved to Manhattan. We had three little kids and we wanted to get them out of the City for the summer. We rented in Amagansett, then stayed at my wife's sisters' in Sagaponack. Then this house came along. It was one of those big summer cottages. Twenty bedrooms, two baths. We paid $50,000 for it. We probably overpaid."

And so Fred Alger embarked on one of the most successful careers on Wall Street. He joined the Maidstone Club in East Hampton, developed his tennis game, worked hard and raised his family.

In 1965 he met one of the most colorful figures ever to grace Wall Street, Bernie Cornfeld. Cornfeld had figured out a unique way to sell American securities to Europeans and had begun to build a huge fortune. His firm, IOS, would collapse in a great heap in 1969, but in 1965, Alger learned that Bernie Cornfeld was putting together his money management team. Alger arranged to meet him at someone's home.

"I got there for our appointment at eight in the morning, and I waited half an hour. Then he came down to meet me. Khaki pants, open shirt. 'Sorry I was late, but I was upstairs balling a girl in the shower,' he said as we shook hands."

Cornfeld announced that Alger should handle a fund for him.

"We'll name it after you." Cornfeld said. "The Alger fund. So if it doesn't work out, I'll have a schmuck to blame."

And so, the Alger Fund was born, as part of Bernie Cornfeld's IOS. It became enormously popular in the late 1960's and made a lot of money for a lot of people, and Alger had no idea when he decided to expand his business in 1968 that IOS was less than a year from destruction.

"I made an application to join the New York Stock Exchange. I had thought we were paying out these fees, if we were on the Exchange ourselves, we could pay them to ourselves."

The stock exchange had a rule that you couldn't be a member if you accepted performance fees and since Cornfeld paid Alger performance fees, Cornfeld resigned the account. And then Cornfeld collapsed in a financial tangle that was to his day what Michael Milken's is to this. The Alger Fund was reborn then, as a fund owned by the Fred Alger Co. And it has been successful since.

"The performance of money invested in my company," Fred Alger says, "is roughly at an annual compound growth rate of 20%. If you had invested $100 when we began in 1963, it would be worth $16,000 today."

The Alger Small Capitalization Fund, over the past five years, was the best performing fund in the country. It made me wonder why this was. I asked him.

"Most money management companies won't research small firms," he said to me. "It is too much trouble. But my background is research and so my company heavily researches a wide variety of small companies and then chooses the cream of the crop. We are able to do extremely well in a small niche of the market."

In 1982, on a Monday, Alger and his wife saw pictures of a giant castle on a hill in France for sale. It overlooked the grand Dordogne Valley and since all three of the children — ages 16 and the twins at 20 — had been going to school in France, the Algers decided to look into it. On Wednesday they flew over to France to look at the castle and that very afternoon, they bought it. They sold the Georgica house in East Hampton. They'd be spending their summers in France.

"My wife would go in the spring and come back in the fall. I'd be there in the summers. I took a five week summer vacation back then."

Though Alger has recently returned to the Hamptons — he has separated from his wife — to this day he has retained an interest in things French. He has daily French lessons at his office at 8:30 in the morning, something he's done every day for twelve years. He is on the Board of the American University in Paris, the American Center in Paris and the French-American Foundation in New York.

Here in the Hamptons, however, he won the Men's B Singles tennis championship at the Maidstone Club in 1979.

Alger has a unique view on America, its economy and where it is headed. Surprisingly, he is very optimistic.

"We are probably more supreme today than any other country ever was," he says. "We lead the world in information technology, pharmaceuticals, biotechnology. The world looks to us. We are the only nation that has successfully dealt with multi-culture.

"I think there is going to be a major revolution in this country, but it is not going to be on the Federal level. The Federal government is becoming increasingly irrelevant. There are a few things they can do, like slow down federal spending and create incentives to invest, but that is not where the problems are. The problems are all on the state and local level. And there are new people coming in with new solutions.

"I believe the entitlement era is now finished. As far as welfare is concerned, medical care, education and housing — all local problems — we are gradually coming around to seeing that responsibility has got to go two ways.

"We need to see that the taxpayers are the clients. Bureaucrats do not want to see this. But there are some young thinkers here in New York, Andrew Cuomo and Andrew Stein come to mind, who I believe will be the leaders of the 21st century.

"I'll give you one example. Education. On an experimental basis in one of the worst districts in Harlem, they give the principal the right to create a curriculum he could sell to the clients — the students. And he got input from the students. A two-way responsibility. The test scores in this district went from rock bottom right up to and past the median.

"I think as people begin to realize how this two-way street works, they will see that our problems are not runaway problems. I think that five years from now in New York City we will see a place that has lower taxes, a rising real estate market, lower crime and better vibrancy in the City. It absolutely can be done."

September 4, 1992

Chapter 23

ALGER HISS

On the last page of his autobiography, *Recollections of a Life*, Alger Hiss describes a chance meeting with an attorney who had employed him when he was just out of law school.

"Years later, after my prison term," he writes, "I ran into John Hall, Esq., at an airport and he greeted me with the kind words, 'Alger, I wish you'd never left us.' I replied, 'Sometimes I wish so myself.' The 'sometimes' of my reply meant that I was satisfied with the bargain I had made with my life. And so I am today."

It has been some life. At the age of 89, with homes in East Hampton and on the East Side of Manhattan, he can look back at a fascinating career filled with accomplishments and catastrophes. He had spent twelve remarkable days in Yalta, in the southern part of the Soviet Union, taking notes for the American delegation, as President Roosevelt, Winston Churchill and Joseph Stalin discussed the future of the world. He had studied law at Harvard as a student of the legendary Felix Frankfurter who later became a member of the Supreme Court. He had been the private secretary to Supreme Court Justice Oliver Wendell Holmes. And in 1945, he was appointed Secretary-General of the first meeting of the United Nations in San Francisco. It was his job to organize this operation for over a thousand delegates, coordinate the agendas, housing and seating, and see to the needs of the translators and members of the press (another thousand people) who needed literature, technical support, guidelines and transportation. He introduced the keynote speaker at the event. He was 41 years old.

And then there were the catastrophes. Accused of being a Russian spy by Whittaker Chambers, he endured sharp attacks before the House

Un-American Activities Committee, led in 1948 by a young Congressman named Richard Nixon. He suffered through two trials, one a hung jury and the other a conviction for "perjury" for denying he had been a spy before a Congressional committee, and then, in the witch hunt atmosphere of the McCarthy era, he served three and a half years in prison.

Finally, there were the vindications. In August of 1992, he received the results of a search made by a Russian general of all the files of the fallen USSR. "Alger Hiss was never a spy for the Soviet Union," this general said, on a videotape played at a press conference at the Algonquin Hotel in New York. "The weight of the burden of this terrible charge can be lifted from his shoulders."

I met Mr. Hiss recently at his East Hampton home. He moves slowly now, but he remains polite and elegant. He was and still is a handsome man. And as he speaks, his eyes twinkle and he smiles a lot. He is thoroughly enjoying himself.

"How did you first come to the Hamptons?" I asked.

"I have always had many friends at *The New Yorker*. One of them was A. J. Liebling who had a summer house here on Springs-Fireplace Road years ago. We'd come out and visit him. I believe the first year was 1960. Then we bought a house on Old Stone Highway in Amagansett and not so long ago we sold that one and bought this house nearer to town."

"What do you like about it out here?"

"Both Isabelle and I are originally from the eastern shore. She is from New Jersey and I'm from Maryland. I'm accustomed to sand, low lying land, estuaries with the sea not too far away. This place beckoned childhood memories. And it is near to New York. I can take the Friday train out and spend the weekend. And every sport is here. I used to play tennis a lot. And my wife and I did a lot of bicycling. This is wonderful land for bicycling, it is so flat. And of course we are a short walk to town."

Hiss spent his childhood in Baltimore, Maryland. But in the summers, he and his brothers would be sent to a farm owned by an aunt and uncle.

"We'd take a big steamer across the Chesapeake to St. Michaels, a town on the Miles River on the eastern shore. The farm was 360 acres and there were cattle and sheep and tomatoes. Canning was big back then and I'd be given 5 cents for every basket of tomatoes I could pick. They'd be taken to a canning factory a few miles away. There was haying in an old haybarn and wheat we'd thresh and stack right after the Fourth of July. Traditionally there would be a hay ride on the night of the Fourth of July for the kids in the community. Also political rallies. This was the time of William Jennings Bryan.

"I remember there was me and my younger brother and two cousins all about the same age. We were the band of four. We'd go swimming in the creek by the front of the house, we'd go boating — aunt and uncle had sailboats with centerboards — and we'd pick corn and peas and lima beans in the garden for dinner and we'd catch soft shelled crabs. On Sundays, we'd all get in this 24 foot motorboat my uncle had — he called it The Yacht — and we'd go off on a picnic. It was a very idyllic life."

Hiss loved to read. When I asked him what he majored in at Johns Hopkins, he said four years of Greek, History, Spanish, French, Political Science and English Literature. Then he went to Harvard Law.

It was here, in the late 1920's, that Hiss was to meet a man who played a great role in his life. He became a student of Professor Felix Frankfurter.

"Felix Frankfurter was far and away the most colorful and controversial member of the (Harvard) faculty," Hiss wrote in *Recollections*. "His innumerable close friendships with leaders all over the country and abroad had already made him a man of national prominence by the time I was his student. He was always conspicuous, despite his small stature...because as he bounced along — short, dynamic, articulate — he was invariably surrounded by a cluster of students."

Years later, Frankfurter would become one of the most respected members of the Supreme Court. But at Harvard, at this time, he held his own court. And he had his favorites. When Hiss graduated from Harvard, he was astonished to get a letter from Supreme Court Justice Oliver Wendell Holmes that, upon the recommendation of Felix Frankfurter, Hiss had been chosen to be Justice Holmes' private secretary for the following year.

Hiss graduated in June of 1929 and went to work for Justice Holmes. Five months later, the stock market crashed. But it did not crash on the young Alger Hiss. He had already been singled out for a remarkable career. And offers from law firms came in from all over. He chose to work in the corporate offices of Choate, Hall and Stewart and shortly after that, the corporate firm of Cotton, Franklin, Wright and Gordon in New York.

But Felix Frankfurter was not through with Alger Hiss just yet. When President Roosevelt invited Frankfurter to Washington, Frankfurter called many of his former students to join in the effort. One of them, again, was Alger Hiss.

"I was just twenty nine. I felt I was just establishing myself as a corporate lawyer when the call came and, oddly, while I was excited about it, so was my law firm. They indicated that after government service they would welcome me back. I went."

Hiss served as an attorney for an agricultural bureau making contracts with American farmers about what crops they should raise. After that, he joined the State Department, where he became an aide to a committee instructed to determine if private enterprise had cheated the government in making military weapons. And it was here that, among the many hangers-on at the hearings, he met a strange young journalist named George Crosley. Crosley was covering the hearings for a paper, and invited him to a cafeteria for lunch on several occasions. He was low on funds. It was the Depression. Hiss lent him money, even gave him an old car after a dealer had offered him only $25 for it as a trade-in. Crosley, it turned out, was a very sick and tormented man who would later accuse Alger Hiss of being a Communist spy. His real name was Whittaker Chambers.

"Crosley used to tell these wonderful stories about all the different kinds of work he did. Once he told me he had labored to place the trolley tracks in the Washington street we were walking along. I knew they had been placed before either of us were born. I decided to carefully end our friendship, which I did."

When World War II broke out, Hiss tried to volunteer, but his superiors in the State Department said he was more valuable in Washington. He stayed.

In the summer of 1944, as the war was winding down and it was apparent there would be an Allied victory, Hiss accepted another assignment. He would be the official secretary at the Dumbarton Oaks conversations in Washington, at which officials from the Soviet Union, Great Britain and the United States would meet to make preliminary plans 'for the establishment of a United Nations.

"The name United Nations came from a joint communique issued by President Roosevelt and Winston Churchill after their meeting in the Atlantic in 1943. There were the Axis forces of Germany, Japan and Italy. And there were the Allied forces. But now so many countries had joined up with the Allies that they became the United Nations. And that's how it began."

The meeting, and Hiss took the official notes, was held in a large estate near Washington. The structure of the future UN was worked out, but several important matters were not agreed upon, for example how the veto would work in the Security Council. It was decided that a further meeting would take place on the Russian peninsula of Yalta later in the year.

"The war was still going on. When we left Washington for Yalta, we were a virtual armada of four-engined transport planes, accompanied by a squadron of fighters. FDR traveled in a plane called the Sacred Cow because it had elevators inside that enabled it to drop down so he could easily get in in his wheelchair. I traveled in a plane carrying much of the delegation from the State Department. It was an overnight flight, because we were going to pass over enemy occupied Greece and we wanted to do that in the dark. We slept in sleeping bags on the floor of the plane. At a refueling stop in Malta we met up with Winston Churchill and the British delegation. I remember Churchill gave FDR a poem. 'From Malta to Yalta we shall not Falta.' And we didn't. We landed at an airfield twenty miles from what had been the Black Sea resort city of Yalta. What a disaster. The Germans had only recently been pushed out. This twenty mile drive went through trees that were blasted, farmhouses burned, great shell holes, detours where the road was out. It took seven hours to get to the old Czarist palace, including one stop for refreshments."

Hiss writes in his *Recollections* book his impressions of the three leaders. Stalin, he recalled, was warm, relaxed, willing to give a little here and a little there. Hiss describes his standing in line with the rest of them to go to the latrine while Roosevelt and Churchill were taken back to their headquarters.

"Stalin was short and stocky," Hiss wrote, "and he usually wore a freshly laundered khaki military tunic with no medals....Churchill, in contrast, was stooped and paunchy in his rumpled garb. Churchill's means of command was his superb eloquence, which could be sharp and wounding as the moment required. Occasionally his eloquence betrayed him, leading him into posturing declamation."

Of Roosevelt, who was to pass away twelve weeks after Yalta, Hiss had this to say:

"Roosevelt had by far the greatest presence. His easy grace and charm were combined with serenity and inner assurance. His posture at the great round table where the participants sat at plenary sessions was one of regal composure. He radiated goodwill, purpose, leadership, and personal magnetism."

It was three years after the war ended when Hiss, still at the State Department, learned there was somebody going around accusing him of being a Russian spy. He went over to the FBI and answered questions, but they did not seem to be satisfactory.

In a series of sensational hearings and trials, the word of Whittaker Chambers prevailed over that of Alger Hiss. Chambers was emotional, crafty, persuasive and desperate. His no-holds-barred accusations of the gentle Alger Hiss were supported by the young congressman from California, Richard Nixon, who saw the trials as a good opportunity to grab national headlines, and by J. Edgar Hoover, head of the FBI. Hiss, back in the 1930's, had on several occasions recommended to his superiors that Hoover resign. Hoover was not one to forget.

Entire careers rode on the need to convict Alger Hiss. And so he was. His State Department career was ruined. He was convicted, disbarred, his first marriage over and he was sentenced to five years in prison. He served it working in the commissary at the Lewisburg Penitentiary.

But for the rest of his life, Alger Hiss never wavered from attempting to get his conviction overturned. Three times his case came before the Supreme Court and three times it was turned down. And so, though he was never legally vindicated, he came to believe that a life well lived amounted to the good fight, regardless of victory.

"I've lived by my principles, and so I have no cause for bitterness or regret," he said.

We are sitting on a sofa in a modest living room of the Hiss house. Some friends come in. I am introduced. They happily embrace this grand old man. They say they are going to take his wife out vegetable shopping. They all leave.

"One of my greatest pleasures today," Hiss says, "is books. My eyesight is too poor for me to read them, however. And so I am read to. I have many readers. I have recently completed the biography of Jean Stafford, who had been the wife of my friend Joe Liebling."

I ask Mr. Hiss what he thinks of the current television era. Literacy is in decline. Everything comes from TV.

"Well, scientists say we have a problem of saving the planet. There are things we have to do in a matter of decades, and this will be hard to do. Bush dragged his feet at Rio. Whether we have a video age or more reliance on traditional methods seems secondary to whether we will have a planet at all."

November 27, 1992

Chapter 24

PAT HYNES

Pat Hynes, a Manhattan attorney who has a vacation home in Southampton, deals in large matters.

"Give me an example of your day," I asked her as we sat down for this interview. "For example, what did you do yesterday?"

"Yesterday? Well, I was representing shareholders who had filed lawsuits against Michael Milken. I was, along with Mel Weiss, one of the lead lawyers. The case is in front of Judge Milton Pollock at the Federal courthouse here in Manhattan and we reached a settlement. The plaintiffs and the Government will be paid $1.3 billion by Mr. Milken and others. That was yesterday."

I wrote this down. "One point three MILLION?" I asked.

"No, billion," she replied.

She's a small woman. A few generations ago, she would have been called the Little Woman. Today she gets called that and she likes it.

"There's an assumption in the courtroom that if it is a woman she won't be that good. I think this is an advantage. By the time they figure that out it is too late."

Pat Hynes loves being in a courtroom and loves the competition. Always has. Seems as if she always will. She's very good at it.

"I learned very early on to think on my feet," she says.

She was born in Flushing and raised in Queens Village, one of three daughters in a blue collar family. Her mother was a housewife. Her father was a quality control expert for manufacturers in Long Island City, Hicksville and elsewhere.

She went to Catholic schools and was the first in her family to go to college. But it was in Catholic school, at The Mary Lewis Academy in Jamaica, that she learned about debating and how exciting it was. She joined the debating team.

"I learned to take a complex situation and simplify it. I learned to take a lot of facts and put them together so that there is a structure that is understandable and convincing."

In her junior year, though her regular grades were good, she spent much of her energy on the debating team. They would go off and debate with other schools. Things like the Farm Subsidy program, pros and cons. She accumulated a whole group of trophies for her efforts, which her family proudly displayed in the china closet in the dining room.

"After my junior year," Pat Hynes said, "I decided it was all too much work. The coach was very demanding and expected you to be very prepared and very good. I considered quitting."

But the coach, Sister Dorothy Mercedes, would not let her. She encouraged Pat, told her she was good at it, that this would be great training for her. And so she continued.

Pat Hynes attended Queens College and then Fordham Law School. This was in the mid-1960's and of 230 students at Fordham law, she recalls, eight were women. She got student loans to pay her way and she also worked two and three jobs. She worked in the cosmetics department at Gertz in Jamaica, she supervised kids for the Board of Education at a playground in Queens and she worked the switchboard nights at the Jewish Center in Rego Park.

"It was a time of great change in the world," she said. "But these changes surely were not yet about women. As it turned out, I broke ground in that department. I made law review, graduated at the top of my class and became the first female law clerk in the Federal Court in Brooklyn. I clerked for Federal Judge Joseph Zavatt in Brooklyn."

She passed the bar. And in 1967 she got a job as an Assistant U.S. Attorney in the U.S. Attorney's office of Bob Morganthau. When she started she was the only woman working there.

I asked Ms. Hynes about these early days of her law practice in the late Sixties. Cities were burning. Students were taking over administration buildings. People were demonstrating against the war in Vietnam.

"I stood to one side of it," she said. "The way the issue got framed, it was such a long way away, why were we involving ourselves? I had serious reservations. But I did not march or anything."

What she did do was work. She figured that as a woman she would have to work harder to prove herself and so she worked long hours.

For the next fourteen years, she was to live in a small apartment on East End Avenue, commute to work, and handle many of the prosecutions for the U.S. Attorney's office. By 1980, she had been promoted to the number three position. She was the Executive Assistant behind U. S. Attorney John Martin. She was getting tremendous experience.

113

Perhaps her most well known case came in an indictment against State Senator Jack Bronston. Bronston was accused of a scheme to defraud a client of his law firm of the opportunity to obtain a lucrative franchise to build New York City bus shelters by promoting the interests of a competitor for which he received $12,500. Bronston hired Louis Nizer. The United States Attorney assigned the prosecution to Pat Hynes. Hynes won and the Senator was sent to jail.

I asked Ms. Hynes to talk more about what it was like at this time when, more likely than not, she was the only woman in the courtroom.

"I'd get a lot of attention. I remember one time I was trying a case for the government involving a mid-air collision. The opposing lawyer said 'I know Ms. Hynes is a very attractive woman...' and the judge, this was Judge Inzer Wyatt, interrupted and said 'I was talking about the attractiveness of her argument.'

"Judge Wyatt, by the way, had a habit of standing up occasionally behind the bench when he found himself getting a bit tired. One day some attorneys came in from the Department of Justice — they were thinking of taking over the case from us — and when I got up to make a presentation the judge stood up. Afterwards, the lawyers asked me if the judges always stand when I go to argue."

In 1982, Pat Hynes was at a judicial conference at the Sagamore Hotel on Lake George. Seating was assigned. At dinner, she found herself sitting next to Mel Weiss. She'd never heard of him.

"But one of my friends had. And as the conversation evolved, it became apparent that the work Weiss did, bringing litigation on behalf of stockholders against corporate enterprises, was very similar to the work I did for the U.S. Attorney's office. 'Pat would be great on these cases,' one of these people said to Weiss. 'This would be a marriage made in heaven.' Frankly, I felt I had proven myself. Nobody could say I could not prevail in a courtroom. Mel Weiss offered me a partnership in his firm."

To go from public service to the private sector meant a considerable increase in income. Pat Hynes decided she was ready to give herself a present. She bought a house in Southampton, in Noyac near the Coast Grille. And she began coming out weekends.

"I love to go to my house in Southampton," she said. "I come out and I read and I relax and I see the trees and smell the fresh air. It is a simple little house. And I love it."

The contrast of the city and the country means a lot to Pat Hynes. During the week she is all business.

"I'm a very high energy person," she said. "I love the challenge. I think I have good judgement on what will make sense to a jury. I'm a good strategist."

"Do you set traps for your opponents?" I asked.

114

"No traps. I just put our case together in a way that is convincing to a judge or a jury. I convince them we are right."

Pat Hynes has become one of the most successful civil trial lawyers in America. Among cases she has won has been one on behalf of the City of San Jose in California. City employees had been making speculative investments with taxpayers' money based on the recommendations of brokers. The brokers made fat commissions, but the City lost over $60 million during the course of a year. The City's accountants, Price-Waterhouse, did not advise the Mayor and City Council of the situation. Pat Hynes spent six months prosecuting Price-Waterhouse and two of the 13 other brokerage firms and she won a jury verdict in excess of $27 million.

Recently, Pat Hynes moved to a Fifth Avenue apartment. At the top of her profession, she has served as a member of Governor Cuomo's Commission on Government Integrity and as Secretary and a member of the Executive Committee of the Association of the Bar of the City of New York. She has taught at Fordham and at Harvard.

She is also active in fundraising for Futures in Education, a non-profit organization which she chairs.

"We raise money to keep the Catholic schools open in Brooklyn and Queens," she said. "They provided me with discipline and a first class education. I want to see that this opportunity continues to be provided to others."

January 8, 1993

* * *

In May 1993, Pat Hynes became a name partner in her firm — Milberg Weiss Bershad Hynes & Lerach. Pat is one of the first women to achieve name recognition at a large national law firm.

In January of 1993, Pat Hynes was married to the well-known trial lawyer Roy L. Reardon of Westhampton Beach and New York City.

Chapter 25

ROGER RESSMEYER

Roger Ressmeyer is one of this nation's most prominent location photographers. He has done the photo covers of three Shirley MacLaine and eighteen Danielle Steel titles. Along with writer Tom Clancy, he recently did a photo essay inside the CIA for *Life* magazine, the first time anyone had been allowed in to extensively photograph Langley headquarters in fourteen years.

He has done assignments in Australia for *National Geographic*, traveling around the globe with 1,500 pounds of photo equipment, and he has done assignments for *Newsweek, Fortune, Rolling Stone, Time,* and a host of others. He has done covers for *People* magazine of Loretta Lynn, Whoopi Goldberg, David Crosby and Huey Lewis. One of his most recent projects is a hard cover book about space exploration, a book photographed all over the world. It is called *Space Places.* The introduction is by astronaut Buzz Aldrin, the second man to walk on the moon. Buzz writes, "Roger has allowed us to experience the human spirit blossoming."

But as I am sitting here talking to him, what I can't help noticing is just how young he is. He's just thirty-eight. He seems to have lived ten lifetimes. And now, for some reason, he has moved to the Hamptons.

"My whole adult life, I lived in San Francisco," he says. "I graduated from college in Connecticut and four weeks after graduation I was on the West Coast. My whole operation has been based there."

"And now you've come to the Hamptons."

"I have moved my entire operation, my photo library, and my studios to Noyac."

"Why Noyac?"

"I used to come to eastern Long Island as a child. I've traveled a lot and the Hamptons are just about the most beautiful place in the world. Furthermore, Noyac is in the hills away from tidal waves and other natural disasters."

This last bit of a comment kind of took me by surprise. But as Ressmeyer began to explain it, it made perfect sense.

"It was October of 1989. Around five o'clock one afternoon, my then girlfriend Jain and I were standing in our living room along with my assistant Dan Walters, giving him directions on how to get home. It was rush hour and he lived in Oakland and we lived in San Francisco in the Marina District, and so we were explaining that he might take a shortcut over the Bay Bridge. Then the room began to shake.

"I shouted, THIS IS IT, THIS IS THE BIG ONE, and I shoved each of them into a door archway while I got into one myself. All Hell broke loose. I like to describe it as being in a Boston Whaler with all your furniture. It lasted fifteen seconds and the earthquake scientists say it measured 7.1 but where we were, on landfill, geologists say the ground motion was the equivalent of a 9.0.

"We had a six room apartment on the second floor of a three story wooden building. Until that moment. My entire life was in that apartment. And it all came down off the walls — pictures, filing cabinets, tables, computers. When the shaking stopped, every room was two or three feet deep in debris. The walls and floors were crooked. And of course all the lights were out.

"The sirens started soon after that. And the fires. Soon the Red Cross set up in the high school down and across the street. There was smoke and chaos everywhere, cars at crazy angles out in the street teetering across huge crevices. The Bay Bridge was down. Dan spent most of the night trying to get home.

"Reaction? I can't exactly tell you I had any intense emotional reaction. Except we were all in the state of shock. The archway just over Jain had separated and looked like one more shake and it would come down. We picked our way out of the building and went across the street. Soon engineers went around putting red, yellow and green stickers on all the buildings. Ours got a yellow sticker which meant get out within a few hours. But I couldn't leave with all my life's work there. So Jain brought an engineer back and talked him into checking more closely and re-stickering it green."

It had only been twenty four hours before that Ressmeyer had shipped out most of the photographs for his *Space Places* book. But there was much more to do. And over the next six months Roger and Jain would camp out in this six room apartment, picking through the wreckage, slowly restoring the filing cabinets and slides. There were two cats and they feared had been buried. But a few hours later, both of them returned.

"One of them had a personality change. He used to be king of the world. Now he needed more attention. He'd seen God."

And so did the Ressmeyers. They thought it through. It was apparent to both of them that with fax machines and telephones and copy machines and Federal Express they could live anywhere. And they had been just about everywhere. They chose Noyac.

* * *

Roger Ressmeyer was born and raised in Malverne, Long Island. His father was a minister. In fact, among his blood relatives there were 20 ministers. At age 8, however, Roger became fascinated with astronomy. In Lutheran High School he built telescopes, and purchased a camera so he could take pictures through his telescope to show in school. Then, he found he could also go out with his camera and take pictures that could appear in the school newspaper.

"I was shooting constantly," he says. "They gave me the keys to the school darkroom." For three years in a row 90% of the photographs in his high school yearbook were Ressmeyer's.

At Yale, however, he studied group dynamics and institutional intervention. This is indeed a mouthful, but then it was the early 1970's and students everywhere were still demanding a say in the curriculum. Roger grew his hair long.

"Those were wild times," he says. "I helped organize a huge protest at Yale in 1975. You may remember it. The Yale administration was trying to kill off the humanistic branch of the school's psychology department. You could get credit through this department for leading protests and studying the process of social change and the administration was trying to stop it. That was the department I was in." Ressmeyer pauses for a moment. "My dad and I weren't really talking at this point."

At Yale, Ressmeyer also had the opportunity to photograph numerous visiting lecturers and performers. He photographed Jane Fonda and Grace Slick.

But as his time at Yale came tumultuously to an end, Ressmeyer began to wonder what he was going to do, degree in hand, after college.

"I came to the conclusion I should leave the New York area," he says. "One of the teachers at Yale had moved to San Francisco and had a short term job I could take as his writing assistant. I took it. I packed my things, spent four weeks with my family in East Northport, and then I was gone."

Shortly after his arrival in the Bay Area, he was introduced to Yippie Jerry Rubin who taught him how not to take no for an answer from the secretaries of powerful people.

On a hunch, he went one day a few weeks later to the headquarters of the band Jefferson Starship, which was an old Victorian mansion on Fulton Street in San Francisco. He had with him some photographs of Paul Kantner and Grace Slick he had taken back east. He wondered if they might hire him to take pictures at one of their concerts.

"Sure, they told me. You have to understand this scene, with all sorts of people hanging around this big mansion. Got a concert coming right up. You be our photographer."

Roger Ressmeyer, at the age of 21, thus got to be the band's official backstage photographer at the big free concert Jefferson Starship gave in Golden Gate Park along with The Grateful Dead. The band's single, *Miracles*, became number one on the charts, and all the magazines wanted his pictures.

"The Jefferson Starship asked me how much do I want? And I said, I dunno, $75 for my time? They said we'll give you $100 plus pay for your film and processing and you have all the rights. I didn't know what rights were. I didn't even know what an invoice was."

What Jefferson Starship did for Ressmeyer, however, was essentially launch his career. They set up a file in the mansion for his pictures, and as they licensed the "use" of them to various magazines, they turned the money over to Ressmeyer and made sure he got a credit. They also invited him to photograph their next concert.

"It was a great time, hanging around with Jefferson Starship," Ressmeyer says. "I traveled with them. I essentially rode with them through their peak. They were just coming into being famous for the second time. And I was the house photographer."

Ressmeyer began to be known as the backstage celebrity photographer and one group told another and told another. It began to be his business. His pictures began to appear in *Time, Newsweek* and *Rolling Stone*.

In the late 1970's, however, the music business began to go downhill. So Ressmeyer branched out. He began doing work for the new science magazines that came into existence at that time. He photographed the first shuttle launch, solar eclipses, scientific breakthroughs, astronauts in training and various Star Wars projects at Los Alamos and Livermore. Three times a year he would come east to visit his family and each time he would bring a new portfolio and visit the Manhattan magazines. He got more assignments from *Time* and *Newsweek*. He got an assignment from *National Geographic*. He photographed the dust jacket of Shirley MacLaine's *Out On A Limb*.

Beginning in 1987 he began shooting heavily for *National Geographic*. It began to take up most of his time.

"My life became sane again," he says. Well, comparatively speaking. He was assigned shoots in Chile, Japan, Germany, Australia, Hawaii and the South Pacific.

Perhaps another reason for his sanity was this woman named Jain. In the late 1980's, he was hired to be the guest managing editor of an annual book publication called "A Day In The Life", this time "A Day In The Life Of California". His job was to oversee 100 photographers going out on 400 assignments throughout the state, all to take place in a 24 hour period.

"Jain was one of my assignment editors," he says. She moved in with him and they were married in the Hamptons on July 28, 1990. She heads up their photo library and agency, Starlight, and handles advance production work on many of his assignments.

After the earthquake, the Ressmeyers then knew, sitting amidst the debris in their San Francisco apartment, that they did not want to live on land fill. But they also knew it would take them as much as six months to put all the pieces of Ressmeyer's career back together again from amidst the chaos. If nothing else, it would take that long just to organize the editing and writing of *Space Places* from little notes and scraps of paper.

They debated moving to bedrock a few blocks south in San Francisco, to Marin County or even Washington D.C. Finally they decided on Southampton. They came out, stayed briefly with friends, rented for a year and then, as the huge Ressmeyer archive was finally fully   assembled, bought their house here and moved in.

Welcome to the Hamptons, Jain and Roger. No big earthquakes here. Yet, anyway.

August 28, 1992

Chapter 26

CARL SPIELVOGEL

Yogi Berra, who achieved fame early in his life as the catcher for the New York Yankees, achieved fame later in life for some of the things he had said earlier on. He said "It Ain't Over till It's Over," and he said "This place has gotten so crowded nobody comes here anymore," but the most popular of the expressions of Yogi Berra, to a young man named Carl Spielvogel, growing up in the Greenpoint section of New York, was when Berra said "you can learn a lot by looking around." Spielvogel took this last phrase, perhaps not so spectacular as the other ones, to heart. And this spring, when he and his wife Barbaralee Diamonstein (the author of eighteen books) bought an oceanfront home in Southampton and moved here from upstate Pound Ridge, he was, by many measures, one of the three or four most successful men in the media business in the nation. His firm, Backer, Spielvogel Bates Worldwide, has offices in 55 countries and has billing of more than $6 billion a year. The Spielvogels are active in numerous public service and charity endeavors in the city and Carl Spielvogel has received many honors from that city, including, last fall, an honor as Man of the Year from the UJA. Among the Honorary Chairmen of the dinner at the Pierre Hotel where this award was conferred last November were Senators Daniel Moynihan, Robert Kerrey, Harris Wofford, David Pryor and Bill Bradley as well as luminaries such as Leonard A. Lauder, Laurence Tisch and Arthur Ochs Sulzberger. A letter from President Clinton was read by his special assistant, Mark Middleton and a pair of President's cuff links was the gift from the White House.

The "look around you" motto has served him well.

A good example of this took place in the late 1950's. At the time, young Carl Spielvogel was 27 years old, and working as a cub reporter at the *New York Times*. His dream, for as long as he could remember, was to be a foreign correspondent for a major American daily. He had started at age 21 at the *Times*, at the very bottom as a copy boy in the City Room and he had worked up through the system, becoming next a news clerk on the Foreign Desk and, finally, a cub reporter. Seven years had gone by.

What he had noticed, looking around that day in 1957, was that the Financial News Editor, Jack Forrest, although scheduled to come in from 11 am until 7 pm, usually showed up for work an hour early, at 10. At the time, Spielvogel was assigned to the Financial News Department and was supposed to work from 11 to 7, too. He began showing up at 10.

"Hey kid," Forrest asked him one morning, "what are you doing? I always see you here an hour early."

"Just getting things started," Spielvogel said.

"I've got a few minutes. Want to have some coffee?"

At this particular time, considerable emphasis was being put on developing a strong financial news section at the *Times*. The editors higher up had become concerned by a strong showing then being made by an upstart competitor — the *Wall Street Journal*. Possibilities were in the air.

"What do you know about the advertising business?" Forrest asked.

"I studied marketing and advertising in college," Spielvogel said.

"We're thinking about starting a six-time a week column about the advertising industry. How'd you like to write it?"

Spielvogel was telling me this story, sitting across from me at a conference table, in his large corner office on the eighth floor of the Chrysler Building. A big smile crossed his face as he remembered this incident, thirty five years before.

"A six day a week column, with my own byline in the New York Times," he said. "I was 27 years old. I thought I'd died and gone to heaven."

Carl Spielvogel was born and raised the son of an Austrian immigrant who owned a fur processing company and died when Carl was 14 years old. Both his parents were strong willed. They instilled in him a very strong work ethic that he would carry with him for the rest of his life. His father, for example, got up to go to work at 4 a.m. every day, then returned home from work at 8 in the evening. Young Carl was taught this was the correct thing to do.

In Boys High School, Carl developed two major interests. Writing and sports. To this day, Carl Spielvogel can sink a two handed set shot from the outside.

"We played most of our basketball games in armories and church gymnasiums," he said. "I was only five foot nine. I didn't get much inside. And so I learned one thing and I learned it real well. From the outside, I could swish a long, low set shot. And I could aim it hard and on a line so it wouldn't arc high and hit the ceiling."

At seventeen, having saved up some money by working in the nearby shipyards, Carl announced that he was going to Cuba for one week.

"Why are you going to Cuba?" his mother asked.

"I want to meet Ernest Hemingway,"

"Who?"

Spielvogel, all by himself, took a train to Miami, stayed in Miami two days, then climbed aboard a B-23 bound for Havana. "On the plane at 9 a.m., they handed me a cup of rum I thought was grapefruit juice, I drank it and it made for a short day." Carl said. From the Havana Airport, laden with books and backpack, he took a bus to the Ambos Mundos Hotel where he had read that Hemingway wrote *Farewell to Arms*. He spent his days at Hemingway's hangout, the Florida Bar. Sure enough, Hemingway stopped in.

"I introduced myself and I told him I was a great admirer of his. He sort of patted me on the head and said that's nice. And that was it. I had met the great man. I could go home."

At the *New York Times*, since nobody had ever written this six times weekly advertising column, there was nobody who could give him advice on what to do.

Spielvogel decided, first of all, that he had better hit the library. He was told on a Wednesday that the column would start the following Monday and that it would run 1,200 words.

"I went to the main branch of the New York Public Library when it opened at 9 a.m. and I stayed there until it closed at 9 p.m. That was on Wednesday. I did the same thing Thursday and Friday and also Saturday and Sunday."

He filed his first column. Soon, he decided, he could have more success with the column if he got on his bicycle. Literally. He went around to the various advertising agencies on Madison Avenue, asking them for information and for news.

"I wore headphones when I was on the phone, because I also had to open 200 letters a day and file 1,000 words."

When he first started at the *Times*, he moved out of his parents' house and took an apartment in Greenwich Village. He enjoyed the excitement of that place, sitting around the White Horse Bar, talking about poetry, hanging out in cafes and jazz clubs. He remembers Gerry Mulligan and David Brubeck and Maynard Ferguson. At the age of 25 he married and had three children, from a previous wife. By the time the offer came around two years later to write the advertising column, his dream of becoming a foreign correspondent had already begun to fade.

123

Just having a bi-lined daily column in the *Times* seemed excitement enough. Until he met a man named Marion Harper, Jr.

"I'd been writing the column for three years. One day I got a call from Marion who was the chief executive of McCann Erickson, one of the world's leading agencies. He asked if I would have lunch with him. We sat in his office for 6 hours. He opened the conversation by saying that as a columnist I was always fighting with him, why not fight FOR him. Six hours later, Marion had fully explained his dream. He envisioned something that was not just an advertising agency, but a marketing and communications conglomerate. He told me that such a company, made up of smaller specialty companies, acquired around the world, could gross more than a billion dollars a year. I had never heard anything like this before and, I was intrigued. One week later, I handed in my resignation to the *New York Times*. I became his assistant and traveled the world."

Those who remember the remarkable and wild ride that Marion Harper took in the early 1960's, with his worldwide firm The Interpublic Group of Companies, Inc. have to marvel at what this young man was able to do and learn. He was 30 years old when he signed on. He and Marion Harper traveled the world selling their concept and purchasing small agencies to make them into subsidiaries of this giant chain. What Harper had noticed, back then, was that public relations and research and marketing and sales promotion were indeed being provided by advertising agencies, but they were being performed for free and in a very non-professional manner. Harper wanted people to pay for these services. And he wanted them done first rate and professionally.

"Marion had converted a former B-26 bomber for business use. It was noisy but it took us where we wanted to go. We went to South America and all over the U.S. Eventually, Interpublic purchased more than forty companies. It ran into financial trouble for a time, but it grew to be a giant. I was with the company for twenty years, and resigned as Vice Chairman."

I asked Mr. Spielvogel for an example of the kind of thinking that could come from an integrated company such as Interpublic.

"Coca Cola is a good example," he said. "We went to Atlanta and we told them they were not in the soda business, they were in the refreshment business. It was a much broader concept. And one step down they were in the trucking business since that was a major item of expense and they were delivering one product. They had, in fact, one of the biggest trucking organizations in the country and they had never thought of it in those terms. The first time Marion told them this, they literally threw us out the door. Today, they are a full line refreshment company, not just soft drinks."

Marion Harper was retired in the mid 1960's when the company ran into financial trouble. In 1979, Spielvogel was Vice Chairman and vying for the top job with Phil Gejer.

"The job went to him," Spielvogel said. "I gave them my resignation. One day there were 6,000 people in 40 countries working for me, the next day it was just my secretary. At the age of fifty, I decided to start my career over again, and took four months to think about it."

One month into his thinking he got a call from Robert Strauss, President Carter's Ambassador for Tariff Negotiations. "I've got Air Force Two," Strauss told him, "and I'm putting together a group to open trade negotiations with China. Would you like to go?" Spielvogel was one of twenty businessmen who went.

While he was away, he received a phone call from Bill Backer.

"I'd known Bill Backer for many years," Spielvogel told me. "We were perfect opposites. I was from Greenpoint, a liberal Democrat, and interested in tennis. He was from Charleston, South Carolina, a right-wing Republican and interested in horses." They talked. Bill had left McCann-Erickson as an award winning creative director, one of the subsidiaries of Interpublic, and they decided that maybe what this country needed was a new type of advertising agency.

Backer and Spielvogel opened its doors in June of 1979, with a great party at its first offices, which were a suite at the Gotham (now Peninsula) Hotel at 55th Street and Fifth Avenue.

"We had lots of champagne and lots of pretzels and plenty of people came," he said. "But we had no clients. June turned into July and July into August. And then, on August 15, I was celebrating the fiftieth birthday of a friend, at lunch at the '21 Club' when a message came that I was wanted on the telephone."

The call was from the Miller Brewing Company. And it was to stun the ad agency business. Miller was taking its entire $85 million account and it was giving it to this tiny new ad agency. No major American corporation had ever expressed its confidence in a brand new ad agency on this level before.

"Within three months we had hired 96 people. We owed the bank $9 million before we received our first revenue. But here we are."

Backer and Spielvogel grew dramatically after that, merged with Ted Bates, Inc. and as I mentioned at the start of this article, it is billing more than $6 billion today, just fourteen years later. I asked Mr. Spielvogel to what he attributed this success.

"Well, I think I understand something many have forgotten. Nothing happens unless it happens at retail. It is nice to win creative awards and rave reviews. But our rewards come when we see our clients' sales and profits grow."

Today, the Spielvogels live on Park Avenue not far from the Metropolitan Museum of Art, where he serves as trustee. He is also a member of the Executive Committee and he is Chairman of the

125

Business Committee of that institution. He is a member of the Board of Trustees and the Executive Committee of both the Asia Society and the Lincoln Center for the Performing Arts, a member of the Executve Committee of Mt. Sinai Hospital, as well as on its Board of Trustees, and he is a member of the Board of the New York Philharmonic. He is also a member of the International Advisory Board of the Business Council for the United Nations and a member of the Council on Foreign Relations. In April 1990 he was appointed Chairman of the Mayor's Committee for Public/Private Partnership and was formerly Chairman of the Mayor's Committee in The Public Interest.

Mr. Spielvogel is a past President of the Board of Trustees College Fund of his alma mater, Baruch College, and was the recipient in 1990 of an Honorary Degree for outstanding career accomplishment. In 1992, Baruch College inaugurated a semi-annual lecture series in Mr. Spielvogel's honor titled "The Carl Spielvogel Lecture Series on Global Marketing Communications." The most recent lecture was given by William Donaldson, President of The New York Stock Exchange on the subject of the "Emerging Global Stock Market." The first lecture was delivered by Ted Turner, the founder of CNN and Turner Broadcasting.

Here in Southampton, the Spielvogel's concluded a three year search by buying a 100 year old Stamford White house previously owned by the Havenmeyers and the Sabatines. They have hired the architect's great grandson, Sam White to help with the renovations.

July, 1994 (Scheduled)

126

Chapter 27

MARTHA STEWART

The thing you first notice about Martha Stewart is just how incredibly beautiful she is. She is not twenty years old anymore, but there is something about the way she carries herself and the way she moves, her wonderful face and smile that can bring conversation to a halt when she comes into a room.

People this handsome — men or women — can be intimidating to those around them, but Martha Stewart will have none of it. She gets right to the point. She is quick and fast and whatever feelings you might have about her remarkable appearance are swept away in unending waves of ideas, jokes, actions, activity and that most wonderful smile. She is nonstop. A mover. And she is having a great time with it although lately it is getting a little out of hand.

"It's the technology," she says. "Ten years ago I had one telephone. Now I have 24 lines, I have cellular phones, I have personally got five computers. The more technology, it seems, the more there is to do."

I am visiting with Martha Stewart in the home she bought last year on Lily Pond Lane in East Hampton. It is, she says, the first summer house ever built on the lane, constructed in 1873 by a Talmadge for an Eldridge — who was a Brooklyn minister. In any case, she has restored it and she has built around this wonderful early Victorian house some of the most beautiful gardens you can imagine. During our interview, someone brought in a vase full of roses from these gardens. The flowers were the size of grapefruits. It was quite amazing.

Martha Stewart is today one of America's taste makers. She has her own magazine, *Martha Stewart Living*, published by Time-Warner, she has a segment on the *Today* show and over the last ten years she has published ten beautiful hard cover books. Her *Martha Stewart Weddings* book is the bible for all wedding planning and has sold close to a million. Her first book, *Entertaining*, shares the same reputation. And so does her book on gardening. Martha Stewart is one of a kind.

I really wanted to know, on first meeting Martha Stewart, where her remarkable taste — which has struck such a chord — has come from. But first, I asked her to define it.

"My books are written for everybody," she said. "Rich or poor, there is something for every lifestyle. And this carries over to everything that I do. For example, on a recent *Today* segment, we went to the studio of Mr. Clatt, who has done tin roofs for me. I was curious what he did when it rained. He said he makes hoods for ovens and so forth. I asked him to make me a desktop out of tin and he did so and it is beautiful. In this segment we showed how he does his soldering, forms edges and so forth. These are ideas for anybody. People like them."

"How would you define good home entertaining?" I asked.

"It is one friend treating friends, it is beauty, caring, simplicity, fun, abundance, good things."

I wrote these things down as notes as she said them and I was startled at how concise each category was. She had just rattled them off.

But where had her interest in taste come from?

Martha Stewart was born and raised in New Jersey, a kid in the suburbs, from a large family with not much money and, as she began to spell it out, with extraordinary parents, particularly her father.

"We lived, from the time I was born until I graduated high school, in a three bedroom house in Nutley, New Jersey," she said. "I was the second oldest of six children. And both my parents were teachers. Well, teachers didn't make much money in those days and so when so many kids came along my father quit teaching and became a pharmaceutical salesman for Pfizer. Somehow, we got by. Everybody had chores to do. Lights were out at nine thirty. Home was run like a drill team with so many kids."

Both parents were European in their mannerisms. Her mother, who Martha describes as a great beauty, was the daughter of Polish immigrants. Her father — and she showed me pictures of him as a young man and he is so stunning with such piercing eyes it is hard to look at him — her father was the son of a Prussian cavalryman in the service of Prince Franz-Josef.

"You'll find this hard to believe," Martha told me, "but when we moved to Nutley, my father joined a European Cavalry Unit in Montclair. They still had cavalry then. (This was in the 1940's.) Father was also a horseback rider, a gymnast, and an expert with Indian clubs. He stayed in perfect physical condition until the day he died."

All the kids had chores. They did laundry. They set the table.

One of Martha's chores was to polish her father's high boots.

Father dressed faultlessly. He wore Harris Tweed. He had herringbone ties and leather shoes. They all had leather shoes. And father dressed his wife beautifully. When Martha was ten she played in her mother's dresses. At ten she was learning about *peau de soie* and *shantung* (Chinese silks). What other ten year old in New Jersey knew about these things?

The two ideas that dominated this household, and it was run in a very demanding fashion, were style and learning. There were, for example, always fresh vegetables in a silver bowl on the dining room table.

"Many of my brothers and sisters, particularly Laura and George, found being raised in such a demanding household very difficult. But I loved it. My father was a perfectionist. I was a perfectionist."

If there were schedules to be kept and chores to be done, then there was one thing you could do that could exempt you from them. You could read. If lights out was at nine p.m. and you wanted to read until midnight, so be it. You were learning. Martha and all her brothers and sisters took weekly trips to the local library. Martha would read five to ten books a week.

Two stories that Martha told me seem further to explain her ultimate fascination with style. One involved her father, who was also the scoutmaster for the Nutley troop.

"He did this every year, on Moving Up Day, the day the Cub Scouts became Boy Scouts. He would strip naked and dress himself in a blanket and headdress. He would paint his face with iridescent paint. And then, at the ceremony, the lights would dim, the curtains would open and there would be father, Big Indian, sitting on the school stage, a somber expression on his face and his iridescent body paint glowing in a blue light, and he would read poetry."

The second story involves Martha's work as chairperson of the Prom Club in her senior year at Nutley High School. She was a mover and a shaker even then and she was editor of the school magazine the *Gauntlet*, she was on Student Council, she was in the Latin Club and for the prom, well, here is what she did.

"I called it Stairway to the Stars," she said. "The gym had a high ceiling so I had netting put up under it, then I had blue angel hair put over that. I hung from it clear plastic stars. I also had a grand flight of stairs constructed. Couples could climb the stairs, they went up toward the ceiling, and then at the top step there was a landing where you could have your picture taken. Stairway to the Stars."

It seemed to Martha that among all the children she was the most curious about everything. Her father seemed to think so. He took her to New York City to museums, to Chinatown. They would wander around Chinatown. At twelve, a schoolmate of hers across the street started to do modeling in Manhattan. Martha wanted to do it too and so her parents took her in to the agency in the City and they took her on. For the next fifteen years, until the birth of her daughter Alexis, she modeled professionally around the city, at first going in with her parents or a chaperone and later, as a high school student, going into the city by herself.

"I became a fashion model," she said. "On weekends, anyway. They paid me $25 an hour which was a fortune back then, certainly more than the 50 cents an hour I made baby sitting."

"How did you get into the city by yourself?" I asked.

"Easy. There was a bus stop right on the corner of our block. It was the number 13 bus and it took me from Kingsland Road through the Lincoln Tunnel to the Port Authority in less than thirty minutes. From there, I could go anywhere."

She never was a front cover model, but she was often a back cover model, for Clairol and other clients. She did a lot of editorial model work for *Glamour* magazine and *Mademoiselle*. They took her on the weekends to Florida and to Canada and, once, to Paris, for the debut of the collections.

"Once the shoot was on Shelter Island, at the house of Perry Como, I think."

Martha Kostyra, her maiden name, went off to Barnard to be a chemist. She wasn't good at it however. And so she changed her major to art history and English. She did her thesis — they had thesis for bachelor's degrees at Barnard then — on Finance Minister Colbert's design for the roof of the Louvre constructed during the reign of Louis XIV.

At age 19, while still at Barnard, she married a Yale law student, Andrew Stewart. Her marriage to him lasted 27 years. She and Andrew were divorced in 1990.

"I moved to New Haven," she said. "I finished up my last year at Barnard while living there. It was an amazing and horrible commute. In retrospect I do not know how I did it. My husband said we should live in Guilford, on a farm 20 minutes from New Haven. What did I know? I was 19. He'd get up at four a.m., drive me to the train station, I'd travel two hours on these horrible wicker seats they had then, you couldn't even sleep on them, get off at 125th Street, then take the subway to Barnard. It was a four hour commute all together. My husband would pick me up at ten p.m." She pauses. "We should have lived in Greenwich."

After college, Andrew Stewart joined a Wall Street law firm and he too commuted. Martha took a job at Pearlberg-Monness, a go-go Wall Street research firm. They had charts on the wall measuring everybody's performance every day. She loved it. But she also found out something fundamental about herself.

"I found out I really liked substance, things. I was successful at

Pearlberg-Monness, we were all successful, but try as I might I could not make substance out of securities. I began to think what else I could do."

She decided upon catering. In 1972, when Alexis was six years old, she opened The UnCatered Affair, out of her home in Westport. She would cater weddings and receptions and bar mitzvahs. And she would do it, by and large, with things that she had produced in her garden. Her home — Andrew Stewart was already quite successful — had six acres of grounds. She grew flowers and vegetables and plants. There were even chickens. She loved being in her garden.

"My idea for the catering firm was that it would cater as if you had done it yourself — the uncatered affair. It quickly became very successful. I did parties at the Met, at the Cooper, I did practically all the previews at Sotheby's. I kept this firm going until 1986 by which time I was doing parties for as many as 2000 with a staff of 200. It was a million dollar business."

Martha probably would have continued with her catering business if it had not been for one thing — her successes — particularly the successes with the magnificent coffee table books that she wrote that Clarkson N. Potter Publishing published — had come to the attention of a large department store chain.

"My husband had gone into the publishing business — first as publisher of Abrams Art Books and then with his own firm Stewart-Tabori and Chang — and though he did not publish my work there is no doubt I learned much about publishing from him. So my first book, *Entertaining*, came out in 1982 and was a smash hit and then I did one a year, *Quick Cook, Pies And Tarts, Hors D'oeuvres*, and in 1986 along came K-Mart."

K-Mart wanted nothing less than to mass produce merchandise picked out by Martha under the Martha Stewart name. Martha saw this as an extraordinary opportunity to have her ideas become known to the mass culture.

"This company talked about billions," she said. "Billions and hundreds of millions as in a hundred million shoppers through their doors every year. I signed on with them. And I designed for them flatware and bedroom and bathroom things and sheets and ensembles and I am still doing this today. Just to give you an idea, when I designed lace for the first sheets I did, K-Mart calculated they would need an amount of lace for the trim that, if you extended it from end to end, would go from New York to Chicago. This blew me away."

K-Mart asked her to close her catering business to devote full time to her books and designing. She did. Her one-a-year books continued and then, in 1989, she thought it would be a good idea to publish a magazine as well.

"I approached Conde Nast that year," she said. "People thought

I was crazy to start a magazine in a bad economic time. But I was convinced that my magazine would fill a need. There was simply no up-to-date how-to magazine on style and elegance in America. Time Warner picked up on the idea. Our first issue we printed a quarter of a million. Now, three years later, it continues bi-monthly and we have just raised our advertising base to three quarters of a million."

It occurred to me to ask if Martha Stewart works in an office.

"I work in my garden," she says. "I have an office, but I don't like spending time in it. I do my best work in the garden. I live in my car. I'm in touch on a portable phone."

Originally, Martha's husband helped her with her garden in Westport. But the time involved soon forced him to tell her he could no longer continue. Martha employs Renato and Rinaldo, two Brazilians who have been with her many years. They live in her barn in Westport.

"Gardens are exactly the opposite of me," she said. "They take time. You have to be very patient in a garden and you can't rush it. I experiment, I try things. This garden here in East Hampton I like a lot because it is only one acre and we can keep it up in just one day a week."

"How about your Westport garden?" I asked.

"It is an out of control garden. Chickens, fruit, berries, vegetables, a great variety in extreme numbers. I love it. And now I have my eyes on a 35 acre piece of land in Fairfield. It is perfect for my next garden. It has a stream, a pond, views, huge trees, everything my Connecticut garden does not have."

How Martha Stewart, your basic Westport resident — four of her six brothers and sisters live in Connecticut — came to East Hampton is another story.

"I was going through a divorce. My daughter Alexis, who had gone to Barnard and had been coming out here summers with her friends said mom, take a place in the Hamptons. When you get a divorce it is a very good place to be. So she rented a house for me on Mill Hill Lane two years ago and I came out and rode my bike around town and thought it was charming and I socialized and I liked it. And so Alexis persuaded me to buy a house."

Alexis, it turns out, is as much a perfectionist as her mother. She is 28 now and has opened a "Fifties" motel in Bridgehampton and will soon open a "Fifties" diner in Bridgehampton but three years ago she told her mother that she, Alexis, could allocate exactly one day to finding a house with her mother.

"I called Frank Neubold, the realtor, and I told him that. I told him, line up ten houses and I'll come out and we'll see them one after another and so that is what he did. The first nine houses were all wrong, for the eighth and ninth we didn't even get out of the car, and then he said he hesitated to show us the tenth because it's for sale but then it is not for sale and it is on again off again and I said let's see it and it was love at first sight."

Martha Stewart opened her Lily Pond Lane house for a fundraiser for the first time last month, a fundraiser for the East Hampton Historical Society, and it was a smash hit. There will be more.

"I like this house because it is spare and uncluttered and light. It really is very beautiful. A beautiful rose covered cottage."

Martha talked proudly for a while about her remarkable daughter Alexis. Alexis, she said, has an extraordinary entrepreneurial spirit. And she is learning a great deal about personal relationships, having to steer her restaurant project past the scrutiny of the Southampton Town Board.

"She has indeed thrust herself into extremely difficult positions. But that is Alexis. You know, I do pre-Martha which is Victorian. Alexis does pre-Alexis, which is Fifties. Same idea."

Our interview was coming to an end. A film crew was arriving to photograph her roses which were now in such full bloom. She'd had messages that Alexis had called several times, wanting to talk to her mother. Otherwise, Martha's staff (based in Westport) had done a pretty good job screening all calls for the two hours Martha and I had spent together.

And so you think that is all about this amazing woman, Martha Stewart? Think again. Her next project is a half hour television show which she is doing for syndication. It's been sold in 80% of the country including Chicago and Los Angeles and here in New York on Channel 2.

If the past is any indication of the future, the *Martha Stewart Living* show should be on the air perhaps the day after tomorrow.

July 2, 1993

* * *

Alexis Stewart's Bridgehampton Motel, done in high "fifties" style, opened in the late spring of 1993. Her planned 50's-style diner at the west end of Bridgehampton was approved by the Town but remains on hold, tied up in bureaucratic red tape in the Suffolk County Health Department.

Chapter 28

ILANA VERED

You may be hearing a great deal about Ilana Vered here in the Hamptons in the years to come. She was here last summer, professionally, for the first time, and she produced a series of classical music concerts at East Hampton's Jewish Center of the Hamptons featuring herself as a solo pianist, and the Tokyo String Quartet.

To many people, the concerts at the Jewish Center (and other locales), called SUMMERFEST, were just that, a series of concerts. To Ilana Vered, however, they were a prelude to the possible conversion of the Hamptons to a major month-long cultural festival that could, sometime in the future, include drama, opera, modern dance and classes. And if you think this is a dream, think again. What Ilana starts, Ilana finishes.

I am sitting with Ilana Vered on a sofa in the second floor living room of the Manhattan townhouse she shares with her husband, neurologist Peter Herman, and I am being served coffee by a maid. A small dog yapped at my heels when I came in and is now, having had me scratch him behind the ears, sniffing my hand and wagging his tail. One is aware, immediately upon entering this 79th street building, that there is an automatic chair that goes up and down along the stairway to the second floor and it makes you wonder about it. It is not for Ilana, a beautiful woman nearing fifty sitting across from me.

"The automatic chair is for this dog's mother. She is quite elderly and can't get up and down. And she's had a serious illness, but we won't give up on her. We give her an injection three times a day."

If you go into another room adjacent to this living room, you will find yourself in a small office with ringing phones and a secretary, handling some of the affairs of Ilana Vered. On the wall are over a dozen major record albums by Ilana, all classical music, some solo, some with The London Royal Philharmonic Orchestra. THE ISRAELI PIANO PRODIGY ILANA VERED reads the text on one.

I mentioned that Ilana Vered finishes what she starts. Some years ago, teaching at Rutgers University, she asked the administration if she could have a hall for a classical concert to raise money for a hunger project. She named it ARTISTS TO END HUNGER. You may have heard of it. The organization, now with offices worldwide, has raised over a million dollars for the world's hungry. As for the single concert at Rutgers, it is now a series of about one hundred concerts, films, dance performances, plays and other cultural events taking up forty five days in June and July every year at what is called by Rutgers their annual RUTGERS SUMMERFEST.

"Why the Hamptons?" I asked her.

The question was answered, not by Ilana, but by Robert Kapilow, who is the associate director of Summerfest and who had wandered in from the office.

"Ilana has a house out there. We just wanted to do something. Eventually we think it could be a performance institute. Like Tanglewood, or Aspen."

Ilana was born in the small town of Natania halfway between Tel Aviv and Haifa. Her mother was a piano teacher and her father was a music teacher and, apparently, as a small child she began to play piano all by herself to get their attention. She was two and a half, an only child.

"Come to think of it, I still play to get their attention," Ilana said. "Maybe that's why I have been playing piano all these years." She laughs. "I think this is a psychological problem that bears looking into."

Playing piano at two and a half is an astonishing thing. It soon became apparent that little Ilana Vered was a prodigy, someone who would make a major mark in the world of music.

"When I was five years old, my parents changed their whole lives for me. I would be the career in the family."

Ilana played recitals and concerts in the new state of Israel. She played with major orchestras. She began to make appearances in the capitals of Europe. When she was twelve years old, her parents moved with her to Paris where she continued her studies at the National Conservatoire. She also continued playing concerts around Europe. And she also played, as a featured guest, in the salons of the wealthy along the Champs Elysee.

Keep in mind that this was post-war Europe and that much of the Continent had been reduced to rubble in battles and bombings. In Paris, however, life went on as before as far as the wealthy were concerned, and part of that life included dinner parties given by private wealthy individuals at which famous entertainers performed.

"I was maybe thirteen or fourteen. I played at the Rothschild's, at the Celetski's. Artur Rubinstein had the apartment next door to Edward Rothschild, who was my benefactor. The dinners? I remember a servant behind every chair. I remember a single egg served floating in a clear gel. I remember the after dinner drinks and then my turn, playing for an hour or two to the polite applause."

When she was seventeen, an impresario took Ilana and her parents on an extended tour of the concert houses of Brazil. She was on Brazilian television. At eighteen, back in Paris, she met a young Israeli medical student named Peter Herman who told her he was in love with her and would marry her. Instead, Ilana married an American violinist. But it was a disaster, and she divorced him and married Peter. They settled in New York City where Dr. Herman took up duties at Mount Sinai Hospital, where he is today.

Still a young Israeli sensation but now in America, Ilana had her debut at Carnegie Hall in 1962 to rave reviews and has been back for concerts there half a dozen times. She performed at Alice Tully Hall. She practiced every day. And her whole life was focused on her career. Until the children.

"I just said one day to Peter I am going to give up the piano. He said do what you want to do. I thought: I have never had a normal life. I never had childhood friends. I never went to public schools. All I knew were tutors. I want this."

This was in 1970 and Ilana, then twenty nine years old, just walked away from the piano to never touch it again. She potted plants. She cooked. She went shopping. She doted on her two children, who at that time were in their early teens. And it was not what she wanted.

"I saw psychologists. I withdrew. I hardly talked unless spoken to. Depressed is a good word. Peter said I seemed to be just half a person. I pressed on."

It took several years. And then, just as suddenly as she had given up the piano, she returned to it. It was the other half of her person. It just had to be there.

"Picking up a career after being out of it for several years is not as easy as you might think," she said. "Especially in America. Especially as a woman."

But come back she did. She returned to Carnegie Hall, she was on the *Today* show, she was on *Donohue*, on Merv Griffin. And her big break came, interestingly enough, in London where, giving a concert, she was contacted by the legendary Leopold Stokowksi.

"It was like a dream," she said, smiling as she remembered it. "He loved my work and I became a soloist for him. I played before Prince Charles at Albert Hall. I went on a world tour. And we made albums."

Many of the albums in the office space indicated Leopold Stokowski conducting the orchestra in the background.

Which brings us to today. She is still playing concerts and making albums, and she is still touring and to be honest with you it seems she loves every minute of it.

"I did have some amazing times," she says, looking off into the middle distance.

One thing that Ilana recalls is the half dozen wars that the Israelis fought against the Arabs since 1948. She is still an Israeli citizen, and like all Israeli citizens, she went into the Army when she was eighteen. And she and Peter have left wherever they are, whatever they are doing, to return to Israel to join in the defense each time war breaks out. After the Yom Kippur War they stayed two years.

"When I was nineteen, I still lived in Paris but I'd fly to Israel for my basic Army training. As an Israeli citizen and as an adult, each time you leave Israel you have to get permission from the Israeli Army that you are not needed at that particular time. I'd have to wait on a bench in a waiting room at the airport while my papers were being reviewed and signed each time. Once I found myself sitting next to Pincus Zuckerman, the violinist. He was there getting his papers signed, too."

Ilana's daughter Ophira, now 25, is an active feminist, on the board of NOW, and attending law school. Ilana's son Marc, age 27, works in Philadelphia as a chef.

Ms. Vered and Dr. Herman have been coming out to the east end of Long Island in the summertime for eleven years. Their first introduction to it was as the guests of Robert and Elizabeth Holtzman (she is active in New York politics), at their summer home in Orient. Since then they have lived on Fire Island, in Southampton and in East Hampton and they have finally settled in a small house in Sag Harbor, which they love.

The future? Well, when you love what you are doing, there is no need to change it, is there? There will be more concerts, more world travel, more benefits and, who knows? Perhaps a performance center here on the eastern end of Long Island.

I left the townhouse filled with a vitality and energy that I felt had been transmitted to me by Ilana Vered. Ms. Vered is charming, full of ideas and seemingly amazed at all the good things that have come her way. She is a rare individual indeed.

August 14, 1992

Chapter 29

DONALD ZUCKER

"Every one of these buildings has a story," Donald Zucker says. "Every one."

We are sitting in Mr. Zucker's office in Manhattan leafing through a prospectus for THE DONALD ZUCKER COMPANY and, on every page there is a different residential apartment building, some twenty stories high, some thirty even thirty five stories high, all built in Manhattan. All together there are about a 18 such buildings, all built or renovated by Mr. Zucker and every one of them has a story to it. Even the one we are in, which houses his headquarters on 55th Street and 6th Avenue.

"Tell me the best story about any one of these buildings," I say.

Don Zucker, the real estate developer, is a stunningly handsome man with an athletic build and a full head of white hair. He moves quickly and animatedly. I would guess his age at about 50. He is 62.

"The best? Let me tell you about a church on West End Avenue."

At the other end of his private office, his wife Barbara says, "Oh I love that story." And in the office in the other direction, Bob Esnard, a former Deputy Mayor, concurs. This is a very big and very unusual office. Bigger than a living room.

"It was called the All Angels Church," Mr. Zucker says. "The membership was declining, they only had thirty or forty members by the time I made contact with them, and they were interested in having me take a 99 year lease on the property. This was at West End Avenue and 81st Street.

"I intended to demolish the church and build a big apartment house. They had no problem with this. What they wanted was for me to build a small one story chapel next to their Parrish House right around the corner. This I agreed to do.

"Putting together a 99 year lease is a very complicated proposition. After five months, we finally had it all together, and we met in the Parrish House, me and the minister and each of our lawyers, and we started to go over the lease, which was as thick as a telephone book. I can tell you the legal fees alone are enormous when you do this kind of thing.

"As we are getting started, the minister says 'I met with the church council last night and we have changed our minds. We have decided not to lease. We want to sell. We have a buyer.'

"The minister's lawyer became very angry. 'You can't do this,' he said. 'We have negotiated with these people in good faith for almost half of a year.' 'Well, we have decided,' the minister said. 'Then you can get another attorney,' the lawyer said. 'I won't be a party to this.' And the minister's lawyer got up and walked out.

"I walked out too, of course, and I caught up with him in the front lobby going out the door. 'Isn't it true,' I said, 'that in order for a church to sell property in New York it has to be approved by a Supreme Court judge?' I asked. 'Yes,' he replied.

"I told my lawyer, 'please watch the records. When the matter comes up, call me.'

"Several months later, the matter came up before Judge Bentley Casell in a courthouse there on the Upper West Side. I went with my lawyer, his name was George Ross, and we sat in the back. In the front, before Judge Casall, there were just three people from the church. This was going to be a very simple matter. But what were these two people doing in the back? They kept turning and looking at us.

"The attorneys from the church presented an appraisal for $1.1 million and then they presented a signed contract for $1.1 million. I raised my hand.

"'Do you want something there in the back?' the judge asked.

"'I am Donald Zucker,' I said, 'and I am prepared to pay $1.2 million for this property.'

"'This is not an auction, sir,' the judge said.

"'I have a certified check to that amount,' I said. And I took it out and waved it and brought it up to the bench. The judge looked at it. 'How can you people have an appraisal for $1.1 million when I've got here a certified check for $1.2 million?' he asked. 'I want you to come back next week. Case adjourned.'

"'The following week we had a repeat performance. The appraisal and contract were for $1.2 million. I came forward with a certified check for $1.3 million. The judge went nuts.

"'Don't you ever come back to this courtroom again with a situation like this,' he said to the church lawyers. 'Either straighten it out or you will never sell this property.'

"Two days later, I got a call from the other buyer. It was Henry Mandell, whose family had built London Terrace apartments back in the 1930's. He invited me to meet him in his lawyer's office.

"'What shall we do?' he asked.

"'Tell you what,' I said. 'We both know the property is worth $1.1 million. Why should the church get an extra $200,000? Either I'll give you $200,000 and you let me buy the property, or you give me $200,000 and I'll let you buy the property. You decide.'

"He took the $200,000 and I subsequently built a 231 apartment building called West River House and did very well thank you. Never regretted it for a minute."

Donald Zucker's office, which I have already said is quite big, is filled with oddities and sculptures and paintings from all over the world. The coffee table is a huge antique bellows, maybe six feet across, with legs under it. There are couches and seating areas. On the top of his desk is a wooden Scale of Justice, except that on the scale on one side are several toy bulldozers and on the other side are little toy bank buildings. Today it seems to be exactly in balance.

Zucker has succeeded as a major Manhattan developer for over thirty years. He has done it with charm and grace, with good business acumen and a firm rule to always build apartment houses from "the inside out." People's homes, he knows, are supposed to be comfortable. They often feature high ceilings, spacious closets, woodburning fireplaces, atriums and skylights.

He is known as well for the magnificence of the lobbies of these projects — the one here on 6th Avenue I came through is all marble and mirrors — woodburning fireplaces and, in the case of the 700 unit Riverside complex, a four level waterfall and palm trees in the lobby.

I ask him what he has underway right now.

"As a matter of fact," he says, "this is the first time in twenty years I have not had one single thing under construction on the island of Manhattan. The times are just not right. They will be again soon. But not right now."

Donald Zucker grew up in Manhattan Beach, Brooklyn, the son of a man in the clothing manufacturing business. He was the photography editor of his high school newspaper. Then he read a book about Bernard Baruch. Baruch was an incredibly successful Wall Street investor, even through the Depression, and he became an advisor to Presidents, beginning with Herbert Hoover. Zucker decided he would go to Wall Street. He would be another Bernard Baruch.

After a degree in business administration at NYU, Zucker actually took a position — as a clerk — at the Wall Street Firm of Hentz and Company, where Baruch had made his mark thirty years earlier.

"There was still a Mr. Baruch there, though he was just a nephew," Mr. Zucker said. "I clerked in the big trading room at this company. I stood in the back and went out to buy the lunches or supplies. One of my jobs was to see that the ink wells where the stock exchange tape came through the machines were always filled. Another job I had was to change the number inserts on the big board at the end of the room if a company had achieved a new high or low at the end of that day. There was no training program then. I remember they'd celebrate when the market had a one million share day."

At this time, in the early 1950's, Zucker still lived at home with his parents in Manhattan Beach. He commuted every day. Then he did a two year stint in the army. At Fort Dix and Fort Jay and Fort Totten he gave lectures about Wall Street and business management from the experience he had already accumulated. He taught high school equivalency to combat officers. He was honorably discharged.

In 1953 he got married. His marriage lasted until 1980 and resulted in three children, all now in their thirties. Since that time he has married his present wife Barbara. They have a five year old and they live on the Upper East Side. They are also about to break ground on an oceanfront home in Sagaponack.

But in 1954 with a new marriage and a first baby on the way, Zucker and his wife rented a tiny apartment. Soon they moved to a two bedroom apartment in Manhattan Beach near their parents. And for the next twenty five years, the Zuckers lived in homes in Woodmere and Lawrence, commuting to Manhattan.

Zucker went to CCNY on the GI Bill for a while and he studied construction, estimating and appraising. Then he worked in a real estate brokerage firm. In 1961, after a stretch working for J. H. Halpern in arranging government guaranteed mortgages, Zucker knew what he wanted to do. He wanted to develop and build in Manhattan. He would arrange financing, hire architects and builders, put up apartment houses and rent them out. He opened an office at 516 Fifth Avenue. It was called the Donald Zucker Company in 1961. It is the Donald Zucker Company today.

Along the way, Zucker has modified his business to change with the times. "If you don't, you don't stay in business," he said. He has branched out into every phase of real estate, including management and brokering. He has bought and developed commercial properties, shopping centers other retail stores, in New Jersey, Long Island and Pennsylvania.

In 1986, Mayor Ed Koch appointed Zucker as his special advisor on construction throughout the City of New York. Zucker worked for the City for three years.

"Without pay," he says. "Not even a dollar."

"If they paid you a dollar it would have been a big bureaucratic mess," said former Deputy Mayor Esnard.

"How much time did you work for the City and how much time did you work for your company?" I asked.

"Full time, both places." He gestured around his big office. "I virtually live here," he says.

Donald Zucker has been coming out to the Hamptons since the 1970's. He used to have a house on Wainscott-Stone Road. He was married in a house on Beach Lane in Wainscott in 1985.

Recently he bought 16 1/2 acres on Millstone Road and another lot on Butter Lane in Bridgehampton. He hired a full time builder. He expects shortly to put up some houses on speculation.

"I think prices in the Hamptons are very good now," he says. "I know it will all come around soon."

He loves to sail and he keeps a 47' sloop in Sag Harbor. He plays golf at a club in Noyac and likes bike riding, photography (still) and jogging. He has always been an athlete. In 1978 he ran in and completed the New York Marathon.

"Where are you living while you are building your house in Sagaponack?" I ask.

"We borrow houses," he says. "In October we borrowed Barbara Slifka's house in Bridgehampton. We come out year-round. We have lots of friends. Dan Brodsky, Sheldon Solow. My wife Barbara has known Pat Wilson since she was three years old living back in Cambria Heights. Pat now owns the Village Toy Store in East Hampton. Her husband Rich is a science teacher. We socialize a lot."

"Any favorite restaurants?"

He thinks for a minute. "Sapore di Mare," he says.

August 20, 1993

Chapter 30

HOLLIS ALPERT

The author Hollis Alpert is an imposing man. Now in his late sixties, he stands a full six foot three and, though he has to look down at you, he cocks his head inquisitively to the side to let you know there is nothing intimidating about that. He is also a gentle sort of man. He speaks softly, and, as he talks, he occasionally flashes a wry bit of a smile.

"The 1950's, when I first came out here, were a whole lot different than now," he says. "You had the artists and the very rich people then — the old money — and you had the local people and that was about it. There were only a few professionals then, no yuppies and hardly any writers at all. If Elaine Benson held a book fair in the 1950's, she'd have hardly anybody. Today there are authors by the hundreds."

Hollis Alpert has written dozens of books in his lifetime, including biographies of Fellini, Richard Burton and the Barrymores and autobiographies where he was either the co-author or the ghost, of Lana Turner and Charlton Heston. His recent books include *The Life and Times of Porgy and Bess* which is a 50-year history of that opera, and *Broadway!*, which publisher Richard Seaver, also a Hamptons resident, has put out on his Arcade subsidiary of Little Brown. Alpert has also written nine novels.

"One of these novels was the very first book about the Hamptons," Alpert says. "In the late 50s I had gotten to know all the artists living out here, and their patrons and their gallery owners and it was not hard to see all the scandalous twinings and intertwinings of everybody. Lots of lovers coming and going — describe it any way you want to. I wrote my book *The Summer Lovers* about all of these goings-on. Called the towns East Nines, West Nines and South Nines and changed everybody's names. It sold over a million copies in paperback and was optioned for the movies. And I guess it was accurate. Mae Rosenberg told me at the time 'you bastard, you got every one of us in there.'"

Alpert was also an early regular in the Artists-Writers softball game, which has been played annually since the early 1960's. Today it is a big media event and is played in the park behind the East Hampton A&P. But back then it was played up on somebody's lawn in Springs.

"By the time the game started," Alpert said, "I was working as the film critic of *Saturday Review*. I'd get up to the plate and Harold Rosenberg would go 'aha, a critic.' And he'd throw the ball at my head."

"I remember playing with de Kooning, Marca Relli, Franz Kline. Philip Pavia always hit a home run when he came up and one time some of the artists, de Kooning among them, got three grapefruits and painted them up to look like softballs and we lobbed one to Pavia and he gished it and said okay throw a real ball so we threw him the second and he gished it and then the third.

"After a number of years Jason Robards Jr. joined the game. And after that it got to be a 'thing.'"

Alpert was born in upstate New York near Utica where his father built this country's first supermarket.

"He had ten checkout counters and ten clerks. It was real busy but nobody had figured how to keep the clerks from pocketing the money from the registers so with ten of them he went broke real quick."

When he was ten, the family moved to Philadelphia. He lived there through his teens, was being groomed to run the family businesses and then World War II broke out. He ran away and joined the Army.

"Best thing that ever happened to me," he says. "The Army literally rescued me. Otherwise I would have gone into business with my Mother."

Alpert only had a high school education, but because he studied "advanced composition" at night after high school, the Army selected him as a combat historian.

"I went to Europe and my job was to write about the history of the war as it was being fought. I had my own jeep and driver, submachine gun and grenades, and I was always getting shot at because I wasn't supposed to be where I was."

Alpert, officially, was a liaison officer at headquarters for Patton's Third Army. He followed Patton all the way into Czechoslovakia and that's where he was when the Germans surrendered. His next assignment was in Paris where General S. L. A. Marshall set him and several other writers up in a mansion on the Avenue duBois to develop research on how the Germans had extricated themselves from the Falais trap near Normandy in June of 1945. And it was here that Hollis Alpert fell in love.

"She was a Russian woman living in Paris. We married. When the war ended she tried to persuade me to live with her in Paris and I tried to persuade her to live with me in America. I really had to make a decision and I just knew I could not live abroad. I took her to America. She tried but she couldn't take it. We separated and she returned to Paris. We were divorced."

Alpert's connection to the Hamptons came about because of his second marriage, which was to Anne Matta, former wife of the painter Matta. She had two children from her prior marriage and was part of the Abstract Expressionist movement based in Greenwich Village and East Hampton. Although Alpert was a writer, all the artists adopted him. Here in the Hamptons, from 1951 to 1960 which was as long as the marriage lasted, he was known as Anne's writer-husband.

I asked Alpert how he came to write his first piece of fiction. He had sold numerous short stories by this time, particularly to *The New Yorker*, *Harper's Bazaar* and *Mademoiselle*.

"Today, it is hard to find a place that will pay you for writing a short story," he said. "But back then there were lots of markets. It was when I was in the Army that I wrote my first piece. I was stuck on the Gulf Coast of Florida, it was just after the war had ended, and I was walking along, talking to a friend, and I was telling him about writing and how a good writer should be able to write 3,000 words on just about anything. Just then a bird flew down and landed in front of us. 'Oh yeah?' he said, 'write about THAT,' and so I did. It was called *The Guinea Hen*. I sold it to *The New Yorker*."

His second short story was also written at this army base in Tallahassee. He had been assigned as defense counsel to a soldier gone absent without leave.

"I talked to him and found that he'd gone AWOL to go home. He was homesick. He had gotten letters from his parents and he didn't know how to read but he was too embarrassed to ask anybody to read them to him so he just took the letters home and asked his parents. I wrote "The Soldier Who Went Home" and *Harper's Bazaar* bought that, too."

For seven years, from 1950 to 1957, Hollis Alpert was on the staff of *The New Yorker*. He lived in Greenwich Village and worked at *The New Yorker* offices on West 43rd Street. His immediate boss was Katherine White, wife of E.B. White, who headed up the fiction department. But he also got to know many of the other legendary figures at *The New Yorker*.

"My office was right near the receptionist," he said. "I met Harold Ross, E. B. White, James Thurber. Thurber was blind then and wasn't doing much. I remember going out to lunch with Joe Liebling. He talked about just how far you could go with non-fiction. Like whether or not you could interview a person over six different times and then write it to make it seem like one."

Alpert married his third wife, Joan, in 1960. She had been a Broadway actress (*Life With Mother* for nine months), then had gone to Barnard, gotten a degree in English Literature and had began teaching at Pratt and Hunter.

Summers, they continued coming out to the Hamptons, living in a variety of places, and then fell in love, as many people do, with the peace and quiet of Shelter Island. They bought a house there in 1967 and have lived there since. (Joan passed away in 1990.)

On Shelter Island, Alpert is part of a nice circle of friends, artists and professional people. He plays golf (for tension, he says) at the nearby Gardiner's Bay Country Club and he writes (to relieve the tension, he says) on a computer set up in a big studio on the back of the property.

He also presides over a group of young writers on the Island.

"I tell them I don't care what you do just as long as you do it as well as you can. I don't believe anyone ought to write crap. Be creative and take chances. You've got the parameters of the medium you are working in. Do your best."

July 10, 1992

* * *

Hollis Alpert sold his house on Shelter Island, but is renting, yearly, a house on Ridge Road in Sag Harbor. "Too attached to the area," he says.

146

Chapter 31

BOB SILLERMAN

I am sitting with Bob Sillerman in the living room of his home on Meadow Lane in Southampton and he is telling me about his childhood. Born and raised in Riverdale — father in the broadcasting business — big business reversal — moved down to the West Side when he was fifteen.

"I went to Collegiate, the Manhattan prep school. Because my dad was having financial problems, I needed to get a job. I looked at the school bulletin board, filled with jobs offered and kids looking for jobs and I thought, maybe there's a job here hooking these two groups up. I created a clearing house. Took a little percentage. Advertised. I was amazed. Hundreds of kids responded. So we put up fliers in Dalton and Brearsley and we expanded it, but I really worried that I wouldn't be able to get everybody jobs.

"Then a friend of mine who was in college told me he could get me a subscription to *Life* magazine cheap. Time/Life was interested in the youth market and they had people all over the college campuses selling magazine subscriptions at a very high discount because they figured if they could start them young they could keep them. All my friend wanted was to help me if I wanted this special offer because I was a high school kid and not yet eligible, but I saw it differently. Here was how I could get everybody on my list employed. I went down to Time/Life, spoke to them, and pretty soon we had all these high school kids out at their schools selling discount magazine subscriptions. Everybody was happy."

As Bob Sillerman is not in the employment agency business today, I asked him what finally happened to this business he started in high school.

"I kept it going through college. Then, when I was 23, I sold it to a San Francisco conglomerate."

"How big was this business when you sold it?" I asked.

"Annual revenue was twenty five million," he said. "I guess I kind of retired when I was 23. For awhile, anyway."

Bob Sillerman, today, is 43, and is the single largest investor in radio stations in America. He owns or has a large part in more than forty of them, many in the major markets around the country, including Manhattan. (Two days after this interview, the *New York Times* reported he is in contract to sell his interest in WNEW-AM. He is keeping his interest in WNEW-FM). He buys them, successful or not successful, persuades management, if he can, that they are more capable than they ever believed they were, and he makes them prosper.

"What do you know that they don't know?" I asked.

"Well, I've been doing this for a long time," he says. "I can bring more competitive techniques to a market, particularly a smaller market. I find that people often have a pre-conceived notion on how to do something. They don't question it. For example, we might find they have been broadcasting the news from 7 to 7:30 every morning because they have been doing it for years. We might do market research and discover that people tend to get up later in the morning now and that 7:30 to 8 would be better. You get the idea. We come in with energy, ingenuity and a can-do approach. I have a whole group of experts and MBA's that are part of Sillerman Companies."

I am struck by how Sillerman's mind works. From his high school days to today, he has been putting things together in new ways, linking things that nobody thought to link. Sillerman tells me, with a little pride, that he is, in fact, the only executive in his organization WITHOUT an MBA. And yet, when he describes his college education, through Brandeis in three years, with a degree in Political Science and the History of Ideas, it kind of makes sense.

"I was trained not to seek answers but to seek questions," he says. "It was the best preparation for business you can have."

And yet, his interest in business came earlier than that. It came in high school when his father, who he adored and who was an early pioneer and legend in the television marketing business had fallen on hard times.

"I saw what happened when we had no money, the pain and the humiliation. I was thirteen. It was so much more fun to be with my mom and dad when they weren't going through this. I determined this would never happen to me."

The man I am looking at today is also someone who keeps himself physically fit. He is a triathlete, he says. And, he tells me, he runs in the *Dan's Papers* Potatohampton Minithon every year and vividly remembers running in it in the early days "when you had the old course, where you had to stop at the railroad tracks to let the train through." This was fifteen years ago.

Later, after our interview, Sillerman takes me through this magnificent 10,000 square foot oceanfront house. There is an indoor swimming pool and an outdoor swimming pool, both oceanfront, and down below, through some glass, I can see a private gym that is about as big as the living room.

There is also something holistic and New Age about Sillerman. I can't quite pin it down. Mind, body and spirit. He talks about one of his friends, an employee at the college, who has recently been sick and how he and his wife will have a dinner for her that night and how they will conduct a healing.

He takes me through this magnificent house that he and architect Mark Matthews took three years to build — the cedar is from Vermont and the cherry is from Wisconsin and the trees were actually brought to the site and cut and finished right here — and Sillerman is rightly proud of the achievement. He shows me how the wood has weathered as he had hoped it would, he shows me the furniture that was handcrafted for his home by Mark Matthew's brother from the same wood, and he shows me rooms from which you can look out over the ocean from one set of windows and out over the Rolls Royce and Meadow Lane to the bay out the other. He does indeed live well, he keeps his body sharp, his mind is active and he is filled with positive ideas. A New Age businessman.

He is also a private man. I met his wife Laura, to whom he has been married for nineteen years. Then Sillerman tells me about some of his immediate neighbors — Kravitz and Forstman and other Wall Street players and he notes that he doesn't know any of them. His friends are mostly people connected with the college — LIU Southampton — and they are close and he has known them a long time.

He tells me about Road D.

He'd been coming out to the Hamptons since he was a little kid. When he'd gotten older, as a teenager and then as a college student he'd come out and stay with friends. Then he discovered Road D, a 100-yard long dead end road in Southampton that is right off Meadow Lane and ends at the beach. There are no beach stickers needed for Road D and he started coming there.

What he found was that Road D was also a favorite spot for LIU Southampton people. Still is. He met Tim Bishop, the Provost, Alice Flynn, the head of Freshman activities, Jane Finalborgo, the Director of Public Relations, Carol Lynch, the Director of Admissions. He has been coming to Road D for the better part of fifteen years, and as he is telling me this, a thought suddenly occurs to me and I look out the window. Yes, indeed.

"Now you know why my house is built here," he says. "I am known, among my friends as Road D Annex. When Road D is full, you can park here and walk down."

Now Sillerman talks about the college. In fact, he is passionate about the college.

"My perception is that people don't understand how LIU Southampton contributes to their lives," he says. "You can't measure the impact by the 1500 people who go there. Just it's being there touches everybody. Did you know that the Marine Science department here is one of the two best in the country? There have been fourteen Fullbright students at the Marine Science department alone. The school is a diamond in the rough. I would like to see the awareness of the college raised so people will view it as a resource and contribute to it as a resource."

Because of his enthusiasm, Sillerman agreed to serve as the chairman of the committee that is bringing the Crosby, Stills and Nash concert to the community on August 31. It is to take place on the soccer field at the college and tickets, available at Ticketmaster, the college administration building, Long Island Sound and Catena's, are $25.

"I hope that this concert will bring 5,000 people to this campus, people who have never been there before," he says.

Bob Sillerman has an apartment in Manhattan on the Upper East Side, an office and staff within three blocks of his home there, and his house on the beach in Southampton. But this house, it is quite clear, is not just a summer home. Equipped with cellular phones and faxes and computers and exercise rooms and swimming pools it is his center, personal and business. Sillerman is here the entire summer. Every weekend the rest of the year. And often during the week off-season as well.

With his interests and enthusiasms and passions he is a little known but very major asset to this community.

August 21, 1992

* * *

Bob Sillerman is now the Chancellor of Long Island University's Southampton Campus. Laura his wife gave birth to a baby girl in August of 1993.

Chapter 32

RICHARD WORTH

On Richard Worth's desk there is a small dartboard. The picture in the center is the same as the person sitting behind the desk. There are darts. You are free to throw them. But at the dartboard, please, not the person.

The statement made by this dartboard gives you a good insight into the personality of this man — rough and gruff and hilariously funny — who is President and CEO of R. W. Frookie, the company that makes sugar free cookies, Cool Fruits, Frookwiches and more than two dozen other food products on grocers' shelves nationwide.

Worth is a big man in his early forties, and when he talks which is close to nonstop, he often gets up and walks around, gesturing with his arms, stopping to look out the window at the sailboats bobbing at anchor in the bay here off Sag Harbor, then starting up and walking around again. He talks about concepts, about whether or not he's been able to do something to bother Nabisco today, about a new product that his wife has whipped up in her oven.

Sometimes he talks about how East Hampton Town Supervisor Tony Bullock chased him out of that town. Worth first moved his headquarters to a house in the woods in Northwest, but was then cited for operating a business in a residential zone prompting his move to Sag Harbor. Worth has been trying to get Bullock to note the economic loss to the East Hampton community when your policy is to chase out business, and to make some changes. He recently appeared before the East Hampton Town Board to present the case of a national businessman looking for a place to move his operation. But, as he says, "it had little effect."

Richard Worth now lives on a handsome estate in the Bell Estate section of East Hampton year around. It is filled with beautiful trees and flowers. He moved here with his new wife Randye six years ago from New York City, and Randye and he have just had a son. But Richard has led many lives.

He was born one of two children of the owner of the first women's ready to wear clothing store in New England — Worth's of Boston. He went to Brookline High School and played on the basketball team and then went to Hobart where he graduated in 1971 with degrees in Psychology and East Asian Studies.

The year he graduated was in the very heart of the hippie era in America and I asked if he was part of it. It had, indeed, been hard to ignore.

"I was not a CLASSIC hippie," he said. "I was very much into counter culture, but whatever forced me into a mold I went the other way."

Among the things that made him go the other way were his studies. He had planned to be a clinical psychologist. But though he had very high marks he was constantly arguing with his professors.

"We studied Skinner and behaviorism and they thought this was the study of man. I thought it was the study of common sense. The study of man, I said, would at least include Tim Leary and the East and a little Freud. I thought there has got to be more than get cheese be happy get no cheese be angry and frustrated. They did not recommend me for graduate work."

The sister school to Hobart in upstate New York was at that time and is today a school called William Smith. Worth married a William Smith girl right after graduation and moved back to Boston with a simple plan. He would go into business for five years, make his fortune, and then go "back to the land." In fact, though the "fortune" part was a bit elusive, that is exactly what he and his wife did.

"We went into the underground irrigation business. At the time, we lived in an apartment on $200 in rent and if we really tried hard enough on $7 a week in food. I was an astounding salesman. I took no prisoners. I was committed. I had this dream. I had this great confidence level. My words to live by were 'Fake It Before We Make It' and 'People Want to Think What They're Buying is Important, Beautiful and Emotional'. So we went in with full scale landscaping plans. And then we did a good job. At the end of one year I sold the business to my partner and we moved to Canada."

Worth had noticed that, on a map, everything to the northeast of Portland, Maine was sort of a big nothing. No people, no towns, no roads. He knew there had to be SOMETHING, but he figured that he would go up to eastern Maine, or across the border into New Brunswick, Canada and if there ever was a place that was back to the land then this was it.

152

"I thought, THAT'LL stop them," he said.

"Stop who?" I asked.

"The Nixons, the Money Greedies, the Jerkos of the last generation. That them."

He and his wife got in their car and drove until they got to a small town just over the border into New Brunswick, Canada, called Rollingdam. Worth went to a local realtor and told him he wanted to see farms for sale and the realtor looked astounded.

"It seemed hard for them to imagine that we would want to buy anything," he said.

Leaving the realtor, he and his wife drove to "the end of the road" where they came upon an old beat up barn, house, four hole outhouse, woodshed, garden, pastureland and ten acres. After some discussions, they bought it.

"The plan was that we would create a living experiment that could be emulated. That first night we slept in a nearby tent camp. We were terrified."

They had reason to be. A couple of suburbanites from America, they were embarking on something that they did not know the first thing about. It was October. The great snows of winter had not yet come. What they could see was that there was no telephone, no running water (there was a handpump), there was wood heat and the nearest neighbor was four miles away. Blueberries could be raised in the summertime on the land and everybody did logging in the wintertime. They had been shown the horse that would haul the logs around with the chains.

"I came to really hate that horse," Worth told me. "And what they did not tell us was that ten acres was not enough land to grow enough to earn a living on. We found that out for ourselves. Eventually, I had to buy much more land."

In fact, the Worths were to stay in New Brunswick on this property for ten years. But in the sixth year, Worth experienced the counter-culture birth of his son in the farmhouse attended by the various potters and weavers and furniture makers that had become his friends. When he realized during this birthing experience that he had almost lost both his wife and his son and they had only barely at the end been saved by an emergency trip to a real doctor and hospital, Worth decided he had had enough of his experiment. But it was to take him four more years to figure out how to get out.

During this time, Richard Worth took on the government of Canada and the Canadian logging interests.

"When winter came and I wanted to sell lumber, what I discovered was that if I wanted to cut trees on my own land I would have to call Georgia-Pacific. If I didn't, they wouldn't buy anything from me. And nobody else would either.

"Georgia-Pacific would tell me what to cut — hard wood or soft, how much they would pay me for it, where it should be delivered and when. I went to a meeting of the Wood Producers of Scharolotte County where I was. People were logging on these terms and making $3,000 a year. I told them you own to six inches under the trees, the government owns the minerals below that and above ground Georgia Pacific runs everything. This is slavery and feudalism. 'What do you have when all is said and done?' I asked them. 'Nothing,' they replied. 'Then you have ME,' I told them. And so they did indeed observe that they had somebody stupid enough to take on the big guys on their behalf and so they elected me Counsel-General."

Worth attempted to set up a meeting with Georgia-Pacific and they weren't interested in taking his calls. He contacted the Canadian government and they said yes, yes, yes, and they did nothing. One year went by. He went back to the Scharlotte County Wood Producers.

"Look, I said, you have two choices. You can continue to act legally which is nowhere and in which case I retire. Or you can act illegally and here is my plan."

Worth told the group he wanted all the loggers to show up with truck loads of logs and throw a big barricade across the Calais International Bridge connecting Canada to the United States. In front of it, they would stick a table and chairs. They would wait for negotiators from Georgia-Pacific. Take your pick.

"To my dismay, the Board of Directors voted that they would go along with me."

The first thing Worth and his group did was to take the $5,500 the government had sent them for a tree-counting survey and spend it on radio commercials announcing what they planned to do. The government contacted Worth and said we gave you that money in good faith. Worth replied that you made us paupers.

Worth met with J. D. Irving, the Canadian billionaire who owns about 30% of the maritime provinces with interests in lumber, transportation and oil. Nothing came of it.

The day before the demonstration, the Prime Minister of the Province came to see Richard Worth.

"He told me you will see that people don't solve their problems in this way here, Mr. Worth."

The day of the demonstration came. All together, instead of the expected 500 trucks and lumber, there came maybe 10 trucks with 20 guys.

"In their eyes I saw fear," Worth said. "So I said to myself, well, the time has come to make my statement and so I put on my hard hat, walked out to the center of this sixth busiest bridge between the United States and Canada, and I lay down in the middle of the road

154

and waited for a tractor trailer truck to come run me over. Instead, they stopped."

It was Richard's wife who put an end to all the proceedings. She came out to the center of the bridge and stood over him and said 'Rich you are going to get killed.'

"And I thought of what Thoreau said to Emerson. Emerson said 'what are you doing down there?' and Thoreau said 'what are you doing up there?' and my wife said 'Rich you are going to die or go to jail for people who ARE NOT WORTH IT.' And so I got up."

He backed out gracefully. He and some of the other loggers halted the trucks in the middle of the bridge and politely invited them to stop by the side of the road on the other side and have a cup of coffee with the woodsmen and look at a leaflet. Many of them did. The upshot of the whole thing was that the price of wood to the woodcutters went up 25% for a while.

Worth tells this story, wandering around his office in Sag Harbor, with the kind of outrageousness and sarcasm and humor that has listeners enthralled. How much of it is exaggeration, how much is real, how much is just Worth telling it like it is, I do not know. But I will tell you this — I could listen to this guy tell stories all day. Besides everything else, he is an entertainer.

Well, he is also, because of this, a speaker at major food industry events. It was shortly after his run-in with Georgia-Pacific and shortly after the birth of his son, that Worth went into the food business, right from there in New Brunswick, Canada.

"My new words to live by were 'Give the People What they Want or What They Don't Even Yet Know They Want.'"

Worth decided that the world was waiting for jam without sugar. It was 1978. He made it with honey at first right there on his farm, he made it with blueberry jam, and he marketed it by selling it to the supermarkets and grocery stores in the area. He made up the name for his little firm. Sorrell Ridge, after a ridge on his property. Today it is the third largest maker of all-fruit jams in America, right behind Smuckers and Polanar.

"We made it on the farm. Then I went down to Boston and I went to a distributor with the product and they said you make it and we'll buy it. And as I was leaving they said 'and also strawberry.' In June of 1979 we broke ground on a factory. By August we were selling out of it."

Sorrell Ridge was a great success right out of the box. But to continue on out of a remote part of New Brunswick, Canada, seemed almost impossible.

"I FORCED New Brunswick Telephone to install us a phone," Worth said. "But it was a ten party line. I had to keep kicking people off."

In 1982, Worth's marriage collapsed, he sold his business to a New

155

Jersey firm called Allied-Old English and Worth came back to America. He spent three years doing consulting work in Manhattan. And then he started Frookie Cookies. Headquarters, at first, were in Englewood, New Jersey.

"I knew the business. And I wanted to get back in it."

He met Randye at a trade show. She was a product and recipe developer looking for work. She had written a number of cookbooks. The rest you know.

"How did we come out to the Hamptons? Well, we got suckered in the way everybody gets suckered in out here. We rented a cottage on Gerard Drive in Springs for a month in the summer of 1985. The first day here I knew I wanted to live here. And so, now we do."

About six months ago, Richard and Randye Worth, very pregnant at the time, came to our house for dinner. Among the other guests were Monte Farber and Amy Zerner, the very successful creators of counterculture artwork, board games and books, who also live in Springs. From this dinner a new product was born.

It will be launched this fall. Along with the Frookie cookies and the Blue Corn Tortilla Chips and the Cool Fruits and the Frookwiches and the Dirty Potato Chips all produced by Frookie you will now find, in your local supermarket a new product called Fortune Frookies.

Monte and Amy have designed them, Richard and Randye have edited them and will market them. Reach into a bag and get your future as told by the I Ching.

One month ago, Monte and Richard went to the Chicago Food Fair to take orders. The two men lived together for a week in a hotel room. Monte, at various times, dressed up in a wizard's costume as part of the promotion. Richard, of course, doesn't have to dress up as anything. He's crazy enough as it is.

July 16, 1993

* * *

Fortune Frookies in three different varieties were successfully brought to market in the autumn of 1993.

156

Chapter 33

RALPH DESTINO

My meeting with Ralph Destino, who is Chairman of the Board of Cartier, Inc., was at three in the afternoon at the Southampton Bath and Tennis Club. When I arrived, promptly at three, I found him at a table — he was there ahead of me — and he stood up upon my arrival and shook my hand. He is a tall man in his mid-fifties, a man of rugged good looks, and he looks exactly how you would expect the Chairman of Cartier to look, right down to the magnificent watch on his wrist.

I began the interview, and, as I usually do, I asked where he was born and raised. The answer was something of a surprise.

"Providence, Rhode Island," he said. "I went to Providence Classical High School. Then I went to Dartmouth."

The Dartmouth part seemed to make sense, but the Providence part confused me, until he told me something that I never knew before about that city.

"Providence was a one industry town," he said. "Jewelry making. On every street corner when I was growing up there were silversmiths or lapidaries or goldsmiths. I think three quarters of the town was involved in jewelry making. I don't remember a time, at home, when that wasn't what was discussed. In fact when I was very young, I thought that was the only thing that people did."

Ralph Destino was the eldest of three sons. His father worked for the National Cash Register Company.

Growing up, Destino took jobs in just about every aspect of the jewelry making business. But when he went off to Dartmouth, and he discovered there were other things you could be besides a jeweler, he concluded he would become a great writer. He took a degree in literature and creative writing.

"I thought creating something called Ralph's Papers might be my calling," he said to me with a twinkle in his eye.

But then, during his college years, he had an opportunity with some friends to come into Manhattan. He had never been to Manhattan before. He was overwhelmed.

"I couldn't believe there could be buildings so tall, streets so wide, stores so vast, people so numerous. It was such a contrast to the small sleepy New England town I had grown up in. I decided the single greatest dream of my life would be to have a penthouse apartment overlooking Central Park."

When he graduated Dartmouth, he moved to Manhattan and immediately fulfilled his dream. He found a single room fifteen feet by fifteen feet, on the top floor of an apartment at Central Park West and 74th Street. Along with a friend from school who wanted to go into the theatre, he rented it. And he took a job at Bloomingdale's to pay his share of the rent.

"Linens and domestics," he said. "I joined the buying department. And it occurred to me that what I really wanted to do was to learn how merchandising and promotion worked, because I knew jewelry and I knew I could go into the jewelry business."

He called his father — his father was only 19 years older than he was — and suggested the two of them open a jewelry business in Manhattan. His dad said he would quit his job and do it. But they would need an office, some financing. He had some friends who would invest. Young Ralph did too.

"This was a dream of mine, going into business with my dad. He was Ralph and I was Ralph Jr. He came down to the City and we opened our business, Ralph Destino, Ltd., out of a single room at 411 Fifth Avenue."

Their plan was simple. Ralph Jr. would make 90 designs in the spring and then 90 more designs in the fall — earrings, bracelets, rings etc. — they would have samples made up at the shops in Providence, and then they would travel around the country with the spring (or fall) collection and take orders from different buyers. The specialty of the firm would be sterling silver, in tailored and geometric designs. The firm prospered.

In the mid-1960's Ralph got married, moved to 35th Street and Park Avenue and fathered a son. Also at this time, Ralph's father developed cancer and died. He was only 51. Ralph Destino Jr. was on his own.

By 1967, the Ralph Destino Company had three lines of jewelry— the Destino line, the John Weitz line and the Christian Dior line from Europe. The firm operated out of two floors at 10 East 34th Street,

158

one block from Destino's home on 35th Street, and it employed 40 people.

And then, without any warning, a watch design by John Weitz became an international sensation.

"He had designed this watch with a heavy gold chain. It was a kind of tough, hairy chested sort of watch, and suddenly everyone in the world had to have one. It was my first experience with status symbols. People had to have tie dyes, bell bottoms and this watch. The orders came thundering in and we could barely keep up with them. We'd order 1,000 made and there'd be orders for 2,000. We'd order 2,000 and the orders were for 4,000. It was incredible."

Within a year, the size of the company Ralph Destino, Inc. had increased four-fold. It was at a whole new level. And so it was that in 1972 that two things happened that were to change Ralph Destino's life.

"The first was that we were approached by Victor Kiam who owned the Benrus Company. He wanted to buy my company. I said I would think about it. And then, there came in the door a man from Cartier-Paris. He said they were expanding their business to the Far East and were looking for someone to head up the division.

"I came home. I told my wife we were moving to Hong Kong. I think she thought I was crazy."

To Ralph Destino, as to almost everyone in the jewelry business in New York, Cartier represented the top of the line, something only to be admired and viewed from afar.

"I had never thought Cartier was something I could be part of. They were prestigious, global. Another league."

Destino sold his company and took on the Cartier job with unimaginable enthusiasm. He and his family moved to Hong Kong, then to Tokyo, Singapore and Sydney. In three years in the Far East, he opened retail outlets and arranged for Must de Cartier products — all made in France or Switzerland — to be sold in stores in Japan, Korea, the Philippines, Taiwan, Malaysia, Guam, Australia and Singapore.

And then, on February 1, 1976, Destino remembers the day, Cartier-Paris bought Cartier USA.

"You have to remember that Cartier is a French firm that is 145 years old. Over the years, a subsidiary of the company in America became independent. Now Cartier-Paris was bringing it back into the fold. They called me and asked me to come back to New York."

Cartier USA became Cartier, Inc., and for the past sixteen years Destino has run it, twelve years as President and four years as Chairman of the Board.

"Cartier is in 91 countries," he says. "Here in America, our headquarters is the mansion built at the turn of the century by railroad tycoon Morton Plant at the corner of Fifth Avenue and 52nd Street.

"There is a wonderful story about how our headquarters came to be here. Morton, age 60, had ordered his home built directly across from the Vanderbilt mansion. It was a gift for his 18 year old wife Maisie. Cartier, at the time, was a small firm located in what is now the Henri Bendel building.

"But in 1916, Cartier put on display a double strand of beautifully formed white pearls, no blemishes. It was for sale for $1.6 million, a huge sum at the time and among the many people who went to see it was Maisie. She returned home that evening and told Morton she would just have to have it. Morton said he wasn't prepared to spend that much money on a strand of pearls and Maisie said she was willing to give up the mansion, which was in her name, for it.

"The idea of a swap, the mansion for the pearls, was presented to Cartier and after Cartier got over the initial shock of it, he accepted the offer. Not a cent or a franc changed hands. Cartier moved its headquarters to the mansion and the Plants moved to the country, which was 85th Street and Fifth Avenue.

"Cartier has actually kept this building up as if it were still a private home. My office on the third floor facing out onto Fifth Avenue for example, was originally a guest bedroom in the Plant family. I'd like to invite you to come by sometime. I will take you through the place."

Destino recounted how Cartier was first founded. Louis-Francoise Cartier was born into a family that decorated and designed stocks for guns. He had a talent for design but hated firearms, so he left the business and apprenticed to M. Picard, a leading Paris jeweler.

"In those days, whether you were successful in the jewelry business really depended upon how you were perceived by the Royal Court of Napolean III. Cartier made things for the niece of the Empress Eugenie. She showed them to Eugenie who liked them and from that time on Cartier's work was in great demand."

At the present time, Destino's job consists largely, as he describes it, of "keeping the flame."

"There are numerous companies that have a marvelous nineteenth century grandeur. But you have to be careful that grandeur doesn't atrophy into Grand Dame. We have to live in our own time. My task therefore is to nourish the richness of our history and still keep the vitality.

"I still write every word that goes into every Cartier ad. We try to conduct ourselves with discretion, manners and form. We do make new products. They must flow from the central reservoir of timelessness that goes back to the integrity of the initial creation."

Today, Destino lives on the Upper East Side of Manhattan, he has a home in Southampton (he's been coming to the Hamptons for more than thirty years), and another at the Palm Beach Polo Club. He is on the board of several companies, also the United Way, the Fashion Institute of Technology, the Jewelry Industry Council (he is Chairman of the Board), and he is Chairman of the Board of the American Cancer Society, New York. Which brings us to a discussion of the fundraising event that is to be held at the Southampton Bath and Tennis Club on the weekend of September 19, 20.

"We'd like to write a check for $100,000 to the American Cancer Society of Long Island," he says. "The event is a weekend tennis tournament, on Saturday at private homes, and on Sunday here at the club which George Semerjian has so graciously given over to us.

"It is mixed doubles, 96 men and 96 women, each of whom will enter by writing a check for $250 to the American Cancer Society. The matches Saturday will be played at 24 homes, eight in Southampton, eight in Bridgehampton and eight in East Hampton. Co-Chairman of the event is former tennis champion Nancy Chafee Whitaker, the wife of Jack Whitaker, and Aaron Daniels who is the retired Chairman of the ABC Radio Network. There will be a Friday night cocktail party at the home of Jon Corzine in Sagaponack and on Saturday an evening at the home of Jack and Nancy Whitaker where all the food and drink are from the eastern end of Long Island.

September 4, 1992

Chapter 34

MAGEE HICKEY

Magee Hickey on television — she is a reporter for WNBC Channel 4 — looks like the girl next door. After you have spent an hour or two with her you realize that is exactly what she is. She is a delight.

Here is how she describes her meeting and subsequent courtship with Richolson Salembier, the man she has been married to for ten years.

"I was twenty and going to Brown, but I was home in Manhattan for the weekend. My sister was dating this guy. He had a friend. So his friend asked me out and we went out on this date and he told me he was smitten with this French babe. Well, that's how I describe it anyway. But at the end of the date we had this passionate good night kiss. It made us both think. And I thought, I'm gonna file this guy."

The next time she saw Richolson Salembier was at Mortimer's seven years later. It was after a wedding and she was feeling blue as many people do after a wedding and she saw him there alone at the bar.

"I thought I'm going over there and talk to him. What could be so bad about that? That night, he told me he was never getting married. The next night he told me he'd never have children. There was something going on here."

Today, Magee Hickey and her husband divide their time between an Upper East Side apartment and the Salembier family home on the ocean next to the Maidstone Club in East Hampton. They have two daughters, age 5 and age 1 1/2. They share the East Hampton home with her husband's brother, a bachelor.

I asked how long they have been coming out to the Hamptons and a twinkle appeared in Magee Hickey's eye.

"My husband is 41 years old and has been coming out to the Hamptons for 41 years. His father just passed away at 76 and had been coming out 76 years. And HIS father had the house built in 1906. So the family has been coming out quite awhile."

The Salembier house is next to the home of Dina Merrill and adjacent to the Maidstone Club. Golf balls land on their lawn.

"My father-in-law had a squeeze horn he would honk. We overlook the fourteenth hole. If he didn't like the man's backswing or something."

Oddly, Magee's husband is not a member of the Maidstone. He belongs to the National Golf Club in Southampton.

"The Maidstone, he says, is a country club. The National is a Golf Course. He's a golfer. Of course, and I remember this well, we would walk down the fourteenth hole to the clubhouse to have lunch with his father and there would be all these women in straw hats and one of them would say 'oh, isn't that little Rickie Salembier?' I guess that has something to do with his being a member of the National."

Richolson Salembier, today, is a respected Manhattan corporate insurance broker.

Magee Hickey grew up at 76th and Park Avenue amidst privilege. She says she did not know it at the time. She went to the Chapin School, went riding at the Clairmont Riding Academy. Her mother was a homemaker and a part-time actress. Her father prospered in the concrete business. Later he went into real estate and today is involved in volunteer work. He raises money for charities, for programs for homeless people, for children with learning disabilities. Sometime next month a shelter in the Bronx is to be built and dedicated as the Lawrence Hickey Shelter.

Magee Hickey has never strayed very far from the Upper East Side. It is as if she has a silver cord connecting herself to it.

"After Rick and I got married, and he is also an Upper East Sider, we thought why not do something really wild and bold? Let's look at the Upper WEST Side. Or Maybe Soho. We stayed on the Upper East Side."

Brown University, in Rhode Island, was just another place for Magee to spend time before finding her way back to the Upper East Side. She was to spend nine years there, however, four at college and then five developing her television career, before she was able to move back home.

Her undergraduate years set her on her career path. "At first I thought I would be a concert flautist," she says. "But there were two little problems. I had no discipline for it. And I had no talent for it. Then I thought I'd be an actress. In private school, which had been an all-girl's school, I had always had the male parts. Nobody quite understood this at Brown. Finally I had a talk with a professor. You are a quick study, he said, you are good with words. You have a short attention span. Why not try radio or television?"

Eventually, she got a degree in "Semiotics," which, she says, is the study of symbols and how they communicate meanings. She'd take courses in film, flute, drama, dance, "a little bit of everything and I'd call it Semiotics."

In her senior year, she got a job with WPRO radio. She also got a job as an intern at WPRI Channel 12.

"They didn't pay me, but I got course credit. I'd go out when they'd cover a story or a fire, set up the equipment, make the phone calls, re-write the story in the van on the way back for the anchor. I also worked at this time as a live-in cook. It enabled me to get a living situation off campus."

Graduating, she took a job at UPI, the press service, working in a tiny office in the Rhode Island State House. There were three people employed by UPI there and each worked an eight hour shift so basically she worked alone, writing stories and sending them out over the wire.

"I learned how to write leanly at UPI," she said. "I remember a News Director at Channel 6 in Providence later on putting this style into words. He said 'tell them what you're about to tell them, then tell them what you're telling them and then tell them what you've just told them.' I remember listening to Dan Rather read one of my UPI stories on Channel 2. It was a story about the death penalty being turned down in Rhode Island. Hardly a word was changed. I felt proud."

She began sending out resumes to the television stations in Providence and going out on interviews. One station told her her hair was too red and her name might have to be changed because "it sounds like a disease." But eventually, Magee Hickey landed what she still calls her "dream job," the six and eleven anchor for the news for Channel 6 Providence/New Bedford.

She stayed on this job for three years — "we liked to say that because of where our tower was we had the strongest signal and blanketed the largest area to the greatest number of fish in New England" — and if you wonder why she finally left it then you have to know about that silver cord around her ankle.

"The next step, I knew, would be an anchor at a medium sized city somewhere — like Cincinnati. I just didn't want this to happen. And I knew that Rick would not want to leave the City. I began to write to every news director in the City of New York. I'd write and I'd call and I'd go down there. And finally I got a break. Channel 5 asked me in for a two week audition. They'd put me on the air and they would pay me and if they liked me they would hire me and they did."

Magee Hickey became a TV reporter, first for Channel 5, then for one year and six months with WABC Channel 7 and for the last seven years with WNBC Channel 4. She is a well known figure on the streets of New York and, to a lesser degree, on the streets of the Hamptons.

"I'll be out with one of my two children on Newtown Lane, no makeup on, hair a mess, and somebody will come over and say you look like a TV reporter but I can't remember her name. Or once, I ran into Peter Kalikow, the owner of the *New York Post* and he said I know you, I used to watch you on Channel 6 in New Bedford. That was in the early days of cable. The Providence stations are what came in to eastern Long Island then.

"And I remember getting a parking ticket from a 'brownie' policeman in East Hampton, and I went down to pay it and the clerk there knew me from Channel 6, New Bedford. It's a strange feeling."

Magee Hickey says she is as amazed as everybody else how the Hamptons have become so overrun with celebrities. "I get excited, too, when I see Christie Brinkley," she says.

We talked for awhile about what it is like to be a street reporter for a New York City television station. Could it be dangerous?

"Absolutely dangerous. We are covering fires, shootings, riots. Sometimes we get there before the police do. For example, we'd learn about a story where a mother is accused of killing a child. The *New York Times* gives the address. We go there, myself and a cameraman and a sound man and the three of us are the only white people in a black neighborhood and I'm the only woman and I've got a notepad and we knock on the door to get a statement. A person not all there could think we're doing police business. The older I get the less I want to do this.

"I remember, pregnant with my first, climbing twelve flights to the top floor of an apartment house to speak to the neighbors of a man, Larry Davis, who'd just shot five police officers, and who was holed up there. No exception was made because I was pregnant. I hadn't expected any.

"Some of the other reporters wear bullet proof vests. Shots would ring out. I've been there when there is shooting. What I have to say is that when the cops say get down they mean get down.

"I am a crier. Sometimes, after I've been talking to people who have lost a child, I cry on camera. Lately, as my kids have become 5 and 1 I find myself trying to talk people out of sharing their feelings. I just don't want them to share their pain."

"There has been a lot of criticism," I said, "of the local New York media covering just murders and fires and drug busts, without looking at some of the more positive stories."

"What we do, basically," she said, "is report inner city news to the outer boroughs. We've had polls, recently, that tell us people would rather see a more positive and more intelligent approach. And we do try to have a story every day that is uplifting, that people can feel good about. Unfortunately, there have been major cutbacks at all the stations. Body bag stories are very easy to do."

"What do you think of all the crime in the City? You've been covering it eight years. Is it on the increase?"

"Well, now they check for weapons at the schools, which they did not do before. I think the problems increased markedly when de-institutionalization was put in effect. But you know, New York takes people from all over the world. And most of them seem happier here than where they came from."

About a month ago, Magee Hickey was given a new assignment, to be the co-anchor of a Saturday and Sunday morning news show. Sort of a local *Today* Show. It is on 9-10:30 a.m. on Saturday and 7-8 a.m. and 9-10 a.m. on Sunday.

"There is no guarantee that I could not be back doing regular street reporting," she said. "The station is trying this out. But it sure is fun. Instead of getting called up at 3 a.m. that a building has collapsed, I go see an off-Broadway play and interview the stars."

How does Magee Hickey and her family spend their time in the Hamptons? They are home-bodies. There is no household help when she and her husband are in East Hampton. It is a time they spend with the children. She'll bike into town and get the morning paper at the Chicken House, stop at Dreesen's Market and pick up sausage.

"Have you ever had this sausage? They deliver it. Not only here but to New York City!" And she'll go to Iaconna's on Long Lane and get a chicken. Later, she'll take the kids to the duck pond and to the playground at Herrick Park.

"I think the Hamptons are probably the most beautiful place I've ever seen."

She goes for walks on the beach — the mile from her house to Main Beach passes in front of the Maidstone Club which, for most of the year is vacant beach — and she collects shells and stones. Back at home there is the barbecue.

"My husband loves to barbecue. He is the cook in the family. In fact, he does more than fifty percent of the housework."

Restaurants?

"Not really. When my father-in-law was alive, we'd go to Gordon's in Amagansett and that other place, what was it? Bountiful Board."

Homebodies. The family that's been here almost a century. And the girl next door.

October 9, 1992

Chapter 35

JOHN CATSIMATIDIS

This is a rags to riches story. I am sitting with a man in his summer home in Quoque who is today the president of a giant conglomerate — supermarkets, oil companies, airline charter companies, real estate — that is today worth about two billion dollars, and he is telling me that when he started this company in his senior year of college he only had about ten cents. His name is John Catsimatidis, he is 40 years old, and the story starts even before that.

"My father emigrated from Greece in 1949 when I was six months old," he says. "We came to the Upper West Side of Manhattan, around 125th Street, and we settled there. He got a job as a waiter."

"What had he done in Greece?"

"My family came from Nissiros, one of the Greek islands. During the 1940's and World War II, the Italians occupied Greece and they impressed some of the residents to work for them. My father tended a lighthouse for the Italians on one of the other islands. I don't know which one."

"But the war ended in 1945. What did he do until 1949?"

"I don't know. Tended goats, maybe."

Andrew Catsimatidis, his wife, and their only son emigrated to America as so many had done before them to give themselves a better life. Greece, like much of Europe, lay prostrate from the effects of the war. America was a new world.

"I went to Brooklyn Tech and took some engineering courses. Then I went to City College and studied to be an engineer. I hated it. I got my degree and knew that I would never be doing that."

He got a job working for a relative who had a small grocery store at 100th St. and Broadway. That was in 1969. Then the relative asked if this young man would like to be partners in the store. Then the relative decided he was homesick and wanted to go back to Greece. John Catsimatidis was the owner of a grocery store.

"I came up with a philosophy. Work hard, and whatever profits I make I will reinvest into the business except ten percent. So if I made $50,000, I took $5,000 for myself. The other $45,000 I found a way to invest back."

He bought a second store. This one was at 87th and Broadway. He ran both of them with the idea that the employees should try harder. He became the first supermarket chain to stay open Sundays, then stay open until midnight.

He named the chain Red Apple. Pretty soon there were five stores and then ten and then twenty, all in the New York metropolitan area.

Today his little company has grown to 130 supermarkets, either Red Apple or Gristedes. His headquarters is in Midtown, but his heart remains on the Upper West Side. He and his wife have lived in the same co-op for twenty years, his parents still live nearby. His father, 89, works at one of the stores.

But the expansion has not stopped with the supermarkets. In recent years he has purchased Charles and Company, a group of specialty shops in New York, and he has bought a chain of Pantry Prides in Florida and the Bahamas, as well as a chain of Grand Unions in the Virgin Islands. He also now owns a big oil company, United Refining, with over 300 gas station in the Northeast, and a company that operates and leases 35 corporate jets. He is heavily into real estate. Not long ago, Mayor Koch named him the "Outstanding Greek American of the Year."

And then there is the *Hellenic Times*, the English language newspaper published in Manhattan for the Greek community.

"About ten years ago, some friends said it was my responsibility as a successful Greek businessman to maintain the losses of the *Hellenic Times*. I bought it and I've been doing that for ten years."

His wife Margo runs both the newspaper and a successful Manhattan advertising agency.

Besides this unbelievable empire built in the space of just twenty years, John Catsimatidis coordinates the annual Columbus and Amsterdam Avenue Festivals, and is vice-chairman of the West Side Chamber of Commerce. Recently, he donated money so the City could start to build a new library in lower Manhattan.

"As for the Hamptons," he said, "we come here to relax." Out the livingroom window there was a lawn and some woods. A long way from the Upper West Side. "We come out almost every weekend in the summer. And sometimes we come out on weekends in the winter."

Twenty years ago, who could have known?

September 1, 1989

Chapter 36

CHRIS WHITTLE

I think Chris Whittle is one of the luckiest people on the planet. Here is is, an easygoing, amiable man in his mid-forties, and on the business side of his life, his company Whittle Communications is involved in the exciting new field of interactive television. Every morning around the country more than eight million school children sit at their desks and watch a twelve minute news summary on Whittle Communications' CHANNEL ONE. Perhaps 5,000 people work for him. He has half a dozen other projects either in the works or out there and flying across the airwaves. Revenues are approaching a billion dollars a year.

His personal life is as lucky as his business life. He lives with his beautiful wife and two young children in one of most magnificent estates ever built in the Hamptons. We are sitting in lawn chairs out on its front lawn right now as a matter of fact. Behind us is this 6,000 square foot, 15 room wood shingled mansion surrounded by porches. Set in a wooded grove, it was built as a summer home for a New York physician in 1932. In front of us, sweeping out across acres and acres of mowed lawn — the estate is more than 16 acres — is a small private dock with several sailboats rocking peacefully back and forth. There is more than a quarter mile of private waterfront on this property. Beyond are the calm waters of Georgica Pond and a half mile away at the end, a clear view of the waves of the Atlantic Ocean crashing down as it tries to break through the closed cut that separates it from the pond.

Our interview lasts about an hour and a half. The children run in and out. Coffee is served out here on the lawn. During the last half of the interview the low rumble of the ocean changes into a sound that is not unlike thunder and lightning. The waves crashing on the beach reverberate up the pond. The sound, stopped by the house and the pine grove, lands on Chris Whittle's front lawn.

"How much time do you get to spend here?" I ask.

"I am here every weekend in the summer," Chris says. "Priscilla (pronounced the Italian way: Pre-SHE-la) and the kids are here. In the winter the family is based in Manhattan where the kids go to the St. Bernard's school. And I commute by plane. On a triangle route."

"A triangle route?"

"Our offices are in Knoxville, Tennessee. Actually, I commute sometimes on a rectangular route. I've been doing it for years. I am here for the weekend. I spend Monday and Tueday in Knoxville, then I fly to Teterboro and New York City for Wednesday and Thursday and then I am back out here. The flights are quite short, actually. From East Hampton to Knoxville is just an hour and forty minutes. The company has a Citation jet plane."

"You said quadrangle."

"And then we have our studios. Mostly now they are in Los Angeles. So sometimes I am out there on Wednesday and Thursday as well."

Chris Whittle was born and raised in Knoxville. He will tell you that because it gets a bit esoteric to explain where he is really from and people have heard of Knoxville. He is from Etowah, Tennessee, which is about 60 miles south of Knoxville.

"Etowah means 'swamp' in Cherokee," Chris says. "There's an Etowah in almost every southern State.

He was born there, he was raised there and he graduated high school there — the Etowah High School Pile Drivers was the football team — and his dad was the town doctor.

There was one Main Street with the stores on one side and the railroad station on the other side. His dad's clinic was in the center of town. Sometimes his mom worked there. He has two older sisters, who today are both married and living in and around Knoxville.
He goes back there a lot.

Chris was an industrious and popular kid in Etowah. He had three paper routes for years and years. He played an instrument in the band and in his senior year was elected President of the school. Often, accompanying his father off on house calls, he would watch as his dad delivered babies — sometimes right on the front steps — and he would see his father get paid sometimes in produce rather than money.

"A few times he got paid in hams," Chris said. "I carried them out to the car."

As the only son, it was naturally expected that Chris would go into medicine and, at first, Chris did not disappoint. He went off to the University of Tennessee as a pre-medical student. Something happened there, however, that got him very much off the track.

170

"It was the late 1960's," Chris says. "Many universities were in a state of unrest. At the University of Tennessee this was played out in a relatively rather tame way — the kids demonstrated for free speech, later curfew hours and more attention to student problems. I joined a group called the National Student Organization, the NSO, which published books on how schools should be reformed. The key aspect was that the kids should become involved in the planning. It should not be just something done to them. They should be part of the process."

Whittle got together with three of his friends at the school, all of whom were small-town boys from rural Tennessee, and they decided to publish a handbook that would bring information to the students at the University. It would be called KNOXVILLE IN A NUTSHELL and it would be a guide to the City in which the University was located. Also, hopefully, it could make money and help them pay their school bills.

"The four of us were Phillip Moffit, Bryant Mayfield, David White and me. We all did a part. Moffitt did the editing. I did sales and marketing. It was, by the standards of those years, quite a success. But because there were four of us we had to divide the profits up and when you got done with it that wasn't much. I think I got $600 that first year. But what it did do was convince us that if we kept at it we could make a go of it. We had gotten bitten by the publishing bug."

In 1969 the foursome graduated and went into business together publishing guidebooks. They would, they thought, eventually put "NUTSHELL" guidebooks in every college town in the country. They rented an old pillow factory in the city — it was in the worst part of Knoxville — and they brought in typesetting equipment. They were in business. The company was called THIRTEEN THIRTY COMPANY, named for the age group that the company hoped to reach.

"We were together for more than six years. Very soon we had COLUMBIA IN A NUTSHELL and we had BERKELEY IN A NUTSHELL. Whatever money we made we put back into the company. And we got friends and investors to put up money. We took it in in increments of $10,000 and we called it 'love money.' At the end of six years we had guidebooks across the nation and we had lost more than one million dollars."

The problem was that each of these annuals did very well by itself. Whittle would travel the country — that was his job, to set up the staffs and teach them research and sales and so forth — but the cost of running the national operation out of a pillow factory in Knoxville swamped them with costs.

"The more magazines we set up," Whittle says, "the more we lost. It was awful."

During this time, Whittle lived in a two room log cabin in a fifty acre woods across a river from the city. This cabin and about a dozen others had been built years earlier in another part of Tennessee in a low area where the TVA planned to build a dam. The land there would be flooded. The cabins were put up for sale. A woman bought them, took them apart, and reassembled them just outside of the City. She called the community Log Haven. After she died, Chris and his three friends bought them all. Two of the partners soon drifted off. But he and Moffit were to live there, each in his own cabin, for seventeen years.

* * *

"One day we got a study from the Harvard Business School sent to us about good and bad names for businesses. We were an example of a bad business. THIRTEEN THIRTY, their study said, was too limiting. We sat down and thought about it. What if we changed things around? We decided that all our different guidebooks should be combined into one national college magazine. It saved our business and completely turned us around. In two years we went from a half a million dollar loss to a half a million dollar profit."

The magazine was called NUTSHELL and it was sent out free to 1.2 million college students. It was, in a nutshell, a Welcome to Your College Experience. There were in it articles on how to finance your college education, how to study, what fraternities were all about. With the success of NUTSHELL, the company published 18ALMANAC, which was sent out to one million high school seniors. And they published THE GRADUATE which went out to 300,000 college seniors. The company, which by 1976 was now doing $5 million and netting $1 million, was in the business of marketing "transition" publications to high school and college kids. There were about 600 people on the payroll in six different buildings around Knoxville.

"And then one day, and this was in 1978, we realized that we were really in the business of publishing magazines for select groups. We can do this for a lot of groups, we thought. What about people in a barber shop or a beauty parlour? What about people in a doctor's waiting room? We began to publish magazines for these groups in these locations as well."

The company, which had now been renamed WHITTLE COMMU-NICATIONS, began publishing annuals in specific and targeted locations. Glossy magazines began to appear in waiting rooms at doctor's offices. I personally remember, some years ago, sitting waiting to get a haircut and looking through a well thumbed glossy magazine targeted specifically for that waiting room and thinking — what an interesting idea.

Whittle also moved into the national spotlight for the first time during that era. In 1977, WHITTLE COMMUNICATIONS bought Esquire Magazine from Clay Felker.

172

"Esquire was losing a lot of money. It continued to lose money for several years after we bought it and to be honest with you there was a time when I thought that it was bleeding so bad maybe we couldn't fix it fast enough. But we did, mostly, I think, because of our understanding of marketing to select groups. We had it prospering by the mid-1980's."

Changes in Chris Whittle's life began to come thick and fast in the mid-1980's. In 1986, he and his partner Phillip Moffit, decided to go separate ways. How they did it was to split up the company. Moffit took Esquire. Whittle took everything else. Moffit then sold Esquire to Hearst Publications and went on to other things.

The following year, at a dinner/birthday party for a friend, Whittle met and fell in love with young Priscilla Ratazzi. The daughter of an Agrelli on her mother's side, the family had major ownership of Fiat in Italy. They also had a house in the East Hampton, on Georgica Pond on the Wainscott side in the Georgica Association. Whittle married her. And this led to a third change.

With all his success, Whittle still lived modestly in Knoxville in the small cabin in Log Haven. He loved it there and considered it his home. Now, however, with the prospect of the start of a family, he would move. He and Priscilla went house hunting in the Hamptons and when they were shown the big mansion on the east side of the Pond by Sotheby's, they bought it.

"You can boat on this pond," Chris says. Then he points down toward the crashing surf. "In fact, on many days we put up the sail on the two catboats, and we just sail across the pond and run 'em into the sand. And that's how we go to the beach."

That same year, 1987, there was still another change. Whittle realized he not only published for groups, he published for groups in specific places. The waiting rooms of doctors offices. The school room. Why not move out of the print media entirely? His company could put satellite dishes on the roof and provide cable wire and television sets in the school rooms and waiting rooms. All of his advertising messages and editorial could come in electronically. In 1987, this was a very daring idea. It was daring then and it is daring now. It was also very difficult to bring about. He had to turn his company around one hundred and eighty degrees.

"How do you tell a typesetter that he is now a cameraman? Well, we did it. And we have succeeded with it. We are, today, at 12,000 schools across the country and we have television sets in 350,000 classrooms. Channel One is seen every morning by eight million people. That's forty percent of all the teenagers in America. To give you an idea of the scope of Channel One, on a good day MTV has 160,000 viewers. We have a major impact on the kids in America."

I ask a question I immediately regret. On the other hand, I'm a journalist and this question immediately springs to mind.

"How do you keep bias out of your newscast?" I ask.

"If the schools didn't like what we put on we would be out in a minute," Chris says.

Whittle describes a typical twelve minute news broadcast. "We come on first thing in the morning, right after attendance in home room. For twelve minutes, the kids watch the news. But this is no ordinary newscast. It is a very hip approach. Our anchors and correspondents are ages 18 to 23. What they have to say is designed to pull heads right up off the desks. They use music extensively, they use maps extensively. With most stories we don't assume anything. For example, if there was something in the news on the streets of Moscow we might show a map of Russia with Moscow highlighted, then move in to show the event on the street itself, describing some of the recent history of that city.

"We have one great advantage over regular classic TV news. Our viewers are there yesterday and they will be there tomorrow. So we can take a whole week to develop a particular story. For example, every day at the beginning of this football season, we have featured a different angle on the use of steroids. Getting the news to these kids in this way is a very exciting thing. This year is our first graduating class. And this year, for the first time, our newscast won a Peabody."

Whittle had further success in doctor's offices. In waiting rooms there are TV sets where announcers offer health tips and promote health products. Actress Joan London anchors this service out of a studio on the west coast. A particular product might be described and she might note that if you want still further information about it you can pick up a brochure right next to the TV set.

Whittle found that he could offer a specialized TV channel in a doctor's private office as well. His original system provided just a twelve minute summary of the day's medical news. But it has expanded.

"We are now putting TVs in doctor's offices with computer keyboards. On the screen, there might be excerpts of a speech made by a scientist at a weeklong heart seminar in Sweden. Press one and you will hear the whole speech. Press two and you will receive the text of this speech over the fax. Press three for a list of the seminar's agenda, press four to continue with the news summary."

If this sounds something like interactive television, well, it is. And now Whittle is going to move it into the classroom.

"There is absolutely no reason not to do this. The idea came to me four years ago. I had been asked to join a business roundtable about the future of American education. What could be done? I was asked to attend this roundtable six months ahead of time so it gave me a considerable time to think about it. What I said was that we needed a new Manhattan Project for education. Ideally, this should be done by the Federal Government because they do have the resources. But I think a private company can do it better. In fact, we'll do it. We have six thousand miles of cable we own already in place in the school. We could easily offer an educational network, something that teachers could build a class around. There could be history, poetry, science. One could start with the Kings of England, then punch up a particular king and get an overview of him, then for further interest punch a number for a detailed event that particular king was involved in. Perhaps an interesting work of literature appeared at that time. You could learn about it on the video. And then, for homework, you could read the book."

Whittle took it even a step further than that. He could build the schools themselves, hire the teachers and bring in this exciting new curicculum. This was going to be a huge program. He called it the Edison Project.

Today, the Edison Project, a part of Whittle Communications, is headed up by Benno Schmidt, the former President of Yale University.

"We have modified our original plan. First we thought we would actually build the schools and charge tuition. But then we realized that the schools already exist. Many of them, particularly in central cities, are in great disrepair. We felt that a better thing to do would be to approach the city governments and offer them the opportunity of letting us run some of these schools. We would charge a fee. But we would agree to invest $3.5 million in the school building to bring it into the modern age. We would provide the technology and the curicculum. We would recruit and train teachers to run the school. We would use existing teachers. We have approached 200 cities. We expect to open our first schools in the fall of 1995, one year ahead of schedule."

* * *

That night, back at my home three miles away, I put one of the Whittle tapes in my VCR. I had a choice of two. One was the news tape designed for doctors. Of course I chose to watch CHANNEL ONE. This was a day that Boris Yeltsin walked through the streets of Moscow, shaking hands with the people. On the screen, he could be seen standing in Red Square amidst a crowd of 5000 or so, listening to a symphony orchestra perform on an outdoor stage Peter Ilyitch Tchaikovsky's 1812 Overture. As the cymbals crashed and the cannons fired at the appropriate places in the score, this is what this 19 year old announcer said.

"Russians are once again firing the cannons..."

Here is what I thought. Wow.

July, 1994 (Scheduled)

* * *

In February, 1994, the School Board of Lowell, Massachusetts announced the Edison Project would take over a school in that city in the fall of 1995.

175

Chapter 37

AYA AZRIELANT

The Aya Azrielant jewelry collection was introduced to the world at the Guggenheim Museum on April 29 at a huge gala hosted by the Israeli actor Topol. The collection can now be found at Saks Fifth Avenue, Bloomingdale's and other fine stores, glorious puffs of 18k gold earrings and pendants and other accessories, hollow in the middle and dazzlingly beautiful, perfect for the working woman who wants to make an impression in gold, but doesn't want to deal with the heaviness of it.

Aya Azrielant's designs are from the beach and the sea. Seahorses and starfishes and blowfish. They come from the land of her youth, Israel. And if she and her husband have just completed renovating a great beachfront home in Southampton, well, for Aya, it is, in one sense, a return to the shells and designs of her early years.

Aya Azrielant is President of Andin International, Inc., one of the largest jewelry firms in the U.S., and I met with her in her offices on the fifth floor of the building that the company occupies there in the western reaches of Greenwich Village. I had expected to find a tough Israeli woman — people born and raised in Israel are called Sabras after a kind of cactus that grows in the desert. What I found was a soft, beautiful woman with a sense of humor. The contrast was startling.

"I am the same age as Israel," she says. "I was born on April 1, 1948. Forty days later the Jews in Palestine declared the founding of the State of Israel. It was the middle of a war. When my parents took me from the hospital where I was born on Mount Carmel back to the kibbutz, they took me in an armored car."

They named her Aya. The letters stand for Aretz Yisroel Ahofshit which in Hebrew translates as The Free Country of Israel. It was a small name with only three letters but it was a name with a considerable amount to live up to. She has lived up to it very well.

Aya's family was among the very first pioneers of what was to become Israel. Her grandfather was Dr. Ernst Rappaport and he had come to Palestine from Vienna in 1919. The Rappaports were one of the ten wealthiest families in Vienna at the turn of the century. Only Ernst decided to emigrate to the dusty, hot land that was Palestine. All the rest stayed, and were ultimately murdered in the Holocaust. But in 1920, Dr. Rappaport helped build the very first kibbutz in Palestine.

Where Aya was born and raised, thirty years later, was the kibbutz north of Haifa known as Ramat Yohanan. Back in the late 1940's and through the 1950's and 1960's, Ramat Yohanan was a commune of chickens and goats and fruits and vegetables. Aya's mother worked in the children's house. She was also a dancer and a musician. She played the mandolin. Aya's father worked in the fields and also did the design and construction of the farm buildings. He was also an amateur inventor. He built devices to keep cows inside fences, he designed toys for little Aya. And sometimes he would go to Haifa and return with 8 mm films of Charlie Chaplin and the Three Stooges. These films would be shown to Aya and her friends with the use of a small projector that operated with a hand crank. The films could be shown in fast or slow motion, forward or backward. The children loved them.

If the images seen on the screen were of another world, they were not all that far away. When Aya was five years old, she went with her mother by boat to visit her mother's family in Paris and Grenoble. Now Aya knew that the kibbutz was not all that there was.

The family soon moved off the kibbutz, living at first in a tiny cottage in a small town, then in a larger house in a bigger town near Haifa. Aya's father worked long hours in construction. Aya was sent off to boarding school where, she says with a laugh, she got a degree in raising chickens. At Haifa University, she studied Fine Arts, Literature and the Bible, and she married a poet. She was 20 years old.

"My husband Yechiel was sent to London by the Israeli government as a missionary to recruit more people to come to Israel. I went with him. And I studied film at Middlesex Politechnic in London. When we returned from London I would be a filmmaker. I would make documentaries. I wanted a career, not just to be a homemaker. But I wasn't sure just what that career ought to be. I did know it should be something creative."

Aya had a daughter, Tama, but her marriage fell apart. Back in Israel, on a filmmaking assignment for the national TV station, she met and fell in love with another filmmaker, Ofer Azrielant, who was to become her second — and present — husband. The two of them thought they

177

might do filmmaking and documentaries independent of the dictates of the government. But they didn't have any money or financial backing.

"Our desire to get money together to do filmmaking is how we got into the jewelry business," Aya says. "Ofer's brother Avi worked for IBM and had gotten this idea to set up a business for himself on the side. He didn't want to leave IBM right away so he continued to work there and Ofer and I joined to help him. Avi was importing small quantities of costume jewelry from Providence, Rhode Island, where people were manufacturing things in small studios. This jewelry we sold door to door. Then Avi and Ofer got the idea that we should try to wholesale it to drug stores. And they got me to agree to be the salesperson to go to these drugstores.

"My mother would come over and watch my daughter, and I would head out with a sample case filled with merchandise and I'd sell it to the store owners. They told me the first day that I should sell it for cash only and that cash would entitle the buyer to a 2% discount. I came back at the end of the day with my pockets and hands filled with money. I hadn't known about checks. When they said cash, cash is what I thought they meant."

The experience of selling something and coming back with cash at the end of the day had another meaning for Aya. This was not like art or film where you did something and then never knew for sure if you failed or succeeded. Selling jewelry and returning cash in hand was instant gratification for a job well done. She liked it. And she became good at it.

As the business grew, it was decided that instead of selling just imported costume jewelry from America, perhaps they could sell fine jewelry made in Israel by local craftsmen. Jewelry makers were contacted and arrangements made. And for the first time, Aya became involved in jewelry design. She would take out a pencil and paper and make a sketch. The jewelry makers would carve it in wax, make the molds and do the castings. And her work sold.

The business grew dramatically. By 1981, Andin Ltd. owned eleven stores throughout Israel, went public and had a large manufacturing plant where many designers and jewelry makers worked. It was at this point that the two brothers had a dispute and decided to split up. Basically, Avi remained based in Israel. Ofer and Aya moved to New York where they set up their headquarters for an expansion worldwide. They called their new company Andin International.

"For the first six months here we just studied the market," Aya says. "Who do we want to target? We decided on department stores and we decided that since the jewelry departments there sold either very inexpensive or very expensive jewelry — $1,000 and up — we would focus on the expensive styles and find a way to create them at just $100

178

to $200. We would create a new market, a new niche. Ultimately, we became very successful at this, bringing high quality jewelry to this mid-range."

Andin International has introduced many innovations to the jewelry business. They were the first to offer all jewelry on a full return of purchase basis. If you couldn't sell it, Andin would take it back. It meant that Andin had to be very careful with what they designed and the buyer was freed of the problem. They were the first to tie their computers in to the computers of the retailers so they could spot trends almost instantly. This gave them a considerable advantage. They were the first people in the jewelry business to do billing enclosures. Order forms and merchandise descriptions were included. They introduced coordinated jewelry — earrings, bracelets, pendants and rings that all matched. And they introduced something called "price point." Your choice for $199. Andin grew into a business doing more than a hundred million dollars a year.

"We employ 1,100 people," Aya says. "We have seven offices around the world, in New York, Tokyo, Bangkok, Bombay, Tel Aviv, Antwerp, and the Dominican Republic."

Ofer and Aya bought an apartment on the Upper West Side and, six years ago, began coming out to the Hamptons. They summered in Westhampton Beach for a while, living on the Bay, but then fell in love with Southampton.

"I love the proximity to water, I like the ocean, bike riding, relaxing. My kids like horseback riding."

Ofer and Aya have two children together, Jonathan, age 10 and Lily, age 5. And Aya has raised them without allowing any toy guns or other toy weapons in the house. "In Israel you live every day with war and weapons. Here, I didn't want them."

Aya's eldest daughter, however, graduated high school and decided, before going off to the University of Chicago, to join the Israeli Army.

"I supported her in this," Aya said.

This was in late 1991. In February of 1992, while her daughter was in the Israeli Army, the Gulf War broke out and SCUD missiles began raining down on Tel Aviv. Aya was terrified. She phoned her daughter and found that she too was terrified. So she flew to Tel Aviv to be with her.

"Practically nobody was flying commercially to Israel that week. Too dangerous. The only other person on my plane was Dr. Ruth. It was just the two of us, the pilot and the crew."

Aya stayed at the Hilton in Tel Aviv. The SCUDs would land with a terrible crash. But amazingly, nobody was killed. She went out to Ramatgan and saw places almost wiped from the earth by the SCUDs. But there were no fatalities.

179

The evening at the Guggenheim on April 29, a benefit for AIDS researcher Dr. Mathilde Krim, was a tremendous success. Accompanying the introduction of the Aya Azrielant collection at this event entitled "Guggenheim in Gold," was an original dance performance choreographed by Daniel Ezralow for dancers and rollerbladers, with visuals designed by Jerome Serlin and Howell Binkley, both of whom had been nominated for Olivier Awards for their sets and lighting of the Broadway production of *Kiss of the Spider Woman*.

As for the collection, one reviewer wrote "Aya has been able to create this breakthrough collection of dazzling earrings and pins using a special state-of-the-art process that allows her to produce jewelry that is not only made completely of gold, but is feather-light, easy to wear and delightfully imaginative."

Look for it in Southampton at Saks.

May 28, 1993

The Aya Azrielant 18K gold collection brought Andin's business to another level by creating a brand name in fine jewelry. The company's jewelry was previously only sold under the name of the store carrying it, without the name brand identification.

By the Spring of 1994 the new line could be found in more than 100 stores in the United States, including Saks Fifth Avenue, Bloomingdale's, Lord & Taylor, Macy's, Rich's and Liberty House. It will soon be seen in Japan and Europe.

Chapter 38

STEPHEN RUBIN

I am in the office of Stephen Rubin, the President of Doubleday Books, and I am seated with him, not at his desk but in comfortable easy chairs that are at the other end of the room, and as Mr. Rubin has had to take an important telephone call here — there's a phone on the coffee table — it has given me the chance to look around. There are a few works of art are on the wall, a rather spectacular view down to Fifth Avenue out the windows, and Stephen Rubin himself. He is a handsome man, about fifty, in terrific condition. He is full of energy and, at this particular moment, full of patience as he deals, long distance, with a negotiator somewhere out in the Midwest. The negotiator has been meeting with an author.

"Well, look, you don't have to appear too eager. So she didn't respond to a million. So what? You don't have to go up to two million right away. What would be wrong with a million and a quarter? Or a million and a half. Look, I know you are in jet lag. Think it through. You don't have to rush this thing. And yes, I know she's talking to the competition. Just take your time."

Rubin hangs up, a sparkle in his eyes. This is one of the things they hired him for, two years ago. To find best-selling authors, negotiate with them, and publish their books under the Doubleday imprint — one of the leading hardcover publishing houses in the world.

His prior credentials were at Bantam Books, where for five years he arranged for the publication of best sellers such as *Destiny* by Sally Beauman, *Free To Be...A Family* by Marlo Thomas, *The Autobiography of Patty Duke*, the best-selling novels of Jonathan Kellerman and many, many others. And according to the press release issued at his appointment, he is considered by his peers to be a team player. "He is recognized as that special publishing professional who gets as much satisfaction guiding people with the follow-through of their work as he does nurturing his own manuscripts," they wrote.

Stephen Rubin has been coming out to the Hamptons since 1966, specifically to Hampton Bays and specifically to the same house, and I intended to get to that. First, however, I asked him about his background, his growing up.

"I grew up in the Bronx. My dad was a metal goods manufacturer, my mom a housewife. But I was eager to get out into the world, and so I left the house as soon as I could."

He got a stipend to attend NYU, found someone downtown who desperately needed a roommate, and went off to college. Two miles from home. But it might as well have been a thousand miles.

"I was a rotten student," he says. "My only interest was in working for the school newspaper, the *Washington Square Journal*. I remember one time I was alone in the office and a call came in that somebody had jumped off a roof. I went out, no credentials, and covered the story. And journalism was in my blood."

He decided on a career path. He would be a Serious Journalist. One summer he worked for UPI as a caption writer. At the newspaper he became editor in chief, completely redesigning it ("we ripped off the *Herald Tribune*"), adding record reviews, winning awards. He was there when Kennedy was assassinated and wrote an editorial. He was out to Kennedy Airport — then Idlewild — to see the arrival of the Beatles.

After graduation from NYU he took a graduate degree in journalism from Boston University, then returned to Manhattan to work once again for UPI. For five years, he did pieces for a service that supplied features to the rotogravure sections of Sunday newspapers, interviews with performers and celebrities such as Judy Garland, Marlene Dietrich, Gregory Peck and Leontyne Price.

"I was considered a bad boy," he says. "I'd get them to say things they hadn't intended to say and later regretted."

In 1969, they closed the section and Rubin, having already established his reputation, became a freelancer. Most notably, he did profiles of classical music artists for the *New York Times*, His editor was Seymour Peck and his pieces brought the classical music section, for the first time, to the front of the Arts and Leisure section.

During this period he met Cynthia Robbins, the woman who has become his lifelong companion. Cynthia was a public relations rep for numerous classical music artists (she is now a literary agent), and, as they attended concerts together, she because she represented the performers and he because he had written a profile for the *Times*, romance bloomed.

Ms. Robbins, back in 1963, had purchased a small house off Springville

Road about five blocks from the Montauk Highway. It had cost $12,500 at that time, an amount even a young person just out of college could afford, and Ms. Robbins occasionally invited people out for the weekend. On one of those weekends, one of her guests was Stephen Rubin.

In 1976, Rubin founded an organization which made a considerable stir in the city. He called it WRITERS BLOC, and it consisted of a group of freelance writers who would meet once a week to propose stories to various publications.

"We signed on different publications. This was a serious attempt by authors to create their own syndicate," Rubin says.

They started with six. Soon there were fourteen, including the *Los Angeles Times*, the *Chicago Tribune*, the *Toronto Star* and the *Washington Post*. Some of the members of the syndicate included Guy Flatley and Helen Dudar. They got an office at 23rd and Lexington and they hired a kid out of journalism school to run it.

"I said I would run it for a year for free," Rubin told me. "In fact I ran it for four years for free. We were well connected and we could deliver. Soon there were 24 newspapers. And then one day, I got a call from *Vanity Fair* magazine offering me an editorship. This was to be the revival of the old *Vanity Fair* and according to Richard Locke, the editor-in-chief, there were to be six editors in six different fields working a round table. They wanted me to be one and they offered me good money. I figured it was time I became a full-fledged adult."

As it turned out, however, the early years of *Vanity Fair*, with Rubin as one of the six, were a virtual disaster.

"They couldn't decide what the magazine ought to be. There'd be Debra Winger and her dog as one photo and there would be, shoulder to shoulder with it, an entire novella by Gabriel Garcia Marquez. The affair foundered. And pretty soon there were new editors and I was the only one left from the old guard. My days were numbered."

Rubin realized that he was at a turning point in his life. Robbins was extremely supportive, he says. And he took his time. He talked with the *Washington Post* and the *Los Angeles Times*. And more and more he realized that Journalism was not what he wanted to do.

"I got a call from Bantam Books. They had a job for me as an editor."

He was a natural at it, and his career took off like a shot. The rest is history.

I did ask Rubin about Jacqueline Kennedy Onassis, a sometime visitor to the Hamptons, who works full time as an editor at Doubleday.

"She is a wonderful person. She publishes Bill Moyers, books by Andre Previn. She has very eclectic tastes. But she takes totally seriously what she does."

A tree came crashing through the living room of the house in Hampton

Bays in a storm in 1987. Rubin and Robbins took it as a sign to rebuild. They rebuilt up and out. Today it is a three bedroom, two bath house with a gym, a swimming pool, plenty of guests, and, Rubin tells me very pointedly, no answering machine.

"Cynthia comes out Friday morning. I go out later in the day. Cynthia is there the whole summer. I come out for two weeks."

He prefers the house in the off-season.

"I am not part of that publishing scene centered in East Hampton and Bridgehampton," he says pointedly. "In the summertime, I never go anyplace. I used to go to the beach all the time. Now I sit by the pool. We have a beautiful garden. I exercise in the gym. Cynthia and I have both become serious exercise people. It has changed my life."

In the off-season, they take walks on the beach. they go out to restaurants. He's a member of the Hampton Athletic Club (HAC) in East Quogue where he plays tennis.

"The Hamptons to me is peace," he says. Both he and Cynthia read a lot. And of course they still go to performances together back in the City.

At Doubleday, Rubin has shepherded numerous books to the bestseller list. These include *There Are No Children Here* by Alex Kotlowitz, *Customers For Life* by Carl Sewell, *The Popcorn Report* by Faith Popcorn and one of the very best sellers of the year, more than 40 weeks on the best seller lists, *The Firm* by John Grisham.

September 4, 1992

184

Chapter 39

TOM PAXTON

Tom Paxton, the folksinger, the bohemian, the rebel, the man who has produced over thirty albums of music so scathing that conservative congressmen turn apoplectic with rage, leads a personal life so upright and decent that it is almost scandalous.

In the early 1960's, as a rising young folk music star in Greenwich Village, he met a young woman and married her. Five years later, he moved to a leafy home in East Hampton on one acre, and twenty five years after that, after concerts in front of screaming fans at Town Hall, Carnegie Hall, Avery Fisher Hall, Royal Albert Hall and at stages in towns and cities all around the world, he is still here. Tom is in his early fifties and Midge is in her late forties, they have raised two daughters who are now at Harvard and Skidmore, they have a lawn and a swimming pool and some gardens, and if you see someone that looks like Tom Paxton in a track suit jogging past the Catholic Church, Guild Hall or the Maidstone Club in East Hampton most mornings, well, that's him.

"I try to run every day," he told me. "I have a bunch of different routes. I go through the park by the A&P. I go down to the ocean. I'll run three to five miles."

He's been in the Stephen Talkhouse footrace at Ashawagh Hall. One year he entered the Dock Race in Montauk.

We are sitting, Tom Paxton and I, on a brick deck by the swimming pool in back of his home. There are lounge chairs, a telephone (which rings once while we are there — a call from his agent), there are shades trees, a picnic table, and there is silence. Hedges and foliage border the property all the way around and it seems almost an intrusion that I, an interviewer, have come here to this private place.

"I love being home," Tom Paxton says. "I'm on the road playing about half the time. The rest of the time I am here. I walk into town. I check the mail. I come back and I go upstairs and work on some songs."

For twenty three years, since Tom and Midge first bought this house a short walk from downtown East Hampton, Tom Paxton has been writing his songs in a study upstairs. He has no regular pattern but he kind of keeps at it on and off all day. He'll jog, read the paper, make some phone calls, return to the work. Once, about six years ago, he read an article in a newspaper that the total number of practicing lawyers in America had passed the one million mark. He went upstairs and with his guitars and computers up there composed a waltz called "One Million Lawyers." It became the lead song in his best selling album *One Million Lawyers and Other Disasters*.

In ten years, we are going to have one million lawyers, one million lawyers, one million lawyers. How much can a poor nation stand?

"Does every idea you get turn into a song?" I asked. "Or what percentage of what you start on turns into something?"

"Oh, if I get a keeper twenty percent of the time I'm happy," he told me.

Before I came to this interview, I invaded my record and tape collection and pulled out something I had bought ten years ago called *The Paxton Report*, and played a bit of it, just to refresh myself with the flavor of the work of an extraordinary man, as if I needed any.

For the few of you not familiar with the songs of Tom Paxton (there must be some), I'll review some of the songs this man wrote for this album. They were written at the end of the Jimmy Carter era. A bit dated. But boy they still hold up:

"I'm Changing My Name To Chrysler" (The government bailout): *I'll tell some power broker, what they did for Iaccoc-er, is perfectly acceptable to me.*

"I Thought You Were An A-rab." (Abscam): *When you handed me the bag of cash, I accepted with a wink, you can catch it on the evening news and I'm headed for the clink.*

"All Clear In Harrisburg" (Three Mile Island): *We might grow us some feathers, just like a lark, stand in the fountain and light up the park.*

"Be A Sport Afghanistan (The 1980 Olympics): *Just because you lost some freedom it's not sporting to complain, still you got an invitation and we're happy to explain, that the Russians will take you there by train. You'll be runnin' round Siberia when they come."*

* * *

Tom spent his early years in Chicago, the youngest of four children and the son of a man in the manufacturing business. When he was ten years old, however, his father's health failed, the business was sold, and the family moved to a small town in Oklahoma, Bristow, where Tom's aunt lived. His father died soon thereafter, and his mother raised him and his brother and sisters modestly on the insurance and the inheritance from the business.

Tom is basically the product of small town midwestern America. He played his first instrument, a trumpet, in the high school band in Bristow. And one summer at church camp, there came a turning point.

"There was a man there who had a ukulele. He played 'Five Foot Two, Eyes of Blue,' and he played 'Ain't She Sweet,' and I thought this is GREAT. How LONG has this been going on. I was sixteen."

His aunt bought him a ukulele and he learned to play these songs. And then, after somebody sat on his ukulele and broke it, his aunt gave him and old guitar. Six strings instead of four.

"I already had a running start with the guitar. I knew four strings from the ukulele. Now there were just two more. I have spent the last thirty years trying to integrate those last two strings."

Three years later, Tom Paxton sat in the back row of an Elizabethan literature class at the University of Oklahoma and on his college note paper he composed his first song. An authentic Elizabethan murder ballad. It was, he says, the very worst song ever composed and certainly the world did not need one more Elizabethan murder ballad. But it was a start.

There was another turning point.

After college — he got a Bachelor of Fine Arts degree in Drama — he joined the Army and got sent to basic training in Fort Dix, New Jersey. This was in 1960 when joining the Army was mandatory, but one option was to serve six months and then go into the reserve. Paxton, serving his six months at Fort Dix, would take his weekend passes in Manhattan. Greenwich Village to be exact.

"It was the height of the coffee house era. The women wore black tights, the men wore black t-shirts. We sat in coffee houses with names like Rienzi's and Figaro's on MacDougal Street and we played chess and we drank cappucino and we listened to folk singers and pondered the meaning of it all. It was, for me, a form of heaven. I began composing, and playing, my folk songs."

Discharged from the Army, Paxton packed up his duffel bag in Fort Dix and moved, like a shot, to Greenwich Village. He got a job. For ten dollars a night, the coffee house known as the Gaslight hired him to sing and play as part of the midnight to 6 a.m. shift.

"I thought, what could be better than this? I composed a song called 'The Marvelous Toy' which became a big hit. Ten dollars a night. The only trouble I had was finding the time to spend this much money."

Paxton lived in the Village and played in the clubs for four years. And then, as a successful New York City folk singer with a following, he became entitled to an album. It came out on the Electra label. It sold well. And then there were more, each with new original Tom Paxton songs, each one designed, as Tom says, "to keep me off the White House guest list."

He wrote "Ramblin' Boy", which the Kingston Trio made into a hit. He wrote "Bottle Of Wine", another hit, "Wasn't That A Party" which the Irish Rovers turned into a hit, and he wrote "The Last Thing On My Mind" which was made into a hit by Peter Paul and Mary and later, by Neil Diamond. "Going To The Zoo" is an early composition but recently recorded by many in the children's music community, including Raffi.

The move to the Hamptons came in 1967. He and Midge had spent the preceding summer out here. And then that winter, they returned to their apartment after taking their one and a half year old daughter to Washington Square Park in her stroller and noticed there was a ring of soot around her nostrils.

We can do better than this, they thought.

And so they have. The girls went through John Marshall School, high school and Kate, 21, is now a senior in college studying art history, and Jennifer, 24, is married, and a graduate student in Medieval Studies in Cambridge.

The future? Some children's tapes and books — there are already four out by Morrow, and more albums, probably at the current rate one every ten months.

"I've been writing songs for thirty years. I'll never stop doing what I'm doing. It makes me happy."

You can hear Tom Paxton performing at the John Drew Theatre at Guild Hall in East Hampton on September 22, two shows, two and four in the afternoon. But don't except too much biting satire. It's a show for the kids.

September 21, 1990

Chapter 40

LANCE LESSMAN

There are a lot of beach bums in their twenties and thirties in the Hamptons. Most of them drive an old jeep, have a pretty girl friend, go to the beach as much as possible and try to keep their lives simple. They might work at a tennis club or a golf course. At night they might pick up money washing dishes in a restaurant.

Someone told me about a kid whose become a different sort of beach bum. He also has a jeep and a pretty girl friend and he tries to spend as much time on the beach as possible. However, where the other kids had gone off to Community College or a State School, he got an undergraduate degree at Harvard and an MBA in Finance from Stanford. In one room of this little beach cottage he has rented in Southampton, a room where the sliders open right out onto the deck, he's installed a computer and several phone lines and a fax. Instead of washing dishes, he moves about fifty million dollars around each day in the financial markets. A couple of million of this is his own, made from wise investments he's made since he was little. (He bought his first stock at the age of 12.) The rest is money placed in his hands by about a dozen rich friends who want to see what he can do with it. In the last two and a half years, he has done extremely well.

I called Lance Lessman last Thursday, the day Iraq invaded Kuwait. "Why don't you come by tomorrow?" he said. "The market is reacting badly to the invasion. I'd just as soon turn the machine off and go to the beach. Come around noon and we'll have lunch at the Bath and Tennis Club."

Lance has rented a cottage in the Murray Compound. This is an enclave of oceanfront beach houses built in the 1920's at the end of a private road with a security guard at the entryway. It is perhaps the most exclusive section of Southampton. It is to Southampton what the Kennedy Compound is to Hyannisport.

So this is what a beach bum lives like when you add a whole bunch of zeros to his net worth. Indeed, the obligatory open jeep was not old and beat up but brand new. There was a hammock, a slate deck, a mowed lawn framing about a hundred and fifty feet of beachfront. Dunes. And the beach and surf beyond.

We rattled up the gravel drive. I knew the house. It belongs to Peter Sichel, President and CEO of Sichel & Sohn Wine Importers of Manhattan. A small stucco and slate beach house indeed all on one floor. He'd rented it this summer to Lance Lessman and his girl friend.

We made introductions all around there on the lawn. Lore Dorr is about 25, tanned, blond, from a family that has a plantation in Beuford, South Carolina. Lance is about 34, thin, wiry, dark haired. He wears shorts and a shirt. He offers us drinks, and scurries around looking for a gin and tonic for my girlfriend Susyn and a rum and coke for me.

"What we could do is hang around here for a little while, I could show you the machine, and then we could go for lunch," Lance says.

We head over to the room with the machine in it. The girls veer out to the slate deck and sit down out there with their drinks to talk about whatever girls talk about. The machine is guy stuff.

Lance turns it on. It's an IBM computer, 386 chip, high speed, and it begins to light up with all sorts of colorful numbers and abbreviations and statements. PLEASE STAND BY. PROCESSING. It sits on a desk messy with letters, faxes and newspapers. There are three telephones.

"How's the Dow?" I ask.

I'm trying to be hot stuff. I'm referring to the Dow Industrial Average on the New York Stock Exchange.

"The Dow is down 63 points," he says, pointing to a little number in the corner. As we speak it drops to minus 66, then minus 67.

Lance turns his attention to some other numbers.

"Here, wait a minute, let me punch up a couple of things, see how some of these stocks are doing."

He presses some keys and watches the screen for a few moments, grunting at this and that. Then he punches up something else.

"Look at this," he says. "I go into this file and I get the news up to the minute. Everything that's happening right now."

"What's happening in Kuwait?" I asked.

He presses some more keys. A whole news story comes up that says President Bush and all western leaders condemn the invasion. There are fears the Iraqis might invade Saudi Arabia.

"Nobody's doing anything," he says. "Tough stuff. Let's turn it off and get some lunch."

We get everybody together, walk down the lawn to the jeep and pile in. The girls in back. Lance and I in front. Lance tells me a bit about himself and about what he does. He's Manhattan born and raised, his late father President of a publicly traded company, his step father a hotel and resort developer. He's come to the Hamptons every summer since he was 5 years old. Four years ago he bought oceanfront property on Meadow Lane, but he hasn't built yet though he has architectural plans. He rents.

He's been with Lore several years. Two years ago, he got a group of investors together with a stake of a million dollars, rented an office in the Seagrams building, and began playing the stockmarket.

Two weeks after he was in business, the stock market crashed. He lost about 20% of the stake. But then, buying and selling, buying and selling, talking on the phone to the traders on the floor, he brought it back. By the end of the first year the investment had risen 50%. At the end of the second year an original investment had risen another 50. Lots more people had climbed aboard.

Lance told me about his third year, the present year which has gone through nine months and is down about 10%.

"It's a matter of making an adjustment," he said. "My title is 'special situation/risk arbitrage investor.' I deal in companies that are asset-rich. Before a year ago, these companies did very well buying and selling one another and if you picked your way in and out you could do quite well. One can still make money in it, but its a matter of getting out of one sort of thing and getting into another. It's a different kettle of fish."

I indicated that I thought I knew what he was talking about.

"And you can run the whole business right here? Right in South-ampton?"

"Certainly over the summer. Over the next decade I see the Hamptons becoming another Greenwich, excepting December through March. Many of the people in the New York region who can dictate their day to day whereabouts already have summer homes in the Hamptons. It's a very easy transition. All you have to do is bring a few more clothes, install a phone system, a computer and fax, and you can work right out here. About the only thing else you might need is a secretary and files and that could be done from an office you're tied in with right in the village."

"Are people doing this now?"

"Well, I am, during July and August. I know of another fellow in Sagaponack who is doing it on the beach. But he has lots of little kids, and he moved his office inland I think."

We had been riding down Gin Lane, now we turned in between some hedgerows to where we were going for lunch. The thok of tennis balls, sounds of children splashing in a pool, rumble of the surf. We parked. And it was here, as we were walking down the brick walk to the outdoor cafe overlooking the beach, that I saw that Lance had not given up his electronic connection to Wall Street. He had a tiny black telephone in his right hand.

We checked in with a maitre' d who said there was a bit of a wait, and we settled in for a few minutes at the bar and ordered drinks. Children were running in and out of the surf. Girls in bikinis were walking by. Lance looked worried.

"This doesn't work," he said. He was pressing various buttons on the phone.

"Ask me a stock price," I said.

Lance hesitated. Then he got it. "International Harvester," he said.

"Sixty four, down a half," I said happily.

"I wish it was sixty four," he said. He tried a few more buttons. "All I can get is Roam," he said.

"Rome? Italy?"

"No. R. O. A. M. It's a form of search."

We got a table and we sat down. Magnificent view, cool breeze, shrimp salad, salad with sesame and Thai dressing. Lovely stuff. We ordered. And then Lance got his telephone to work.

"Lance please put that away," Lore said.

Lance ignored her, writing down some numbers on a piece of paper. His complexion had turned ashen.

"You know you're not supposed to be doing this," Lore persisted.

"I've only done this once before in a year," he said. He wrote down some more numbers. "I don't care." Then he wrote down some more numbers.

"I have to go," he said. "I'm terribly sorry. The market is collapsing. I must be by the machine. I'm sorry to ruin lunch."

He stood up. I was right with him.

"I'll go with you," I said. "I'll pick up my car at your house, come back here and we'll finish lunch. And we'll have them pack a lunch and bring it back to you."

"If I can eat anything."

We walked at a brisk pace out of the club and out toward the jeep in the parking lot.

"Market is down over 150 points," he said.

In other words, it had fallen almost a hundred points while we were driving to the club. No wonder he was upset. I did some mental calculations. The Dow is usually about 2800. Dropping 150 points is a loss of about 5% of its value. And if Lance were dealing with $50,000,000 of everybody's money, then since I'd spoken to him yesterday he had lost $2.5 million, two thirds of which was during the drive to lunch.

"Ever wonder how people could jump out of windows in the Crash of '29?" I asked.

Lance said nothing.

"Well, this is nothing like the big crash in 1987," I said. I was trying to cheer him up. "How many points did it drop then in one day?"

"About 400," he said. "I guess the question is whether they can stop it. But it is in free fall."

We got back to the beach house, and Lance scrambled up the lawn ahead of me, ran inside and turned on the machine. He began laughing.

"It's a rally," he said. "They've got it."

I knew where to look for the Dow. It read minus ninety. On the way back the market had rallied sixty points. The phone rang.

"No, I'm here," Lance said over the telephone. "I went out for lunch for awhile. But I'm back now."

He listened for a few seconds, then said goodbye and hung up.

"I'll stay here a few minutes," he said. "Things have settled down. There may be some interesting opportunities. But maybe I'll be back for lunch."

He never was. I left, drove back to the beach club, we finished lunch and we brought one order, wrapped in silver foil, back with us in the jeep. Lance was heavy into concentration on the machine on our return.

Well, I thought, he isn't your usual beach bum, but then this isn't your usual Wall Street day. I might try to catch him on a more normal day.

Later in the afternoon, I called Lance to thank him for lunch. (It had been taken care of, the waiter said, when I tried to pick up the check).

"Actually, I should thank you," he said. "If we hadn't gone to lunch, I might have panicked and done some very stupid things and lost a lot of money."

I thought about this. Appetizers worth hundreds of thousands, main courses worth millions. I figure Lance owes me.

August 1990

Chapter 41

Fred W. McDarrah

LARRY KRAMER

I am sitting in the East Hampton kitchen of writer Larry Kramer and he is serving tea and apples. We talk for about two hours and he tells me about the various books and plays he has done, about the group ACT UP he had founded, about what it is like to be homosexual in America and that he himself has been HIV positive since 1988. It is an emotional interview. He is a man of passions and he ranges over a wide variety of subjects. It is also a conversation interrupted by three phone calls, all of which he answers animatedly, raising the aerial on the cordless phone, leaping about, pushing on his wire rimmed glasses, running upstairs to set the fax. All of these calls are about his current play, the smash hit autobiography *The Destiny of Me*, currently playing at the Lucille Lortell Theatre in Manhattan.

"How's the house tonight?" he asks during one phone call. The answer pleases him. There are some people coming with passes. He doesn't know them. Where should they be put? "In the balcony," he says.

Hanging up after another phone call, he tells me that the call was from his director and that the play has apparently been chosen by *Time* magazine in their annual year-end roundup of "The Best" in America. "I haven't got the details," he says. He is a happy man.

He asks me how I enjoyed the play. My wife and I had seen it two nights earlier. I told him it was wonderful and moving and extraordinary which it was and he likes that too.

Larry Kramer's interest in literature and theatre began when he was seven years old. Saturday mornings he would go to Sunday school at the Washington Hebrew Congregation. After school, he would go to a matinee. By himself.

"I saw all the different touring companies at the National Theatre. I saw Uta Hagen and Anthony Quinn in the touring company of *A Streetcar Named Desire* at the Shubert. And I went to the Arena Theatre, which may have been the first theatre in the round in America."

His home life growing up in Washington, D. C. was a disaster. His father, an attorney working in a government customs office, was a tyrant at home who constantly demeaned his son. His mother, apparently trying to compensate, was smothering. The net effect, an environment of brutal intimidation and control, created a very difficult childhood for this small and sensitive boy.

He went to Yale, majored in English Literature and was in the Yale Glee Club.

"Yale was not my favorite place. It was a jock school back then in the Fifties. I was no genius academically and I was certainly no athlete. If I couldn't have sung at Yale I think I would have killed myself, successfully killed myself, that is."

The correction comes because he DID try to kill himself. And the event is in his new play.

"When did you learn you were gay?" I ask.

"In eighth grade. When I was a freshman at Yale I told my older brother. My mother learned about it when I was thirty. My father died unenlightened when I was 35."

Years after college, when he was 43, he wrote a smash best seller novel entitled *Faggots*. It was published all over the world and sold millions. This was in the late 1970's in the middle of the sexual revolution.

"At the time, the Playboy philosophy ruled all," he says. "There was tremendous peer pressure to outperform everyone else. Both gay and straight. Well, I wanted more than that. I wanted a true love. Everybody I knew wanted that. But having so much sex made love impossible. And so I wrote *Faggots* which was a condemnation of promiscuity. This was very controversial."

"I remember all that promiscuity in the straight world at that time," I say. "I didn't know about the gay community."

"Promiscuity was all we had. We had no rights. We couldn't will property or inherit property. We couldn't marry. We weren't allowed to raise children. We weren't even allowed to be next of kin in a hospital. We had nothing. But we did have our penises. So we tried to make a virtue of it and it backfired."

In 1957, this slender, mixed up young man graduated Yale with his degree in English Literature. He got a job as a messenger boy for the William Morris Agency, but they fired him. They thought he was too pushy. Next, he saw an ad in the Help Wanted section of the Sunday

Times for a trainee at a motion picture company. He applied. It was for Columbia Pictures. And it was no training program. They wanted him to operate a teletype machine.

It is often said that talent is one thing but luck is another. The job with the teletype, it turned out, was to be his luck.

"At first, I thought I'd turn the job down," he says. "It was too demeaning operating a teletype machine. But the head of Personnel, Gloria Weinstock, told me 'Larry Take This Job, Trust Me. I Can't Tell You Why.' I took it."

The whole thing became quickly and amazingly apparent. Several years before, the President of Columbia Pictures had been Harry Cohn who was, among other things, a penny pincher. He didn't like people in the New York office making all these expensive telephone calls to the West Coast. So he found a cheaper way to communicate. It could be done by teletype. So he had the teletype put in the office right next to his own. He'd keep an eye on it.

"Cohn was gone," Kramer says, "but here I am, right out of college, in control of the communications of all the Vice Presidents of Columbia Pictures. They all have to come to me. I am right next to the new President, Abe Schneider. I get to know Mr. Schneider and I get to know everybody else too."

Kramer remained in this job for two years. He lived in Greenwich Village, just a short bus ride to work. But in 1961 the government of Great Britain, still recovering from the bomb damage of World War II, passed laws to attract the film making business. A tax would be charged on every ticket sold at every British theatre. The tax would be given directly to any studio producer making a film in England. Columbia opened an office in London. And Kramer was asked if he'd like to go and be a production executive.

"My job was to find stories, writers, scripts, books to adapt, directors and producers and put them all together in various combinations to get them to make movies. I stayed in London ten years, from 1961 to 1970 and we made wonderful productions. *Lord Jim*, *The Guns of Navarrone*, *Dr. Strangelove*, *The Bridge Over The River Kwai*. When I first got there, there was still war damage all over London. My office even had some. The metal window frames were distorted. You couldn't even close them all the way. I worked in a coat.

"This was also a time of big change for me. I was psychoanalyzed, five days a week, on a couch. I realized I wanted to be a writer, but was afraid to do it. So I wrote a screenplay."

Kramer took on one of the most difficult of books. He decided to make a movie out of D. H. Lawrence's *Women in Love*. He went to his studio — he was working for United Artists by this time — and they approved it on a budget of $1.5 million. It came in at $1.2 million.

"I got an Oscar nomination for writing *Women in Love*. Glenda Jackson won an Oscar. It also starred Alan Bates. All together there were six Oscar nominations. Ken Russell directed it. He is a crazy man. For all the success of the film, I didn't TALK to him after that."

The stunning success of *Women in Love* in 1969, Kramer's first screenplay out of the box, also coincided with the end of the era of great films being made in England. The cost differential was no longer great. The moguls wanted to build up Hollywood again. And so Kramer took this opportunity, riding the success of *Women in Love* to return triumphant to America.

"I had been away so long. I missed the Sixties which were a mess, but I'd missed them anyway. I came to New York and DROVE across country to the Oscar nominations."

Returning to America, however, was not as easy as he had at first thought. Back in New York City, he found himself confused and depressed. He hardly knew anybody.

"Some friends, Ruthie Mitchell and Florence Klotz said, 'Larry, we have a house in Bridgehampton. Go out and live in the house for the winter. Take some time off.' "

It was 1969.

"It was so beautiful here then. Now it is a place to BE, they say, which I hate. It is STILL beautiful here. It just seems nobody notices. In 1969, I stayed at my friends' house in Hayground. Nobody came out that winter, nobody. It was so peaceful. I jogged. I replenished myself, I walked the beaches. On a Saturday night I'd go to the one gay bar in the area, which was known as the Potting Shed, in Sagaponack, and there'd be one other person there."

After that winter, Kramer entered what was surely, for him, one of the most disastrous periods in his life. He decided he would be a screenwriter. And he offered himself up for hire to the movie studios.

"I made a lot of money in the Seventies," he says. "Because of *Women in Love*, I was thought of as a person who could lick problem books. I was paid well, but none of these projects got made. When you are a screenwriter, you are lucky if one out of a hundred gets made. They pay you like a king and treat you like a slave. A grotesque feeling. I remember one time, I came in and the producer's secretary was rewriting my scenes from the day before. The producer's secretary! And I couldn't do a thing about it."

Kramer would fly to Hollywood and they would put him up in a suite at the Beverly Wiltshire. He was hot.

"Once I was at the Beverly Wiltshire and these producers showed me this script that I absolutely did not want to do. So I told them no. So they offered me more money. I told them no again, so they offered me still more money. I finally agreed to do the screenplay after they offered me $200,000, plus six round trips to London where I still had so many friends, plus a car and a suite of rooms and all expenses in Los Angeles. So I wrote it."

"Was it ever produced?"

"No. Yes."

"What was the name of it?"

"I'm not going to tell you."

Faggots was published by Random House for the New American Library in 1978. It was, he says, what he did when he "finally had the courage to break away from lotus land." He had given up screen-writing, never to go back to it.

Kramer took an apartment in New York City. He lives there to the present day.

Beginning in 1979, Kramer began to see that his friends were dying mysteriously. Nobody knew what they were dying of. The doctors were puzzled. And then, in 1981, they discovered the disease called AIDS.

"I co-founded the Gay Men's Health Crisis in 1981," Kramer says. "Originally it was supposed to be an activist organization, not the Red Cross kind of thing that it has become today. I wanted somebody to DO something. You didn't have to be very intelligent to put two and two together to see what was going to happen if nothing was done."

"What SHOULD have been done?" I ask.

"The people needed to be warned, given the facts. But it never happened. This was the year, you may remember, that there was Legionnaires Disease and there was Toxic Shock and there was the Tylenol scare. These three were on every TV program. Within 24 hours, everybody in the world stopped buying Tylenol. But in this City, where it had all started to get out of control, there was silence. What needed to be done, basically, was to warn people of the danger and let them make up their own minds. It never happened.

"People thank me today when I speak. My message was Learn the Danger and Cool it. Those who didn't are dead those who did are alive."

In 1985, Kramer wrote the play *The Normal Heart*. Today it is being made into a movie, due out next year, starring Barbra Streisand. In 1987 he formed ACT UP, the AIDS protest group that sometimes leads protests and performs acts of civil disobedience. In 1988 he wrote the book *Reports From The Holocaust* and in 1991 he completed his current play *Destiny of Me*.

He is currently working on a book.

"Probably my last," he says.

December 18, 1992

198

Chapter 42

CHRISTIAN WOLFFER

Christian Wolffer, at 54, is one of the most successful businessmen in the Hamptons today. He owns SagPond Stable, a 150 acre property in Sagaponack that has a grand prix ring, stabling for 75 horses and a recently completed indoor riding rink that occupies a half an acre — the largest ever built in the Hamptons. He owns SagPond Vineyard, which has its own winemaker and which last year harvested its third crop and turned it into 36,000 bottles of 1992 Chardonnay and Merlot. He also has an extensive international real estate development company called Euro Investors, Inc. which has projects all over the world. It was here, at Euro Investors headquarters in Bridgehampton, that I caught up with Mr. Wolffer to talk to him for an hour or two.

First of all, I should report about the office. It is just the eastern half of a former service station on the corner of Butter Lane and the Montauk Highway. A small plaque by the front door identifies it. Inside, there are fax machines, copiers, secretaries and office managers, maybe six people all together, and they are busy running a nerve center for a giant organization around the world. Eight telephone lines come in. During our interview, Mr. Wolffer was interrupted twice to talk on the phone. And each time he switched to a foreign language, each language different from the other.

"How many languages do you speak?" I asked after the second.

"Many," he twinkled.

I was lucky to be fit in. Though Mr. Wolffer conducts himself in a leisurely manner, he explained that tomorrow he would be going to Atlanta, the following week he would be in Mexico and after Thanksgiving he would be going to Hungary and other spots in eastern Europe. He has numerous developments in eastern Europe.

"How did you ever come to base an international conglomerate in Bridgehampton?" I asked.

"For many years," he said, "we had offices in Manhattan. I had a townhouse in Manhattan too. One day when the children were three and six I realized that since almost all of our projects are in places other than New York, there really was no reason for me to be there. I could move to our farm in Bridgehampton. And if I shut the Manhattan office and the townhouse I could have all the limousines and helicopters I could want."

Christian Wolffer is tall, kindly, almost gentlemanly. He smiles a lot. He is barrel chested and speaks with a German accent. He is the kind of man that young children would climb up on and call papa.

He is from Hamburg. Born in 1938, he was one of four children in a wealthy German family. His father specialized in importing spices from the Orient. There was the main house there in Hamburg, three miles from the City Center. There was a beach house up on the North Sea and there was a farm they owned in the eastern end of the country.

All of this Christian Wolffer talks about but, in fact, only saw in pictures shown to him by his parents. Because when he was just one year old the roof fell in. World War II started and within a very short time he and his three brothers and sisters and his mother and father were to come to live in very dire circumstances.

"Father had us evacuated to a little village on Lake Costanza," Christian says. "He stayed at home in Hamburg, but he did not join the regular army. He was an invalid then and they put him in a uniform and he became part of the home guard. Hamburg was firebombed while we were away. Tens of thousands of people killed. In 1943 we were told we won the war. I was five years old. My mother took us children back to Hamburg. But it was a lie. So we returned again to Lake Costanza."

If times were hard during the war, they got even harder afterwards.

"We lived in basements sometimes. We couldn't go out. All the valuables, all the watches, paintings and so forth were traded for food. A lot of farmers wound up with very valuable pieces. Fur coats and things. Even so, it was very hard for them to feed us through this war."

In 1952, when he was fourteen, his father went bankrupt and Christian Wolffer had to go out and work. He got a job as a trainee at a bank, then a trainee at an import-export company.

"I had one pair of pants, one jacket and two ties," he says.

He became a trainee for a chemical company, BASF, and they transferred him to Mexico.

"I couldn't get a college education," he says. "So what I had to do was be a trainee. I was twenty years old in Mexico City. I made $100 a month the first year, $125 a month the second year, $175 a month the third year. I'd be broke by the tenth of every month and I had to rely for the rest of the month on friends. Of course there was nothing from home.

"What I realized was what my parents had was no more. They would show me the photographs of the big houses and cars. And we were living so totally differently, sharing bedrooms, sharing towels. What were my priorities in life? I became aware that I would need to do something about myself."

Wolffer came to manage a group of salespeople in Mexico. He may have been the youngest sales manager in Mexico. In 1958 he moved back to Germany to take a position in a reinsurance company — this is a company that insures insurance companies — and he learned about risk taking and how to analyze it. Then he went back to Mexico and joined the Intergrafica printing company. He was in charge of a sales force selling printing equipment throughout Mexico, Colombia and Venezuela and he did so well with this that when the company began to go downhill in the late 1960's, he took half ownership of it. He moved to Munich where it was headquartered. And he got married.

"I married a German girl," he says. "We had twins, Mark and Andrea, who are now 26 and living and working in Europe. I was married for four years."

Wolffer went off on his own in 1972. He went to Hong Kong for a few months to expand Intergrafica, and when he got back he had a fight with his partner and he sold out to him. Then, not wanting to compete with him, he decided to start something totally new. He set up his first real estate investment company, and, putting together projects for European investors, moved to Canada.

"At first, I acted as a real estate broker, selling buildings for sale to European investors. Then I began developing commercial real estate projects. I built the first indoor squash and tennis centers in Canada. I built two in Montreal, one in Toronto and one in Edmonton. And I got management people to take care of them."

In 1976, new laws were put into place in Canada making it unadvantageous for Europeans to invest there. The following year Wolffer closed his firm and opened Euro Investors, Inc., with offices in New York and Atlanta. He has been running Euro Investors for fifteen years now.

"We have major land developments in Hawaii, Orlando, Seattle and Mexico," he says. "Also in Hungary where we are doing a redevelopment project. In Manhattan we only did one project you might have heard about. It is Curzon House, located at 6 East 62nd Street. It is a condominium."

As Wolffer stretched his wings worldwide, a small farm in Bridge-hampton, owned by the Janucick family, came to his attention. He bought the fourteen acres of this farm, including some old barns and the farmhouse, for $167,000. This was in 1978.

"I had come out to the Hamptons several times," he says. "It reminded me of a place very similar, in Sylt, on the North Sea. I had wanted a lot of open land. Maybe it was because my parents had open land like this in eastern Germany. It gave me a certain satisfaction."

Wolffer bought more land around this small farm as it became available. Soon, 14 acres had become 150. He hired Dai Dayton as the farm manager.

"She came along when I was advertising for my household," he says. "She answered this ad and told me she had a horse and a donkey and a set of twins and I said I had no barn for the animals but I could put a shelter up in a pasture for them. This was twelve years ago. When it was clear to me it was going to work out I built her a house on the property."

The original farm, back ten years ago, included six horses that Wolffer owned, eight horses boarded in and, beginning in 1984, a tree farm.

"A storm came and killed the tree farm. I was very upset by that. But I thought why not grapes? Really, wine grapes are a weed, a very hardy plant."

Wolffer remarried in 1980, to Naomi, an Englishwoman who he had met in Manhattan. They had two daughters who are, today seven and ten.

"And then I realized I did not have to continue to live in Manhattan. If people wanted to see me they could come on out."

Wolffer says he will never develop his farm. He likes the open land. For the moment, the winery and the horse farm are being supported by Euro Investors. But the way he has set them up he expects that some time soon they will be self supporting.

Wolffer enjoys tennis, skiing and horseback riding. He leads a big social life with clients and investors, in addition to his family life. Favorite restaurants? He mentioned Mirko's in Water Mill, the Old Stove Pub in Sagaponack and the American Hotel in Sag Harbor.

"And my wife's home cooking," he says, "is the best."

November 27, 1992

Chapter 43

CONNIE COLLINS

It must have seemed like a strange marriage. The groom was Paul Brennan, the son of a Bridgehampton potato farmer. The bride was WNBC News reporter, Connie Collins, the perky woman who stood in front of burning buildings, whether in the Bronx or Afghanistan, and spoke into a microphone for the six o'clock news. How could this be?

Well, the marriage has lasted twelve years. And there are two children, Ashley age 11 and Sayre age 8. And now, after spending many years raising their family "together apart," as Connie Collins puts it, they are truly together again. Besides Mrs. Collins' apartment in the city and Mr. Brennan's house in the country, they now work just five buildings apart. Mr. Brennan is a partner in Braverman, Newbold and Brennan Real Estate at the corner of Main Street and Newtown Lane in East Hampton. And Connie Collins is on assignment from NBC, working as Director of Community Affairs and freelance producer for the new East Hampton radio station, WEHM. The offices for WEHM are down by the post office. Literally five buildings away from one of three offices of her husband.

Connie Collins met Paul Brennan through a mutual friend, Marilyn Salinger who worked for WCBS. Ms. Salinger had bought her house from Paul Brennan. Now she was having a dinner party and she invited both Paul Brennan and Connie Collins.

"You're cute," Connie told Paul.

"You're cute too," he said.

The rest is history. Connie Collins says she recognized the same small town person that was in her, the small town person that was in another place in another time, in her early growing up days in Virginia.

* * *

It is not too much to suggest that Connie Collins grew up as the ultimate all-American small town girl. She was born in 1947, and from the day she was born until her graduation from high school and subsequent marriage to her high school sweetheart, she led a very sheltered suburban existence.

"For my first eighteen years, through William Byrd High School, I lived in the exact same house with my parents in the small town of Vinton, Virginia," she said. "Vinton, Virginia, a town so small it shouldn't have had a name."

We are sitting over coffee in a restaurant. She likes her own little anecdote. Her eyes twinkle.

But not only did she live in a small town, she lived for these first eighteen years in a section of Vinton, entirely surrounded by homes built by uncles and aunts and cousins. Her grandfather had bought a two acre parcel adjacent to his every time his wife got pregnant. She got pregnant five times. As these children grew, grandfather gave these parcels to the children. Most of them built homes there and lived in them. Grandfather also bought the side of an adjacent mountain. Breaking this up into lots, he gave these to his grandchildren.

"I grew up with not only my mother and father and older brother, but with all these relatives. My parents and their brothers and sisters hung around together, they played bridge together, went to the local high school football and basketball games together. They always knew where we were and what we should be doing. And a lot was expected of us."

What was expected was success and to remain in the area. Connie became a cheerleader for her high school teams, nicknamed the Terriers. She became editor of the yearbook. And she had a column in the high school newspaper called "Connie's Corner."

"My family wanted nothing more than I should grow up, become a school teacher, get married and raise a family next to grandfather."

But what Connie wanted to do was get on the other side of that mountain. There was a whole world out there, people who talked in foreign languages, had interesting ideas, went about living on this earth in different ways. Connie called it a "lust." A lust for learning, maybe.

Connie tried the proscribed path. Ultimately, she failed. For many years, she was viewed as a big disappointment to her family.

"I remember getting married," she said. "I was twenty and I was marrying my high school sweetheart who had a job working for the county in the next town. I was married at home and there were 11 bridesmaids and I remember standing on my father's arm before the ceremony knowing I had made the wrong decision but I Can't Stop This."

I asked Connie what had become of her first husband. I also wanted to know about what had become of her brother, what her father did and what her grandfather did. All had remained in the fold.

Her older brother was married, divorced and remarried, and now lives in Troutville, Virginia. Her first husband continues as a government employee and lives in Richmond, Virginia. Her father, for his entire life, managed a large cafeteria in Roanoke, Virginia.

"Roanoke, the Star City of the South," she said, twinkling again. "Roanoke has, on top of a hill, the largest man-made star in the world. It is made of neon lights and steel. When somebody died, for example in an auto accident, it would be lit up red. It was, otherwise, white. They also lit it up red for Christmas. For deaths and for Christmas."

Her grandfather, who certainly was an extraordinary man, had been a "small town man with big dreams," Connie said. "He had the first car in town." He had died when she was nine. But his influence lived.

When Connie graduated from high school she did go over the mountain, but not very far over. She went to the University of Richmond. That was where her boyfriend had a job working for the highway department. She majored in journalism and she gained a respect for accuracy in reporting. At the University, she was the student, they selected one a year, to work at the *Richmond News-Leader* as a reporter. She wrote on the women's page. She still remembers her first by-line and the story that was picked up by the Associated Press and sent all over the country. It was called DO BLONDES HAVE MORE FUN?

Graduating, she worked for a while for Blue Cross and hated it. Then she worked as a producer-writer for the consumer affairs show *Tell Doug* on WWBT-TV in Richmond. She would research problems people called in about regarding used cars, wheel-chairs, home appliances. On the air, Doug would solve the problems.

"It was actually Connie solving the problems," she said. "But Doug had the show so it was *Tell Doug.*'"

There was only one woman reporter at the TV station at that time. All the rest were men. But then one day the woman reporter left the station for a job at a bank and Connie Collins, age 23, slipped into her shoes. She became one of the general assignment reporters. She was to stay here for two years.

During this time Connie's marriage began breaking up. She wanted to go off and see the world. He wanted to stay in Richmond. When they finally decided to get a divorce there was the awkwardness of the little house they owned on the tree lined street. It was actually Connie's house, paid for with the money she got by selling the parcel of land on the mountainside her grandfather had given her. That had been her first statement about moving out and seeing the world. Now there was another. The divorce. So it was Ray Collins that moved out.

Connie continued working at the station while living, alone now, at the house she owned. It began to gather, as she put it, assorted baggage and guilt. She rented it out. She took a studio apartment with a kitchenette in Richmond.

In 1973, her college alumni sponsored a twenty-one day trip to Europe to twenty-one different cities. Connie took three weeks off work and went on this tour. And it was while on this tour that a pivotal experience in her life happened. She told me about it, sighing happily at the memory of it.

"I fell in love," she said. "It was on a Greek island and the man I fell in love with was a young Greek doctor, poet, philosopher, carpenter, revolutionary. He asked me to leave the tour and stay with him but I wouldn't. But when I got home to Richmond, he began writing to me. He loved me and wanted me to come back. He wrote again and again. One morning, I got another letter from him. When I arrived at the news room I found the news editor jumping up and down. It had been a slow news day and now there had been a murder. Something to cover. It would do wonders for their ratings. I considered that in one hand I had a letter from a man in a foreign land who loved me and in front of me there was a man jumping up and down because someone had been murdered. I made a decision."

She wrote back that she was coming, she was moving to Greece. She gave notice, wrapped up her affairs in three weeks and flew to Athens to be with him. He was in Athens because, as it turned out, he still had to take some tests to become a full fledged doctor. They stayed there a month. He passed. Now they moved down to a small fishing village for a week to help out with the olive harvest for his 96 year old grandmother.

"We were in a car, driving to Sparta, when we heard on the radio that the students had taken over the university in Athens. We would go to Athens. He was the leader of the student underground."

Connie says that she never did fully learn to speak Greek. She could understand it however. In Athens, as tanks roamed the streets, she was asked to lean out the passenger side window of a car roaming aimlessly up and down residential streets shouting DOWN WITH AMERICA. She refused. Then the government announced that all Americans would have to leave the country. She went, borrowing ten drachmas so she could pay the airport exit tax before boarding the plane to Kennedy Airport.

"I arrived at Kennedy, called my parents to tell them I was okay, borrowed money on my Visa card so I could have some cash and took a taxi to Manhattan. From the window of this cab, the skyscrapers of Manhattan looked terrific. I had come from tanks and gunfire and all this anger. Now there was all this energy and exhilaration. I decided I wanted to be in New York."

It was 1973 and she was 26 years old. She took a room in a town house on Beekman Place, with a Pullman kitchen, a cast iron stove and a roll up mat for sleeping on the floor, and she bought the *New York Times* to look through the want ads. She would try to get back into television.

This wouldn't be easy. She sent out resume after resume and they all came back. She got a job at the American Cancer Society as an assistant director of public relations so she could have food on the table while she looked. She knocked on TV network doors, sent out tapes. But nothing happened. It was her Southern accent, she was told. People don't trust people with Southern accents.

She quit her job and got a temporary job for Christmas at Saks Fifth Avenue. And then one day she met with a friend who worked at WCBS. "Don't say you want to be a reporter," he said. "Everybody wants to be a reporter. Tell them you want to be a researcher, a writer, a producer, anything but be an on-camera reporter."

It was a devious tactic. But it worked. She immediately got two job offers, one at WABC and the other at WNBC. She took the latter. And she has remained there for seventeen years.

At first, she did production, working on the *Betty Furness Show*. But then Jimmy Carter got elected. And she wrote a letter to her superiors suggesting that perhaps people did find credence with Southern accents. They put her on as a weekend newscaster for News Center Four, the first two hour news show in the country. And, oddly enough, it was because she worked the weekend shift that she became nationally known.

"There was a lunatic named Son of Sam running around New York City shooting people. He only killed on the weekend, and it turned out this was his shooting time because he had a crazy Madonna-Whore complex and this is when his victims, lovers, went out on dates. It was the major story in the City."

Connie rented an apartment on Central Park South, where she still lives today. For seventeen years, she has walked to work to the NBC building in Rockefeller Center. She became a general assignment reporter for NBC News and she also did "essays," two or three minute spots where she would focus on a particular topic and do a more in-depth story, one with more human interest, "the other side of the story," she said. People in welfare hotels searching for apartments. Healthy but destitute mothers, fighting fiercely from the gutter to keep custody of their children.

I asked her to describe some of the most striking memories at WNBC during the past seventeen years there.

"I remember the scream of a father when police showed him his daughter's body. It was in Bay Shore. She had been in the wrong place at the wrong time with the wrong man. They had brought her in with a sheet over and she was laid out in the police garage and they had walked him over to it. It was a scream, a pain you hear from your heart.

207

"I remember doing an essay on Gail Rubin, a 39 year old New Yorker who had been killed by terrorists on the beach in Haifa. She had been photographing birds. I went to her parent's Fifth Avenue apartment and her father took me by the hand. Look. This is who they killed, he said, and he showed me a wall of photographs. I know this person, I thought. I felt as though I had a dart shot through my heart. I wrote a letter to the family after filing this report. I went to the funeral. The family read the letter there. They said I was the same person as their daughter."

It got to her. There was no denying it, listening to her talk. She sometimes suffered post traumatic stress syndrome she told me. But she did it. It was her job to do the tough, drug and gunshots and violence stories that pass for the local New York TV news.

And then came the dinner where she met Paul Brennan in 1980. She had been coming out to the Hamptons off and on for half a dozen years by that time, visiting friends, renting, enjoying the sylvan beauty of the place.

"I still remember the first year I came to the Hamptons. It was a blind date. He drove me to the Hamptons for the day, to East Hampton, and I remember us making the turn at East Hampton Town Pond and I gasped at how beautiful it was. I told my date that some day I would live here. This was in 1975."

For ten years, Paul Brennan and Connie Collins lived the following marriage: he'd drive in with the family on Sunday, spend the night and drive out alone on Monday. Then he'd drive in on Friday, pick everybody up and come back out to the Hamptons on Saturday.

They still commute back and forth to the City. But now the focus is changed because 11 year old Ashley is in the Hampton Day School in Bridgehampton and 8 year old Sayre is at the Amagansett Public School.

"I'm so happy to be working with this radio station," Connie said. "It's informing and entertaining and a lot of fun. A lot different than reporting all that carnage. I hope people enjoy us."

June 11, 1993

* * *

Connie Collins is the recipient of the 1994 LTV East End Media Award.

208

Chapter 44

ANTONIO CICCONE

I am sitting in the art studio of painter Antonio Ciccone, age 52, surrounded by much of his work in progress. There are huge canvasses of nudes, ten feet tall, some religious paintings, works of his wife and children. On a wooden box he has set up the obligatory cheese and crackers and red wine for this interview and we share some.

"A book came out this year about my work," Ciccone says. He hands me a huge, coffee table hard cover volume that must weigh over ten pounds. CICCONE it says on the front. Inside are over 800 paintings and photographs, about half in full color. It is an impressive volume.

Outside a tall window, I can hear the motorscooters and traffic on the narrow alley of this street, the Via de Serragli, just a ten minute walk from the Uffizi Gallery and all the Botticellis, Michaelangelos and da Vincis. It is nine thirty in the morning and the Italian city of Florence is already bustling with activity.

The book is another matter. Here is a painting of Larry Rivers of Southampton, here's another of Dr. Ken Cairns of Southampton, here's a photograph of Ciccone at the opening of the Gordon Peavy/Albert Sharp dance studio in East Hampton, here's Ciccone in the art studio of Fairfield Porter. There is an art review from the *New York Times* praising his work, but there are other art reviews from the *Southampton Press* and the *East Hampton Star* and there are by-lines by Ty Stroudsburg-Boracci, Debbie Tuma and Helen Harrison. And now I see posters here in Ciccone's Florence studio and they are in English and they are from the Bologna-Landi Gallery in East Hampton and the Elaine Benson Gallery in Bridgehampton. Antonio Ciccone, born and raised in the south of Italy, is a part of the Hamptons art scene.

There is something else interesting, for me, anyway, and that is that Ciccone and I were born only months apart. When I meet someone almost exactly my twin I am curious about their upbringing. We were both six years old when World War II ended. We both remember Truman and Eisenhower and the Korean War. What was it like for Ciccone? While I was raised in a cushy American suburb with mowed lawns and cars in the driveway, here is what it was like for Ciccone.

"I remember the Americans bombing Foggia, a good sized town on a hillside near our village. I could see the smoke and hear the explosions. But that was the closest the fighting ever got to our village. Neither the German nor the Allied soldiers were particularly interested in us.

"San Giovanni Rotondo was a little, dirt poor farm village in the heel of Italy with carts and horses and chickens and goats running around. I was the oldest of nine children. I lived there until I was fourteen years old."

At fourteen I was an eighth grader at Millburn Junior High in northern New Jersey. Dwight Eisenhower was President.

"My working life started when I was five. My father had a cart and would collect vegetables and other goods from the farms surrounding San Giovanni Rotondo and he would bring them into town and sell them to the merchants there. When I was five he told me if I stayed in town I'd get spoiled. He bought me ten lambs, nine female and one male and he took me and the lambs out to my grandparent's little farm two miles from town — it was not unusual for kids to be raised by their grandparents then — and he told me take care of the lambs and bring them to market.

"I remember when it came time to sell the lambs it was so hard for me. The lambs were my friends. I really had no other friends.

"I started going to school back in San Giovani Rotondo when I was six. The school was near to a convent presided over by Padre Pio and I sometimes went to chapel there. For awhile there was this lady from the north of Italy with a house nearby and she would invite poor children to her home, then to mass, then back to her house for breakfast, and I used to go because of the breakfast which was, to me, a feast. We'd arrive at 4 a.m. and she'd line us up and march us to the convent. We'd return at 6 and have breakfast and she'd march us off to school. That would be at 7:30 a.m.

"When I was twelve, my father decided I was not studious enough for him. I should stay in the town and be a farmer. Have cows. Sell milk. I had other ideas."

Antonio, from as early as he can remember, drew and painted. He'd draw in charcoal on spaghetti paper. He'd paint murals on the sides of walls. Once, he painted a ten foot saint from a little card of the saint handed out in church. But his father did not encourage him. Painting

210

was for people who didn't have anything else to do.

"My studio? It was the stable. I'd work in there with the donkeys and the chickens. My father didn't like it. I'd have to sneak away there."

At the age of twelve, Ciccone figured out a way to make his father happy and at the same time get him to allow him to paint, however grudgingly. He'd be a professional house painter. And then he could paint pictures on the side. At the age of twelve he spoke to a neighbor who needed to have his house painted, got some advice from someone who knew how to mix the pastes and paints and, for free, painted the place. People liked the work. Soon, he was painting houses all over town, for money now, and he'd turn this money over to his father. Everyone was happy. And Antonio could paint on the side.

"When I was thirteen, I went to confession and I told Padre Pio that what I really wanted to be was a painter. I had brought a roll of drawings and I showed them to him. He said 'have patience and you will see that one day divine providence will help you.' The help came the next year."

By this time Ciccone's paintings were on walls all over town and so it was that when the wealthy Fancelli family from Florence came down to see Padre Pio they saw Ciccone's work, inquired about it and offered to take him back to Florence to live with them. In very short order, this poor village boy from Puglia was living in Florence and studying at the painting studio of Annigoni and at the drawing studios of Simi.

If you look at the photographs and self-portraits of Ciccone at the age of nineteen, you see a handsome dark haired young man with flashing black eyes who might have just melted the heart of a young American girl studying Italian art abroad in Florence. And that is what happened.

Linda Merrill was also 19 then. Tall and patrician with flaming red hair, she was a member of a prominent WASP family in Washington — her father was First Consul in the American embassy in Paris — and they had a summer home on the ocean in Wainscott, Long Island. (Linda's aunt, Edith Siter, founded the East Hampton Nature Preserve.) Linda was attending the same drawing class one day with Simi as was this exotic dark haired young Italian man. He was working on a religious painting in acrylics and he thought she would be the perfect Mary Magdalen. Would she pose for him?

It was an incredible love affair. And when Linda Merrill became pregnant and came home to Washington, her family thought that though Linda said she would have her baby they would just make the best of it and that would be the end of it. They were wrong.

"We wrote letters endlessly," Antonio told me. "But it was not until three years later, in 1965, that I had any chance to see her again. A man came to Florence who owned an art gallery in Palm Beach, Florida.

He was looking for young artists with talent. And he came to Simi's studio and saw my work, bought some and took them back to Palm Beach. Then he wanted to bring me to America for a show."

The art dealer was a man named George Vigouroux and his bringing Ciccone to Palm Beach for the 1965 "season" caused a sensation. Here in the book were photographs of Vigouroux meeting Ciccone at the airport, an event actually covered in *The Shiny Sheet* newspaper, of Jackie Kennedy getting out of a car to view Ciccone's work, of Mr. and Mrs. Cornelius Vanderbilt Whitney inside the gallery at the opening, of Ciccone making a charcoal drawing of the wealthy John Newberry. You have to remember that Palm Beach is not exactly a major art center of the world, but has dozens of local artists of what you might call the Suburban Housewife Set. Here was a handsome young Italian with a heavy accent who could draw like the wind. The Palm Beach Gallery was set up with Ciccone's work in one half and the work of 30 local artists in the other. OLD MASTERS TOUCH GIVEN BY CICCONE headlined the *Palm Beach Daily News*. Antonio Ciccone was the sought after darling of Palm Beach.

Ciccone's handsome dark eyes were elsewhere, however.

"I wanted to go to Washington to claim my family," he told me. "I wanted to see my daughter."

Vigouroux also had an art gallery in Nantucket and it was in Nantucket that millionaire Malcolm Forbes saw Ciccone's work. He loved it. He sent his yacht out to Nantucket to pick up a particular painting. And he asked Vigouroux if Ciccone could come up to New York City to paint his portrait. It did not pass Ciccone's notice that Washington was enroute between Palm Beach and New York.

"The first time I went to her house," he told me, "her parents weren't there. So that was easy. After that, it was not so easy. Can you imagine? A foreigner from Italy, not even Italy but SOUTHERN Italy, come to claim your daughter and her child? Although I must say that it did help that I could paint."

The plan was that Ciccone and Linda Merrill would be married in a big social wedding in Washington. Linda and Antonio objected but it seemed to do no good. And yes, they could first fly back to San Giovanni Rotondo so Ciccone could introduce Linda and Tiana to his family. But then they should return. And perhaps, since they were not yet married, they should travel on separate airplanes, Antonio on one and Linda and Tiana on another.

Linda and Tiana and Antonio flew together. And they were married in a small ceremony at the Palazzo Vecchio in Florence. They set up housekeeping nearby and once again Antonio began to paint.

It was in 1968 that Antonio and Linda and Tiana moved to Wainscott and they did it for a very interesting reason. Antonio and Linda had made a decision to enlarge their family by adopting children from all over the world, and in Italy it was by law not possible to do this before the age of forty. It was legal, of course, to do this in the United States.

The Ciccones moved to the Hamptons and lived here for thirteen years and if you were here at the time you probably remember them. They lived at the oceanfront house on Beach Lane in Wainscott at first, then on Little Plains Road in Southampton and then for many years on Meeting House Lane just a short walk from downtown. Ciccone rented Larry River's barn as his painter's studio.

What a sight they were in town. The tallest was Linda with her flaming red hair, then came Antonio Ciccone with his moustache and goatee and smock, and often as not in boots and beret, and then the seven children. There was Tiana, the Italian-American, Kim of Vietnamese descent, Pablo of Korean descent, the Penny and Jerry, both of black background, Lisa from Puerto Rico and Dario of mixed background. In 1975, which was about midway in their thirteen years in Southampton, these children ranged in age from three to sixteen. They went to the Southampton Elementary School, the Middle School and the Southampton High School. Also, in the case of Pablo, Jerry and Lisa, Our Lady of Poland up by the Southampton railroad station.

"There was some prejudice," Antonio told me. "But I suppose considering that it was a small town, we got along pretty well. I do remember one day walking down Main Street, all of us, and I am towing a little red wagon full of children which I have attached to my belt with a rope, and some kids shouted 'hey guys Halloween is over, take off the masks,' but you know I suppose we did look pretty funny each one of us so different from the other."

Where Ciccone really wanted to be, however, was in his beloved Florence, the cradle of the Renaissance, where he could receive his inspiration from the ages. In 1980, he and Linda and the children moved here. They have been here ever since.

Amazingly, twelve years later, all the surviving family is still in Florence. (Young Jerry was killed tragically in a motorcycle accident.) They are ages nineteen to twenty nine. Three of the children still live at home, one is living with friends, one is living with her fiance and one is married and living with her husband. They work, all that are old enough, in Florence, respectively as a furniture restorer, a hairdresser, a homemaker, the manager of a local Mexican restaurant and as a sometimes secretary to Antonio. None is a painter.

Ciccone's work has been described in the *New York Times* as follows: "The art of Antonio Ciccone is spindrift. Like the windblown sea spray, it is elusive, poetic and wispy, resisting convenient descriptions. (Mr. Ciccone) is a virtuoso of pictures, a man of many styles, an energetic artist who doesn't settle for one vision of the world...Just when the

213

observer thinks he has seized its essence and summoned the vocabulary to articulate his perception, it moves mercurially off in another direction, doing unpredictable things the observer has not anticipated... (He) has made some extraordinary drawings, drawings that his Italian forefathers would be proud of. He can use a hunk of charcoal as if it were an extension of his body."

Currently, Mr. Ciccone is working on a massive painting for a church in Italy.

September 4, 1992

Chapter 45

HENRY KALLAN

If ever there were an example of the American experience, of what freedom and democracy can mean for one individual, it is exemplified in the person of Henry Kallan. I am sitting in the busy office of Mr. Kallan in the Hotel Wales on Madison Avenue and 92nd Street, and I am listening and watching as he directs his staff members in the ongoing – and almost completed – $5 million renovation of this place. Mr. Kallan is President of this 92 room hotel. He is about forty-two years old, he is married with an apartment in the city and a house on First Neck Lane in Southampton, he is handsome, athletic and filled with energy as he directs what is becoming a wonderful transformation from a formerly rundown eyesore into this magnificent restoration of a Victorian masterpiece.

"The original Victorian grandeur was all right here," he says. "But it was just buried under layers and layers of paint. We have recovered more mahogany, more ironwork, more cherubs and angels that anyone could have ever thought possible."

It does not go unnoticed that Mr. Kallan speaks with something of an accent. It is not quite German and it is not quite Austrian and when you ask him about it, you learn it is from Czechoslovakia. And when you ask him a little bit further, you learn that just twenty-two years ago, when he was merely twenty years old, he fled Czechoslovakia just before the Russian tanks moved in to quell the Prague Spring. Without a penny in his pocket, and without even the knowledge of his parents, he and a friend took a train to Austria where, for the first week, he slept in the back seat of a parked car. One year later, barely speaking English, he was working as a busboy in what was then the Gotham Hotel in Manhattan. And he was studying English and business administration at NYU. Soon he was promoted to waiter. Then to front office clerk. And as the years went by, he was promoted up and up and up, simply because he was likeable, creative and he was good at everything he set out to do. As I said, this is a classic American success story.

Henry Kallan is now co-owner of his own hotel. It is hard to imagine how anything could feel better for a man who worked his way up through this industry, always in the employ of someone else, always the man from a foreign land. And as he walks me through this magnificent project, at a pace so brisk I can hardly keep up with him, the enthusiasm and pride for everything that is ongoing here cannot be contained.

"Look at these wooden columns, look at this detailing. We've restored the old gas fireplaces to their original states, though of course we cannot use them, and as you can see we have all these rooms and all these suites filled with antiques. I spent $50,000 on the closets. They are filled with hooks, shelves, drawers and tie racks. These rooms: they are homes away from home, full suites or just individual rooms. Look here. Look at this cast iron. It was covered with paint. Now look at it."

The place is magnificent. We go up to the roof, where Henry is overseeing the construction of a roof garden that overlooks the Central Park Reservoir. Weddings and receptions will take place there amidst tents and potted plants. We go to the second floor, to a grand drawing room where there is to be a Steinway piano, where the windows look out on flowerboxes and the park, and where sofas and overstuffed chairs set the mood for the breakfast buffet to be served there.

It is to become a beautiful hotel in the European tradition. And Mr. Kallan, a European, knows all about that hotel tradition.

"What I did, in 1967, was bribe an Austrian official. My friend and I, we went to the Austrian embassy and I gave this man there a little money, and he gave me a visa to Austria even though I did not have the proper papers to leave Czechoslovakia. Many people were leaving then, and we all knew it couldn't last. What you did was take a train to Yugoslavia, and from there you transferred to a train to Vienna. We got to Yugoslavia, but then we got on the wrong train which was going to Munich, and so we got off that and onto the right train. And then, coming into Austria, an official looked over our papers and, thank goodness, he just asked for the Austrian visas. Had he asked for the Czech papers, which we didn't have, we'd have been denied entry. We probably would have been sent back to Yugoslavia, then returned to Czechoslovakia, and jailed. We were lucky."

Henry Kallan's first job in the west was as a helper in the kitchen of the Hotel deFrance in Vienna. From here, saving up, he managed to get himself to New York City to the Hotel Gotham. And then, when the Russian tanks actually rolled into Prague, he sent money to his childhood sweetheart from high school in Bratislava. He got her out in the nick of time before everything closed down.

"I'm just curious about one thing," I said. "Since your parents didn't know you were leaving, when did they finally find out?"

Henry Kallan looks at me funny.

"The next day," he says. "When I got to Vienna. I called them on the telephone."

"Oh."

Kallan's big break came ten year later, in 1978, when he was the assistant to the General Manager at the Summit, the 800 room Loews Hotel owned by the Tisches. At that time, the City of New York was on the brink of bankruptcy and a number of major hotels were virtually insolvent as well. One of these, the Gotham, was owned by the late Sol Goldman and the late Alex DeLorenzo and it owed so much in back taxes and its prospects were so poor that DeLorenzo wanted out. In fact, according to Kallan, he simply walked away from it.

"Sol Goldman had a brother Irving who lives in Bridgehampton and had money, and Sol called him and offered him DeLorenzo's half for $150,000. Irving accepted, but only if he, Irving, could have the right to run the place. Sol agreed. And that's when Irving called me."

At the time, Kallan was twenty-seven years old but as assistant to the General Manager at the Summit he had already shown what he could do. Kallan and Irving Goldman met.

"You're too young to run a business for me." Irving said. "But if you can, if you can turn it around, you can write your own ticket. If you can't and you fail. You're fired. What do you say?"

Kallan said he would do it, and with his whirlwind management style and with his light European touch, he brought it back into profit within twelve months. Most interesting was the reaction of some of the waiters. There are many old time waiters in these big Manhattan hotels and here at the Gotham some of them had been there for forty years. And some of them remembered this immigrant from Czechoslovakia who had worked there as a busboy nine years before. They were all rooting for him.

After the Gotham, the Tisch brothers hired him back to turn around the Warwick. And after he did that and after the Tisches sold it to a Hong Kong family, he helped this Chinese mercantile family build a chain of ten hotels, of which four are in America. Then came the opportunity at the Hotel Wales.

"The way it came about was that a friend of mine, who is an attorney, came upon this rundown hotel for sale. He approached me, we went into partnership, and I became the manager of the hotel."

Kallan recently purchased the Old James Nederlander estate on Southampton's First Neck Lane. Before that, he lived in a home in the Northwest section of East Hampton, and before that he stayed in a cabin on Three Mile Harbor Road. The Hamptons were a sylvan retreat for his growing family. He and his childhood sweetheart have been married twenty-two years, have a daughter off at college and a nine year old son.

And the Hotel Wales has been a big hit. The neighbors loved seeing a derelict turn into a restoration. Paul Newman, who lives in the area, stopped by to see how it was going and to cheer them on. And, ultimately, it was something that was just waiting to be done. This hotel sits in the midst of the residential Carnegie Hill district, with grand mansions up and down on either side of the street. Many of Manhattan's major museums are only a few blocks away. And the prices to stay at the Wales, beginning at only $125, are surely modest by any comparison.

In the meantime, Henry Kallan has never lost his perspective, never forgotten where he is from, and how he got to where he is.

"I think if you take care of yourself, work hard and be fair, people will recognize your talents. Here in America, I see where people lose their jobs and they go on unemployment. I don't understand it. Here many like me leave their country to make a new life and people here they won't even relocate to New Jersey or Connecticut. I think it is a virtue to never be too proud, never be unwilling to do or try anything, never be impressed with yourself. Once you think you are 'there', wherever 'there' is, you lose it."

And Henry Kallan, grateful for his own success, sees his responsibility as helping others. He has helped and sponsored twenty-one other immigrants from Czechoslovakia, taking responsibility for their housing, their jobs, their food.

"When I was at the Warwick, I sponsored a man. I remember him there with his wife and two kids, tears in his eyes. Today he is managing the Copley/Plaza in Boston. This is my religion. Some people go to church. My helping people in from my homeland, this is my church."

"What became of your friend? The twenty year old you crossed the border with?"

"He has some restaurants in Dallas. Four of them. Mexican, Italian, seafood, steakhouse."

And that's an American tale.

June 29, 1990

* * *

Henry Kallan sold his interest in the Hotel Wales in 1992 and purchased the Elysee Hotel with its famous Monkey Bar on 54th St. and Madison which he then put through another beautiful restoration.

Chapter 46

THEODORE W. KHEEL

Theodore Kheel, the well-known labor negotiator and mediator, has been coming out to the Hamptons with his family for over 25 years. I interviewed him the other day, and when I arrived at his East Hampton summer home, the first thing we did was conduct a negotiation.

"Where would you like to sit?" he asked. "In the living room? Out on the deck?"

The living room seemed a little dark for such a bright summer day, but the deck was completely in the bright sun.

"Is there a shady spot on the deck?" I asked.

We wandered out and looked around but there was none, and then I saw something that was a remarkable compromise. It was a treehouse in the middle of the recently-mowed back yard, an open platform about eight feet up accessible by wooden ladder.

"I built that for my grandchildren," he said, "But there is good shade up there."

"Looks good to me."

And so that's where we went. Ted and I each grabbed a wrought iron lawn chair, I went up first and he handed them up to me then climbed up after and we both sat down. Both of us were in shorts and t-shirts.

"Where shall we begin?" Ted asked.

At that moment, his wife came out onto the rear deck and looked up at us. "Well, this is a first," she said. And then she climbed up and joined us.

"Begin at the beginning," I said.

As Mr. Kheel began to talk, about graduating college and going to law school during the Depression, I did some addition. He had looked to me, a man with a crew cut, a firm handshake, a nice smile and an athlete's build, that he was possibly in his late fifties. I think we all do this when we first meet someone, figure their age roughly from the way that they look. Now, I realized, if he went to college in the early thirties, he had to be in his seventies today. And there we were, sitting like kids up in this treehouse.

"I got into labor relations by accident," he said. "Jobs were so hard to find back in the Depression. I got out of law school, and couldn't find a "decent" job for two years. I was employed during the time but for a pittance. Finally, I got lucky. There was an opening at the National Labor Relations Board for a young lawyer and I got offered the job. My first day on the job, this man comes in and asks how much money I'm making. Two thousand a year, I told him. You're entitled under our union contract with the NLRB to two thousand six hundred he said. And I'm the lawyer that represents everyone that works here. You file a grievance.

"Now, I didn't want to file a grievance. I was perfectly happy making two thousand a year, perfectly happy to just have a job, but he saw this look on my face, and he said 'if you don't file the grievance, we'll do it for you,' and so I filed the grievance. The next week I was making two thousand six hundred."

Shortly afterwards, the Second World War broke out, and somehow, somewhere down in Washington, the name of this young man who had challenged the establishment in his first day on the job, came to the attention of the powers-that-be. After a stint settling strikes that interfered with the war effort, he was named as Executive Director of the National War Labor Board, a job with tremendous power nation-wide during the 1940's. And by the end of the war, he was a man with a national reputation for solving disputes.

We looked out from the treehouse. Coming across the lawn from the garage to the house were three young people about twenty. They wore bathing suits and carried towels and had just come from the beach over the dunes.

"Grandchildren," Mr. Kheel said. "And their friends."

Everyone waved.

I asked Mr. Kheel who was the most fascinating person he ever knew. He has dealt with heads of state, presidents, mayors and million-aires. And he launched in to this remarkable story about President Lyndon Johnson.

"I was at our home in Riverdale one evening watching the news on television, this was in 1964, when the phone rang. My wife got it. On the news, a commentator was saying that the railrods were threatening a retaliatory nationwide railroad lockout to begin the next day to counter a strike against one railroad the unions had called and it could start any day and it would paralyze the nation, but that President Johnson announced that he had gotten the unions to end their strike and the railroads to postpone the lockout for 15 days and that he was going to call in new negotiators.

"Now I thought this was a kind of odd way of putting it because the unions and the railroad people had the negotiators and they weren't going to change them, and if you called in anyone it would be mediators, to help them out.

"Anyway, my wife handed me the phone and on the other end, this voice said, 'Mr. Kheel'? and then when I said yes, he said, 'The President of the United States.' And then, there was no mistaking the voice, there he was. 'Ted,' he said. He called me that like he had known me all my life, 'Ted, we need new negotiators down here. Can you be here at 10 a.m.?' And of course I was out of the house in 20 minutes and was in the Oval Office the very next morning.

"When I came in, there was a long table set up, and the President sat me right on his right. Then he presses a button and in comes Pierre Salinger, his press secretary, and this huge array of press photographers. And then he put his nose in my face and kept it there as Salinger counted 'sixty, fifty-nine, fifty-eight, fifty-seven,' and so forth and the flashbulbs popped until he had counted right down to zero. And then they scurried out. He had given them one minute.

"The next day, in the morning papers, there was the picture, 'President Johnson confers with Mr. Kheel about railroad problems.' And that's exactly what it looked like.

"To my right at the table was George Taylor, a university professor who had been called in as my co-mediator, and as all of us began to talk, the phone rang next to the President and he answered it. It was a call he had put through to George Taylor's wife, Mrs. Taylor who was in the hospital.

"The President stopped the discussion. 'Mrs. Taylor,' Lyndon Johnson said. 'Your husband is a great countryman. He should be by your side and he's here instead serving his country. Here I'll put him on.' The President held out the phone, it wouldn't reach much, and Mr. Taylor had to lean across me, he actually had to lay across me right on the table, and he picked up the phone. 'Hello, Edith,' he said. 'I'll call you later.'

"The whole time the President was looking away so he wouldn't appear to be eavesdropping. You don't disturb a phone conversation between husband and wife after all."

The negotiations went on for days, first in a room in the White House, then in Blair House — an adjunct to the White House. A few times, President Johnson would stop in, unannounced, to see how

221

things were going. Once he came in with Walter Lippman, another time with Steichen, the photographer.

"Want to see what a bunch of tough guys look like?" Johnson said to Steichen.

Thirteen days later, an agreement was reached. Recommendations Kheel and Taylor made had staved off what might have been a national disaster.

"How did you do it?" I asked. "What makes you so good at this." As recently as a year ago, Kheel worked negotiating the sale of the *New York Post* from Rupert Murdoch to Peter Kalikow.

"Are there secrets?"

"No secrets," Mr. Kheel said. "But it is an art. A mediator's chief function is to clear the air and try to educate everyone. You can't appear to favor one side or the other, even if in your heart you do. You present yourself as the advocate of the settlement, and you identify the strengths and weaknesses of everyone's positions, and you create scenarios. What happens if we do this? What are the consequences of that? People have attitudes, bitter feelings. What do you do? You can't shout at them. You can't appeal to their patriotism. You appeal to their self interest. Now look at what would happen if we do this."

"Who was the toughest negotiator?" I asked.

"I've never been discouraged by toughness. But I have been discouraged by stupidity. It is hard to work with stupidity. And the hardest thing of all is to cope with irrationality. That's impossible. The Ayatollah? Terrorists? With irrationality, there is just nothing you can do."

Mr. Kheel told me briefly about some of the other negotiations he has been involved with. He had been the advisor to Mayor O'Dwyer in New York City for a number of years. "Now he was remarkable," Kheel said. "He could sense what was happening, grasp things in a moment." He was involved in the labor negotiations between Mayor John Lindsay and Michael Quill. And, at the President Kennedy's request, he smoothed over a controversial attempt by Phil Graham of the *Washington Post* to use his friendship with the President to intervene in the 1962-63 114 day newspaper strike in New York City over the strenuous objection of the New York publishers. "I remember talking to Mr. Kennedy in Palm Beach from a pay phone in New York and got disconnected when the operator said my time was up, five cents more please, and I didn't have the nickel."

Mr. Kheel delights in telling these stories. His eyes sparkle and he grins happily. It was a lovely summer morning there, up in that treehouse.

After a while, the three of us (Mrs. Kheel is a beautiful and dignified woman who would put her two cents in when her husband couldn't remember a name or a detail), all climbed down and walked across the lawn to the house for a lunch of cold cuts and fruit in the dining room with children and grandchildren.

Both Mr. and Mrs. Kheel are proud of their beautiful old house, which was originally built by John Drew, the famous actor, for his daughter to live in. It is down the street from the main house that Drew lived in.

"This had been a group house at one time." Mr. Kheel said. "Although it was some group — Betty Friedan, Bob Hirschfield, Arthur Herzog and some others — and then it was sold to Jerry Lawton who painted the interior white and he sold it to me."

I asked how he had first come to the Hamptons.

"My wife and I were married in Bellport, not too far from here," he said. "And we just wanted someplace to go on vacation near the ocean. So we came out to the Sea Spray Inn right on the beach — it has since burned down — and that's where we stayed off and on for many years. Our daughter was a waitress there. A Hot Cross Bun girl."

After lunch, we toured the house. It is of a modest size, though it is bright and airy. The living room, Mrs. Kheel opined, had been built for play readings or for rehearsals. In the attic, they had found many personal effects of John Drew's grandson, John Drew Devereaux, who was a well-known actor in his own right. There were clippings from his Broadway performances. There were his letters from Europe when he had been a soldier.

"We cannot locate Mr. Devereaux," Mrs. Kheel said, "though we think he is still alive. But if he or his estate do not want these effects, we think they should be donated to the East Hampton Library or to the museum. So we are just holding on to them."

There was a picture in a frame, taken at the Kheel's fiftieth wedding anniversary, of the whole family together, children and grandchildren, and there must have been 50 of them. What a warm, loving home this certainly is.

I left the Kheel home deeply touched at having been allowed to become a part of it, even as a luncheon guest, even for a morning.

As for mediation and negotiations, perhaps this was Mr. Kheel's secret: love.

A grandson was walking down the driveway with a surfboard.

July 28, 1989

* * *

Since the article appeared, the Kheels were unsuccessful in tracking Devereaux down and donated the letters to the East Hampton Library.

Chapter 47

WILLIAM SOKOLIN

About five years ago, William Sokolin was up in the Town Clerk's office in East Hampton to get a beach parking permit when he noticed a sign on the wall. It was a warning about drunken driving. And it noted the penalties involved with drunken driving in such far away places as Central America, Africa and the Canary Islands, some of which involved life imprisonment or physical mutilation.

Sokolin, who is in the business of selling wine, jotted down some of these extraordinary penalties, and a few days later wrote about them in a newsletter he publishes. Shortly thereafter, he came upon an article that said drunken driving laws were being tightened up in California. He wrote to the Legislature of California, enclosing the reprint of the extreme penalties. A few weeks later he got a call from a Dr. Franzblau of the California branch of the American Medical Association. The AMA had been asked to recommend some new laws. Dr. Franzblau wanted William Sokolin to know his letter had made a considerable difference. The laws would be stiffer in California because of what Bill Sokolin wrote.

William Sokolin, Jr., Wine Merchant, is like that. He is always thinking, always writing. He writes, he says, three hours every day. Letters, articles, books. He's written several hard cover books. Not bad for a man who simply owns a wine shop on Madison Avenue in Manhattan.

But the story of the material posted on the East Hampton bulletin board does not just stop there. Some time ago, Sokolin was entertaining Lily Sokolin and her father Boris, some relatives from Moscow visiting the United States, when he learned that Lily's mother (Boris's wife) was ill in Moscow and in need of medication only available in America.

William Sokolin phoned Dr. Franzblau in California and arranged to have the medicine available. But how to get it to Russia? Gorbachev was visiting George Bush in Washington at the time, and so Sokolin wrote to him. One week later, an aide to Gorbachev called. Get the medicine to Washington. They would get it into the Soviet Union in the diplomatic pouch. Sokolin air mailed it to Washington, and off it went.

Here are excerpts from a letter written by the Soviet Ambassador to the United Nations, written to Bill Sokolin and dated June 14, just eighty days ago.

"I am glad we are on the way to becoming friends now. Looks like the world is getting smaller, and our two countries are getting closer at last.

"It gave me great pleasure to be of assistance to you. I hope your relative in Moscow has the medicine by now and is getting better.

"Thank you for the gracious gift of Mouton Rothschild 1981 — what better way to toast our common future! And I take it as a heartfelt welcome to New York, since I have been here for only about one month...

"Yuli Vorontsov, Deputy Foreign Minister and Ambassador."

Bill Sokolin is a handsome sixty years old, lives with his wife and family on the Upper West Side and in Bridgehampton, and has a wine shop on Madison and 33rd Street that delivers. They deliver to the Hamptons, to Saudi Arabia (yes!), to Ireland, even to France. I interviewed him in the little room he keeps as an office in the back of his wine shop.

"Today? We have a delivery to Quogue. And we have one to Tokyo. Why do we have a worldwide clientele? Because we have a policy called 'feel good.' Eleven cases of forty one we shipped to California were broken? Don't get excited. We'll be your friend. All fixed at no charge."

Bill Sokolin's father emigrated from Moscow to New York in 1921 and went into the grocery business. In 1934 he got a license and opened a liquor store. It is the very same store that his son runs the wine shop out of now.

Bill went to private school, then to Tufts where he studied History, then into the military.

Bill's father died in 1959 and at first it appeared the store would be sold. But then Bill, who had been in Europe, stepped in and said he would run it. He had fallen in love with fine wines from Europe. He decided to stop selling liquor and instead sell just wine.

At first, the business plummeted. But after about two years, it was apparent that Bill Sokolin was on to something. America was learning about French wines and Italian wines. Business began to look up. He was one of only a few wine shops in New York City. He decided he would learn just about everything there was to know about wines.

Bill and his wife and two young children summered in Bordeaux in the Summers of 1971, 1976 and 1981 and Bill came to appreciate the long history of winemaking. He would buy old wines that were hundreds of years old and he would sell them more for their historical value than their taste.

"In France I learned that Thomas Jefferson had purchased one hundred and eighty cases of Chateau Margaux. This was in 1788. He was Ambassador to France at the time, and he kept ninety cases for himself and he shipped the other ninety cases off to Congress. He had paid the equivalent of 14 cents for each bottle, but what he really bought it for was to inform America that if they drank wine, if they eliminated hard alcohol, they would have a country that would thrive.

"Jefferson wrote 'no country is drunken where there is good inexpensive wine. None sober where ardent spirits are the drink of the day.' And he wrote 'the greatest public service I have performed for my country was the lowering of wine tariffs. Greater than if I had paid the national debt.' In 1774, Thomas Jefferson and George Washington chartered the Wine Company, whose purpose was to make America a temperate wine drinking country."

Sokolin is serious about this. He truly believes that wine drunk in moderation is good for the soul, but liquor drunk in moderation causes trouble and chaos. He writes a newsletter he mails out to his clientele whenever the whim strikes. Health and historical connections are the theme of his newsletter.

And then, while visiting a friend in the wine business in Manchester, England, named Tim Littler, Bill Sokolin came across a bottle of 1787 Chateau Margaux: the very wine that Thomas Jefferson had bought. It had been certified by the maker.

Sokolin did not buy this bottle — it was being offered for sale for hundreds of thousands of dollars — but he did suggest to Tim Littler that he, Sokolin, would be willing to showcase it in the window of his wine shop if he could have it on consignment. Littler agreed.

"A month later, Littler flew into Kennedy Airport with the bottle in a satchel," Sokolin recalls. "It was about five p.m. He got off the plane, handed me the satchel, and I said would you care to have some dinner, and he said no, he was going right back, and he did."

Sokolin displayed this rare bottle as he said he would, and it got publicity in the *New York Times*, and there were offers made for it. And then, on April 24, 1989, there was a party at the Four Seasons Restaurant to celebrate the opening of the new vintages of wines for the 1987 year and Chateau Margaux was there, and Sokolin thought what a nice thing it would be to take the bottle there and show it

226

to them.

At the Four Seasons, he set it on the center of the round table at which sat the contingent from France, then he took it off and was walking with it to another table to show it to former baseball player Rusty Staub when he felt it bang against a marble serving tray. Then he felt that his jacket and pants were wet.

"It couldn't have happened," he said. "But it did. A huge chunk of glass had broken on the side of the bottle and over half the contents were on my trousers, in my shoes, on the rug. I was in shock. I excused myself. Took a cab home. I thought I would have a heart attack. Fortunately, the bottle was well insured and the value of it, well over a hundred thousand dollars, went to Mr. Littler in Manchester."

William Sokolin also tasted what remained of the wine as there still was some in the bottom of the broken bottle. It didn't taste like much.

"I buy and sell these old wines not for their taste," he told me, "but for their historic value. Imagine what it feels like to be in the presence of a bottle of wine that Thomas Jefferson had."

Not everything that Bill Sokolin does, however, turns out successfully. After writing to Gorbachev about the medicines, the next day Bill Sokolin wrote to Gorbachev about drunkenness in the Soviet Union. He paraphrased what Jefferson had said, that a land prospers where there is good inexpensive wine, and that a land declines where ardent spirits are the order of the day.

He got no personal response to this one. But a month later, he got the form letter. Thank you for writing. The President appreciates hearing your comments. Feel free to write again.

"I've been talking to people about opening a wine shop in Moscow," Sokolin says. "Could happen." And knowing Bill Sokolin, it will happen.

August 24, 1990

Chapter 48

TONY DREXEL DUKE

180 boys arrived last weekend at Boy's Harbor, the camp for underprivileged city kids on the shores of Three Mile Harbor in East Hampton. These boys, however, are between the ages of sixty and seventy-five, and if they are sleeping in the bunk beds in the cabins that the little kids usually sleep in, it is perfectly okay because the camp does not open until next week and these 180 boys have been invited here by the camp's owner, Anthony Drexel Duke, for an extraordinary time.

The occasion? It has been exactly forty-five years since Tony Duke was the Commander of a World War II LST transport ship. These 180 boys, mostly teenagers forty-five years ago, were all under his command aboard that ship and it was during the last two years of that war that Lt. Commander Duke got them through the D-Day invasion of France with the Nazi shore batteries shooting at them, and the following year at the amphibious assault of Okinawa in the Pacific, where tens of thousands of Japanese fought to the death.

The reunion has been two years in the making. And Commander Duke, who was in command in 1944 and 1945, was in command again as probably the only person with an estate and grounds large enough (he has 180 waterfront acres) to accommodate the assemblage.

The first of these former sailors began to arrive around noon on Friday, coming in campers, rented cars, station wagons or whatever. There was Robert Reed from Commerce City, Colorado, who had been a chief motor machinist mate on the ship and who arrived with his wife Ruth. He is now a retired truck mechanic. There was Cliff Sinnett from Portland, Maine, who had been a lieutenant aboard the ship and works today as an investment banker, and who came with his wife Charlotte. There was Charlie Pierce, now of Del Ray Beach, Florida, another lieutenant who recently retired as an IRS T-man investigator for the government. And there was Woogie Barth, a former electrician's mate on the ship who drove up from Chalmette, Louisiana. He is a retired New Orleans police officer. All together, they came from 28 states. One man left Oregon by car three days earlier, drove across country, and pulled into East Hampton Friday morning.

There was a registration procedure upon arrival with the men and their wives and families being assigned a bunk or cabin, and then around five Friday afternoon there was a get-acquainted cocktail party in the camp mess hall, which was festooned with banners and bunting, photographs of English warplanes and American destroyers, even a wooden model of LST-530 itself. A few of these men had kept in touch over the years but most had not and the emotions of getting together, all together, after all these years, was quite overwhelming. A banquet was held Friday night, poems were read, speeches made, and stories told. The men received identical blue T-shirts with the inscription USS LST-530 in white letters across the chest, and they received blue peaked caps with a silhouette of the ship stenciled across it. There were proclamations, personally addressed to each of them from Commander Duke, and there was a letter read to the entire crew, sent from the present-day Secretary of the Navy.

Commander Duke was asked to reveal some of the secret information from the War, some of the things he could not even tell his crew at the time, and at great length, he did.

"This is about Operation Tiger," he told the men. "You never knew about this. We had crossed the Atlantic as you know and our battle plan was to participate in the invasion of Europe, crossing the Channel from England to Nazi occupied France, which is what we did. But, as part of the preparations for this invasion, there was something called Operation Tiger and it was so tragic and so terrible that my lips were sealed about it right up through the beginning of the 1970's, when, finally, the Freedom of Information Act enabled much of what happened to be made public.

"Fortunately, we arrived just too late to participate in Operation Tiger. We were supposed to have been in it. But we missed it.

"Operation Tiger was a rehearsal of the invasion, designed to develop our coordination. Two destroyers and six LSTs loaded with troops went to sea off the English coast and proceeded to start a practice landing on an English beach called Slapton Sands in Devonshire.

"Several German E-Boats showed up, however, and began firing their torpedoes and before it was all over two of the LSTs were at the bottom of the sea and over 1,000 soldiers and sailors had lost their lives. The action was so disastrous that it could not be made public at that time, and Admiral Moon ordered all the survivors put in isolation until after

D-Day, at which time, the parents of those who died were told, inaccurately, that their sons had lost their lives in the invasion."

The men listened spellbound as their Commander related this event forty-five years later. Then they told stories of their own. For example, there was the time, in the English Channel, when Junior Kinnamon, now a farmer in Pasco, Washington, knocked down a German plane in the English Channel with his anti-aircraft gun.

"It was after sunset and I knew our planes were not supposed to be in the air. And there he was coming in. I said, 'blow that s.o.b.' and I did."

Another man described a dalliance with a lady in the back of an English theatre, and he publicly thanked a shipmate here at Boy's Harbor for getting him out of there and back to the ship before curfew. His wife and the other wives looked on. What could they say? The stories went on until four o'clock in the morning.

LST-530 was christened in December of 1943 in Jeffersonville, Indiana and Anthony Drexel Duke, age 25, a commissioned officer and a descendant of the tobacco fortune Dukes of North Carolina as well as the Drexels and Biddles of Philadelphia, received the task of commanding her.

The ship plied down the Mississippi River to New Orleans after fitting out, picking up crew from the states along the shore.

On D-Day, the first day of the massive invasion of Europe, Duke's LST-530 was in the front line, transporting 580 British troops from the Eighth Army to a landfall, supposedly, at an Allied designated beach called "Gold."

But every man remembered what happened. The German artillery, 88's, was too devastating at "Gold," and so they veered to starboard and landed the men at a beach called "Juno." After that, during the next weeks, they made 41 trips across the Channel, ferrying a total of 30,000 soldiers, assorted jeeps, tanks, ammunition and aviation fuel from England to France as the soldiers fought their way inland.

Now the men talked about their next operation, which was making an emergency trip across the Channel to Brittany where General Patton had run out of ammunition, fuel and supplies. It was a hot trip, with once again the German artillery trying to sink them and prevent the landing, but the ship got through and returned safely.

"I never told you this either," Tony Duke said, "but I had been asked to 'volunteer' the ship by Admiral Nasmuth, and so I did."

"Well thanks a lot," someone shouted back at him now, forty-five years later. This got lots of laughter.

Saturday, some of the men went off golfing at the Maidstone Club, which had graciously lent its course to Duke and his men, and some of them went sailing or fishing from the Duke's lobster boat *Simbar*, and some of them drove into town to go shopping, but for many of them, it was a time of sitting around and swapping stories and discussing what had become of each of them. The wind was up, the leaves rustled in the trees and it was a simply magnificent spring day.

There was a luncheon, in the early afternoon a group photograph in front of the mess hall, everyone in t-shirts and caps, and then it was down to the Duke residence by the water for more discussions and a memorial service for those that had passed on. In the evening, there was dinner, dancing, and the arrival of a Navy band, which serenaded the men with songs that were popular so long ago.

With the Normandy invasion complete and the bridgehead in France secured, the attention of the American authorities turned to the Pacific, where the Japanese Empire extended over two dozen countries and several thousand miles in every direction. Even a portion of Alaska was under Japanese control then.

Commander Duke brought LST-530 through the Panama Canal to Hawaii, where, at the great Naval base, he joined up with the American Pacific fleet determined to break the Japanese hold in the Pacific.

The American strategy consisted of a succession of Naval assaults on Pacific islands slowly getting closer and closer to the Japanese mainland. The two most infamous of these were the bloody battles for Guadalcanal and two years later Okinawa, where American troops fought for weeks and months, for the most part to the last Japanese man.

LST-530 was in the assault on Okinawa, now bringing in American marines rather than English soldiers. Duke remembered a dreadful time, when they were anchored off Okinawa in Buckner Bay, and a Japanese Zero airplane flew in undetected beneath the cover of the radar. The Japanese were desperate at this time, and the pilots of these planes, called Kamikazes, were committing suicide by attempting to fly their aircraft directly into American ships to destroy them in great conflagrations.

"This one, you all may remember, came right at us, and as we trained our guns at him and began firing, he veered away, and slammed into LST-534 directly astern of us. She was beached when hit and suffered fire and casualties."

And then there was the final action of the war. Commander Duke had brought his ship and his men to a rendezvous point off the north coast of Japan. "You men didn't know this," he now told them, "but the ship had been selected to participate in what was to be the invasion of the Japanese mainland for the final battle." There were 150 ships assembled that day when, as the men remembered, the word went out that a great Atomic Bomb had been dropped on a city in Japan and the Emperor was surrendering.

"Somebody, somewhere, you will recall, decided to begin firing into the sky. Pretty soon virtually all the ships were firing their anti-aircraft

231

guns and artillery shells into the air and I knew what might happen. I ordered you all immediately below. And sure enough the shrapnel and flak came raining down and the radio wires were hot with demands to cease firing. But there were casualties and these were hushed up too."

But there were no casualties aboard LST-530, not then, not ever, except for a cook who had suffered a heart attack in the European campaign. Commander Duke had brought them through unscathed.

At this meeting, Duke learned, for the first time, that some of his crew had named children after him. Officer Howard Benson of McMinneville, Oregon, named a son Anthony Benson after his chief. Anthony is now a Reverend in Eatontown, New Jersey. And Carl Deakins, another crew member now living in Lithonia, Georgia, has a son he named Anthony Duke Deakins. These are the things people do in their lives when they've been through an experience such as this.

Sunday there were individual photographs taken of the men for a yearbook to be printed and mailed, and there was a barbecue and farewell speeches. The men now, from all walks of life, laborers, merchants, professional men and bankers, got in their cars and station wagons and, after tearful farewells, drove away to resume their regular lives.

This week the other kids arrive. The camp will come alive with the voices of young children.

May 25, 1990

Chapter 49

STEVE FRANKFURT

Steve Frankfurt, the legendary advertising man, works in Manhattan and lives in Quogue. He commutes between the two. I suppose a lot of people do this, but none of them do it like Steve Frankfurt. Because Steve Frankfurt is at work before he gets to work.

"I started doing this eighteen years ago," he told me. "We had begun coming out to the Hamptons for the summers and we fell in love with the people, the ocean, the smell of it, the peace and quiet. Our daughter was four years old then and we thought, wouldn't it be wonderful if we could move out here full time so she could go to school here? I said I didn't think I could make the drive day after day, but I'd try. After a while I tried the train, then the Jitney, even a seaplane a few times. It's a long pull, two hours, no matter how you cut it. And then I figured it out."

One of Frankfurt's longtime clients was Chrysler. He bought a big Dodge van and he had it outfitted as an office, with a telephone, a video monitor and VCR, a kind of living room affair in the back with wall to wall carpeting and, up front, a driver. He began this in 1975 and with a change of vans every three years, he is still doing this today.

"My driver is a retired police officer. I get up at 6:30 in the morning, pick him up at his house, and then he drives me in. He helps out at the office and around town all day. Then he drives me back. I am actually at work before eight in the morning. In my van."

I can attest to that. A few days after this interview, which was conducted at the offices of Frankfurt, Balkind in New York, the phone rang at my home at eight in the morning. It was Steve Frankfurt, on the job, calling me from his rolling stock on its way into Manhattan,

233

asking if he and his wife might get together with us this weekend. We set it up.

Steve Frankfurt literally changed the face of television advertising back in the 1950's and 60's, responsible for all sorts of fresh and new commercials that had never been done before. "Bet You Can't Eat Just One" was done on his watch for Lays Potato Chips. "Wings of Man" was for Eastern Air Lines. But if many other early creative geniuses developed imaginative new advertising in this period, none of them did what Steve did. At the age of 36, he was named President of Young and Rubicam Advertising in Manhattan, then the second largest ad agency in the world. Billings were $500 million and 2,500 people worked in offices in New York, Los Angeles, San Francisco, Chicago, London, Frankfurt and Paris and Milan.

"How did it feel to head up this company at that age?" I asked.

"I was terrified," he said. "They were all older than me."

All together, from the time he started at the age of 24 until the time he left, Frankfurt was to work at Young and Rubicam for more than fourteen years. After leaving Y and R, he set up his own company, FCI, then sold it to Kenyon and Eckhart where as chief creative officer he helped the agency's billings double. What he likes doing best is full corporate image work including advertising, promotion, marketing, identity and logos, even annual reports. In his long career he has directed the unique graphics for, among others, the motion pictures *All That Jazz*, *Superman*, *Alien*, *Rosemary's Baby* and lots more. Some of them certainly are memorable. Who can forget the monster pushing his way out from behind the glimmering opening title of *Alien*?

Frankfurt was born and raised in the Bronx, where he went to Music and Art High School and then, later, Pratt. His father was an attorney and became Deputy Controller of the City of New York. His mother was the secretary to the head of Republic Pictures and there were two incidents in his early life that, I think, go a long way to explain the future career of Steve Frankfurt.

One was his visits to the Madison Square Garden rodeo.

"My brother Mike and I were the envy of the neighborhood," he said. "Our parents would take us to cowboy shows at the Garden and before the show we would get to have lunch with Roy Rogers, who my mother knew because of her work at Republic Pictures."

The second was a job he got while studying at Pratt. Through friends of his father's, he worked as an usher at the fledgling CBS television studio on 50th and Broadway. He worked not indoors but out of doors, on the street, dressed smartly in his CBS uniform with the eye logo, white gloves and a long black cape, talking to people passing by, urging them to come in, have some free tickets, and go sit in and watch the Jackie Gleason or Ed Sullivan shows.

234

Frankfurt was thus bitten by broadcasting, by the logos and corporate uniforms and costumes, and by the glitter of celebrity and by entertainment. Also, while at Music and Art, he came to associate the excitement of the creative process with the smell of paint. After Music and Art, for example, he went to NYU for a year to study liberal arts. But he didn't stay. There was no smell of paint at NYU. He transferred to Pratt.

It is interesting that even today, he is around the smell of paint. His wife, Kay, is an accomplished painter and works in a studio at the house. She has been married to Steve since 1969 and is a success in her own right. She does volunteer work for the Parrish Art Museum. She was the driving force in the design, development and construction of a children's playground in Westhampton, and she is active with the library there. For her efforts, the Family Counseling Service named her "Woman of the Year," three years ago. The "Man of the Year" that year was Angier Biddle Duke.

Steve Frankfurt did not start out in advertising. Graduating from Pratt, he got work as a colorist for the UPA Corporation, which made children's animated cartoons such as Mr. Magoo. Often, he would deliver story boards from UPA to advertising agencies around the City and he remembers these agencies as big, institutional, forbidding places where he very likely would never work.

But he got fired from UPA because, he says, he "wasn't fast enough." They needed someone who could crank the stuff out and that wasn't Frankfurt. They replaced him with Jules Feiffer.

Much of the UPA work was for television, then in its infancy. There were TV cartoons. TV advertising tended to be either people standing up holding a product and pointing at it. Occasionally, there would be some kind of animation.

When Frankfurt left UPA, he left with the probably inaccurate reputation that he could run an animation department. He received an offer from Hallas and Bachelor in London, offering him the job of running such a department for the TV commercials they were doing there. Frankfurt hesitated to take this job. He was only 23 years old at the time. So he spoke to a friend at UPA.

"Take the job," the friend said. "And call me every morning from London and I'll tell you what to do."

So Frankfurt did take it, but then there turned out to be a six month waiting period before he could be brought in. There were permits involved, and union approvals. Because he had to eat during this period, Frankfurt began to offer his services out as a freelancer to advertising agencies. And from this came an offer from Young and Rubicam to help them with a fledgling TV art department.

"You have to understand that at this particular time, nobody wanted to work for TV. TV was something you did when you couldn't do

235

good print. But I loved TV. And this job was wonderful. I was learning more and more every day and being paid for something I loved to do. I told London I would not be going."

The work that Steve Frankfurt did at Y and R and later with his own agency and at K and E is legendary. He did the titles to the 1961 movie *To Kill A Mockingbird.* He did ground breaking work with Bufferin and Excedrin commercials, with Sanka and with Johnson and Johnson. The campaigns for all of these products are considered part of the history of advertising in America. Many of them are now available to be seen in the Museum of Broadcasting on 52nd Street, and some are even in the Museum of Modern Art.

"One of my campaigns in the Museum of Modern Art was shown in just one city in America and then for just 48 hours. The product was Modess. Feminine products had never before been shown on television and I decided we would do one in the most tasteful manner possible. The screen shows one large dot. The camera pulls back and you see there are several dots and then many dots and finally you see that it is an image of a woman. A voice then says 'Modess...because.' And that is the entire commercial. We put this TV commercial on in Johnstown, Pennsylvania and people called the station almost instantly. How dare we put this product on television. We took it off. And that was the start of advertising for feminine products on television."

Frankfurt works today, besides in the screening room and living room affair in his van, at offices occupying two townhouses on East 58th Street. His own office, while not large, has a seating area at one end and a desk at the other, and is filled with the memorabilia of a long and remarkable career that is still in full flower. (His brother Mike, by the way, was also bitten by the entertainment bug. His firm, FGKS, is one of the major law firms in entertainment, publishing and advertising.)

Frankfurt takes out a thick, softcover book that looks like it might be the annual report for *Rolling Stone* magazine. It is filled with vivid colors, excitement, drawings and collage.

"It's the annual report for DuPont this year," he says. "Like it?" This is Corporate America? It knocked me out. Thank you, Steve Frankfurt.

July 30, 1993

Chapter 50

BARBARA CORCORAN

This is a profile of a person who does not physically come to the East End. She prefers going, in the summertime, to upstate New York, where nobody knows her and she doesn't have to talk to anybody. And so it is that here in the Hamptons she is talked about and discussed and wondered over. She is, by many measures, the most successful real estate lady in the City, she is self made, only forty-five years old, and of the 140 brokers that she employs at her firm, the Corcoran Group, almost a hundred of them have places here in the Hamptons and are here weekends to talk about her. Thus she is here in spirit. And people want to know — is there really a Barbara Corcoran?

Well, there is. She is small, pretty, Irish (well half-Irish) and funny and she is always in motion. When I met her in her skyscraper Manhattan office the other day, her first words to me were to ask if I would do her a favor. She was throwing a surprise birthday party for her secretary and when I left could I leave carrying the shopping bag filled with salads and desserts she had made? She did not want her secretary to see it.

"We'll pretend I am taking you over to see our new West Side office," she said. "That would make sense for an interviewer. I love surprises." And she saw my smile and shoved the shopping bag toward me.

This is the same woman who, four years ago, pulled off one of the most dramatic real estate sales that New York City had ever seen. She had taken over something called the MacArthur Portfolio, a collection of buildings in Manhattan, about ten of them, all owned by the MacArthur estate. But monthly maintenance fees on the apartments in these buildings — 175 of them — was so high that nobody could sell them. Nobody but Barbara Corcoran.

Everybody remembers the day. Using some of the most innovative selling techniques imaginable, she dazzled the New York real estate community by selling all 175 apartments within twenty four hours. Total gross: $1.3 million.

A brief description of how she pulled this off might be in order here. She stopped all construction at every building. She stationed her people in front of them with blank contracts. She announced that all the apartments would be going for exactly the same price, the good and the bad, and she announced that all of them would go on sale at 9 a.m. that morning. Then she sent out invitations, privately, to all her broker friends, inviting them to come and bring their friends and relatives. She enclosed a treasure map of the buildings. And she said that all apartments would be sold as-is, so there would be apartments with kitchens and spectacular views and there would be basement apartments with no kitchen appliances installed yet, and these were all priced the same. Contract signing and ten percent down were required within sixty minutes of reserve. It was, for a whole day, pandemonium. But because no matter when anybody got there there was always one apartment better than another, it worked.

Barbara Corcoran lives every day. She is full of excitement and ideas and when you ask her to tell you a few, her eyes twinkle and she says let me tell you two good ones and two catastrophes. As she explains her disastrous attempt to replace the word EXCLUSIVE with the word CENTRAL throughout her firm, so that "exclusive listings," would be called "central listings," she seems almost as pleased that it all went down in flames as she might have been had it succeeded. It was the trying that counts.

The word pandemonium, which I used earlier in this account, comes to mind when describing Barbara Corcoran's growing up. She was one of ten children, born and raised in a tiny town by the George Washington Bridge on the New Jersey side. The town was Edgewater and it was then and is now one and a half miles long and two blocks wide. The ten kids, born within a span of sixteen years, lived at first in the ground floor apartment of a three family house with an aunt and uncle on the second floor and the grandparents on the third floor. Father moved from job to job working as a plant manager in printing companies. And at night he washed trucks for United Parcel. Mother was a full time housewife. And Barbara was number two. As in, number two, the second oldest.

The ten kids lived in three bedrooms practically the whole time Barbara was growing up. But when she was sixteen, her aunt and uncle moved to the Jersey Shore.

"That was heaven. I got to move upstairs to an almost-my-own-bedroom. I just had to share it with Ellen (number three)."

Barbara remembers school mornings as a precision drill. Mother had made the lunches the night before, and they were all lined up on the counter in size order. Mother also lined up everybody's white shoes in size order. They would just run over, leap in, and they were off.

"Living as we did," Barbara said, "was about as close to real life as you could get. There was a pecking order. Some kids got other kids to do their dirty work. There was always somebody to be your friend. And if you had a fight with one brother you could move on to another brother. And of course all of us were very protective of one another."

The values of the family were school, church and family. Barbara was only one of two children in the family who went to college, and her parents almost pulled her out. They felt it was more important that she learn to work for somebody and that she contribute financially to the family. ("I felt like a traitor," Barbara said.) They also objected because the Catholic college she attended, St. Thomas Aquinas in Rockland County, had a very liberal theology teacher who was presenting ideas the family did not agree with. But Barbara stayed. And she got a B. A. in English and Philosophy.

Her decision to go off to college seems even more extraordinary because she bumped through Leonia High School academically at the bottom of her class.

"I was dyslexic and didn't know it," she said. "I flunked Spanish four times. Twice regular and twice in summer school. Finally, I barely got through with C's and D's."

"Why did St. Thomas Aquinas take you?" I asked.

"They took almost anybody. I guess they looked at me and thought, well, she seems nice. And I was a worker. I had all sorts of jobs, salesgirl, waitress. I once counted that through high school and college I worked twenty seven different jobs. I was determined to get through."

But if school were a trial, at home she was a star. She was funny, the center of attention. She liked this and though she would go to college she would stay home and commute the half hour to it. Every day for four years she did this. And she was determined never to fail again.

In her sophomore year of college, Barbara Corcoran was working as a waitress at the counter of the Fort Lee Diner when in walked Ray Simone who sat down and ordered a cup of tea. Simone was ten years older than Barbara, divorced, in the construction business and raising two young children. He and Barbara became a couple. And in many ways, he became her father figure. For the next ten years he was her boyfriend, confidant and, shortly, her business partner. He gave her the courage, she says, to do what she wanted to do.

"What I wanted to do after graduating college," she said, "was move to Manhattan. IT was in Manhattan. I didn't know what IT was, but IT was there and there was more of it there than anywhere else."

She moved into Manhattan to the Barbizon, found two girlfriends and the three of them rented an apartment on East 86th Street. She went job hunting.

"I had a job working the telephone for a firm that placed temporaries. We all had pseudonyms. I'd call at random to a business and say 'hello, my name is Barbara Buttons and I was wondering if you have any temporary jobs you want filled?' I never made one placement. People would hang up."

Then she got a job she liked. She was hired to be the receptionist in the office of a large apartment building on the East Side owned by the Giffunni brothers. She ordered supplies, took tenant complaints. The Giffunnis owned and managed twenty different buildings in the City. One of the sons, Vincent, rented out apartments and had a limousine he drove around in. Barbara thought real estate must be a gold mine and on weekends became a salesperson for Vincent Giffunni. She made more on the weekends than she did during the week.

"But what I really liked was being outside. And being able to do what I wanted on my own time. At the office I felt guilty if I came in at 9:08. Or I'd take a holiday off without asking and then pretend I didn't know that holiday was a work day. Outside, I was free."

Against the advice of Simone and the Giffunnis, she left her job and opened her own business. She called it The Flower of the Week Club. Here she was, twenty four years old, and at 5 a.m. every morning she would go down to the flower district on Sixth Avenue between 24th and 28th Streets and buy flowers for her customers. She had thirty seven customers, all of whom agreed to purchase a spray of flowers a week. But Barbara had not worked out the numbers properly. And she gave credit where she shouldn't have. After eight months at this, she gave it up.

Rather than go back to work for the Giffunnis, however, Barbara decided that if they could do it she could do it. She sat with Ray and he gave her $1000 as start-up money. She would open a real estate firm in her apartment and use Ray's money to pay her rent for four months while she got the business off the ground. Thus it was, twenty years ago, that she went into the real estate business. The firm was called CORCORAN AND SIMONE and if Ray Simone remained in New Jersey to run his firm there he was always there at the end of the telephone for advice.

Her very first account was her landlord.

"Ray had given me this beautiful, bright coat and I was wearing it and the landlord of my apartment building saw it on me and apparently thought I was a hooker. He served me eviction papers. I went to see him. And when I showed him I was in the real estate business,

240

he said okay you can stay, and maybe you could rent some of our apartments. We get three or four a month. And that is how I got started."

Barbara then and now gives the impression of being trustworthy, fun and enthusiastic, and, I guess unless she is wearing her hooker coat, nice to be around. She'd put ads in the New York Times advertising the apartments and she rented them. She was good at it. The Giffunni's gave her more apartments. She rented those too.

Five years later, in 1979, she had fifteen sales people, an office just off Fifth Avenue at 60th Street, and what was perhaps the worst personal crisis in her life.

"Ray Simone fell in love with my secretary," she said. "He'd tell me he was taking his toothbrush because he had to stay overnight in the City and I'd believe him. What did I know. Her name was Tina and Ray would not let me fire her. He promoted her to Relocation Manager or some other meaningless title. I moved everything out of his apartment. A salesperson working for us named Kathy Gilson had a walkup studio apartment on East 79th Street and she said move in and I did. She had broken her arm skiing and the deal was I'd carry the groceries and do the cooking. I was there three months. She never charged me rent."

As for Ray Simone, he married Tina and fifteen years later he is still married to her. He is forgiven by Barbara. He meant a great deal to her for ten years.

How they broke up the firm was interesting. They picked sides. She took the first sales person, he took the second, she took the third. It was like choosing sides for a football game. They flipped for the firm's phone number. Ray got it.

Barbara's new firm, called THE CORCORAN GROUP, took the eighth floor at 964 Third Avenue at 58th Street. She was continuing to do rentals, but now, quite by accident, she got into sales.

"We had started calling on bigger companies and one of our accounts was Union Carbide. We were handling the placement of their younger renters. One day, by mistake, they sent us an employee who was not looking to rent but to buy. They really were using another firm for that purpose. But here he was and he came in as my account and I showed him an apartment to rent and he said he really wanted to buy and I said come back tomorrow. That night I called the owner ads in the Times, got some listings and the next day sold him an apartment for $58,500."

From that moment, business for Barbara Corcoran took off like a rocket. Today, her firm no longer does rentals at all, just sales. And though she is the sole owner of her firm and figures are not available, her 120 salespeople probably do an annual gross somewhere around a hundred million dollars. Only one other firm in the City, Douglas Elliman, does more residential sales business than the Corcoran Group.

241

I wondered how Barbara had survived all the shakeouts and reversals that had finished off other firms in the last ten years. Ray Simone's firm failed in the downturn of 1982 for example.

"I think it is fear of failure. I am always afraid, always fearful that failure is just around the corner and so I am always planning how to keep away from it. For example, seven years ago, in good times, I said this good market will not last forever and so we cannot be complacent. We must become equal in size to our competitors. Otherwise, when the market turns we won't be here. So we grew, and we got through."

Corcoran is always innovating, always changing with the times. Seven years ago, when cash was tight, she decided to start something called the Corcoran Report. She still publishes it. It is a newsletter about the current state of Manhattan real estate and it gets all sorts of publicity in the daily papers and all sorts of calls to her salespeople. But in fact the Corcoran Report was started because, that year, Barbara could not afford to buy ads and was trying to think of other ways to drum up business.

This year, she has opened a real estate gallery next to Zabars on Broadway on the West Side and a second on Hudson Street in Tribecca. They are entirely computerized, with screens everywhere. Punch in what you are looking for and you see the interior of apartments for sale throughout the city on the screen. There are, in fact, nine screens in the window so you get the idea of what is inside. Now Corcoran is working on what she calls "phase two" where ALL the listings in her entire firm are on videotape so prospective buyers can simply take the videos home.

Barbara lives today with her husband Bill. They have an apartment on East 69th Street and a house in New Jersey where her husband has a brokerage firm. And she frequently gets together with her family. Once a year, all the sisters go off for a weekend, no husbands or children, to a ski resort or a dude ranch and this is a favorite time for Barbara.

And of course there is Thanksgiving and Christmas though with her parents now in Florida and the children scattered all over they only get together in bits and pieces. Her brothers and sisters are, today, an airline reservationist, a printing salesman, a nurse's aide, a catering business owner, a roofing business owner, a building contractor, a Gal Friday and a housewife. All together they have 19 children.

It's even bigger pandemonium. And Barbara Corcoran still loves it.

July 16, 1993

* * *

Barbara gave birth to her first child, in March of 1994.

Chapter 51

MARTIN H. LANDEY

The Hamptons is considered by many New Yorkers as a measurement of success. Achieve a certain level in your chosen field and you will find a home on the east end as a base for beachgoing, cocktail parties, gallery openings, dinners. Achieve an even greater level and you move up: your vacation home will be near the ocean on landscaped property with a pool and possibly a tennis court. And then there are the leaders in their fields. Men or women who have revolutionized the thinking of certain professions, who have reaped the rewards, and who relax in grand mansions by the sea. Martin Landey is one of those who, by every standard, has achieved just that. Beginning with the founding of his advertising firm in 1966, Martin turned what was then contemporary thinking about the business on its ear. The way products are perceived today — products such as Absolut Vodka, Fortunoff, the list is long — is largely the result of the revolutionary thinking of this man. But more about this later. For now, listen to Martin Landey talk about how he spends his weekends in the Hamptons, commencing from the arrival at his home, an eight bedroom hundred year old home in Westhampon Beach with two swimming pools and two tennis courts. And keep in mind this is not a man who is twenty five years old.

"I get in to Westhampton Beach around 3 p.m. Thursday, go to the house, pack. I'll be out on the water Friday for the next three days and two nights. Where I go next is to Pell's Dock at Shinnecock where I have a 47 foot Buddy Davis called INDULGENCE. I am joined by a couple of guys who are also avid fishermen — Jim Lockwood from Hampton Bays, Jim Henry from Freeport, maybe a few others — and off we go.

"Where we fish is out by the continental shelf, 150 miles out. It might take us seven hours to just get out there depending on the weather. Last weekend for example, we were out at Veeche Canyon about 90 miles south of Nantucket. We'll put out seven riggers, nine lines, troll for fifteen hours or so, drift the night, troll the day. We'll fish for big eye tuna or yellow fin and blue marlin fish that weigh in at around three hundred and fifty pounds sometimes.

"Yeah, we're a different breed. There's no Coast Guard, no radio. We're out there on the edge for three whole days, totally self sufficient. You never know what will happen. It can be very rough. Or not long ago we had a fog so thick we didn't know bow from stern."

Martin Landey does this every weekend. He is a fisherman and needs to be near the ocean and he chose Westhampton Beach not for its social contacts or for the charm of the village but because it was the shortest drive from New York City where he could have access to the great ocean, the great Kaleidescope of marine life, as he puts it, becoming part of the natural process.

The weekend ends Sunday afternoon when he arrives back at Pell's Dock between three and five. The fish often will be sold to buyers on the dock, some of them Japanese who sell the fish for Sushi. The boat is hosed down, refueled (the weekend consumes almost 1000 gallons of fuel), the men pack up and say goodbye until next week.

"Jim Lockwood and Jim Henry are pretty much regulars when we go out," Martin says. "But we can be as many as five. Sometimes I take my Gucci loafer friends but they usually get sick. Don't come back."

And that's how Martin Landey spends his weekends.

Landey revolutionized the advertising industry in the mid-nineteen sixties by taking a completely new approach. Prior to this time, advertising was driven by research findings. The idea was to find the product benefit and then point out the difference. A toothpaste would have Gardol, something that doctors recommend. A car would have a synchromesh transmission, something that would make it ride smoother.

I don't mean for a minute to suggest that Martin Landey was alone back then in the mid-nineteen sixties coming up with new ideas for the industry, but consider just what he did.

"We came at the problem with the belief that people cared how things were perceived. We became involved with branding, imaging, bonding."

That was what he did for the Fortunoff Department Store.

"We approached Lauren Bacall. She hadn't been doing much since her early successes with Humphrey Bogart, and we asked her to provide an identity for this store. Fortunoff's. 'The Source.' Here was a beautiful, sophisticated, no nonsense lady, a real New Yorker. Someone who wouldn't want to overpay."

Then there was *Cosmopolitan* magazine.

"We've provided an identity for *Cosmopolitan* — 'That Cosmopolitan Girl' — they have used now for twenty seven years. We imaged the magazine. It is an insight into the id, the libido of the reader."

Landey's firm launched Absolut Vodka. They hired photographers to photograph the most magnificent and most remote places in the world for Grand Marnier and they published these photographs with the caption "there are still places on earth where Grand Marnier is not served after dinner."

Other successes included Bank NatWest, Oldsmobile (The Good Olds Guys), Kodak, Coty and more recently Walker's Shortbread, *Harpers Bazaar* magazine, Putnay Bank of Greenwich.

Landey was born in Boston but raised in Manhattan the son of a stockbroker. He lived on the Upper East Side. In 1966 he founded the firm of Martin Landey Arlow at 777 Third Avenue and by 1983 had built it, along with his partner Arnold Arlow, into a firm billing one hundred million dollars. He sold the firm then, but, unhappy with how it was being run — the new ownership spent too much time tending to financial issues and not enough time taking care of the needs of clients, he says — he left and took up a consulting position. "I had a non-compete clause for three or four years," he says. "It was boring as can be." Now he is back with a new firm, Cox Landey Partners, and he already is billing thirty five million, about a third of what the old firm did. The firm is working for Hickey Freeman, for Acura dealers, for Bobby Jones, for Eastman Kodak, and for the Hearst Corporation "And back to work is wonderful."

Out in Westhampton Beach, guests at the house sometimes include his 92 year old mother out from Manhattan, or his daughter Kate who is an attorney, running for the U.S. Senate in the California primary or his daughter Jennifer, who works with him at Cox-Landey.

"She has a summer home in East Hampton. But she comes over."

And then there is the fishing. Landey first threw a hook in the water at the age of three. He is not going to stop now. He's been coming to Westhampton Beach for twenty five years. Come Friday noon there he will be at Pell's Dock, throwing gear and provisions on board for his three days on the "edge" through storm, fog or hail. He'll see you Sunday.

September 1990

Chapter 52

DAVID MAHONEY

David Mahoney, the Bridgehampton summer resident, is sitting up in my office and we are remembering the best athlete ever to come out of the Bridgehampton School system: Carl Yastrzemski. Yaz became one of the greatest baseball players of all time. Playing for the Boston Red Sox, he dominated baseball for more than a decade, achieving the highest batting average, hitting the most home runs, winning the Triple Crown and leading the Red Sox into the World Series. When he retired in the early 1980's, this son of a potato farmer was greeted back in Bridgehampton with a huge parade and a giant sign across the Montauk Highway by the IGA. People have talked about him here ever since.

The time Mahoney and I are talking about, however, is before that. It is 1955 and Yastrzemski is a sophomore in high school in Bridgehampton. David Mahoney, the owner of his own Manhattan ad agency, had bought an oceanfront summer mansion just a few years before. One of the Yastrzemskis was his gardener.

"I'd find out when there was a baseball game and I'd wander up to the school and watch him play," Mahoney said. "Boy, he could hit that ball a mile. He was something to see."

"When I was growing up in New Jersey," I said, "I remember there was a kid who could hit the ball a mile. His name was Fred Wynn. He'd always get chosen first. I never did find out what happened to him."

"This was not the same," Mahoney said. "There were kids like that at the school. Yaz would hit it over THEIR heads."

It seemed unusual to me that a wealthy summer person would take the time to wander up to the school and watch a sandlot baseball game back then. But then I did the arithmetic. This tall friendly Irishman sitting in front of me is today 70 years old. He was, back then, 32. An early summer resident of the Hamptons. And a kid just beyond growing up himself who probably would have gone in and played himself if they had let them.

I think the common knowledge about all the summer mansions down on the beach in the Hamptons, and many of them have been here for more than a hundred years, is that they are either owned by wealthy families who hand them down from father to son, or they are in the temporary possession of New Yorkers whose careers have gone meteor-like through the roof. The mansions are one of their prizes.

The career of David Mahoney fits neither of these categories. He came to the Hamptons at the age of 30, having only recently overcome a childhood of poverty. He stayed. Over the years, much like the career of Carl Yastrzemski on the sports pages, David Mahoney made a lot of ink on the financial pages. When he retired ten years ago as CEO of Norton Simon, having lost a huge corporate battle with Beatrice, he reportedly settled for about $40 million. He was 60. His next career, which he began immediately, was in medicine and science as the Chairman of the Board of the Dana Foundation. It would pay $1 a year. He would spend the rest of his career giving back to the world that had so amply rewarded him. He would help in furthering medical research into the functioning and the malfunctioning of the human brain. He is doing this today.

David Mahoney was seven years old when the Crash of 1929 wiped out just about everybody in America. It was a searing event. David's father, a first generation Irish-American, was not terribly well off in the first place. He was a crane operator. And beginning in 1929 an out of work crane operator. David's mother worked sometimes as a telephone operator. But beginning in 1929 there was very little of that either. The family had to leave their home in the Bronx, and move to a tiny bungalow down on the beach at Locust Point, just opposite City Island.

"These had been summer homes for fishermen," Mahoney said. "Now there were no jobs and almost no money and these bungalows could be rented for $20 a month."

"How could the landlords rent them so cheap?" I asked.

"The landlords were broke too. Lots and lots of blue collar families moved into these bungalows and I remember my youth — I lived there from the time I was nine until I graduated high school — as a lot of games and sports. The way out, we kids thought, was to excel in a sport. We played our hearts out. And many of us did excel. Hank Greenberg lived in the Bronx and became a professional baseball player. George Sternweiss too. Both excellent players. I was six foot one by my senior year of high school — I went to St. Francis de Chantal

247

Catholic school — and I excelled at basketball later at La Salle Military Academy. We got to the finals at the Glens Falls Tournament in my senior year. And I was offered a basketball scholarship at the University of Pennsylvania."

Mahoney vowed, like many people who were raised during the Depression, that their goal in life would be not to be poor. At Penn, he would study business at the Wharton School. He was there two years when World War II broke out and he enlisted in the infantry. They sent David Mahoney to Okinawa and then to mainland Japan for the occupation. He was mustered out of the Army as a Captain.

Mahoney intended to return to Wharton, but there was such a crush of returning American youth that it would be almost a year before he could be re-admitted.

"Colleges were operating 24 hours a day to accommodate all the returning G.I.'s," he said. "I decided that if I had to wait a year I would, in the meantime, get a job."

He had moved back home to Locust Point to be with his parents. He was only 23. Now he thought up an interesting idea for an advertising campaign for a product, determined its ad agency in Manhattan and applied for a job there. Impressed, they hired him. He started in the mail room, was promoted within the year to account executive and two years later to Vice President. At the same time, he finished up his college education at Wharton, which is in Philadelphia. He'd work all day at Ruthrauff and Ryan, then he'd take a train to Philadelphia, study all night, and take a train back. He received his degree in 1945.

Around this time, he fell in with a columnist by the name of Robert C. Ruark. Ruark, who was also well known for his numerous works of fiction, wrote a column about this young 25 year old Vice President of a major advertising agency. In fact, he wrote four columns about him. "Mahoney," he wrote, "is a pretty striking example of the fact that opportunity is not dead in these parts and we need not substitute, as yet, socialism for hustle."

Mahoney hung out with Ruark first at Houston's Hotel Shamrock and later at the celebrated Monkey Bar of the Elysee Hotel, where Ruark, as many well known writers of the time, lived.

In 1951, Mahoney went out on his own, setting up his own advertising agency in the Chanin Building. He was 28 years old. This afforded Ruark the chance to write still another column. And clients rushed to seek work at David Mahoney, Inc. It was, at the time, what would today be known as a "boutique" shop. He soon was employing 25 people and billing a substantial sum for the time. Among his clients was Good Humor, Virginia Dare Wine, Noxzema and Schrafts.

And so, Mahoney, by standard accounts, had achieved his success. He married Powers fashion model Barbara Anne Moore and the following

248

year, at the age of thirty, purchased a house in Bridgehampton at the beach. He wanted, he said, at the time, to live near the ocean. And so he did.

Mahoney went from success to success. An article in *Fortune* magazine, written twenty years later, noted that if an investor had purchased stock in the companies that Mahoney either headed or was associated with during those twenty years, they would have become extremely wealthy. Surely Mahoney did. But he did it on his own, not as an investor, the poor son of Irish-American immigrants. One of the happiest moments of his life, Mahoney says, is when he was able to buy his parents a new home. It was right where they always lived, in Locust Point, near all their friends. But it was no bungalow. Another thing that gave him pleasure was to be on the Board of Directors of the New York Telephone Company, later NYNEX. Also the University of Pennsylvania. His mother had been an operator at one. He had gone to school at the other.

Although the David Mahoney Co. was a considerable success, after only five years he decided to accept an offer to become the President of the Good Humor Company. The Chairman of the Board of that company was so impressed with how Mahoney was handling the account that he decided to step aside so that a "marketing" whiz could take it for a ride. He offered Mahoney twice what he was making working for himself. Mahoney thought about it and he decided that if Corporate America was where the big money was then he would join Corporate America. He sold his ad agency for half a million dollars — a considerable sum for the time — and he took up the reins of Good Humor.

As everyone knows, the measure of a Chief Executive of any large corporation is whether the bottom line goes up or down and whether the stock goes up or down. Mahoney's marketing prowess, within five years, left Good Humor four times the size it was when he took it over and the stock doubled and doubled again. He was invited to become number two man at Colgate-Palmolive and from there he was offered the Presidency at Canada Dry. Soon he was President of the parent company, Norton Simon, which he led through much of the consolidating period of the 1970's and early 1980's. He presided over the purchase of AVIS rent-a-car and half a dozen other businesses. When he was himself forced out in a corporate battle in 1982, he had turned what had been a business billing in the hundreds of millions of dollars into a business billing three and a half billion. And the stock had gone way up.

Personally, there were other developments in David Mahoney's life. His summer home on the ocean was washed out to sea in a big storm in 1962. He bought another, several blocks up the street, on Ocean Road. In 1975, his wife passed away. He remarried Hillie Merrill and with her has raised his two children from his earlier marriage, Barbara and David, and also two stepsons. He has homes here in Bridgehampton, in Manhattan and in Palm Beach. Here in the Hamptons he is a member of the Shinnecock and National Golf Clubs, also the Meadow Club and the Bridgehampton Club where he is an associate member. He served as Chairman of the Board of Phoenix House, the American Health Foundation and he has been on the Board of the Urban League.

Mahoney's current major interest, as I mentioned, is the Dana Foundation and its subsidiary, the Dana Alliance. Upon leaving Norton Simon in 1983 he realized that if he wanted to make a complete change with what he did with his life he now certainly had that opportunity. He was 61. He had left the company, heralded by his associates and admired by his competitors, with more money than he could possibly spend. What would he do?

Mahoney decided that he would retire from business. From this point on, he would find a place for himself with a charity.

Mr. Mahoney became Chairman of the Charles A. Dana Foundation in 1977 and in 1993 Mr. Mahoney became Chairman of the Dana Alliance for Brain Initiatives. With his marketing skills, he would attempt to bring the activities of this organization to the forefront of the American consciousness.

"I became fascinated with just how little we know about the human brain," he said. "Here is an organ weighing just three pounds that is made up of billions and billions of cells and what do we know about it? Almost nothing. We know about the diseases of the brain, the tumors, the Alzheimer's, the Parkinson's, the strokes and so forth but ten years ago we could only describe them when they occurred. Treatment was remedial. Essentially, whatever happened, happened. I knew there was a lot more going on here than just behaviorism."

Mahoney, as Chairman of the DANA Foundation, began speaking out about the brain. And he put his money where his mouth was. He made an outright gift of more than a million dollars to the brain research institute at the University of Pennsylvania and they named a research institute after him. He did the same thing with Harvard. Harvard reciprocated with the Harvard Mahoney Institute.

To his surprise, dramatic progress began to be made about the workings of the brain. There were genes discovered, chemicals discovered.

"One in five people will have brain illnesses in their lifetime and everyone will in their lifetimes suffer a neuroscience problem." Mahoney said. "And yet, less than a billion dollars is being spent by the government on brain research. It is an incredible situation. I thought about the fact that dramatic progress was being made which nobody seemed to know anything about. And I thought we should do something dramatic."

Three years ago, Mahoney assembled a large team of neurologists for

250

a weekend at Cold Spring Harbor here on Long Island. He put a question to them. If dramatic progress was already being made, what would be ten things, ten specific things, that would very likely be discovered or solved about the brain in the next decade?

"I didn't want any vague promises. Nothing about spend the money now and we will see what we can do. I felt a list of ten things would be very dramatic."

Here is the list the neurologists came up with.

1. Identification of the genes defective in familial Alzheimer's and Huntington's diseases.

2. Identification of the genes responsible for hereditary forms of manic-depressive illness.

3. Development of new medications and therapeutic strategies to reduce nerve cell death and enhance recovery of function after strokes and other forms of brain injury.

4. Development of new drugs and other measures to alleviate the effects of multiple sclerosis, Alzheimer's disease, motor neuron disease (Lou Gehrig's disease), Parkinson's disease, and epilepsy.

5. Identification of new treatments to promote nerve regeneration following spinal cord and peripheral nerve injury.

6. Development of new and more effective treatments for manic-depressive illness, anxiety disorders, and forms of schizophrenia that at present resist treatment.

7. Discovery, testing and application of agents that will block the action of cocaine and other addictive substances.

8. Development of new treatments for pain associated with cancer, arthritis, migraine headaches, and other debilitating illnesses.

9. Identification of the genes that cause hereditary deafness and blindness.

10. Elucidation of the neuronal mechanisms involved in learning and memory.

And now, David Mahoney has taken his show on the road. Three weeks ago, he appeared on stage at LIU Southampton before a packed house with Nobel laureate James D. Watson, co-discoverer of the double helix structure of DNA, and Dr. Max Cowan, known for his pioneer work on the early development of the brain.

"Our lecture was fitted in that Sunday between Forstmann's Huggy Bear tennis tournament and the Hampton Classic Horse Show and it was sold out. I guess our efforts are working."

As a result of David Mahoney's marketing efforts, it is possible that whatever is learned about the brain will come about sooner than had he not been involved. That, in itself, marks the capstone to this man's very remarkable career.

September 24, 1993

Chapter 53

MARQUETTE de BARY

If there ever was a story about how someone with entreprenureal spirit came to help out where the helping was needed it is the story of Marquette de Bary, the financier, and a small Southampton college radio station called WPBX.

"We have a summer home quite near the college, on Hill Street," Mr. de Bary told me, "and the station became quite a favorite of mine. I do remember the first time. It was about six years ago. I was in the bathroom one morning shaving and I was listening to Paul Sidney holding forth with some of the local news, and I just turned the dial and there it was. Classical music. Right there in Southampton. I told my wife we ought to set all the radios in the house to this station and we did."

Little did Mr. de Bary know that the WPBX radio station was in serious trouble up at the college. It had been funded by the parent school, Long Island University, some years before. But then there hadn't been that many students who wanted to run it. After awhile, it went off the air. Radio station equipment was actually missing for a while until somebody thought to ask a janitor where it was. "Oh yes," he said, "I worried about it, so I put it into a closet."

It was only a year before de Bary heard it that it was back on the air, although in a limited edition. It pushed out only 100 watts. It had an antenna just 90 feet high. It could be heard only in the immediate Southampton area. Not much further.

The de Barys held a dinner party a few months later in honor of a friend of theirs who had known Angier Biddle Duke when he was Ambassador to Spain. Duke was now the Chancellor of Southampton

College. They'd get them all together.

In the course of the evening, de Bary mentioned that he so enjoyed listening to WPBX, the college radio station. Duke looked him right in the eye.

"I've been looking for somebody like you," Duke said.

Duke had just been made Chancellor. And in his inaugural address he said he wanted to make a priority of finding a way to bring together the town and the college in real ways. One of these ways, he now told de Bary, was with the radio station.

"We need to increase its power," Duke told him. "We need to bring people in from the local community to have programs on it. We need to make it a major source of communication throughout the entire East End."

Mr. de Bary, in 1986, took on this job. I was talking about it with him, now, in 1991, in his offices on Madison Avenue where a crowd of employees work in a large bullpen watching the financial news on computers, talking on phones and placing orders. Marquette de Bary has been, all his adult life, in the business of capital formation. His firm also serves as stock and bond discount brokers. Indeed he could put the necessary pieces together for the local college radio station.

"We estimated that to increase our signal to 1000 watts and to build a taller antenna, we would need $30,000," he told me. "I thought, who do I know who could spare $1000 if it was for a good cause, and I sent out 40 letters. I got the $30,000. Then we learned the cost really was more like $40,000 and so off we went again. We just muscled our way through.

"We founded a group called Friends of WPBX and I began spending two mornings a week there. What I wanted to do, since the college students handled the programming and did the programs in the evening, was to expand the loyal core of community volunteers who ran the station while the students were in class. I was on the phone a lot. Some of our best programming, still going on, is Ellen Samuel's "Gardening Guidelines," which tells you, each weekend, what you can do that weekend in your garden. Barbara Phillips, the wife of the former President of Dow Jones, joined to do a show on Hampton Happenings and Hillie Mahoney, wife of David Mahoney — chairman of Norton, Simon, created Hillie's Health Hints. If you couldn't go on the air, you could finance a show. I remember that Jerry Finkelstein, who owned the New York Law Journal, financed one."

The aerial went up and the new generator came in. WPBX could now be heard, loud and clear, for a distance of sixty or seventy miles.

"I wanted it to have national programming," he told me. "That meant getting programming from either the National Public Radio or the American Public Radio. I looked into it. And what I found was that

253

for us to be eligible we had to have a certain annual budget. We didn't have it. We were too small."

But de Bary got a very ingenious idea. If he could put a price tag on the work done by the town volunteers at the station, he could add that in and the total would make the station eligible. He got back on the phone. He talked to the powers that be at National Public Radio in Washington but without success, to his great regret.

"We chose American Public Radio," he told me. "It was cheaper and it had more of the sort of programming we had in mind. Although there is quite a bit on National Public Radio that I wish we had."

Today, the station is thriving. You can hear it just about wherever you go on the East End, at 91.3 on your dial, broadcasting local fare, classical, jazz, progressive rock, features and news. Marquette de Bary has made something where there was nothing.

"One of our biggest successes is our annual Jazz Festival," he said.

"And do please mention Bill Beutel and Kristi Witker. They were so supportive. We'd have Christmas or mid-term parties for the students at our house and he'd come and give pep talks."

de Bary continues to live at Whitefield in Southampton. He lives in Manhattan and he and his wife Patricia have a Paris apartment.

"Have you ever been on the air yourself?" I asked.

"From time to time, I did some interviews," he told me. "Also some obituaries."

de Bary came to Southampton, for the first time, as it turned out, because of his marriage to his present wife Patricia. She had lived there before, raised children there.

de Bary was born and raised in the New York area, started on Wall Street during the Great Depression and did advanced studies at night at NYU. He then studied at Columbia, at the Institute of Banking and at Wharton. He did service in World War II in the European theater with the 62nd Fighter Wing, then returned home and started his own firm in 1962.

He has a brother, Theodore, who was a Confucian scholar and recently retired as head of the Far Eastern Department at Columbia University. And he has two sons and a daughter. One son is with the firm, his daughter is raising a family in Virginia, and the other son is in the Balearic Islands busy being a vegetarian.

As for other charitable pursuits, he leaves much of it to his wife, who remains extremely active. She was a co-chairman of the Southampton Hospital summer party for a number of years. And in the city she is active with the New York Botanical Gardens where she just finished a successful fundraising that exceeded a million dollars.

October 25, 1991

254

Chapter 54

IRV GIKOFSKY
"Mr. G"

At ten minutes to five, Mr. G, the CBS weatherman, came down the hall and shook my hand there in front of the receptionist's desk. He was wearing jeans, a sports jacket he says he bought in East Hampton, a red tie and white shirt. We were on the ground floor of the vast CBS broadcasting studios on 57th Street between 10th and 11th Avenue in Manhattan. He'd be on the air in ninety minutes.

Mr. G's real name is Irving Gikofsky and I found this out after he had led me back down the hall and through a maze of studios, engineering booths and offices to the room where he has his own desk and computers and I noticed that on the wall was a completion certificate from the New York City Marathon in 1989. It was made out to Irving Gikofsky.

"I run about six marathons a year," he said. "I love to run."

I would have judged Mr. G to be about thirty two or thirty three years old. He's a friendly, handsome man, bubbling with self confidence — you have to be likeable and credible and an up guy to be a weatherman he later told me — and he certainly is all of those. He is tanned, as if he had just come back from a Caribbean island vacation, and he is slender and funny. And he told me he is forty six.

"It's in the genes," he said. He meant it with a G.

I asked Mr. G how he had become the weatherman for CBS.

"I was never in the minor leagues," he said. "My first job in television, it was right here."

In fact, the story of how he came to be on CBS is a true Cinderella story. A Long Island boy, he grew up in Brooklyn and then Kew Gardens where he went to Francis Lewis High School in Queens and then to Hofstra where he got degrees in History, Education and Meteorology. He studied with the legendary teacher Eliot Shapiro, who imbued in him a sense of the true needs of children. He got a job teaching, in one of the toughest sections of the Bronx, at I.S. 31.

"I taught biology for a year," he told me. "But then I started to set up a weather station. It was a true professional weather station with every computer, every dial and gauge imaginable, and I ran it every day, from 5:30 in the morning until 1:15 in the afternoon. Or I should say the kids ran it, seventh graders, and after a year it became a full fledged weather bureau. The kids were from a disadvantaged neighborhood. We were giving the weather, officially, for WNYE, the public radio station in New York. People started writing stories about it.

"One story appeared on NBC. Another on CBS. Trisch Riley, a reporter for CBS, said to me I was absolutely made for television and I said look, I hang back, I'm shy. You know, it was true. In my high school yearbook, I wouldn't even have my picture taken. I got sick that day. My yearbook says HALL PATROL, CAFETERIA MONITOR, GYM and above it is an empty box. I began to wonder about this and why I did it and how I might be made for television. I began to appear in some of the reports about the weather station instead of hanging back. I liked it.

"At this time, I was single, I had a bachelor apartment in Whitestone and I would drive to the Bronx to school. I was in my early thirties. One day in 1977 they did a piece on our weather station on Frank Field's show on NBC and Larry Schultz, the producer, said the same thing to me. 'You are made for television.' I thought about it.

"One day I saw an ad in a daily newspaper in the city that read WANTED, TALL DARK HANDSOME STUD-LIKE WEATHER MAN. MAJOR MARKET. I thought, I'm six feet, I'm a bachelor, I'm having a wonderful time. I didn't do anything about it. I couldn't afford an agent. But then one day I decided I WOULD do something and I went to a talent scout and she got me an interview for a weatherman's job at a station in Altoona, Pennsylvania, paying six thousand dollars a year. I auditioned. I didn't get the job. But I kept the tape of the audition. Then I got an audition here at CBS and at first they were unconvinced but then they came up to the Bronx and sat in the back while I taught my kids, and they offered me a job.

"I did the weekend weather. For two years, I continued teaching in the Bronx but then on Saturdays and Sundays I did the weather for CBS. I worked seven days a week but I loved it, both the teaching and being the weatherman, and so it didn't seem like work to me."

Eventually, CBS wanted him full time and he gave up teaching in the Bronx. That was twelve years ago.

"Did the weather station continue?" I asked.

"It continued on for three years after I left, just slowly dying. It was so frustrating to see. There was another teacher interested in continuing it at a school just a few blocks away — he was also interested in meteorology — but it was just too hard to transfer the program from one school to another."

"What do you think about what is happening to education?"

"I'm truly frustrated. We constantly lose sight of the ball. We can't ever forget that the human being has the longest extended childhood of any species. Our kids need shoulders, someone to make the world safe, for maybe sixteen years. But we constantly interrupt our kids with adult problems or adult problems using kids as scapegoats."

I asked Mr. G to describe some of the things that have happened over the past twelve years as the weatherman at CBS.

"Well there was one day I kept garbling a particular word. I would say there is a leading edge of cold hair moving in our direction. I tried it several times. All I could say was hair. I have no idea why. Finally, I said this is Boy G brother of Mr. G. I didn't want anyone to know it was me."

"Once I wore a blue shirt that was exactly the same shade of blue as the blue in the trick photography we use so it looks like I'm standing in front of this huge weather map. I could see it on the monitor, it was raining on my shirt, there was a thunderstorm moving toward my belt. It was wild.

"I remember the morning Hurricane Hugo struck Charleston. It was coming up the coast, right at us. Boy was this important. Usually, the weatherman is more important than the story, but not this day.

"I do visit kids in schools a lot. I just came back from visiting a school in Morristown, New Jersey. It's nice to see the kids and it's nice for them to see someone on television. I answer their questions about the weather.

"One time I visited this school of first graders and all the kids were laughing and happy to see me except this one who was crying and howling. We asked him, what was wrong what was the matter and he said I thought Mr. T was coming and who the heck are you? Oh well. And many kids, especially that age, haven't really figured out television. They say HOW DID YOU GET OUT OF THE BOX? I can't answer that question.

"I've been coming out to the Hamptons for fifteen years on and off. Years ago I'd come with the guys and we'd rent a house with a farm behind it and I'd pick lettuce from the ground, here I was a Queens boy out in the country and it was so healthy I'd get sick. We'd lie on the beach and I'd get too much sun and we'd go dancing. I am afraid of the water so I never went swimming and I have no rhythm so I can't really dance, so finally, what I'd wind up doing was strolling through town or reading or sometimes fishing off a boat where the lines get tangled up.

"I love the Hamptons. They've always had a special feeling for me, that someday I would 'arrive' and I'd have my own place. I used to think of this in terms of job success, but now it is a relaxing spot for me, with interesting people. I saw Paul Simon in East Hampton the other day and I walked into a parking meter."

August 2, 1991

* * *

Mr. G is currently the weatherman at WPIX Channel 11 in New York.

Chapter 55

CHARLIE MOSS

Charles Moss has written some of the greatest advertising slogans of all time. I Love New York. Quality is Job One. (Ford). Flick Your Bic. He also looks like a Marx Brother. He is fifty-one years old, wiry, funny, animated and with a great shock of wiry black hair, and about as imposing looking as Jay Leno or David Letterman. He and his wife own one of the grand old houses near the ocean in Wainscott — it used to be the old Wainscott Post Office — but where I met with him and spoke with him was at his well appointed office at the advertising agency Wells, Rich and Greene where he is the corporate creative director. Pictures of his wife and children, and the Wainscott house, were hanging on the walls there. But as for the man who ruled this roost, he might have been the man delivering the coffee so informally was he dressed.

I asked about the house.

"Alan Schneider sold it to me. This was fourteen years ago before he got rich and famous. It had been the old post office in Wainscott, and they wanted to sell it but they wanted it moved off the land. Alan had found some land across the street. I hired Brownie to move it. And we've been there ever since, overlooking the Pond. Actually, I am very lucky because Ronald Lauder is my neighbor and he has bought up all the adjacent land and has kept it from being developed. We call the whole area Lauderville."

"How long had you been coming to the Hamptons?"

"I first rented a beach house in Westhampton Beach around twenty years ago. But then I didn't come back for awhile. Then I met Susan. We lived together in Manhattan and we rented this wonderful little bungalow on Sagaponack Main Street. That was such a wonderful time. I think we paid all of $2000 for the whole summer there. There was a bed, a sofa, a little deck where we ate dinner. We'd eat dinner looking out over this vast potato field and we said we had the biggest dining room in the whole world. We had friends on the other side of the field. Sometimes they would walk across to us, sometimes we would walk across to them. What a wonderful summer that was.

"The next year, and this was fourteen years ago, we decided to buy. I had proposed to Susan and we had decided to buy a house on Ocean Road in Bridgehampton — the sellers were happy, the agent was happy, the price was right — and then, suddenly, in our apartment in Manhattan, I got cold feet. I broke out in sweats. Susan came home and she had bought a big cow bell that would hang on our kitchen door there that she would ring to announce dinner. It was inscribed 'I'll be there.' And I looked at this and I told her I had bad news. I couldn't get married and buy a house at the same time. It was just too much. And so we decided to get married and NOT buy the house which is what we did and we bought this other house another time, about six months later."

Charlie Moss has an older son, in his early twenties, from an earlier marriage who is working as a copywriter right there at Wells, Rich and Greene, which Charlie describes as a really strange feeling since it reminds him of himself twenty-five years ago. He and Susan also have two adopted children, Korean children named Mary and Sam who are now five and six. They are cute as buttons and their picture is right on the wall there alongside the picture of the Wainscott house. "We've expanded the house as our family has expanded," Charlie says.

As for his career, Charlie Moss describes it beginning in Union, New Jersey at the age of eleven. He was born and raised in this Newark suburb and when he was in grammar school he became fascinated with the kids in the school plays. On his own, he tried out for the plays, he got parts and he performed. His teachers encouraged him and from the seventh grade on he was going to a dramatic school in Manhattan, commuting from his home in New Jersey. His parents were very supportive, and he played many roles as a child actor. He was on TV, he was in a movie at the age of twelve — *The Little Fugitive* about a boy who runs away to Coney Island — and he soon developed a whole range of talents from tap dancing to singing to ventriloquism to telling jokes.

By the time he was seventeen, however, he decided to put his theatrical career on hold for awhile and he went off to Ithaca College where he got a degree in English literature. Back in New York he went through a disastrous attempt to get back into his career as an adult child actor, and then one day he found himself taking a course at NYU in advertising design with Bob Levenson. Levenson saw the talent in him and encouraged him, after a six month stint in the armed forces, to give him a call and he would help Charlie find work. Levenson was true to his word and Charlie Moss, the wild, wild haired Charlie Moss, soon found himself as a copywriter at Doyle Dane and Bernbach under the tutilage of Mary Wells. Mary went to Jack Tinker and Partners, Moss followed, and it was here that he was to develop the first of his advertising campaigns that was to make him famous.

"I did this campaign for Braniff," he says. "All the airplanes were painted in different bright colors, and the stewardesses dressed in layers of clothing which they would remove, layer by layer, during the flight. Every ten minutes or so they would have a different look, it was a kind of a fashion show. I called it the 'Air Strip.'

"I must say that today there wouldn't be a chance of getting this on the air, what with equal rights and all, but back then, the passengers loved it. One would get on a flight to San Antonio and say I'm getting off in Houston, will I miss anything?"

A career was launched.

Looking around the office, it is clear that this man simply loves what he is doing. There is a TV set in one corner with cassettes alongside to view commercials. There are campaigns lining the walls. Moss tells me there is a new campaign about to be launched for Hertz that he has done, "America's Wheels" it is called, and we should see it soon.

Besides Wainscott, the Moss' have an apartment on Fifth Avenue. Charlie rises at six, works out at the Cardio/Fitness Center right in the office building at 9 West 57th Street across from the Plaza and is in his office by nine, ready to go for the day, and ready to consider the Hamptons for the weekend.

September 14, 1990

Chapter 56

WILBUR ROSS

Andy Warhol said that everybody gets fifteen minutes of fame in their lifetime. For Wilbur Ross, who has spent most of his adult life as a behind-the-scenes financier, this came one year ago when he was negotiating with Donald Trump about the Taj Mahal in Atlantic City.

"I have met many of the financial people who did these deals in the 1980's," Ross says. "Trump is one of the most colorful of them."

Wilbur Ross is 53, looks like an accountant, and is a very mild mannered, quiet sort of a guy. He is also Senior Managing Director of Rothschild, Inc. and as such was tapped as the point man for the Taj Mahal bondholders, as angry a group as there could be as they watched their holdings in the Taj teeter toward bankruptcy.

"I negotiated directly with Mr. Trump to work out the restructuring," Ross says. "I was on television a lot. We came close to a deal, then it would fall apart and the Taj seemed like it would fall into default. We were negotiating for twenty-four hours and then, at just five minutes to six p.m. on a Monday, six was the deadline, I received a message that Trump would not negotiate with me anymore but with some other unnamed bond holders. I went on television. I told reporters it was a big public relations stunt. And then I got a call from my mother in New Jersey who is 78 years old. 'You look awful,' she said. 'I saw you on TV and you need a shave. And if you're getting fired why does it have to be so public? If you'd only been a lawyer like I always wanted you to be you wouldn't have to hang around with people like that.'"

Eventually, the deadline was extended and Donald Trump came around again. A deal was finally hammered out.

"A lot of the Taj Mahal bondholders wanted retribution against Mr. Trump," Ross continued. "But I didn't feel that way. I felt he had considerable value. We'd go down there and when we'd walk through a casino everything would stop and people would look at him. He was like a mini-dictator. I'll tell you, people who gamble at these Casinos want to be paid. When they see Mr. Donald Trump walking through, they know everything will be okay."

Ross peers at me over his round bookkeeper glasses. "Actually, Trump and I have very different styles," he says. "We did not get along."

It is, perhaps, Mr. Ross' style that led him into finance in the first place. After a childhood in North Bergen, New Jersey, he went to Yale to major in English and become a writer. He joined the Yale Literary Review and they took a look at him and said I don't know about his writing but I'll bet he can sell ads and they sent him out. And he sold ads. Whatever literary publications he became involved with, he wound up as business manager.

"I never did find out if I could be a creative writer," he says.

But he did get involved in a prank. In his senior year at Yale, he and a few other guys decided to hold a contest to give away blind dates. They contacted four girls at four different schools and after getting each of them to agree to a blind date, invited them for homecoming weekend to Yale. Then they put an ad in the Yale daily. SHE IS COMING, it read. Write an essay of 50 words or less and you could win this blind date.

"It kind of blew up in our faces," Ross says. "*Life* magazine covered our contest rather than the scholar of the house competition which they usually did. Somebody wrote a letter suggesting we were in violation of the Mann Act. What finally happened is that we scrapped the contest and dated the four girls ourselves."

From Yale, Wilbur Ross went to the Harvard Business School where he earned an MBA. And then, after a stint in the Army, at the invitation of one of his former teachers at Yale, he joined a small Wall Street firm specializing in money management. He moved to Manhattan. He would make a career on Wall Street.

Ross also bought a small house in Southampton at this time. Having come out summers before to group houses, he learned from a realtor named Isabelle Crockett that a house in the estate section of Southampton, on First Neck Lane, could be bought for just $42,000. The bank would roll over the mortgage from the prior owner. All he needed was $2,000 down.

"This house is two doors down from where I am today," Ross says. "I bought it. We had a great time back then. This was in my bachelor days. We had beach parties, I went careening around, stuff like that. I guess it is not much different than today but maybe it is in one respect:

we didn't have this sense of having to get one millimeter ahead of the next person all the time."

At his job on Wall Street, things took a strange turn, one which would have profound implications for Ross' future. The principal of the firm, Imre DeVegh, died. And the firm was sold to one of the wealthy families that had been a client. After awhile, this family decided to merge the firm and at the same time to get out of the risky venture capital business. This had been a sideline of the business.

"Raising venture capital was what had excited me in the first place," Ross says. "We had raised money to back a company that made art reproductions for museum stores. We raised money for a fellow who thought he could make transistors out of cellulose. We invested in something called TRG, a laser company that we later sold to Control Data. Some of these companies failed. Some succeeded. Now somebody had to talk to these companies and get them to find other backing because we were pulling out. They gave this job to me."

Ross talked with bankers and investors. He fought and argued and cajoled and compromised.

"I learned a lot looking in on companies that are all screwed up," he says.

Eventually, his old firm wanted him to go into research. He declined. He liked dealing with start ups and venture capital and businesses in need of being turned around. And so he joined Faulkners, Dawkins, where, after a stint in research, he got put in charge of venture capital and public offerings.

"I remember being very attracted to an air freight firm out west. I met the people and they seemed very disciplined, had a particular market in mind and a specific plan. They seemed very determined. We put in seed money and I got investors to put in more. It prospered and today it is Airborne Freight Company.

"Then, I took a gamble on Wein Airlines in Alaska and we raised money for them and in three months, to my horror I found they had gone through half of it. I found myself every weekend flying up to Alaska to help them straighten things out. Then they discovered oil in Prudhoe Bay and it turned out Wein had the exclusive on the route to Prudhoe. My Alaska commute came to an end."

Ross prospered, married, had two daughters. In 1976 he was hired by Rothschild as managing director to run their corporate financing. At the very first meeting, he was told that they had raised $75 million for a small company called Federal Express, that Federal Express was on the ropes, that the banks were closing in and it was his job to persuade the banks to hold off for awhile. He was 36 years old.

"Twelve months later, Federal Express went public," Ross says. "Now they are a giant thing."

264

Since 1976, Ross has often been the point man in dealing with companies where a possible change of ownership is at hand. In the late 1970's, Rothschild often represented the sellers of companies in $50-100 million transactions. But beginning in 1983, when the buying and selling often involved junk bonds, Ross and Rothschild made an interesting decision.

"I was convinced all of this was not going to work out," Ross says. "I became something of a curmudgeon. We decided to position ourselves for the shake out. We believed this whole junk bond business was going to crater."

And indeed it did. It took much longer than either Ross or Rothschild figured, but when it did the crash was heard round the world.

"It made no sense," Ross says. "At first, Michael Milkin had shown, and it was true, that the bonds of reputable companies that had gone bad, called junk bonds, were much less risky than previously thought. But it was one thing to deal in these unrated bonds. It was another to say that if unrated bonds fared well then we could CREATE out of nothing unrated bonds. And yet that is exactly what they did. They created a whole new currency, a flawed currency, and then they used it to buy and sell companies. What used to be creditors were now equity holders. And when the equity proved worthless, the stockholders — who were actually victims — were caught holding the bag."

Ross decided he would work for the victims. When a company would get in trouble, he'd call up the major stockholders and try to get them to band together to fight the management that had gotten them there.

"These were called 'work outs.' We'd be there to work things out. And there was never enough money to go around, so who gets what?"

Ross represented the stock and bond holders for Revere Copper and Brass, for A. H. Robbins, for Texaco.

"Sometimes it was trench warfare," he says. Sometimes, negotiating on behalf of the stockholders, he would insist that management provide the stockholders an attorney and an investment banker so the playing field would be more level. He got seven hundred million for the stockholders of A. H. Robbins. The stockholders of Revere Copper and Brass threw out the management, took control of the company and sold it at a profit.

"That battle with Revere kind of put us on the map," he says. And a year later he was leading the negotiations with Trump.

"I must say I found him tough, quick and articulate and a very good bargainer," Ross says. "And I think, everything considered, and I don't know his whole picture, he has made out quite well. He's still in there playing. And these are very tough times."

In recent years, Ross has represented stockholders and bondholders in battles against TWA, Continental, Orion and, most recently, the real estate firm of Olympia and York.

"I think this whole country is in a work out," he says. "If we're not careful, the real junk bonds are going to turn out to be Treasury bonds."

But is there a way out of this mess?

"Yes, I think there is. But it isn't going to be easy. This administration's policies have been an abysmal failure. There is lots that needs to be done."

Very upset with what has gone on in the 1980's, Wilbur Ross has on occasion become very active in the Democratic party. He supported Senator Bob Kerrey of Nebraska during the primaries, had him out to his house in Southampton. He recently put together a party for Ted Weiss, Congressman from Manhattan's West Side, at the Southampton Bath and Tennis Club where he is a Chairman of the Board. Larry Rivers played. He has had similar events for Senators Kennedy and Moynihan.

Ross has been an active supporter of the schools that his children attended, Yale and Sarah Lawrence. He organized the first parent fund raising group for Sarah Lawrence. He is President of the Board of Southampton's Parrish Art Museum and he is Chairman of the Board of the National Museum of American Art in Washington, D.C. He is a collector of 19th Century American Art.

Today, Wilbur Ross lives in Southampton and on Manhattan's West Side. In the Hamptons, He plays tennis and often dines out. He says two of his favorite restaurants are Basilico in Southampton and the Old Stove Pub in Bridgehampton. He and his wife come out to the Hamptons weekends year around.

July 31, 1992

Chapter 57

D. A. PENNEBAKER

D. A. Pennebaker is known nationally as one of this country's premiere filmmakers. And he is known locally for having virtually populated Sag Harbor. Since 1950, Mr. Pennebaker has been married three times and has produced eight beautiful children. His own house, with his present wife and two children (age 6 and 10), is on Spring and Garden Streets. His first wife Sylvia lives on Madison Street, his son Frazer who works with him lives on High Street and Linley, who runs Provisions in Sag Harbor, has a home in Noyac. Most of the other children are either in school or in and out of Sag Harbor. As for Penny, as he is universally known, he is out there for three or four day weekends as much as he can.

Penny today is almost seventy years old. And yet, meeting him in his Manhattan brownstone, it is sort of a footnote. He is so filled with film projects and travel and raising young children and relating with his own children and his attractive wife, filmmaker Chris Hegedus, to whom he has been married for twelve years, that it is hard to imagine what age he is.

He has been collaborating with Chris Hegedus making films since 1976. "Chris does things I cannot do," he says. "She learned filmmaking before I met her and she is brilliant."

The brownstone is on 91st Street off Broadway and there is a ground floor of offices and screening rooms, a second floor filled with editing studios, a third floor with more editing studios and a basement for the archives. Half a dozen people are running around. The phone is ringing. Projects are going on all over the place. Yet this brownstone is not where the Pennebakers live. They live in another one, a few blocks away. And as we speak it is a weekday and the children are off at school.

The whole thing is known as Pennebaker, Associates. And Associates it is indeed. On the second floor, I meet his son, Frazer, who occupies a room filled with computers overlooking the street.

"I could not do this without Frazer," Penny says. "He handles the whole business side and is executive producer on most films."

For those unfamiliar with his work, Penny is probably best known for having made the movie *Monterey Pop* about that 1968 rock concert and *Don't Look Back* the Bob Dylan film. They both still show up at theaters around the world.

Currently, and there have been about fifty films between that one and this one, Pennebaker Associates is busy editing a movie called *War Room*. Scheduled for release November 3 at the NY Film Forum, it is the detailed story of Bill Clinton's campaign for President. The name for the film comes from the name of the room where George Stephanopolis, Stan Greenberg, Mandy Grunwald, James Carville and many others orchestrated Clinton's successful run. Pennebaker had been invited, based upon his reputation, to film the goings-on in this room throughout the campaign as the three men and one woman bounced from one crisis to another in engineering their candidate's six percentage point victory over George Bush.

"When we started this project," Penny says, "and it was originally proposed and produced along with Frazer, by R. J. Cutler and Wendy Ettinger, we had no idea whether Clinton would even win. It might have amounted to nothing."

D. A. Pennebaker was born and raised in Chicago. His father was a commercial photographer specializing in advertising work. He and Penny's mother were soon divorced. His mother moved to New York.

"I remember twenty four hour train rides between New York and Chicago," Penny says. "I wore a tag with my name and address on it."

He was raised primarily in Chicago, attending many different schools there. He has vivid memories of his father and his work because there were times that Penny was in it.

"I recall one time he had to take a shot of a lifeboat sinking. It was done in a studio and I was a survivor in the boat. A set of the ocean had been constructed. There were hoses turned on us, spray and water everywhere."

At his uncle's house, Penny did his own form of construction. Using hammer and nails, he attacked a big pile of wood in the yard and made giant model airplanes, big enough to sit in. They didn't fly but you could climb in them and pretend to fly. He also made a full scale model wooden boat.

268

Penny went to Salisbury Prep School in Connecticut, then Yale where he majored in engineering.

"I thought engineering was building things out of solder and wire which sounded kind of fun. Instead it was mostly about mathematics."

He left Yale to serve in the armed forces during World War II, ending up in the Naval Air Corps. And he studied more engineering, learning about radio equipment and transmitting equipment. When the war ended, he went back to Yale, finished up, got married and began his family. He lived on East 17th Street between First and Second Avenues across from the park. And he worked as an engineer for a Manhattan firm for six months, then opened his own electronics company in a loft on Murray Street. It was called Electronic Engineering Co.

"We made radios, phonographs, amplifiers. I helped design and manufacture a reservation system for American Airlines. This was in the late 1940's, so they were not the big airline they are today. Our project involved a big metal drum coated in ferrous oxide that the airline kept in its Pittsburgh headquarters. It was kept in a cool box to keep the heat down and it stored data. It was an early form of computer."

Penny saw that his future might include opening a factory somewhere out in the suburbs. The idea did not appeal to him.

"I didn't know what I really wanted to do," he said. "I just knew I had to earn a living. I had a problem there."

What he did want to do quickly made itself known. Around 1950, he saw an art film called NYNY made by Francis Thompson.

"You have to realize that film cameras at this time weighed forty pounds or more. Most films were big deals made in a studio. What got me was a person could make it all by himself. No actors, no studio."

Pennebaker met Francis Thompson and, in his spare time, began helping him out. He would carry equipment, help set up the camera. Later they made films at the Stock Exchange, at the YMCA, at the Girl Scouts. Many were just poetic fantasy films. And most were heavily narrated. This was before the time that a small filmmaker could coordinate film and sound on hand-held equipment.

There was a whole sub-culture of filmmakers in New York City at this time, and Pennebaker, who was in his mid-twenties, became part of it. Films would be made, sixteen millimeter, and be shown at theatres around Manhattan. Maybe fifty or a hundred people would attend.

"Everybody involved in this became friends," Penny said. "We'd hear that a film would be showing on a Saturday morning at Amos Vogel's Cinema 16 for example, and we'd go. Nobody took sides for or against. We all just went to see. Sometimes a very nice guy at the *New York Times* would review these films. Why I don't know."

Inevitably, Pennebaker tried his own hand at making one of these films. The movie he made, five minutes long, was called *Daybreak Express*, after the Duke Ellington jazz record that Penny chose for the background. The camera films the Third Avenue El (it was scheduled to be torn down and was torn down later that year), and it is dawn and commuters are on their way to work. A very arty film, it was raved about wherever it was seen. It is still being shown today. "A friend knew a guy who owned the Paris Theatre at 58th Street and 5th Avenue. I went to see him. He was not much for short films, he said. But if I could blow it up to 35mm, he would rent it from me for $25 a week, or buy the thing for $100."

It was the first money he had ever been offered for filmmaking. And it was his very first film.

"I couldn't part with it. So I took him up on the rental idea. It lasted for quite a while."

Pennebaker is modest. It lasted for years and became a cult film. It was one of the most extraordinary short films ever made.

Penny's real work began about three years later. He was contacted by Bob Drew at *LIFE* magazine. He wanted to start a film section for the magazine, sell films to TV. They hired Pennebaker and they hired filmmakers Al Maysles and Richard Leacock, who had studied physics at Harvard and they put the three of them under the direction of Bob Drew, a *LIFE* editor. He would give it a year or two. The idea was to create candid realism in film journalism. *LIFE* had approached ABC television about it. Television was still in its infancy, but it was getting off the ground.

Pennebaker, Maysles and Leacock immediately went to work. How were they going to cover late breaking journalistic events with equipment that weighed in excess of forty pounds? Between Leacock with his physics training and Pennebaker with his electrical engineering training, things rapidly began to take shape.

"One of our first assignments for *LIFE* was *Primary*, about the Presidential primary, then we did *On The Pole*, the Indianapolis 500 then *Yankee No*, about Fidel Castro in Cuba then a film covering the inauguration of President Kennedy. The idea was that we would mingle with the crowd, be backstage, get on film what everybody was saying. Somehow, we had to get sound to synchronize with moving pictures in a package that a cameraman could carry around all day. If we could get sound to playback to an accuracy within one frame in 16,000 that would solve the problem. One day, I read an advertisement for a Bulova watch. 'Accurate to one in 16,000,' it said. I went to see them. Could they make a clock for us? We worked with TRW to develop an entirely new kind of motor for our camera. And I went to see a company that was building batteries for the space program. They were lightweight all right, but there were serious recharging problems."

Eventually, Pennebaker and Leacock developed a system where little marks were electronically put down on the tape like pickets defining a fence. Their package, which featured a film magazine capable of just ten minutes, weighed under twelve pounds. Nobody had ever seen anything like it before.

They fanned out with the new equipment for the Kennedy Inauguration in Washington. Whether it was the new equipment or the untried coordination, the effort was a disaster. Pierre Salinger wanted to do something, they did tapes with John and Elaine Steinbeck, with John Galbraith. Pennebaker was with a crew following Scottie Lenihan and F. Scott Fitzgerald's daughter. Then, because there was more than a foot of snow on the ground, they repaired to a bar where they commenced an interview with a man because he looked like, although he wasn't, Dwight D. Eisenhower.

"In the end it all came to nothing," Pennebaker told me. "I kept the footage and tried to work with it, maybe make a comedy out of it. But I couldn't even do that."

Some people connected with *LIFE* rented houses for the summer in Sag Harbor. Among them were Lincoln Barnett and Bob Osborne. They'd work four days a week at *LIFE* then spend three days in Sag Harbor.

Pennebaker had actually been coming to Sag Harbor since 1960 when his friend writer John Sherry (*Maggie's Farm*) rented Jean Snow's house. In 1961, Pennebaker and his wife bought a house there.

"I bought the house without ever even seeing the inside of it. There just didn't seem to be a need. It was late at night. We'd been up late at John's. I had to run back to New York to work at *LIFE*. I figured that whatever was inside would be just fine, which it was.

"Incidentally, up until then, I did not know you could buy a house without having all the money up front in advance. Mortgages were a big revelation to me. I think we bought that house with just twenty five hundred dollars down."

There were more projects attempted with the new equipment. And these achieved considerable success. In fact, perhaps their greatest success resulted in their leaving *LIFE*. It was four years later and Drew, on behalf of *LIFE*, had declined a proposal to film a confrontation between Governor Wallace of Alabama and Robert Kennedy. Leacock and Pennebaker together with reporter Greg Shugar did it anyway, and when it was apparently going to be a big hit, it became a Bob Drew project again. The project, including footage of students and Nicholas Katzenbach in addition to Kennedy and Wallace, was called *Crisis*. It ran one hour on ABC.

Leacock and Pennebaker set up a studio of their own on 43rd Street in Manhattan and began their own projects. They filmed Timothy Leary's wedding, did a film on jazz musician Dave Lambert and another called

Happy Mother's Day about a set of quintuplets.

In 1966, Leacock and Pennebaker made a film entitled *Don't Look Back*, which followed the first European tour of Bob Dylan. The following year, they made *Monterey Pop*, about the festival in California which they distributed themselves. They also made a film with Van Cliburn and Company, a behind-the-scenes look at the original cast recording session for a Broadway show by Steve Sondheim. The collaboration ended and Leacock went up to MIT to teach and Pennebaker kept going in New York. They also worked on a film here in Water Mill and East Hampton called *Maidstone*. Pennebaker was one of the cameramen on this piece. Another was Nick Proferes. The film itself, a critical disaster, was directed by Norman Mailer.

Pennebaker commented to me that his film studio in Manhattan could grow and grow. That is the normal evolution of things in the film business. But Pennebaker is interested in staying small. He turns down a lot and, since 1970, he has turned out two or three films a year, including *Delorean*, the story of automaker John Delorean, *Sweet Toronto* with John Lennon and Yoko Ono, *Rockabye*, *Depeche Mode 101*, and *Dance Black America*. Most of these later pieces have been made together with Chris Hegedus. Their most celebrated work together was *The Energy War*, which documented President Jimmy Carter, Energy Secretary James Schlesinger and various senators and lobbyists struggling to put together a national energy policy in the late 1970's. Harvard's Kennedy School of Government cited *The Energy War* as "one of the best political films ever made."

After thirty years of filmmaking, the basement archive of D. A. Pennebaker is filled with films of some of the most celebrated individuals of our time. Many of these films have been completed and released. Others have never been released. Chris and Pennebaker are constantly going through these archives for films to re-release material. In 1991 they released *Comin' Home* with Janis Joplin. There is more to come.

Through this all, D. A. Pennebaker continues to come back to Sag Harbor. Among other things, at his home on Garden Street, he makes things in a workshop in the back for his young children. Things made of lumber that a kid could bang together with nails and a hammer and sit on.

It was something he did, years ago, in a suburb in New Jersey. Now he wants it for his kids.

September 3, 1993

* * *

The War Room was nominated for an Academy Award in 1994.

Chapter 58

SUSAN ISAACS

Susan Isaacs is a sweet, straightforward unassuming woman. She is in her mid-forties, soft and motherly looking. There is nothing about her that would ever lead you to believe that she is a cult figure. And yet, when she gets up to talk in front of an audience, as she did recently as part of the Writer's Lecture Series on the lawn of the Library in Bridgehampton (the place was jammed with her readers, mostly other women), people sit there enthralled at her every word.

For Susan Isaacs has struck a chord. She struck it for the first time in 1976 when she wrote her premiere novel *Compromising Positions*. At the time, she was a Long Island housewife with two small children and an attorney for a husband who said he would support her in doing whatever she wanted. And so she took her typewriter into a basement office he had set up for her and she wrote this book, and they made it into a movie starring Susan Sarandon and Raoul Julia, and it became a Book of the Month Club selection. And then after that she struck this chord with a total of five more best sellers one after the other. Her new book, *After All These Years*, came out last month, and to judge by the critical reviews, she has done it again.

I think that if Susan Isaacs were slender and glamorous she would not be receiving the virtual adulation her many fans heap upon her. But Susan Isaacs in person is like one of the heroines in her books. She is a conventional but upwardly mobile nouveau riche suburban housewife who broke the mold. In her books, these housewives tend to get themselves into trouble, and then, instead of finding some man to get them out of it, take a deep breath and go off and straighten their lives out for themselves. Usually, they solve murders. In the case

273

of Susan Isaacs, she went off and became a famous novelist with a home in Sands Point and a summer home in Bridgehampton.

But if Susan Isaacs' modus operandi were only to take women characters out of the house and make true heroines out of them, it would mean very little unless she could write. She can indeed write very, well.

"After nearly a quarter of a century of marriage, Richie Meyers, my husband, told me to call him Rick. Then he started slicking back his hair with thirty five dollars a jar English pomade," are the first sentences in *After All These Years*. Something is very wrong with Richie Meyers and you simply must read on to find out what it is. You do find out. In the middle of the night, a few pages later, the heroine comes upon him sprawled dead on the kitchen floor with a knife through his belly. The novel has begun.

When you talk to Susan Isaacs, and I interviewed her at a table at the HSF Restaurant in Bridgehampton, she occasionally says things that are very hilarious. You will be reading some of them in this interview. Mostly, however, she is perfectly ordinary. You'd never know.

She was born in the Flatbush section of Brooklyn, and except for two extraordinary trips, remained there through high school. She graduated Forest Hills.

Her father was an electrical engineer. When she was 12, he received a change of job and promotion that required the family to move to Cincinnati. They were to remain there for three years.

"I hated it," Susan said. "Here I was, at this perfectly difficult age where your breasts finally become larger than your nose although not by much, and I am this Brooklyn kid with dark curly hair in a school in Cincinnati where everybody has a blond page boy. There was only one group of kids in Cincinnati and you were either in it or you were out of it and you can guess where I was. Finally, when I was 15, we moved back to Long Island, to Forest Hills. It was so nice, lots of kids and lots of groups, not just one standard of excellence."

She was an only child. Her mother had the normal expectations.

"I should marry well," she said.

But her father wanted her to have a profession. He took her fishing, showed her how to build shelves. Why be a nurse when you can be a doctor? he asked. She liked him a lot.

I mentioned that the year she moved to Cincinnati was the year the Brooklyn Dodgers moved to Los Angeles.

"Yes," she said darkly. "There was Walter O'Malley who owned the Dodgers and there was Adolph Hitler who was the head of Germany."

Isaacs went to Queens College as a pre-med major. But she was not committed to it and when calculus did her in she moved to economics where math once again did her in.

"I had two goals. I wanted to do anything to avoid becoming a teacher. And I wanted to be Somebody. So I became an English major. I read H. L. Mencken and Jane Austen and Elizabeth Bennett and these writers became my heroes."

She began writing short little pieces for the college paper. She wrote a defense of sororities and fraternities.

"I wrote a Menckenesque defense. It was unbearably smug."

She became involved in the upheavals of the 1960's. When the school banned Malcolm X and Benjamin Davis from speaking she joined a student strike. Andrew Goodman, one of the three freedom riders who was killed in Mississippi, was in the same graduating class at Queens College.

At the age of 20, not quite through with her senior year, she dropped out of school. She went with her parents to an assignment that her father had designing a naval base in the Philippines. She was there six months.

"Here was American military life in the Philippines. There were servants, clubs, everything these officers couldn't afford to have in the United States. It was a colonial system and I got a job teaching in an American school there to the spawn of these people. It was pretty disgusting."

Back in New York City, she did not return to college but instead took a job at *Seventeen* magazine as an editorial assistant. She wrote advice to the lovelorn columns, answered reader mail, typed and proofread.

"I was the only person there from a City college," she said. "Everybody else was from an Ivy League school and had rich parents and this was because *Seventeen* magazine paid salaries that were abysmal. All these other kids were being essentially supported by their parents to work there. So I went and asked for a raise. Why? the editors wanted to know. 'Because I need the money,' I told them. They gave me one."

She stayed at *Seventeen* for three years and rose to the level of Senior Editor. She shared an apartment early on with three other women on her $75 a week salary but shortly she found that with her pittance wages she could not afford even that and so she went home to live with her parents.

In 1967 relatives fixed her up on a blind date with Elkan Abramowitz who was a young lawyer working as a Federal prosecutor in the United States Attorney's office.

"That was enough of a reason not to go out with him right there," she said. "But I went. He sounded very nice on the phone. We went on that first date to a New York Mets Old-Timers Day and we both got teary eyed when Campanella got wheeled out. We had, it seemed, a lot in common."

Isaacs and Abramowitz were married in 1968 and honeymooned in the Caribbean. The following year, Isaacs became pregnant. She did stay on at *Seventeen* for a while and they did offer her a nice maternity leave but in the end she decided to leave. Her son was born. She began freelancing articles to national magazines, writing them between duties taking care of her husband and son and now she had another child on the way.

"I remember selling an article to *New York* magazine on low phosphate detergents. I felt so terribly chic. I also freelanced an article to *Seventeen*. It was called 'How To Write a Letter To a Boy.'"

She also did volunteer work speech writing for New York City politicians running for office. She wrote speeches for John Lindsay, Herman Badillo, Bob Morganthau and for Donald Manes. She was in great demand because for each of these politicians she tried to capture their real "voice." She was, apparently, quite successful.

But the real change in Susan Isaacs' life came when her young daughter finally was old enough to go to nursery school. Isaacs was free to do whatever she wanted, so long as she was back at her Manhasset home by the time the kids came home. She decided she would try her hand at writing a novel.

"At first I was overwhelmed with all this self-effacing girl crap. Who am I to write a novel? I had to work at overcoming all this insecurity and wimpiness. What helped was that this character came to me. She was a housewife, a woman in my head who wanted to solve a murder. I had this very strong urge to bring this character to life. It was so weird.

"So what I'll do, I thought, is I will take a course in novel writing at the New School. But Elkan's hours were so crazy he could not guarantee he could be home when the courses were being given. And somebody had to be home to mind the kids. So this was not going to work. And then I thought: Dostoevski wrote novels and he didn't go to the New School and so then I bought a book called *Writing a Novel*. It broke this seemingly impossible task down into small and manageable steps."

She began writing. Her husband, who loved the way she put words together, built this basement office for her and after he would go off to his Manhattan law practice she would go down there and plug in her electric typewriter. It made a pleasing hum. A surge protector warmed her feet. The dog would curl up on the surge protector. And in the next room the washing machine would go into the spin cycle.

And so it was that the story *Compromising Positions*, about a suburban housewife named Judith Singer, a woman "with dark hair and high cheekbones, as if Mongols had a go at her great great grandmother at the siege of Minsk," came into being. She has a stuffy husband, two kids, and then one day finds out that her periodontist has been murdered. She goes out and, rather than take the problem to the authorities, solves the murder herself.

276

"I sent this manuscript off to a friend of Elkan's, an old fraternity brother who was Managing Editor of Simon & Schuster and he read it and he said he didn't want to negotiate with us because he knew us but that we should get an agent. He recommended Gloria Safire. And as it turned out, my novel became the first one to be published by Times Books who, up until that time had been doing these big boring books on things such as Romanian saints."

It is most unusual for a first novel to find a publisher. In this case, however, people found this manuscript so sensational that before the book even came out the movie rights were sold, the foreign rights were sold, it was selected as a Main Selection of the Book of the Month Club and there were arrangements made for a big paperback sale.

"So there it was," Isaacs said. "I had a career."

Not a whole lot has changed since then. Isaacs has prospered and Abramowitz has prospered. (He is currently the lawyer for Woody Allen.) They moved to Sands Point. The kids grew up. And she keeps writing novels.

She wrote *Close Relations*, then *Almost Paradise*, then *Shining Through* which became a movie by David Seltzer starring Melanie Griffith and Michael Douglas, and she wrote *Magic Hour* which is currently in the works to become a movie.

I asked her what she thought the reason was her writing was so successful.

"Most people censor themselves," she said. "I lack that censor in my writing. And people come up to me and say 'you write the way I think' and I guess I do. I just come out and write it."

I asked her how she came to find her second home in the Hamptons.

"This is hard to believe, but until twelve years ago, I had never been east of Exit 70 and the Long Island Game Farm in Manorville. But then, one day, my husband and I were invited out east to a book party. We went for a wonderful walk on the beach the next morning and I found myself falling in love with the place. We rented for a number of years — in Springs, Wainscott and Bridgehampton — and finally bought a house in Bridgehampton. It has a big den. I work on my novels there on a laptop computer

"It is so nice here in January and February. Half the town has left. It is so peaceful and quiet."

It is amidst such peace and quiet that murders take place in the head of Susan Isaacs. She writes them down. And her characters solve them. Then she starts another novel.

August 27, 1993

Chapter 59

NORMAN JAFFE

Ten years ago, I decided to design my own home in East Hampton. I had architectural training at Harvard, but I had never gone into practice. Instead, I made my career with this newspaper.

At the time, I did some drawings and I thought these are okay but I really could use some first rate advice. I thought I would go see Norman Jaffe. He was a world class architect who lived in the community and his residential work was remarkable. Some of his homes had won major awards from the American Institute of Architects and one in particular, overlooking the ocean in Montauk, had been given the nationwide Honor Award by the AIA. This was a rare achievement.

Normally, I would not have approached an architect of such stature for a little advice, but I had known Norman by then for almost fifteen years. Occasionally, I would run into him in the Bridgehampton Candy Kitchen drawing on a napkin. I would sit with him and we would talk. He was a man dedicated to his work, a man frequently lost in thought. I had always found him gentle and kind, quiet and almost regal in bearing, someone totally self contained. He was the epitome of a man committed to his profession. I admired him. And I had befriended him.

When I went to see him ten years ago about my house, Norman gave me about twenty minutes of his time. He made large strokes with a broad marker on tracing paper over my drawings. My designs, which were flat and dull, burst into life. I couldn't believe what he was doing and the changes he was proposing.

Twenty minutes was all I ever wanted from Norman Jaffe about my house. I had asked it as a favor and he had freely given it. I did not want to take advantage of it. But one week later, a letter arrived in the mail from Norman Jaffe. I had never before received one from him. In it, he wrote more design ideas and then he wrote that he had been giving my project more thought and that given its spectacular site high on a hill overlooking a harbor, he suggested that before I made even one more drawing I go up on that hill and imagine the spiritual qualities of the place — colors and textures and how the sun would bathe down on it — in short, feel all the emotions. And then I should go back to my drawings.

I relate this encounter because it helps to better get the sense of just how remarkable Jaffe was. He often said he had no interest in money. Once, he said that the longer he lived the more he came to respect things made by nature. He devoted his life to design and how things felt and looked.

Norman Jaffe was the architect for literally dozens of homes in the Hamptons and in Montauk. People lined up to give him commissions and this was in spite of what came to be known as War Stories — where Norman had designed a stone wall and had it built and then walked down to the site, stared at it for awhile and decided it would have to be taken down and moved about three feet further out. The homes he designed had a spirit about them — they brought out enormous feelings from the people that were in them. People wanted them.

In recent years, Jaffe's practice expanded out of residential architecture into institutional and commercial architecture. He designed the interior space of the Laundry Restaurant in East Hampton (this is a remarkable room), he designed a hospital in Bosnia. He designed the "Gates of the Grove" chapel for the Jewish Center of the Hamptons in East Hampton, a project that has been photographed and written about around the world. He recently completed a building at 565 Fifth Avenue in Manhattan, which won critical acclaim from the *New York Times* architectural critic Paul Goldberger.

Jaffe's personal life seemed even more extraordinary, if that were possible. He was a tall, handsome six footer. And when I met him years ago, when he was in his thirties, he had just suffered an unimaginable tragedy. His wife had been killed in an auto accident. He was a widower, left to raise his son, Miles, alone. Miles, at that time, was in grammar school.

And yet, Jaffe never talked about his personal life. He dedicated himself to his work. And he did what he had to do. Twenty years later, in his fifties, he met Sarah Stahl, an attorney. They were married and by this year, when he was 61, he and Sarah had two children, Will Isaac, 7 and Max, 4. Miles, now 35, was married and had children of his own. He worked with his father.

This summer, the Jaffes rented their house in Montauk and lived on Shelter Island. But sometimes Norman would stay late at his Bridgehampton studio and would sleep in a barn on the property that

279

had been restored. He did this last Wednesday, August 18. Early in the morning on August 19, he drove down to the end of Ocean Road in Bridgehampton and parked his Mercedes in the driveway of a friend. Then he went out on the beach alone, sat and meditated. Then he went for what he believed would be a brief swim.

We know this because Jaffe was in the habit of making this visit and swim before work. He would return to his car, towel off and then visit with his friend for awhile, having coffee. Then he would go up to his office on Corwith Street. This particular morning, however, he never returned to retrieve his car.

By 2 p.m. in the afternoon, his friend, finding the keys still in the car with Jaffe's wallet on the front seat, and finding Jaffe's clothes on the beach, began a search for him. There is no lifeguard at this beach and Jaffe, thin and ascetic, is not a strong swimmer. The police were called and a search begun. But Jaffe has not been seen since.

I miss my friend. Today, after many days of searching land and sea, after articles in the *New York Times* and other publications, the family issued a press release stating that Jaffe is presumed drowned. Memorial services have not yet been planned and remembrance of him can be made through donations to ICROSS East End (the International Community for the Relief of Starving and Suffering), c/o Bill Hattrick, Prudential Securities, Southampton, NY 11968.

August 27, 1993

* * *

A few weeks after this was written, the remains of Norman Jaffe's body washed ashore. He is buried in a cemetery in Springs.

Chapter 60

KATHE TANOUS

In late July, when Iraq was threatening Kuwait with invasion, there was a global affairs conference at the Southampton Campus of LIU. It had been scheduled for months, and among the prominent panelists were Connecticut Congressman Christopher Dodd, former senator and presidential candidate Eugene McCarthy and communications mogul Robert F. X. Sillerman. Mr. Sillerman had just finished explaining the astonishing new development where television had come to dominate politics. The upheavals in Russia could be explained that way. People in the Communist world could watch James Bond movies, see all the Porsches and Mercedes. It was all in their homes.

"Then why don't we just let western television do it's thing in Iraq and Saudi Arabia?" someone in the audience wanted to know.

Mr. Sillerman swallowed hard. "It doesn't work in the Persian Gulf," he said. "There is no Western television there. These are ancient feudal states where the government controls everything. Even what's on TV."

* * *

Kathe Tanous today is a respected American painter. Married for over a dozen years to Bob Levenson, the creative director of the Scali McCabe advertising agency, she leads a busy life between her Manhattan apartment, her Florida condominium and her East Hampton home. Kathe is a California girl, born in Los Angeles and raised in a house on a suburban street in Burbank. She is quick, funny, thoughtful. She has a brother and sister, a father now retired who worked for Walt Disney, and a mother who took care of the house and wrote children's books. In the early 1960's she went off to study art at the Chouinart Art Institute in L. A. and it looked as if this all-American girl was about to embark on an all-American life.

But then there was the blind date. He was handsome, dark and Arabian and his name was Hisham Mooslie and he was an exchange student at the University of Southern California. She fell for him immediately.

Kathe Tanous and Mohammed Hisham Mooslie were married in 1963 at her parent's home in Burbank. They were married by a minister which today Kathe thinks is a little odd since he was a Muslim, but on the other hand, Hisham had plans to stay in the United States. He now had an American wife and a taste of America and he liked it. Perhaps they would settle near Burbank. Kathe's father was a Lebanese.

No one, however, had reckoned on the immigration laws and even though Hisham was now married to an American, he was told he would have to leave. It would take almost two years for the papers to go through channels admitting him to America and during that time Hisham would have to be out of the country. He packed. He would return to the Persian Gulf.

Kathe was 21, newly married, and couldn't imagine being away from her husband for two years. Had she stayed in America and waited for him the two years, her life might have taken an entirely different turn. Instead, however, she packed too. She would go with her man, wherever life took her. She had no idea that within a matter of weeks she would be living in a harem in a palace in the middle of the desert in northern Saudi Arabia.

* * *

"The taxi arrived at four o'clock in the afternoon in front of our hotel in Amman, Jordan. Hisham had told me we would be going to the palace of a Saudi prince. It was his brother-in-law. His sister had married this man who was a nephew of the King. I guess I imagined some kind of fairy tale.

"I packed a bag of oranges and some bread. We went downstairs and there was this beat up old taxi in such bad shape the doors were held shut by rope. They untied them and we got in and they tied them back up and off we went. And on, and on, and on through the desert. We were in that taxi for twelve hours. At four a.m., far across the desert we saw a few lights in the distance. The palace. We were there.

"To tell you the truth, I find it hard to remember today just how big this place was. I remember it had many rooms and it was surrounded by a high wall. There was, indeed, a bedroom for us, but then I remember the bathroom next to it was just a hole in the floor. We went to sleep. And when I woke up, in the morning, I found that my man was gone and all there was was a note. See you at lunch."

After dressing, and putting on the traditional black Arabian chaldor

282

and veil over her clothes, Kathe was taken through a courtyard, past the nursery where there were women servants and children running around, and into the room where she was now told she would be spending her waking hours. It was the harem.

"The harem is not exactly the way Americans think of it," Kathe said. "Women are kept separate from men in Saudi Arabia. They are not to be seen in public. Here was a large room where all the women in the compound stayed all day to be separate from the men. There were the wives of the Prince, only in this case he had only one wife, there were his sisters, female visitors, there was me, there were women servants and, five times a day, there was a blind priest who would come in and lead us in prayers where we prayed to Mecca. He was supposed to be blind anyway, because unless there was a special occasion such as my first day of arrival, men were not allowed in the harem where they might see what was going on.

"In fact, nothing was going on. Here it was, my first day on the job so to speak, and I knew some Arabic, at least enough to get by, and the women were at first so happy to see me. What did I want? Tell them anything I wanted? At this time I had long hair that came all the way down to my knees. I had been on a twelve hour taxi trip, I was filled with dirt and dust. I wanted a shower. This caused great laughter. Water was available only two days a week and then only for two hours a day. That was when you took a shower. It was a beginning."

Here's what the women did all day in the harem. They tried on their clothes. They polished their jewels. They listened to the radio. They ate pumpkin seeds from a little pouch and spit out the husks. They would play with the children. Girl friends would come in and they would gossip. They would go out (driven in a car by a male servant to the airport and thence to Damascus) and they would go shopping. Covered in their black chaldor of course. And that was it.

"There was almost nothing there for me to do," Kathe said. "I wrote endless letters to my friends back home. I sang Beatles songs. I sang lots of Beatles songs."

This first day on the job was in her honor. The main meal of the day, the noontime meal, would be this celebration and both her husband and his brother-in-law the Prince, Prince Abdullah Sudary, would attend to welcome her. An oil cloth was put down on the Persian rug on the floor, and a huge platter of food brought in and put on the floor on top of that. It consisted of a big mound of rice, boiled goat, cinnamon, oranges. Kathe followed everyone's lead. When in Rome etc. She sat on the floor, right leg under. She leaned on her left hand. (You don't eat with your left hand. Your left hand is unclean.) And she reached into the platter with her right hand and scooped out whatever food she wanted, brought it to her mouth and ate it, pushing it toward her mouth with her thumb.

"This was the only time we all ate together during the time I was there, which was the time I was able to stand it, which was about two months. After this first meal, there was a dining room where we ate the big noonday meal. This is how it worked. First the platters of food were brought in and set on the floor. Then the men came in and ate. Then they left and the men's falconers came in and ate. Then it was the turn of the male servants. Then they left and it was the female servants, the family and children. We got whatever was left.

"I remember one day we came in and there was almost nothing left. Some watermelon and a few pieces of bread. Nothing we could do. We went hungry."

Kathe did get mail from the outside world, but there were problems. She could receive nothing that had anything to do with the barer parts of a woman's body. Magazines were gone through. Sections were either cut out or blacked out with magic marker.

"A *Time* magazine I once got, I remember, had a piece about some new stained glass windows by Mark Chagall. The pictures were allowed but the text was all blacked out. Because he was Jewish, I guess. Another time, my mother sent me the comics from the Sunday *Los Angeles Times*. It took six months. Apparently they had to translate every word."

Toilet tissue, however, did get through.

It was two months later, just when Kathe was about to tell her husband that she could not take it anymore — they did spend every night in their room together — that word came that the Prince had been named a minister in the government and everyone, the approximately forty members of the palace, would be packing up and moving to the capital, Riyadh.

"There were these two twin engined planes. One for the men and one for the women. I still remember this great procession of the women in their black chaldors, black heads bobbing along toward the ramp."

In Riyadh they did live in a large, western style house with a walled garden. Kathe met some Americans who lived in the American compound in the city and in the mornings she would sometimes arrange it to go shopping with them. By this time, Muna, the wife of the Prince, had come to hate her. Kathe was different, she was American, she had married her brother. She had ruined him.

"There was one spice, I found, I could hardly tolerate in this new environment. Coriander. Muna had everything made with lots of coriander. She put it where it had never been before. I tried to spend as little time in the harem as possible. I had made friends with a fourteen year old servant girl named Tifaha (Apple), and she would come to my room night or day and she would whisper 'the Americans are here,' and I'd run out and hop in Suzy's VW Beetle and off we would go shopping."

The law was, and is, that every woman in public wears a black chaldor and on the approach of a man pulls down the veil to completely cover the head and face. Here were two American women, out of their Volkswagen and into the Souk, quickly pulling down the veil at the approach of even a stock clerk.

"Once we left our veils off in the souk. There are religious men there, called Metawas, and the punishments are very severe for removing the veil. One saw us and after us he came swinging this big staff. We raced back to the VW, climbed in, slammed the door and there he was pounding on the roof as we roared off."

One day everyone went out to watch a man beheaded in the town square and a woman stoned to death for adultery. But Hisham insisted she not go see it and she stayed home.

Once she was invited to make the lunch and she made mounds of tuna fish sandwiches with canned tuna fish from the market, mayonnaise and bread and everyone seemed to love it.

Once she got a temporary job at the French Embassy. There had been some survey made, it had been made in Arabic, then translated into French then translated into English. But the English was very bad. They hired her to make it into good English. She put on her chaldor, went out to the car where the servant drove her toward the embassy and, as they approached, she did what she was told which was to lay down in the back seat so nobody would see she was going in to work there.

She had taken up painting. It was something she wasn't supposed to do — women weren't supposed to do ANYTHING — but she had done it anyway and had bought masonite and house paint and house paint brushes and she had painted scenes of the desert and scenes of Riyadh. And that, really is how her marriage, and her time in the Persian Gulf, came to an end.

"I knew exactly what I was doing. I had done this painting, secretly, where nobody would see. Then one afternoon, my husband was bringing some important ministers home for coffee. Just before he arrived, I took out this painting and I hung it in the living room. He and his men friends came in and there it was. A painting of a naked black woman sitting cross legged, staring out at the viewer. He went into a rage. He tore it off the wall, ripped it into little pieces and he threw it over the wall into the street."

* * *

It was not easy for Kathe Tanous to remember all that had happened in this wrong turn she had made in her life twenty five years ago. It was so hard to believe any of it anyway. We were sitting, she and

285

I, in Bobby Van's Restaurant in Bridgehampton as she told all this and toward the end she brought out her black chaldor so I could see what it felt like and how one looked through it to still be able to see what was going on while no one could see in. I put it on. The waitresses and the diners were hazy here in Bridgehampton but it was indeed possible to see out.

Recently, Hisham called Kathe to tell her he was in New York and she went out with him for lunch at the Plaza. He had remarried — another American woman — and had three boys, and was living in Riyadh but also had homes in London and Brussels. He had prospered too. And he said a lot had changed in Riyadh since she was there.

"But I don't think so," Kathe said. Here in the restaurant she brought out a recent issue of *Time* magazine and turned to a photograph of some American soldier shopping in the Souk. There were some women, completely covered over in their chaldors. And there was the description of the Metawa, the religious men who severely beat them if they pulled up their veils.

September 28, 1990

Chapter 61

GLADYS NEDERLANDER

Mention the name Gladys Nederlander to anybody and they say oh that's the woman who produces all those Broadway shows. Indeed, as I walk down a corridor through her second floor offices just off Eighth Avenue, I pass posters of all her Broadway productions — *The Goodbye Girl, Legend, Sunset, Caesar and Cleopatra, West Side Story* (with Debbie Allen). It is understandable that people would see her that way.

To me, however, this lovely blonde woman is the wife of New York City theatre owner Bob Nederlander, and the thing that immediately comes to mind when I think of her is a story she told at dinner about how she and Bob came to buy their house in East Hampton, and how this turned out to be, in addition to a house purchase, a marriage proposal.

It helps the story, I think, if you know Bob. He is from Detroit — his whole family is from Detroit — and though he now lives with Gladys on the Upper East Side, Michigan just oozes out all over him. He is small, thin, and he looks out into the middle distance a lot. He doesn't say much. He appears to be somebody looking forward to going hunting in northern Michigan.

And so it was that Gladys, who had been dating Bob for several years and has many friends in the Hamptons, suggested one day two years ago that they go out to the Hamptons to visit some of them. Nederlander balked. He didn't want to go.

"I know you don't like being around people you don't know," she told him, "but you'll see, you'll have a good time."

They stayed at the home of Sue and Roy Pollock, and on Sunday morning, as an activity, it was suggested they go out and look at some real estate for sale. TV sports personality Fred Raphael was selling his house. The price was more than $1 million. It was supposed to be a beautiful place.

"Why are we looking at this house?" Bob asked the Pollocks. "You've already got a house. And I certainly don't want to come out here. It's a two and a half hour drive. And it is even farther from Michigan."

What could be the harm in looking, somebody said.

Realtor John Golden from Sotheby's came over and took the four of them to the house. Fred Raphael was there and showed them around. It was right on Georgica Pond, had beautiful grounds, trees, lots of room.

At one point, Gladys overhead Bob and Fred Raphael walking off to one side and talking.

"Yes, except for those lamps of my mothers," Raphael said.

"After all, Gladys and I are going to get married," Bob said. This was news to Gladys.

The two of them came over.

"I'm buying it," Bob said. "I'm writing a check."

"I thought you said this was too far from Detroit?" Gladys said. "And are you going to marry me first or are you going to buy the house first?"

"I'll call you," Bob said.

And that's how Bob and Gladys Nederlander came to buy a house in the Hamptons. And, incidentally, get married.

Gladys Nederlander was born and raised in Westwood, California. Her father was in the advertising business. UCLA, just two blocks away, was her playground. She lived a normal, suburban California childhood until the age of fifteen when her father died.

"Shortly after the funeral, a friend of my father's, Ray Morgan, who also owned the advertising agency my dad worked at, came over and said there was this new thing called TV and they were producing a show. Perhaps I'd like to have a job there. They needed a kid."

This was in 1944. Gladys took a bus to Hollywood 45 minutes away and reported to Earle Carol's nightclub. This was on a Saturday at 9 in the morning. They were setting up TV cameras and lights and a stage for the production of the premiere of something brand new — a daytime television show to be called *Queen for a Day*. It would be on television from 10 to 11 in Los Angeles, which would be 1 to 2 in New York. And by noon they would have the entire nightclub put back, all the tables and chairs and so forth, so the club could operate that evening.

"Apparently, they had debated whether or not to have the show on radio or on this new thing called TV. Radio was the major market in 1944. This was a big gamble for them."

Teenager Gladys made chalk marks on the floor and stood on them while people looked through the cameras to see if the shadows were right. She ran errands. She helped gather up the audience from outside, by bribing them with offers of donuts and coffee inside. And she sometimes appeared on television herself, bringing things to the participants.

"Jack Bailey was the MC," she said. "Dinah Shore was often on the show. And sometimes when we couldn't find anybody interesting in the audience to be Queen for a Day, they had me call my mother. Mother was Queen four times."

Gladys worked weekends and summers with the show, and when she graduated high school and then got married (to song writer Freddie Stryker), she continued coming. She was in and around *Queen for a Day* for four years, right through the birth of her first child.

"On television, when I was pregnant, the camera went up, and up and up. You weren't supposed to show pregnant people on television then. Today, I tell my kids about it, and they say mom you were the first Vanna and I guess I was."

Gladys married Freddie Stryker after falling in love with him because, she says, he was the first person she ever met who could play piano like Carmen Cavallero. She was married to him ten years. They had a son, who today is an educator living in Maryland, and they had a daughter who today is a nutritionist living in Palo Alto. It was a good time.

"I remember, for my son's fifth birthday party, Freddie arranged for western movie star Tex Ritter to come and entertain in full cowboy regalia. Freddie knew everybody in the music business. We went to Europe. We went to Argentina on behalf of Decca Records which was doing a big push down there. We were entertained by Evita Peron."

When her marriage fell apart, she moved with her two young children to Palm Springs. It was on the advice of her doctor. Her son had asthma. Here, she decided that perhaps she should open a gift shop. She went out to the biggest and most well known resort in Palm Springs at the time — Charlie Farrell's Racquet Club — and she asked Charlie Farrell if she couldn't open a shop there. There was everything else. There were tennis courts, a big swimming pool, bungalows where everybody stayed. A restaurant.

Farrell told her no. "He said he didn't want one. That everything he ordered, hats and clothes and boots, were all in one size — his — and were in pink. But I talked him into it."

Gladys' at the Racquet Club was to remain in business for six years. Every celebrity in Hollywood visiting Palm Springs, all the writers, producers and movie stars, would shop there. Today, thirty five years later, we are sitting in her office above the Great White Way, and Gladys smiles as she fondly remembers it.

"People would come in for a can of tennis balls and go out with a $300 shirt. I'd have Cary Grant over on one side of the store and the head of U.S. Steel at the other side. I still remember what was written about my shop in the *Harper's Bazaar* at that time. 'Glady's Shop is crowded with the Who's Who of Stage and Screen. Cash register never stops. Macy's should have it so good.'"

In 1961 the President of Universal Pictures, Milton Rackmil, came in to buy a sweater and, as Gladys put it, went out with a wife. Soon thereafter, Gladys closed her shop and moved back to Los Angeles. Her son was thirteen, her daughter ten. She sent them to Chadwick Prep School in Palo Verde where they would be educated. As for her and Milton, it would be a new life. For her, anyway.

"Stick with me, kid, and you'll see every airport in the world," he told her. Indeed, in 1961, this was quite a statement. Propeller driven planes were only just then leaving the scene. The new Boeing 707 had only been on the market for a year.

"He did prepare me for what this was all going to be about," Gladys said. "We were going off to promote motion pictures around the globe."

Milton Rackmil would take the can of film containing their new release — for example *Ben Hur* — and he'd put it under his arm and he'd climb on an airplane and off they would go. They flew on all the major airlines and everybody knew them. Seats 2A and 2B. A certain brand of scotch. Always, there would be somebody from the airline to greet them. They would be accompanied on these worldwide jaunts by the movie stars in the films. Henry Fonda. Cary Grant.

"My job would be as follows. We would be in London and we would set up in a hotel suite with a screening room. I would greet people at the door. On my right was a bar and a bartender. Behind me, very discreetly, would be an assistant with a small notebook. People would come in and I'd say Oh Armando Sante! And what would you like to drink? And how is your wife? What was her name? And Armando would order a campari and soda with a dash of vodka and say that his wife Belinda was fine and I would go get him his drink. Meanwhile, my assistant off to one side would be writing in the notebook. Armando Sante, campari and soda with a dash of vodka and Belinda. Six months later, when he would walk in again I would greet him with oh Armando, waiter, get Armando a campari and soda with a dash of vodka. And Armando, how is Belinda? I still have six of these little red Gucci notebooks somewhere.

"Milton, meanwhile, would be talking to people about the film. This was a time, if you recall, that everybody was worried that movies were on their way out, that television was about to replace movies and why would anyone pay when they could get entertainment free in their living rooms?

"Milton was adamant that movies were here to stay. How could you all be so dumb, he would say. People will always go to the movies. Where else are you going to be in the dark alone with a girl you have the hots for and you could hold her hand or feel her leg?"

Gladys' life became Milton's. Everything seemed so important. She remembered how they would fly into Tokyo and there at the airport there would be geishas with flowers and crowds of people waving clackers and American and Japanese flags. It was quite impressive.

"Then one day we are in Tokyo and we are with our publicity man and he asks how we liked the welcome. It seems he would set up a sign next to a bus in downtown Tokyo and people would come over and he would offer them free tickets to the movies if they would come out to the airport for a few hours and cheer and wave flags."

Ten years later, in 1972, her marriage to Milton ended and she moved to New York City. She bought a townhouse on East 62nd Street from Francois and Oscar de Laurentis. Francois had just had it decorated. Gladys could be in New York, or Washington — it was just a $29 shuttle flight away — and she could be near her son who was starting at the University of Pennsylvania.

One day, she had coffee with her dear friend, Broadway show producer Roger Stevens. What are you going to do with your life now? he asked her. I think I'm going into the TV business, she said. No Gladys, go into theatre. You've read so many scripts. Theatre is the place for you.

Roger became the Director of the Kennedy Center in Washington and one day he and Gladys talked about what she might produce in Manhattan and she mentioned how much she had liked *West Side Story*. Her daughter had heard the music and liked it. But it seemed a shame that it was gone forever and would never be back. Why not revive it?

"You'd have to get Sondheim and Robbins and Bernstein and Arthur Laurents," Roger said. "How are you going to ever get these four men in the same room at the same time? Hmmm. Maybe Lenny could help us."

'Lenny,' it turned out, was Leonard Bernstein. They went to see him. The rest is history. *West Side Story*, produced by Gladys Racklis, ran for twenty two months on Broadway and then toured Europe. It was the start of her next career.

Gladys now took me for a short tour back through the hallways of her offices to look, once again, at the posters. There was *Caesar and Cleopatra* starring Rex Harrison and Elizabeth Ashley.

"Ming Cho Lee did the scenery. We had a 20 foot high sphinx. We sold it to a motel in New Jersey after the show closed."

There was the show *Perfectly Frank* of the music of Frank Loesser, there was *Sunset* with Alexis Smith which opened and closed in Buffalo. (I learned, Gladys said.) There was *Solitary Confinement* starring Stacy Keach.

"Roger had called me from Washington and said you've got to see this script. It's about a millionaire living in the penthouse of a hotel whose only contact with the outside world is with people whose images he brings up on TV screens. He talks to his lawyer, his accountant, his priest, his chef, his secretary. Late in the first act he lies down on a bed and goes to sleep. Then two TV's come on all by themselves. It is his lawyer and his accountant and they talk to one another about killing him. It is great.

"And the people who saw it loved it. But the critics hated it. How dare we bring TV to the theatre? they asked. People shouldn't go to Broadway and wind up watching TV. It previewed for three weeks and then it closed."

In the Summer of '92, Gladys produced *Death and the Maiden* starring Glenn Close, Richard Dreyfus and Gene Hackman with Mike Nichols directing. And this year she produced Neil Simon's *The Goodbye Girl* with Bernadette Peters and Martin Short. It ran three and a half months.

Currently, she is working on a show about Abbie Lane and Xavier Cugat. On board already are Joe Layton as the director, Arthur Kopit and Morey Yeston (who did 9) as music and story writers.

"We should have it all set in the next few weeks," she said.

She and her husband are here in the Hamptons almost every weekend year around.

"We love it here," she said. "We love the tennis and the walks on the beach and the friends we've made. With fax and computer we can conduct business here. And no matter how upsetting things get you walk outside, take a look at how beautiful this place is and everything is just fine."

October 22, 1993

Chapter 62

KEITH REINHARD

A handsome new summer "cottage" has gone up on Ocean Road in Bridgehampton. 8000 square feet in size, it is the creation of architect Francis Fleetwood, has a pool, tennis court and lovely grounds of three and three quarters acres. The keys to the front door were handed to Keith Reinhard and his wife Rose-Lee, the new owners, in the spring. The Reinhards and their seven children have been coming out here for six years.

I am sitting with Keith Reinhard in a large corner office in a Manhattan skyscraper that befits the Chief Executive Officer of a multi-billion dollar corporation. Mr. Reinhard sits across from me at a conference table and offers me some coffee from the service that is on the tray between us. He is not what I thought he would be. He is slender, athletic looking, alert and, as I quickly learn, funny. He looks like an overgrown kid. But then, the corporation he heads, DDBNeedham, is an advertising agency, one of the eight largest in the world. Maybe there is something appropriate about this.

I ask Keith when he first thought about being an advertising man and what I get is a childhood. Keith Reinhard was born and raised in a small house in the small midwestern town of Berne, Indiana, population 2000.

"As soon as I was old enough, I wanted to get out of it," Keith says.

The problem was not family. He had a loving family. The problem was that there were so many things he wasn't allowed to do. His was a family of Mennonites. Berne was a town filled with Mennonites in a farm region surrounding them filled with Amish. Everything and everybody had to conform to rules.

"We had no television, no advertising, you couldn't go to the movies, you couldn't even go dancing. Sinful. Against the rules of the Church. It wasn't as strict as Amish. We did have cars, we did have electricity and we didn't have to wear the Amish clothes. But it was a close second."

Who knows what it is that makes one person accept the peaceful ways and rules of the Amish and the Mennonites while another rebels. Genetics? Environment?

"Well, I am today a very lousy dancer. But I'll tell you, I am an excellent skater. In high school, if you went to a roller skating party or an ice skating party — one of the few kinds of parties we were allowed, then you could touch girls. You'd go with them on the bus to the rink and when you got there, you could hold hands. You could do that."

People in Berne either worked the farms or worked for one of the seven furniture factories in town. The Mennonites were largely from Switzerland, and the Swiss were known as craftsmen. Keith's father worked as an upholsterer, but when he died when Keith was just 3, his mother had to go to work to support Keith and his younger brother. Fortunately, grandfather lived in town and, in many ways, became the surrogate father for the young man.

Still, it was Keith's plan, somehow, to get out and the plotting began early. It began, Keith thinks, when the V8 truck made a delivery to the grocery store where his mother worked and where he sometimes helped in the stockroom. He would unload the boxes, and, there would be the cardboard full color promotional posters for V8 Juice, and he would take them home and up to his room and put them under his bed. There was lots going on in the outside world he wanted to know about.

"We'd listen to the radio," Keith said. "That was tolerated. I figured there were two ways out, either I'd be a commercial artist or I'd be a radio announcer. But I didn't know anybody in radio. And one day, when a kid who recently had moved to town from Detroit told me he had an uncle back in Detroit who was a commercial artist, I went with him to visit this uncle and as we sat there in his studio and I saw him airbrush the fenders of an automobile for a General Motors advertisement, all I could think about is how could it be possible they could pay you to do something that was this much fun. I was hooked."

Keith spoke to his grandfather about art. His grandfather said it is frowned upon by our religion since it could be construed to be a form of creation, certainly presumptuous at best. How about music? Music sings the praises of God. You could play at church. I will get you whatever music instruments you want.

I'll play the drums, Keith told him. They didn't let drums into the church.

Eventually, Keith's hard-working mother scraped up $600 so at night he could take a correspondence course to become an artist. It had been right there on the back of the *Popular Mechanics* magazine. A full page ad headlined DRAW ME. Keith could draw the silhouette of this woman pictured there, he could send it in, and they could tell him what it would take for him to become an artist.

"And that's how I learned to draw," Keith says. "A two year correspondence course I took while in high school from the back cover of a *Popular Mechanics* magazine."

The day after he graduated high school, Keith was out the door and headed toward New York City. It was an odd trip and there was a certain deceptiveness about it. A friend of his, Jerry Sprunger, had a father who had the Ford dealership in town and since they were graduating high school, this father was willing to give them a 25 year old Ford pickup truck which if they wanted to, they could fix up and drive east for a visit to see the sights in New York. Jerry Sprunger, Chet Smith and Keith, along with a fouth graduate, Max Lehman, painted this old truck robin-egg blue and constructed a wooden enclosure on the back with three plank beds in it. They'd go to New York City, see the sights, and they'd come back. Keith, of course, planned to go to New York, see the sights, and stay. But he didn't tell anybody that.

"We were one of the few vehicles ever thrown off the New Jersey Turnpike," Keith told me. "All we could do was thirty miles an hour. It was below minimum. They threw us off."

Eventually, they came through the Holland Tunnel and on the West Side in the mid-40's found a parking lot with a chain link fence around it. Here is where they slept every night for four days.

"I tried everything," Keith told me. "From a pay phone, I called every commercial art studio in the yellow pages. I couldn't even get an appointment." On the fourth day, they returned to Berne. "New York wasn't ready for me," Keith says.

It had been a taste, however.

This had been in 1953. Later that year, Keith got his first job in a commercial art studio as an apprentice in Fort Wayne, Indiana, making a dollar an hour if there was something he could do. He cleaned brushes. He delivered packages. After saving up some money, he went to Chicago looking for work. He stayed at the YMCA and got a job at Kling Studios, one of the largest commercial art studios in the country. Virtually all the work was for advertising agencies.

It took the next ten years for Keith to finally break into advertising agencies with his art portfolio. He tried and tried. He went back to Fort Wayne and worked at a studio there. He worked for a company in Bloomington, Indiana. He got married. (A New York girl. Nice choice.) But nothing he did seemed to get him out of just doing studio work.

At one point, he went off and made a movie. He'd never made a movie. But when a friend told him this religious organization that put together basketball teams from religious schools and took them around the world wanted to make a movie out of it, Keith put in a bid. A very low bid. They gave him the project.

Keith traveled with the team to Guatemala, Nicaragua, Brazil. Eventually, his 35mm production, which he wrote, scored, narrated and even illustrated, was produced at a length of 48 minutes.

"One of the highlights of this trip was our team playing in Quito, the capital of Equador. There is a famous shortwave radio station in Quito that broadcasts all over the world. At the game we were playing there was another game scheduled and this was the University of Quito versus the San Francisco Dons starring Bill Russell. What with the altitude problems, these little Equadorans were running the Dons around and making a very close game out of it. I sat on the sidelines. In the fourth quarter, one of the commentators for the shortwave radio station got too sick to continue. They called me in. I narrated the fourth quarter of a Bill Russell basketball game for listeners all over the world."

The movie, called *Venture South*, came in way over budget. When the religious organization offered Keith the opportunity to buy a print of the film, he didn't have the $400. He doesn't have a copy.

"It was just last year that I finally threw out of my attic all the outtakes from *Venture South*," Keith told me. "I'd been saving them all these years."

In 1963, Keith made an application to work for the ad agency Needham, Louis & Brorby in Chicago. Then he became very ill. From a hospital bed, he was struck by the fact that the people at Needham would call him asking when he would be out. They really seemed interested in him. When he was well, he went to see them. He carried with him a forty page portfolio of his artwork.

"It absolutely didn't come out the way I had planned," Keith told me. "I presented all this art work and they looked at me and said — Did you ever think of being a writer? They hired me as a writer."

Ten years it had taken. But now, at long last, he was in the advertising business. He was 29 years old.

"My very first job at the agency was to write 26 humorous radio commercials for State Farm Insurance. I had no idea what to do. I went to my supervisor. He told me just sit and type. When you laugh, show it to me, and if I laugh, we have something. If not, go back and write some more."

As it turned out, inside this commercial artist there lurked one of the greatest ad writers of all time. Keith won't tell you that. But his credits will. Keith wrote commercials for McDonald's. He wrote, "You Deserve A Break Today," and he wrote "Two all beef patties special sauce lettuce cheese pickles onions on a sesame seed bun," which practically every kid in American can recite today.

"I love hearing it in foreign languages," Keith said.

He wrote "Like a Good Neighbor, State Farm is There," which is still used by that insurance company, and within five years, at the age of 34, he was creative director at Needham, Harper and Steers. There were mergers, changes. Keith was divorced and remarried.

"I married the best account executive I ever worked with," he says. In 1980 he was named President of NH&S/Chicago and, in 1984, Chairman and CEO of Needham Harper worldwide.

The move to New York City came in 1984 when he was named Chairman and CEO. He would preside over a company with 93 offices around the globe from a suite of offices on Park Avenue.

"When we got here, we heard everybody has a house in the Hamptons in the summertime and we didn't understand it. But then came our first August. It was so hot. Now we knew."

They rented a place for one year on Millstone Road in Bridgehampton, then bought one of those modern oceanfront houses on Dune Road in Bridgehampton.

"It was a builder's house, and I was very happy there," Keith says. "But Rose-Lee wanted something larger, a dream house. And so that's what we had built."

Keith's seven children range in age from 29 down to his little girl Elizabeth who is four. Ask him and he will pull out a large frame of photographs, mounted about four feet across, that he can stand up on his conference table. It shows all his children, in order, from oldest to youngest. They are in New York, Chicago, California. They work as a computer programmer, an art director, a model, a standup comic and inventor. Rachel, who is 10, last year won her first ribbon in the Hampton Classic Horse Show in Bridgehampton. There's a lot going on here, a lot of pride.

I was curious to know if by becoming Chief Executive Officer, Keith had given up doing the creative work he is known for. He has not. He has surrounded himself with men who are very strong in the financial and media sector. Keith keeps going, he seems to just love to keep going, by hopping around to the different offices of the agency around the world brainstorming with his men there. He's developed a whole new concept of producing advertising, something called R.O.I., which has been published as a college textbook by Prentice Hall. R.O.I. stands for Return on Investment. But it also stands for Relevance, Originality, and Impact.

"Oh yes, I still work at it," he told me. "You know that Volkswagen campaign called Fahrvergnugen? It's been out over a year. It was worked up right at this table we are sitting at. Something I worked on for months."

Keith's agency writes commercials for Seagrams, for Volkswagen, for Audi, for American Airlines, Amtrak, Hershey's and dozens of others. And if his energy and enthusiasm are transmitted throughout his agency as he transmitted it just across this table to me, there will be dozens more.

July 26, 1991

* * *

Since the interview, DDB Needham has expanded in size to 120 offices in 53 countries including China and the new markets of Central Europe and the former Soviet Union. The agency has won worldwide assignments from IBM and Johnson & Johnson and has reached a worldwide billings level of $6.2 billion. DDB Needham also set new records for creativity at the Cannes Festival of Advertising, winning 23 "Lions" in 1992 and 26 "Lions" in 1993.

After 51 years of widowhood, Keith's mother, Agnes, has remarried and moved from Berne to LaPorte, Indiana where she and her new husband are active in the Presbyterian Church.

Chapter 63

RICHARD GOLTRY

Richard Goltry is a tall, intense, brooding sort of man in his late thirties with his hair swept down over his forehead. He looks off into the middle distance a lot, he sometimes shambles when he walks, and he has been known, when walking down the street, not to notice you. In short, he is a man often lost in his own world, a creative type, and so it is not surprising to find that he is an excellent painter and graphic artist, and that, among other things, he created the absolutely smashing and original logo of SOHO, N.Y. that has come to symbolize that community as well as many other designs. It is also not surprising that he finds himself around a fiery, alert and determined young Israeli woman in her early thirties named Devora. He's been with her for almost nine years and he had the good sense to marry her. Together they make an extra-ordinary team.

Richard grew up in Oklahoma. His mother was a Las Vegas chorus girl, his father left the family at his birth, and he was taken in by grandparents who owned a farm in Muskogee, Oklahoma. He was raised a country boy.

But then his mother returned. He had a new father and together the family moved to Staten Island where Richard spent the rest of his youth amidst the Italian-American community there. And it was in this environment, a displaced country boy, that he found himself as an artist.

"Mostly what I found was that being an artist meant driving a cab," he said.

It also meant having his own rock band and going to art school. And it was at a class at the School of Visual Arts on 23rd Street that Richard met Devora Avikzer, the young Israeli girl he was to marry.

299

She was a filmmaker and sculptress.

At that time, Richard painted in oils. And with Devora working as a salesgirl in a clothing store on East 57th Street, he began painting on t-shirts as well as canvases.

"What had happened," Richard said, "was that I had fallen six months behind in my rent and had to move out. She asked me to move in. I set up a drawing table in one corner. We'd go down to Orchard Street, buy some t-shirts, and I'd do paintings on them. Why shouldn't original fine art be on t-shirts? Then Devora would take them up to the store and make a display of them and we'd sell them for fifty dollars."

"With the store owner's consent?"

"It was pretty much an absentee ownership. But one day he came by and there we had the display in the window and he didn't much like it. Even though we paid him for each shirt sold. So we stopped."

At this point, Devora and Richard had saved up about $1,500. They decided to go into business for themselves.

"I made up four different designs," Richard said. "We got a silk screen printer. And Devora and I would drive around Manhattan in this silver Grand Prix, and we'd sell t-shirts to any store we could."

Devora was the businessperson. Richard stayed in the car. Devora would show the designs, take the orders, and she'd write them up on an order form.

"How soon can we take delivery?" the store owners would ask.

"Immediately," she would say. And she'd skip out to the car and fill the order.

Devora Goltry is Israeli born, one of eight children, of a Moroccan rabbi who settled there many years ago. She served in the Israeli Army and at the age of twenty, sponsored by one of her brothers who had already moved here, came to America for a career in the arts. She saw Richard for what he is: a fine artist. She would be his commercial half.

Before Devora and Richard got married, Richard converted to Judaism. It was not a difficult decision. He was an Oklahoma boy born and raised, and a Staten Island Italian-American, and now he wanted full acceptance in Devora's family. Further, he had been attracted to the religion.

"I went to this bearded rabbi in Borough Park in Brooklyn," he said. "He gave me a hard time at first. But when he realized I was serious, we got to work. I went to him for four months before I could convert."

The business from the silver Grand Prix thrived, but then the Goltrys discovered Manhattan street fairs. They made a handsome booth out of wooden dowels — like something you'd see in a Benetton store — and in showcasing the t-shirts this way they began to make over $1000 a day. Soon they had given up driving from store to store, and they were not only doing street fairs, but assembling and disassembling their booth in the street markets of Soho. It was the mid-1980s.

"We had four markets going at one time," Richard told me. "Boy did we work hard. We'd get up at 5 a.m. and begin assembling booths outdoors in ten degree weather. But people loved my silk screened shirts. We were a great success."

And then Richard designed the Soho logo. He dashed it off in fifteen minutes one day, showing it to Devora. What did she think? Very nice. They put it on a dozen t-shirts. They went in a flash.

For some reason, perhaps because it was so dazzling, the Soho section of Manhattan adopted it as their own. For two years, Richard and Devora found themselves as the center of attention in Soho. And it was only after that that others tried to copy the logo, which Richard and Devora had to take legal action to prevent.

"Why is it popular? Beats me. I just do what I do. No philosophical explanation behind it."

From this point on, the Goltrys became a classic American success story. They opened a shop on Broome Street, another on Wooster Street, then decided to print their own t-shirts and so opened a printing factory/showroom/office in what had been an old 8,000 square foot sewing factory on Greene Street. They opened in Tokyo. They called all their shops FORAVI.

"The landlord loved us," Richard said. "We completely made it over. It looks like a palace."

Also smart looking is the FORAVI store on Main Street in East Hampton, which the Goltrys opened this spring. They designed it with Soho-looking columns on the street out front. It is one of the most striking store renovations in town. And, among other things, the Goltrys are selling t-shirts with an original Richard Goltry East Hampton logo.

For a number of years, the Goltrys would take off for three or four days and stay at motels in Napeague. Once, a big deal for them, was a four day stay at Gurney's.

And then, last year, they bought an oceanfront house in the Beachhampton section of Amagansett. The surf pounds on the sand out front. And out back down toward the street, Devora grows a vegetable garden, much as her mother did in Israel.

"My sisters and brothers and their families come and stay with us in the summer," Devora says. "I hope to have my mother and father here soon."

Though Devora's parents have come and stayed with them in Soho, the Goltrys have not returned to Israel. Yet. In the meantime, Richard has his eye on a small cabin on the property, which he hopes to clear out soon with a yard sale, and inside set up easels and canvases as a place to work.

"And you know what I saw the other day?" Richard says. "Walking down the street, a woman wearing one of my hand painted t-shirts from ten years ago. I couldn't believe it. And it looked good as new."

August 3, 1990

* * *

Richard and Devora had their first child in January 1994.

Chapter 64

ROBERT GARDINER

Every summer weekend for twenty years, millionaire Robert David Lion Gardiner of Main Street, East Hampton would be driven in his limousine down to the marina he owned in Three Mile Harbor. He would board the ancient wooden motor yacht anchored there, he would raise the Jolly Roger, and he would roar out into Gardiner's Bay, and then tie up at the dock of Gardiner's Island and clamber ashore.

Gardiner's Island is a magnificent, almost untouched island, and on its 3,300 acres there are farm buildings, stables, a manor house, an old English windmill painted white, even a dirt airstrip. It is the oldest privately owned island in America, dating back to 1639 when King Charles I of England issued a patent of ownership for it to Lion Gardiner. And it is visible offshore of much of eastern Long Island, from Amagansett, Montauk, Shelter Island, Greenport and Orient.

Robert David Lion Gardiner, during those years, took on the title that had been awarded to his ancestor in 1639, "Lord of the Manor." He described himself, correctly it seemed, as the "Sixteenth Lord of the Manor," and he reveled in telling and re-telling the fascinating history of the place to whatever guests he took with him on his yacht, be they politicians, royalty from Europe, friends or newspaper reporters.

This twenty year period spanned 1962 to 1982 and many of us who lived here through that time remember it well. It all came to an end in 1982 as a result of a horrendous family squabble amongst the Gardiners, and for the next decade, Mr. Gardiner did not go at all. Now, at the age of 81, he is back. (He is holding a press tour of the island on July 18.) And the amazing thing, in retrospect, is that he was legally prevented from going to the island in 1982 in the first place. As a matter of fact, the current appellate court ruling handed down last week restoring Mr. Gardiner's rights, expresses similar amazement that such a ruling had ever been handed down.

Everybody back then in 1982 accepted the logic of the old Surrogate Court ruling. Sarah D. Gardiner, who had owned the island outright before her death in 1951, had set up a trust fund to pay the expenses of the island. She did not have any children but she had a young nephew and a young niece. They could enjoy the private island and fish and swim there and hold parties and even live there and, it was expected by Sarah Gardiner, they would then hand the island down to their heirs for future enjoyment.

The nephew, of course, was Robert David Lion Gardiner. And the niece, well, she married a man named Creel, moved away, and seemed not to express much interest in what went on on the island.

All the trouble started in the late 1970's when the annual upkeep of the island, what with maintenance people, repairs and taxes and so forth, began to approach a million dollars. The trust fund, which was administered by the United States Trust Company, had been instructed to pay these costs from interest and returns on investment. But now, the costs were so high the trust fund could no longer do that. The lawyers therefore moved to the next few paragraphs of Sarah Gardiner's will, which said that if money were not available then the trustees could lease the island out, or sell it (though the will said it should be sold to a Gardiner, even though he might offer less). Or perhaps, the attorneys for the trust fund thought, Mr. Gardiner, who had the exclusive use of the place, should be required to pay. He had long since made a fortune as a shopping center developer, primarily in Bay Shore, where he had developed the Gardiner Mall.

The Surrogate Court heard the Trustees' case and ruled, in 1982, that the upkeep of the island would no longer have to be paid by the trust fund since the fund didn't have it, but would instead have to be paid by heirs to Gardiner's Island. It was noted by the court that there were now exactly two heirs. There was Robert David Lion Gardiner, of course, and there was the young Alexandra Gardiner Creel, the daughter of Robert Gardiner's sister who had recently died. Robert David Lion Gardiner of East Hampton and Palm Beach was instructed to pay his half. Alexandra Gardiner Creel, who had just married a prominent Manhattan museum curator named Robert Goelet, would pay the other half. It was a court order.

The Goelets, of course, must have been quite surprised back in 1982 to learn that they would now have to foot a bill of almost a half a million dollars a year. But a court order was a court order. On the other hand, they were certainly now going to make use of the island.

In the first year after the court order, the whole thing fell apart.

304

Gardiner accused Mr. Goelet of trying to run him down with a jeep on the island. A judge ruled that Gardiner could have the place two weeks and then the Goelets could have the place two weeks. And then Gardiner announced he would not pay anything at all. The Goelets went to court. A judge banned Robert Gardiner from setting foot on the island. And that was the end of Mr. Gardiner making his summer weekend trips out to his island.

Until last week. The appellate court, ruling on a demand by Robert David Lion Gardiner that he was the sole owner of the island, instead confirmed that there were two heirs, himself and Alexandra Creel Goelet.

But then the court went further. It said that it could not understand how, if Sarah Gardiner did not specify that upkeep should be paid by her heirs, how the surrogate court in 1982 could demand it. Also, if it couldn't demand it from Gardiner and Goelet, then of course it could not dare to suggest that one party, by not paying it, lost the right to set foot on their own property.

And so, up goes the Jolly Roger, and off Mr. Gardiner motors to the island. In one sense, he is a very happy man because for the full ten years, the upkeep, all of it, was indeed paid by the Goelets. The future is another matter.

I do hope that at the luncheon for the press this Saturday, Mr. Gardiner tells what is one of my favorite stories. No, it is not about Captain Kidd burying his treasure on the island. And no, it is not about Mr. Gardiner, at the coronation of Queen Elizabeth in 1951, presenting her with a copy of his receipt of the treasure as it was returned back in the 1680's. (It did not match her copy.)

The story I like is Mr. Gardiner, sitting in a lawyer's office, with officials from Sterns Department Store, who were to become the largest tenant in the proposed new Gardiner's Mall. The lawyers had asked to see a title search. They wanted one of those long, long legal documents showing how the Bay Shore property had been bought and sold from landowner to landowner, guaranteeing, finally that it did indeed belong to Mr. Gardiner as he said it did.

At this meeting, Robert Gardiner reached into his briefcase and took out a scroll. It was the original deed, on parchment, in which the Crown deeded the land in question to Lion Gardiner. He unrolled it and handed it to the department store attorney. It was dated 1639 and it was signed by King Charles I.

"This is the whole title search?" the lawyer asked.

July 17, 1992

Chapter 65

WAGS

Meet Wags. Movie star. Mystery dog. Like all of us, he must have had an early life in which events took place that shaped his career and made him what he is today. But nobody knows about it and Wags isn't telling. In 1987, Wags just appeared on the scene, full grown. He has been here since, a total as of this writing of seven years. So he is at least eight years old. Maybe he is twelve. For reasons I cannot fathom, veterinarians cannot tell the ages of dogs closely. Vets have looked at Wags teeth and they have looked him in the eye, and the closest they can come is to say that he is "full grown," or when I first got him that he was a "full grown young male." Then they stick him with a hypodermic needle which is what they almost always do when I bring him to the vet and Wags pants and wags his tail and completely ignores the fact that somebody is sticking a needle in him. Nobody else in our family can do that.

Wags was given his name, this time, — he certainly must have had a name before 1987 — by the caring and wonderful people at the Animal Rescue Fund in Wainscott. Back in the autumn of that year, Wags had been seen walking forlornly around the Main Street of Bridgehampton. Merchants had noticed him. He was wet and tired and hungry. They would feed him. And they reported him to the Southampton Dog Catcher, known these days as the Southampton Animal Control Officer.

It did seem incredible that this dog could have been a stray. He was, and is, magnificent. He is ninety pounds and from a quick look appears to be a beautiful sheepdog. (Whether he is or isn't purebred we will never know.) He is grey with white markings, he has fabulous Clydesdale feet, all feathered and ruffled, and he prances when he walks as if he were in a show. And when he is happy he wags and wags his tail so vigorously that the entire back end of the dog moves back and forth.

The Southampton Dog Catcher took Wags in and because this dog was so beautiful, called the Animal Rescue Fund. The Dog Catcher keeps dogs for only thirty days after which if they are unclaimed they are put to sleep. The Animal Rescue Fund, on the other hand, will not destroy any animal they take in. This one they knew immediately they would take in. They brought him over to the Animal Rescue Fund, put him in the kennel there, and they bought advertisements in the local newspaper and they put posters up around town asking if anyone had lost this dog. Nobody answered. After thirty days, they named him Wags.

Sometimes, I wonder what his name was before it was Wags. Perhaps he had been a spy for the CIA and he responded to "K58." I tried that one time. He did not respond. What he did and does respond to, very clearly, is "Wags." He looks up and comes running over. That's his name alright.

"Fido? Radar? Spot? Lucky?" I tried them all. Nothing. The past is dead and buried.

Staying on this topic for one more minute, the only real clue we have to go on here is that Wags was found in October. There is a real problem in the Hamptons involving dogs at the end of the summer. People come out here from the City in the spring and they rent houses for the summer season and sometimes they get a dog. In the fall, they go back to New York City. Sometimes they just drive off and leave the dog behind to fend for himself. He'll find a nice farm house is perhaps what the thinking is. What a cruel thing. The town winds up with many strays.

Anyway, so much for Wags, the formative years.

We move to today.

Like most dogs, Wags is faithful and dependable in all things. Whatever he does, he does. And you can count on him, day after day, to do things the same way he had done them before.

Fortunately, other than a recent addiction he has developed which I will talk about in a moment, his patterns and habits are as magnificent as his beautiful grey and white coat.

He sits when you ask him to sit. He gives you his paw. If you throw a ball he looks at the ball and then he looks at you and wonders what it is you wanted him to do about that. He loves children. He likes to be patted and snuggled with and sung to and he wags his tail and if you get close enough he will lick you in the face just for the pure fun of it.

He is sad when members of the family go away. He'll lie by the door. He gets into moods of friskiness where he will bump you with

307

his nose and then bark and then run around the sofa and then run around again hoping you will chase him. He likes you to grab his feet, push him down, roll him over on his back and rub is stomach. He will jump up onto couches and chairs and beds when invited to do so. He understands that as a general rule he is not supposed to do this and he treats all furniture accordingly. But he also understands that there are certain sofas and chairs and beds he can jump up on and there is no problem about that and with those he jumps up whenever he wants.

He loves to go for a ride in a car. He prances about excitedly whenever a member of the family puts on a hat and coat and he can show utter dejection if he is told to STAY and to SIT and on this trip he is not coming. He will shuffle over to the front door and he will lie down and look at you as if you have just condemned him to being shot at dawn. You can feel very guilty backing the car down the driveway and glancing over every once in awhile to get this sorrowful look.

He does have his idiosyncracies. He will go over to a door and bark at it once apparently in the belief that this will open it. After a fashion, if the door does not open he will bark at it again. Usually, somebody comes over and opens it for him.

From the outside coming in he prefers glass sliding doors. At glass sliding doors he can see who might be about inside. If nobody is about he will lie down next to the slider. If somebody walks by inside he will bark once and then he will paw at the door. If this does not work he will paw harder — it is not much different than a human knocking at the door — and if this does not work and a person is still visible inside he will begin to bodily hurl himself against the slider — WHAM, WHAM. Eventually, whoever is inside gets the idea.

He eats lying down. I have never before seen a dog do this. He will come over to the dog food in his bowl in the evening and he will suddenly collapse noisily onto the linoleum. He makes a grunting or aheming sound when he does this. And you can hear the unmistakable sound of parts of his body hitting the floor in some sort of sequence. Bump, thump, whoom, crack, bump. He puts the bowl of food between his two front paws while in this position and usually for the longest time he will just stare at it. Then he will eat it.

Pretty weird, no? You have to see this.

I mentioned that Wags has an addiction. This is a recent development. Somewhere along the way, I think it was about a year ago, I started giving him milkbone dog bones. He loved them. You could hold one out — I get the boxes with the big, big bones in them — and he will sit down obediently and just barely control himself in waiting for you to lean forward with the bone so he can gently take it out of your hand. Then he is off with it. He wants to go outside. You let him

308

out and he runs off. He goes to another part of the yard and he lies down kerthump and he eats it.

The addiction developed after a few weeks. He began to demand them. He would come over and bark once, then kind of poke you with his nose in the back of your knee. It was a demanding poke. If no bone were forthcoming he would bark again and poke again. A look of irritation would cross his face. And then, finally, if the bone appeared, this expression would turn to ecstasy, he would grab it and off he would go.

I give him milkbones now only once or twice a day. He is very upset about this.

I did mention that Wags is a movie star. This is not a joke. Two years ago, a film crew from Germany came to the eastern end of Long Island and wanted to cast a dog running through the dunes with some children. Wags got the job as the dog. They paid him $300. It is not easy from an accounting point of view to deal with money paid to a dog by a German movie crew. But somehow we managed. Wags certainly didn't mind. As long as those milk bones keep coming he could care less about the money. We later saw him on screen. It was a TV commercial for Audi. Wags was visible trotting through the dune grass for about a second and a half.

Wags believes he has been put on this planet to perform a job. His job is me. Wherever I go he follows me around — sometimes he runs ahead leading me to where he thinks I am going to go — WRONG, WAGS — and part of this job is, as much as possible, to keep me and everything associated with me herded into one place.

For example, if the two of us are in my van and somebody, for example a gas station attendant, comes over to ask me if I want high test or regular, this dog goes nuts with barking in the back seat. He will not stop. For awhile, I had a van with curtains on the windows. When a gas station attendant would come over Wags would commence to tear the curtains off the windows. Not good. I'd literally have to grab him by the collar and hold him steady while the gas tank was being filled. He'd shake and cut back on the barking but it was still apparent he was very upset about the situation. Somebody was messing with the outside of the car.

I thought for awhile that this had to do with strangers coming by, but then I went out and put gas in the car for the first time at one of those self service stations. I was amazed to see he did the same thing. He barked like a lunatic inside the car and nothing I said or did could make him stop. To some extent this was even a bit embarrassing. How could the owner of a car be treated like an intruder in front of all these gas station attendants? Hey everybody come over and look at this.

I developed a theory. The car was the enclosure inside of which were the sheep (me and the other members of the family.) The shell of the car was the equivalent of the fence. If somebody was out there messing with the fence it was his job to bark like hell. If he didn't, everybody could get out. He's a sheepdog after all.

Sometimes I will sit at a computer for two and three hours and will write and write. It wears Wags out. He falls asleep on the floor nearby. This is an exhausting business taking care of Dan. But he does the best he can and that is good enough.

Photo Credits: Julie Warner p. 45, copyright © 1991 Warner Bros. Inc.; Dani Shapiro p. 57, Ruven Afanador; Erica Abeel p. 70, Jerry Bauer; Lee Bailey p. 88, Tom Eckerle; Rusty Leaver p. 97, David Allen; Roger Ressmeyer p. 116, Starlight Photo Agency; Martha Stewart p. 127, Chuck Baker; Stephen Rubin p. 181, Alex Gotfryd; Tom Paxton p. 185, Irene Young; Tony Drexel Duke p. 228, Mary Hilliard; Susan Isaacs p. 273, Ingrid Estrada; Dan Rattiner p. 310, Joan Jedell